Musicology of Religion

SUNY series in Religious Studies
Harold Coward, editor

Musicology of Religion
Theories, Methods, and Directions

Guy L. Beck

Cover Art: "Homo Musicus" by Kajal Dass Beck

Published by State University of New York Press, Albany

© 2023 State University of New York

All rights reserved

Printed in the United States of America

No part of this book may be used or reproduced in any manner without written permission. No part of this book may be stored in a retrieval system or transmitted in any form or by any means including electronic, electrostatic, magnetic tape, mechanical, photocopying, recording, or otherwise without the prior permission in writing of the publisher.

For information, contact State University of New York Press, Albany, NY
www.sunypress.edu

Library of Congress Cataloging-in-Publication Data

Name: Beck, Guy L., 1948– author.
Title: Musicology of religion : theories, methods, and directions / Guy L. Beck.
Description: Albany : State University of New York Press, 2023. | Series: SUNY series in religious studies | Includes bibliographical references and index.
Identifiers: LCCN 2022037717 | ISBN 9781438493114 (hardcover : alk. paper) | ISBN 9781438493091 (ebook) } ISBN 9781438493107 (pbk. : alk. paper)
Subjects: LCSH: Music—Religious aspects. | Music—Philosophy and aesthetics.
Classification: LCC ML3921 .B425 2021 | DDC 781.1/2—dc23/eng/20220810
LC record available at https://lccn.loc.gov/2022037717

10 9 8 7 6 5 4 3 2 1

Affectionately dedicated to my Parents

Contents

Preface — ix

Introduction — 1

Part I
Theories and Methods

Chapter 1 Religious Studies and Music — 43

Chapter 2 Social Sciences and Music — 89

Chapter 3 Musicology and Ethnomusicology — 121

Part II
New Directions and Paradigms

Chapter 4 Philosophy and Music — 143

Chapter 5 Theology and Music — 165

Chapter 6 Liturgical Studies and Music — 217

Chapter 7 Cognitive Studies and Music — 241

Part III
Homo Religiosus and Homo Musicus

Chapter 8 Musicology of Religion — 263

Appendix A	Resources and Current Outlook	303
Appendix B	Glossary of Terms for Musicology of Religion	311
Works Cited		317
Index		349

Preface

The creation of a book proposing a new academic field is not a common occurrence. Sometimes it may be facilitated by unique personal circumstances that compel an author to meticulously gather information, hunker down, and "make it happen." In this case, the extended time and space provided by the COVID-19 pandemic offered an immediate wake-up call to initiate, pursue, and complete this project, which had been lying dormant as an idea for years.

I outline the lengthy process of the book's inspiration, gestation, and final consummation below in the Introduction, weaving my acknowledgments into the narrative, along with how my parents provided the necessary foundations. Here I want only to say that the entire process has been a marvelous journey of intellectual discovery and attentive listening, through which *Musicology of Religion* has come to fruition.

I wish also to take the liberty of saying thanks here to those most instrumental in aiding this project to completion. Professor Harold Coward most kindly encouraged me to submit this book to his Religious Studies Series at SUNY Press. The robust combination of traditional scholarship and innovative vision characteristic of SUNY Press made it the perfect venue. In that regard, my sincere thanks go to Mr. James Peltz, associate director and editor-in-chief of SUNY Press, for his patience and expertise in handling the manuscript for review and revision. Thanks as well to all of the staff at SUNY Press for all their hard work and assistance.

My artist wife Kajal has been a devoted companion and emotional support through the ups and downs of this project, including a hurricane. For all these moments, and for assistance in the envisioning of this book through her cover art, I am most grateful.

Introduction

Music has been a major part of all religions. It has powers to alter and match moods, to sustain and evoke emotion, to induce trance or ecstasy states, to express worship, and to entertain.

—John Bowker, *The Oxford Dictionary of World Religions*

Music magically modulates the spirit as well as the world that resounds with it. Music is the most effective sign of the human spirit and its transformative capacities.

—Lawrence E. Sullivan, *Enchanting Powers: Music in the World's Religions*

In all societies, music is found in religious ritual—it is almost everywhere a mainstay of sacred ceremonies—leading some scholars to suggest that perhaps music was actually invented for humans to have a special way of communicating with the supernatural.

—Bruno Nettl, *Excursions in World Music*

The citations above are from distinguished scholars of religious studies and musicology. While one might expect their positions to reflect a consensus in these fields, they are in fact exceptions to the general academic silence regarding the combined phenomenon of "religion and music" as a special field of study and research. Over the years, the focus areas of religion and music have remained in separate corners of the academy, seemingly operating in "compartments" rather than "departments." Until very recently there have been minimal opportunities for presenting original research on religion and music at academic conferences, few monographs on specific religious music, and minimal attention to music and chant in standard reference works in religion as well as teaching materials. Recognizing the vital importance of music throughout the world's religions, this book is a call for a permanent remedy to the current situation in the form of a new discipline, Musicology of Religion, which will provide an umbrella field for the growing interest and rapidly accumulating data on music in religious thought and practice.

Current Situation

Before outlining the basic parameters of Musicology of Religion, we take account of the current situation in the study of religion and music. A neglect of music in the field of religious studies has perpetuated, as has the avoidance of religion in musicology and the social sciences. Published reference works and theoretical compendiums in religious studies fail to give proper emphasis to music. The monumental *Encyclopedia of Religion and Ethics* (Hastings 1908–1921) contained a lengthy article (v. 9: 5–61) on music in ancient and living religions. Yet, excepting *The Encyclopedia of Religion* (Eliade 1987), recent works of this type have normally omitted music: *The HarperCollins Dictionary of Religion* (Smith 1995), *Merriam-Webster's Encyclopedia of World Religions* (Doniger 1999), and *The Routledge Handbook of Research Methods in the Study of Religion* (Stausberg and Engler 2013). On the side of musicology, *The New Harvard Dictionary of Music* (Randel 1986), *Rethinking Music* (Cook and Everist 2001), *Systematic and Comparative Musicology: Concepts, Methods, Findings* (Schneider 2008), and *Theory and Method in Historical Ethnomusicology* (McCollum and Hebert 2014), works that continue to shape the discipline, have generally sidestepped religion. Religion is also absent from *Musicology: The Key Concepts* (Beard and Gloag 2016). And while music has also been ostensibly linked with individual social sciences, as in *The Anthropology of Music* (Merriam 1964), *Introduction to the Sociology of Music* (Adorno 1976), and *The Psychology of Music* (Deutsch 1982), in each case there is little mention of religion or reflection on the enduring presence of music in nearly all religious rituals and human cultures.

Regarding academic conferences, past annual meetings of the American Academy of Religion and the Society of Biblical Literature have rarely touched upon music as a feature of religion. Professor Albert L. Blackwell, in *The Sacred in Music* (1999: 11), shared an anecdote from these meetings that mirrors my own experience: "More than seven thousand scholars attended the meeting. We gathered in over seven hundred different sessions for seminars, workshops, and lectures on almost every imaginable subject relating to the academic study of religion. Of these seven hundred sessions, however, only three bore any relation to music."

The teaching of religious studies also displays a lack of attention to music, with only passing references in textbooks and films, and few college-level courses on religion and music. For a survey of the presence or absence of music in publications on religion, including college textbooks, encyclopedias, handbooks, and other reference works, see the Introduction in Beck (2006). Briefly restated, most of the standard college textbooks in religious studies and world religions have omitted discussion of music and chant in religion: Smith (1958 [1991]), Parrinder (1971), Fenton (1993), Nielson, Jr. (1993), Hopfe and Woodward (2001), Fisher (2002), Noss (2003), Ellwood and McGraw (2005), Livingston (2005), and Young (2005). Interestingly, postcolonial critiques of "world religions," such as Tomoko Masuzawa's *The Invention of World Religions: Or, How European Universalism Was Preserved in the Language of Pluralism* (2005), fail to account for the overriding presence of music in nearly all forms of religion.

Moreover, music is conspicuously absent in theoretical guides, dictionaries, and anthologies dealing with methods in the study of religion. Beginning with the omission of "music" among the vast "Index of Scholarly Concepts" in Jacques Waardenburg's otherwise monumental work of 1971, *Classical Approaches to the Study of Religion: Aims, Methods, and Theories of Research*, this tendency has continued in *Critical Terms for Religious Studies* (Mark C. Taylor 1998), *Guide to the Study of Religion* (Willi Braun and Russell T. McCutcheon 2000), and *Theory and Method in Religious Studies: A Selection of Critical Readings* (Carl Olson 2003). Most regrettably, the dictionaries of relevant terms in religious studies by Aaron W. Hughes and Russell T. McCutcheon, *Religion in 50 Words: A Critical Vocabulary* (2022) and *Religion in 50 More Words: A Critical Vocabulary* (2022), fail to include music, sound, or chant.

Studies in religious experience, despite the influence of William James and Rudolf Otto, have not continued this area's emphasis on music. After the brief inclusion of music in William James's classic text *The Varieties of Religious Experience: A Study in Human Nature* (1902), succeeding academic works in the field of "religious experience," including Wayne Proudfoot's *Religious Experience* (1985) and Ann Taves's *Religious Experience Reconsidered: A Building Block Approach to the Study of Religion and Other Special Things* (2009), have sidestepped the presence of music. Proudfoot gives extensive coverage of the thought of James and Schleiermacher, who also highlighted music, but avoids music in his own analysis.

One might assume that works in theology would include music, yet standard references such as *Baker's Dictionary of Theology* (Harrison 1960), and *New Dictionary of Theology: Historical and Systematic* (Davie 2016), have not mentioned it. Foundational works in systematic theology in recent times have also surprisingly left out the musical dimension of religious practice and worship, such as Geoffrey Wainwright's *Doxology: The Praise of God in Worship, Doctrine and Life: A Systematic Theology* (1980) and George A. Lindbeck's *The Nature of Doctrine: Religion and Theology in a Postliberal Age* (1984). Important ecumenical works have also neglected this important dimension, including Wilfrid Cantwell Smith's *Towards a World Theology: Faith and the Comparative History of Religion* (1981), Leonard Swidler's collection *Toward a Universal Theology of Religion* (1987), and Paul F. Knitter's *Introducing Theologies of Religions* (2002). Multivolume projects by leading scholars in comparative religion and theology, such as Editor Robert Cummings Neville's three-volume effort (*The Comparative Religious Ideas Project. Vol. I: The Human Condition*; Vol. II: *Ultimate Realities*; Vol. III: *Religious Truth* [2000]), while holding great expectations, have failed to deliver on music.

Despite these omissions, however, prominent Christian theologians of the twentieth century have displayed their love of music and its quality of transcendence, one even aspiring to hear music in heaven. The great Swiss Protestant theologian Karl Barth (1886–1968), despite not taking note of music in his monumental work *The Epistle to the Romans* (1922), confided in his 1956 collection of essays on Mozart, *Wolfgang Amadeus Mozart* (1986: 16), that he placed the great musician above theologians in the afterlife: "I even have to confess that if I ever get to heaven, I would first of all seek out Mozart, and only then inquire after Augustine, St. Thomas, Luther, Calvin, and Schleiermacher." Barth (1986: 38) even affirmed his own unique perspective that views beautiful music as a means of proclaiming the Word of God: "He [Mozart] just does it—precisely in that humility in which he himself is, so to speak, only the instrument with which he allows us to hear what he hears: what surges at him from God's creation, what rises in him, and must proceed from him." The Roman Catholic theologian Hans Kung (1928–2021), though also not discussing music in his works, articulated the notion of music's capacity for transcendence in *Mozart: Traces of Transcendence* (1993: 33):

> Mozart's music—seems to show in its sensual yet unsensual beauty, power and clarity, how wafer-thin is the boundary between music,

which is the most abstract of all arts, and religion, which has always had a special connection with music. For both, though they are different, direct us to what is ultimately unspeakable, to mystery. And though music cannot become a religion of art, the art of music is the most spiritual of all symbols for that "mystical sanctuary of our religion," the divine itself . . . for me Mozart's music has relevance for religion not only where religious and church themes or forms emerge, but precisely through the compositional technique of the non-vocal, purely instrumental music, through the way in which this music interprets the world, a way which transcends extra-musical conceptuality.

Not to be ignored by theologians, the great Lutheran composer J. S. Bach was considered a theologian himself by Yale theology professor Jaroslav Pelikan in *Bach Among the Theologians* (1986). Pelikan (1988) even likened theology to a "melody." Yet according to Jeremy S. Begbie (2005: 719), "In modern theology, music is conspicuous by its absence. The theology and literature interface is well served and the same increasingly applies to other art forms, not least the visual arts. But music has attracted little attention." It is thus timely that theology address music and its abiding effect on religious experience.

While the greatest amount of theological study has emerged within the Christian tradition, the rapidly growing field of comparative theology holds promise, not as a confessional exercise, but as a theoretical discipline for cross-cultural study that transcends boundaries. Oxford professor Keith Ward, in *Religion and Revelation: A Theology of Revelation in the World's Religions* (1994: 50), was one of the first to define comparative theology: "Comparative theology is an enquiry into ideas of God and revelation, of ultimate reality and its disclosures to human minds, as such ideas arise across the full spectrum of human history and experience." Several issues and directions in the field of comparative theology are further developed in Francis X. Clooney, S. J., *Comparative Theology: Deep Learning across Religious Borders* (2010a), and *The New Comparative Theology: Interreligious Insights from the Next Generation* (2010b). The broad approach of comparative theology has been fully stated by Catherine Cornille in *Meaning and Method in Comparative Theology* (2020: 1): "Comparative theology forms an integral part of every religious and theological tradition. Throughout history, religions have developed their beliefs, practices, and overall sense of identity through a process of borrowing, refuting, and reinterpreting elements from other religious traditions." Though not yet discussing music in depth, the new developments in comparative theology provide optimistic points of entry for the inclusion of music in the wider frame of theological discourse.

Conversely, the field of ethnomusicology shows a paucity of coverage of religion in both teaching and research. The teaching of ethnomusicology and world music in hundreds of institutions of higher learning in America employs a catalog of textbooks designed to expose the eager student to the sounds of foreign singing and instrument playing. In most texts, however, the emphasis is on the visual and tactile elements with colorful illustrations of natives in full attire performing their music in exotic venues. Four of the most popular world music textbooks—Alves (2012), Bakan (2007), Miller (2016), and Shelemay (2001)—make no mention of "religion" in their indices and include little to no discussion regarding the use of music in relation to the transcendent or the divine. Two other texts, May (1983) and Titon (2016), contain only fragmented references to religion, primarily in the context of magic or tribal dance. The exception is Bruno Nettl (2001: 10), whose citation in the opening is an important defense of universalism in music and one of the pillars of support for the Musicology of Religion: "In all societies, music is found in religious ritual—it is almost everywhere a mainstay of sacred ceremonies—leading some scholars to suggest that perhaps music was actually invented for humans to have a special way of communicating with the supernatural."

Despite these anomalies, both religion and music, however defined, are claimed to be "universal human phenomena," occurring in all forms of culture and civilization. Scholars of religion routinely discuss the concept of *homo religiosus*, "religious human," as an indication that religiosity is embedded within human nature. Musicologists have adopted the idea of *homo musicus*, "musical human," noting that to be fully human is to be "musical." What behooves our attention is not simply that religion and music are universal but that religion and music have been inextricably bound together throughout history and geography. In fact, new research in ritual studies suggests that humans are also *homo ritualis*, "ritual human," a template that graphically reveals the link between religion and music. Yet it is surprising that the widespread and consistent association of music with religion has still largely eluded the eyes and ears of scholars, both in religious studies and in musicology. And despite the plethora of ethnographic data available on music and religion collected by social scientists and ethnomusicologists, many salient aspects of music and its almost universal association with religious rituals and ceremonies around the world have not been sufficiently analyzed and interpreted. Targeted research by ethnomusicologists and anthropologists has often shown how musical performances consolidate various human communities, reinforce identities, enunciate boundaries, and strengthen hierarchies. And yet for decades the overall role of music in religious practice as well as the relation between religion and music as a meaningful locus for understanding religious experience has eluded religious studies scholarship. This situation has been recognized by two prominent scholars in *The Encyclopedia of Religion* (1987): Ter Ellingson, in "Music and Religion" (1987: Vol. 10, 171), "There is no integrated study of this subject on a worldwide scale"; and Alexander L. Ringer, in "Religious Music of the West" (1987: Vol. 10, 216), "The well-nigh universal interpenetration of music and religion notwithstanding, there exists no overall treatment of the subject in English." These observations are also present in the 2005 second edition.

We note at this point that the combined expression of "religion and music" may appear "problematic" and require clarification. Christopher I. Lehrich (2014: 24) offers insights into perceptions regarding the study of "religion and music" in different fields of study:

> One rarely speaks of "religion and music" in general terms. Instead, the phrase shifts to "religion in music" or "music in religion." The direction of subordination depends on one's home discipline: scholars of religion subordinate music, musicologists of religion. Either way, the secondary term divides: within the set of "religion," "music" defines a subset. From this point, subdivisions accumulate rapidly: music and religion, having become music in religion, breaks into "music in religions of South Asia," thence a chain of increasing particularity.

Despite these issues, what is lacking is a consistent methodology across disciplines that starts with the premise that religion and music are bound together in fundamental ways.

The principal conundrum underscored here is that religion and music are each deemed universal by their respective domains yet neglected in the other's repertory of scholarship and educational materials. This situation may be said to have morphed into an invisible elephant in the room within academic circles. One side mostly avoids discussion of the other, giving the appearance of a lacuna of information and method when it comes to the two in combination. Moreover, all of this is complicated by the current popular interest in music, religion, and spirituality, with the attendant presumption that they are intrinsically related.

Our response in this book is to first examine the principal viewpoints on religion and music in selected disciplines in the academy, namely religious studies, the social sciences, philosophy, theology, liturgical studies, and cognitive studies, and then to make the case for the creation of a new realm of information and research with suggested methods. An example from the lore of the ancients is appropriate here. A Buddhist version of a famous parable tells how several blind men are invited by a king to his palace to describe an elephant. The blind men, after each touching a different part of the elephant, describe the elephant as a plow, a granary, and a winnowing basket. To the king's surprise, the blind men cannot agree with each other's interpretation of the elephant, and none can describe the elephant in entirety. Like the blind men and the elephant, scholars from the stated areas do not necessarily agree with each other when it comes to religion and music, and none of the disciplines alone can do the pairing of the two justice. However, due to the growing consensus of interest in the subject, both in academia and in the popular sphere, and the combined expertise of scholars from a variety of disciplines, eyes and ears appear ready to open to the new field of Musicology of Religion.

Popular Domain

> Music is a holy place, a cathedral so majestic that we can sense the majesty of the universe, and also a hovel so simple and private that none of us can plumb its deepest secrets.
>
> —Don Campbell, *The Mozart Effect: Tapping the Power of Music to Heal the Body, Strengthen the Mind, and Unlock the Creative Spirit*

Notwithstanding the apparent separation of religion and music in the academy, the opposite situation occurs in the popular domain. A spate of books over the years has comported to present a unified spirituality or religious dimension of music for either specialized audiences or for general popular consumption. One of the first for Western classical music was R.W.S. Mendl's *The Divine Quest in Music* (1957). A rising interest in the religious lives of the Western classical composers, often passed over in the standard biographies, later resulted in Patrick Kavanaugh's *Spiritual Lives of the Great Composers* (1992).

In this vein a rapid rise of interest has occurred in music and spirituality, coinciding with the New Age Movement. As such, New Age books on music have imbibed the spirit of esotericism and mysticism. One early work for esoteric readers was of theosophist Cyril Scott (1879–1970), *Music and Its Secret Influence throughout the Ages* (1933), many years later followed by David Tame, *The Secret Power of Music: The Transformation of Self and Society through Musical Energy* (1984), Peter Hamel with his popular *Through Music to the Self* (1987), and R. J. Stewart, *The Spiritual Dimension of Music: Altering Consciousness for Inner Development* (1990). As part of New Age, music therapy has become a significant factor in the elevation of sound and spirituality. Spearheaded by the New Age music of pioneer Steven Halpern, the concept of 'sound healing' was established by Halpern and Louis Savary in *Sound Health: The Music and Sounds that Make us Whole* (1985). Later, Don Campbell's *The Mozart Effect: Tapping the Power of Music to Heal the Body, Strengthen the Mind, and Unlock the Creative Spirit* (1997) became a very popular work, along with his earlier anthology of articles on music therapy, *Music Physician for Times to Come* (1991), which is a useful introduction to the healing powers of sound and sacred music. Many other books as well as audiovisual media on music therapy and spirituality continue to enlarge upon similar themes.

Driven by the pursuit of esoteric interests and spiritual "harmony," the theme of Pythagoras and the harmony of the spheres has aroused popular attention. Jamie James's *The Music of the Spheres: Music, Science, and the Natural Order of the Universe* (1993) provided a useful introduction to this normally arcane subject. Blending the mathematical with the musical, James's book revealed the order of the universe as understood by scientists and composers who, in the words of the description, "perceived distances between objects in the sky mirrored (and were mirrored by) the spaces between notes forming chords and scales. The smooth operation of the cosmos created a divine harmony that composers sought to capture and express . . . and to what extent it survives today—from Pythagoras to Newton, Bach to Beethoven, and on to the twentieth century of Einstein, Schoenberg, Stravinsky, Cage and Glass."

In the mid-1990s, an unexpected surge of interest in Gregorian chant occurred following the Angel recording of *Chant* in 1994, sung by the Benedictine monks of Santo Domingo de Silos in Spain. The tranquil sounds of the monks helped bring much-needed peace to many, though few knew anything about Gregorian chant or understood the language in which it is sung. As a companion book to the Angel CD, Katharine Le Mée, in *Chant: The Origins, Form, Practice, and Healing Power of Gregorian Chant* (1994), discussed the historical and liturgical sources of the chant and provided information on the latest research on its therapeutic qualities. As explained by the author: "The calm, measured, almost transcendent sound of the monks singing these ancient melodies seems to put us in touch with our true selves . . . The sudden popularity of this music today—after 1,300 years—is indicative of the deep spiritual hunger manifesting everywhere." Within a few years, the chanting of diverse religious traditions gained in ascendency, coinciding with the commercial popularity of "world music."

Robert Gass and Kathleen Brehony, in *Chanting: Discovering Spirit in Sound* (1999), responded to the growing market for world music and religious chant with a comprehensive presentation of chant in Hindu, Christian, Buddhist, Jewish, Islamic, African, Shamanic, Goddess, and Native American traditions, including notations of twenty-five chants. Stressing the therapeutic effects of chant cross-culturally, the authors explain: "The ancient art of chanting has long been embraced by the world's great religious traditions as a path to healing and enlightenment, but only recently has Western science begun to recognize its therapeutic effects on the body and mind. *Chanting* provides a fascinating introduction to this powerful and increasingly popular practice and shows you how to use chant in your own life as a powerful tool for relaxation, body-mind healing, and spiritual self-discovery."

The interest in New Age forms of music was accompanied by a deep interest in Middle Eastern and Asian forms of spirituality and music. The Islamic Sufi message of the mystical spirituality of sound and music reached early audiences through Hazrat Inayat Khan's *The Sufi Message of Hazrat Inayat Khan* (1962), complemented by the extraordinary popularity of Pakistani Qawwali singer Ustad Nusrat Fateh Ali Khan, as well as the Turkish Whirling Dervishes representing the teachings of thirteenth-century mystical poet Jalalu'ddin Rumi. Regarding the Whirling Dervishes, Shems Friedlander (1992: 130) has summarized their spiritual approach to music according to Rumi, who was respectfully known as Mevlana ("our master"): "The teaching of Mevlana depends upon and is expressed in three elements: dance, music, and love. In his works, Mevlana admires music and accepts it as high art. According to him, music begins where speech ends, and it has the ability to contain and expose what words are unable to do. The language of music is universal. It is the language of lovers."

After years of propagating Haṭha Yoga (physical and physiological Yoga) in the West, a new wave of interest also occurred in Hindu practices of Mantra chant and Yoga, as expressed by Russill Paul in *The Yoga of Sound: Healing & Enlightenment through the Sacred Practice of Mantra* (2004). A native Indian Christian by birth, Paul proclaimed that America is ready for the spirituality of the Yoga of Sound:

> My hope is that yogis and spiritual seekers in America will earnestly take up the study and practice of the Yoga of Sound. I truly believe that it can contribute an essential element to the spiritual depth that people are seeking . . . I feel that it is time for American yogis and spiritual practitioners to reintroduce the yoga of sacred sound. Such a study will empower the American soul, infusing the growing practice of yoga in this country with a mystical system for reaching the highest goal of samadhi [liberation]. (2004: 237–238)

This emphasis on Indian sound had been prefigured in an earlier attempt to awaken society to the value of listening and realizing cosmic sound in the form of Nāda-Brahman by jazz producer and writer Joachim-Ernst Berendt in *Nada Brahma: The World is Sound; Music and the Landscape of Consciousness* (1987: 5): "Human beings with their disproportionate emphasis on seeing have brought on the excess of rationality, of analysis and abstraction, whose breakdown we are now witnessing . . . Living almost exclusively through the eyes has led us to almost not living at all." Other popular works fitting into this category of Indian sound and spirituality include Cynthia Snodgrass, *The Sonic Thread: Sound as a Pathway to Spirituality* (2002), Patrick Bernard, *Music as Yoga: Discover the Healing Power of Sound* (2004), and Richard Whitehurst, *Mahamantra Yoga: Chanting to Anchor the Mind and Access the Divine* (2011). To document the rapidly growing phenomenon of collective devotional singing known as Kīrtan, and to build upon the introductory work of Linda Johnsen and Maggie Jacobus in *Kirtan! Chanting as a Spiritual Path* (2007), Steven Rosen collected dozens of lively conversations with leading performers in *The Yoga of Kirtan: Conversations on the Sacred Art of Chanting* (2008). For exploration into the subtle joys of Kīrtan, see Pranada Comtois's *Prema Kirtan: Journey into Sacred Sound* (2022).

Populist authors and musicians in the West have also promulgated positive views on the enduring nature and intrinsic value of sound and music for the human species. Oliver Sacks, in *Musicophilia* (2007: x), opines regarding the perennial human capacity for music: "This propensity to music—this musicophilia—shows itself in infancy, is manifest and central in every culture, and probably goes back to the very beginnings of the species. It may be developed or shaped by the cultures we live in, by the circumstances of life, or by the particular gifts or weaknesses we have as individuals—but it lies so deep in human nature that one is tempted to think of it as innate." Also worthy of mention, a multivolume project by musician Justin St. Vincent, *The Spiritual Significance of Music* (2009–2012), gathered hundreds of interviews of musicians from around the world testifying to the spirituality of music in their lives. These publications amount to an ever-expanding public interest in the "spirituality" or religious dimension of music, regardless of religion, genre, or geographic location, which begs for a more intellectual or academic venue for research and scholarship.

Envisioning Musicology of Religion

I pause at this point for a personal and professional narrative on how this project on Musicology of Religion was conceived and generated. The narrative progresses through several phases, beginning in New York City where I was born, then to Upstate New York, Denver, to India and back, then on to Florida, Syracuse, and lastly to Louisiana in pursuit of an academic career in religion and music. Throughout the journey, my parents were instrumental in their support and encouragement. With roots in Minneapolis, they began their professional lives in New York City where my father, Harold Cooke, worked as a professional musician: composer, vocal arranger for Broadway shows, and pianist at the famous Blue Angel. As a close friend and colleague of fellow Minnesotan, piano legend Cy Walter, he was well connected with a coterie of popular musicians and composers in Manhattan. I was told that he opened for singer Mabel Mercer on occasion. There are faint memories of our house being filled with lively conversation and the music of George Gershwin, Cole Porter, and Benny Goodman from the Great American Songbook. My mother, Dale Hanson, worked as an interior designer at Raymond Loewy's firm in New York. As she was also musically trained, I took piano lessons and sometimes even visited places where my dad was playing. However, things were about to change, but not without a silver lining.

When I was about age ten, my mother married again, to George A. Beck, an accomplished industrial designer working for General Electric Company in Upstate New York, and who soon partnered with her to form the successful design firm George A. Beck Associates. But while my parents would have been pleased if I had taken up design or visual arts as my two younger brothers had done, they recognized that I was becoming more passionate about music. In fact, it was my good fortune that our new home featured a grand piano and a treasure trove of classical sheet music and records. Now living in a quiet rural area, I was able to continue my music training uninterrupted, this time with an emphasis on classical piano. Listening to the symphonies and concertos of the great masters, I was drawn to the beauty and richness of the European classical tradition. As a teenager, my desire to play the piano pieces of Chopin, Brahms, and Debussy led to private lessons with Professor George Mulfinger at Syracuse University's Crouse College of Music. Simultaneously, the elegance of sacred music made its impression as I was greatly moved by the singing of the *German Requiem* of Brahms in high school chorus. During church attendance, I also noticed how the rousing hymns were enhanced by beautiful organ music and its association with priestly rituals, gestures, and the tranquility of contemplative pauses. And in my senior year, playing bass guitar in a dance band enabled me to realize the dynamic effects of rhythm on groups of my peers. Thus, due to the exposure and support of music from my parents, an entire range of experiences increased my love and attraction to this great art, both sacred and secular. Yet what was missing was a mature understanding of why music was so attractive to me, and by extension, to humanity. I suddenly needed answers to a host of new questions that kept me thinking and pondering for years to come.

As an undergraduate student at the University of Denver in the late 1960s, I began, like some of my friends, to search for the meaning of life. Enrolling in courses like Introduction to Religion and Introduction to Philosophy, I subsequently took related courses in Sociology of Religion, Anthropology of Religion, and Psychology of Religion, which eventually led to a BA in the social sciences. My courses dealing with religion contained no discussion of religious music or ritual and music, and a required course on Western culture, "Arts & Ideas," included little or no mention of religion. And in those days there were no courses in ethnomusicology or world music. As I had already recognized the importance of sacred music in Western music history and was even beginning to appreciate non-Western sacred music, I was hoping for further guidance. Yet at the undergraduate level this was not forthcoming.

After university, some extraordinary life experiences in Asia made the connections between religion and music more vital, realizable, and worth investigating. Disenchanted by the moral decline of American youth on college campuses in the wake of the countercultural explosion, I had begun seeking alternative lifestyles and directions. My chosen path involved the practice of devotional Yoga (Bhakti) that included studying Sanskrit and listening to Indian music. In search of deeper knowledge and experience of Indian culture and religion, I decided to spend an extended period of time in India. Initially surprised by the direction of this quest, my parents nonetheless encouraged me to see it to completion.

Arriving in early 1976, I sought out "holy places" in northern India where there was vibrant devotional music, including Rishikesh, Hardwar, Jaipur, Prayag, Mathura, and Vrindaban. To penetrate further into this element, I spent months listening attentively to music in the Hindu temples in the Braj region in Uttar Pradesh, but also at Sikh Gurdvaras in the Punjab and other remote areas of the country. In several cases, I was assisted by devotees of the International Society for Krishna Consciousness (ISKCON), founded by His Divine Grace A. C. Bhaktivedānta Swami Prabhupāda, who, beside introducing me to the devotional music of Bengal Vaishnavism in West Bengal, guided me to other communities employing music in religious worship. However, to understand the complexities of the melodies and rhythms of the music, I realized I needed to undertake formal training in the classical music of Dhrupad and Khayal, available only in big cities like Kolkata and New Delhi. Attending weekly lessons from exponents of different schools of music in these cities over several years, I eventually rose to the standard of all-India performance, earned an academic degree in Hindustani vocal music, and appeared on Indian national television.

Although I had studied the music of several musical *gharanas* ("traditions"), I ultimately concentrated on the Agra Gharana, one of the oldest and most esteemed lineages in Hindustani music (see Vijay Kichlu 1987). In all these endeavors, I was overwhelmed by what I sensed were experiences of the divine or the sacred as manifest in music, whether classical or devotional. Thus for me religion and music often felt synonymous. The depth of insight given by my principal gurus and teachers was extraordinary: Sangitacharya Sailendranath Banerjee of Seniya Gharana (Tansen Music College, Kolkata), Shri Ashish Goswami of the Patiala Gharana (Kolkata), Dagar Brothers of the Dagar Dhrupad lineage (New Delhi), Pandit Arun Bhaduri of Kirana Gharana (Sangeet Research Academy, Kolkata), and Pandit Vijay Kichlu of the Agra Gharana (Founding Director, Sangeet Research Academy, Kolkata). In addition, I was able to hear live performances of great maestros like Pt.

Mallikarjun Mansur, Pt. Kumar Gandharva, Ustad Latafat Hussain Khan, and Smt. Hirabai Barodekar, among many others. Being blessed with a largesse of practical knowledge and experience, I was considering a professional Indian music career, yet my academic background took the upper hand as I began to contemplate the larger comparative issues and theoretical questions related to religion and music. My conviction deepened that music and religion were intimately bound together in multiple ways, not only in India but perhaps on a worldwide scale. If this were the case in Hindu and Sikh traditions, I asked, then what about other religions and cultures?

To pursue serious issues and questions regarding religion and music in an academic setting, I needed to return to America. But before departing from India in 1980, I was further blessed to have married my talented wife, Smt. Kajal Dass, in a traditional Indian ceremony. Besides directing her own art school in Kolkata, she held multiple exhibitions of her art in places like the famed Academy of Fine Arts. Continuing her work in America, she published a book on Indian decorative design (see Kajal Dass Beck 2016). After arrival, we first settled near Tampa, where my father, Harold Cooke, had retired from his career in music. He gladly pledged his assistance to my proposed plan of academic teaching and research in religion and music and helped with many arrangements. It was a wonderful reunion, as he also gave me cherished piano lessons and shared personal experiences from the good old days in New York.

For graduate studies, I enrolled in the University of South Florida in Tampa, which had just started a new MA degree program in religious studies. After acceptance into the program, I was trained in biblical literature and religion under Professors James F. Strange and William Shea, and in eastern religions and literature under Professors Daniel E. Bassuk and George Artola (visiting from University of Toronto). At USF, I was introduced to the field of ethnomusicology by Professor Patricia Waterman. As widow of Richard Waterman, one of the founders of the Society of Ethnomusicology, Patricia taught me the basics of the subject, including the most important thinkers and sources. By 1982, I was ready for doctoral studies.

In 1983, we moved to Syracuse to be near my mother who had retired from her career in interior design. Applying to the Department of Religion at Syracuse University (1983–1990) upon the recommendation of Prof. George Artola, I studied several years (1983–1990) for the PhD in Religion, South Asia, under Professors H. Daniel Smith, Agehananda Bharati, and Richard Pilgrim. During this time, foundations were provided in history of religions by Professor Charles H. Long, along with training in theology and philosophy of religion by Professors James Wiggins and David L. Miller. At SU, I also earned an MA in musicology in 1986, which included training in world music from ethnomusicologist Professor Ellen Koskoff (visiting from Eastman School of Music), and courses in the European classical tradition from Professors Howard Boatwright, George Nugent, Eric Jensen, and English musicologist Wilfrid Mellers (visiting from University of York). In preparation for my dissertation on sacred sound in Hinduism, I spent the summer of 1988 in India, conducting university-sponsored research and study under several renowned scholars, primarily Professor Gaurināth Śāstrī and Professor Govinda Gopāl Mukhopādhāya. My research and study at Syracuse University culminated in the publication of two monographs: *Sonic Theology: Hinduism and Sacred Sound* (1993), and *Sonic Liturgy: Ritual and Music in Hindu Tradition* (2012). For interested students and scholars, the basic themes and ideas from these books have become accessible in an online course, "Hindu Devotional Music and Chant," offered by the Oxford Centre for Hindu Studies, Oxford, UK.

In 1990, I began my teaching career in Religious Studies, and was in turn invited to create courses in religion and music at several institutions, including Louisiana State University, College of Charleston, Tulane University, University of North Carolina–Wilmington, and Loyola University New Orleans. But as time passed, a persistent issue kept emerging—if religion is approached from the different methods in the social sciences, why is there not a separate field where religion is approached purely through the lens of sound, music, and music-making? And therefore, just as one encounters sociology of religion, anthropology of religion, psychology of religion, and archaeology of religion, I came to envision "Musicology of Religion." Yet more steps needed to be taken on the journey before this vision could be realized.

A close precedent for this book was the preparation of an anthology on music in world religions. Professor Harold Coward of the University of Victoria (British Columbia) kindly invited me to serve as editor for the volume, soliciting other authors who were also performers. The outcome was *Sacred Sound: Experiencing Music in World Religions* (Beck 2006), which has since become a popular textbook for courses in world religions and music, covering Judaism, Christianity, Islam, Hinduism, Sikhism, and Buddhism. Although preceded by the anthologies of Joyce Irwin (1983) and Lawrence E. Sullivan (1997), the 2006 volume for the first time included recorded examples by the authors themselves, enabling students to listen to sacred music and learn simultaneously. But I also soon recognized a growing need for an accompanying text that outlined the study of religion and music as a special field of research and publication. Hence, *Musicology of Religion* may serve as a useful companion to the 2006 book.

As I continued in my teaching, I was surprised, and glad, to discover that colleagues and mentors in Asian studies shared my predilection for the combined study of religion and music. During a 1992–1993 Fulbright Research Grant, I had the opportunity to record and document a large body of the Hindu temple music that had earlier attracted my attention to the close relation between religion and music. In his foreword to the published song archive, South Asian studies scholar John S. Hawley offered these kind words:

> The strong relationship between music and religion is well known to millions of the world's citizens—people who belong to a host of contrasting religious traditions. Some of these religions go so far as to take a stand *against* the power of the tie between religion and music, so as to rescue the holy word from the vanities, distractions, and deformities that might pollute it if allowed a musical manifestation. When a religion embarks on a sonoclastic campaign of this sort, however, that effort only serves to underscore the strength of the connection that is sought to be dismantled. One of the ongoing embarrassments of the field of Religious Studies is that we represent this bond so feebly in the classroom. All too few Religion departments have a course called "Religion and Music" or some variant of that title. Yet every department should, and Guy Beck, taking a single religious tradition as his example, shows us why. (Hawley 2011: xxi)

Taking these words to heart, and recalling the generous assistance of my professors, gurus, music teachers, and especially my parents, I made the final decision to take up this project of *Musicology of Religion* when I received the invitation by religious studies scholar Robert A. Segal of the University of Aberdeen to contribute an article on Music for the second edition of *The Wiley Blackwell Companion to the Study of Religion* (2021). This was a vital stimulant, and incidentally may also serve as a thumbnail introduction to *Musicology of Religion*.

Theories and Methods

Academic interest in religion and music, while currently on the rise, has been late on arrival. Awareness of neglect was acknowledged over fifty years ago in *A Dictionary of Comparative Religion* (1970: 457), edited by S.G.F. Brandon: "The connection between music and religion is so generally recognized that it is surprising to find how little work has been done, particularly from the side of comparative religion, in relating the phenomenology of the two." The avoidance by anthropologists, musicologists, and ethnomusicologists of the religious significance of music was also noted by Brandon (1970: 457): "Musicologists, ethnomusicologists and anthropologists have assembled details of instruments, scales, rhythm, harmony (if any) and performance from many ethnic and religious areas. But, although so much is known about the practical function of music in various contexts, little attention has been paid to its significance as an aspect of religious action." Brandon also took notice that historians who have examined the development of music have sidestepped the enormous importance of religion in music-making: "Histories of music, which normally cover more or less the same ground, beginning with "primitive" music and proceeding, via the ancient civilizations, music in the Orient and the West, frequently tend to overlook the religious significance of their material" (457). Moreover, music was minimal in ritual studies, as noted by Sharpe (1971: 57): "The study of ritual, and its means of expression in art, music, and drama, has been seriously neglected by scholarship for far too long, with a consequent distortion of perspective. This whole area needs to be considered afresh."

When it comes to the study of religion and music, there are multiple perspectives. To clarify the process of understanding throughout, I have chosen to apply a typology of two theories of religion originally posited by historian of religions Eric J. Sharpe, in *Understanding Religion* (1983). The first position is the "Window Theory" of religion that considers the world, as reflected in religion or religious experience, as a "window" or opening to a possible transcendent or supernatural realm: "[A]ll things in the world and in human experience are evidence of the divine." This position is characteristic of the areas of history of religions, phenomenology of religion, and theology. Though traceable to ancient thinkers and to the influence of Kant, one finds its modern expression in terms of religion in the thought of Friedrich Schleiermacher, Wilhelm Dilthey, Max Muller, Rudolf Otto, Gerardus van der Leeuw, Mircea Eliade, and others. For music, these thinkers favor aesthetics and endorse the notion that music itself is much more than an art or skill, in fact a veritable "window" into a higher realm of reality. By contrast, the second position, the "Mirror Theory," views religion as a human projection, a social construction, or a product of historical and cultural processes. This position has dominated the social sciences and many of the humanities. Although the influences of Hume and Comte are evident here, the more accurate point of origin is Ludwig Feuerbach, a student of theology who rejected traditional Christian teachings and is the founder of the modern secular view of religion. The critiques offered by Karl Marx, Sigmund Freud, and Emile Durkheim are examples of the Mirror Theory, as each is indebted to Feuerbach in varying degrees. Regarding the role of music, it is conspicuous by its absence in works reflecting the Mirror Theory.

This book comprises eight chapters that trace the course of the Window and Mirror approaches since the nineteenth century in religion studies, social sciences (especially anthropology), musicology, ethnomusicology, philosophy, theology, liturgical studies, and cognitive studies of musical perception, religious experience, and brain function. In each of these fields, there is a reprisal of theoretical and methodological development from early twentieth-century interest in universals to the current postmodernist focus on particularity and back again to the contemporary revival of universalistic concepts and methods. The general argument is the cumulatively historical one that posits that this pattern obtains in each of the constitutive fields of religion studies and musicology, thereby justifying the coalescence of universalistic and particularistic music and religion theories and methods into a new discipline. Although some critics aim to pit one side against the other as rivals, the endgame is not to supplant relativism with universalism, or universalism with relativism, as the extreme in either direction is disadvantageous. What we are seeking here is a balance, or "creative tension," that allows for free inquiry and a diversity of options in the study of religion and music.

Providing context, I will now introduce the Window Theory and its association with the development of religious studies in its early phases when religion was considered as a universal or near universal element in human experience. Early pioneers in the phenomenology of religion also viewed music as forming an integral part of religious experience and in the dimension of the sacred or holy. A lesser-known fact is the direct influence of sound and music on the lives and works of thinkers instrumental in establishing religious studies and the phenomenology of religion. The foundations were laid in the early nineteenth century by liberal theologian Friedrich Schleiermacher (1768–1834), who single-handedly refashioned theology for the modern world. And while Schleiermacher is also credited with establishing the groundwork for the academic study of religion, with its stress on religious experience, recent studies have noted that he was also deeply engaged with music in his life, and that he made major contributions to aesthetics.

In the early twentieth century, Edmund Husserl, the founder of the philosophical school of phenomenology, became a major influence on multiple areas of academia, not the least of which was the phenomenology of religion. Interestingly, Husserl learned from German musicologists and their analyses of tonal experience. Moreover, he was influenced by Schleiermacher, who was himself impacted by Spinoza. In fact, a continuous line of understanding of the importance of self-consciousness and the world of human experience can be traced from Spinoza to Schleiermacher through Wilhelm Dilthey, and to Husserl and Otto.

As a pivotal figure in religious studies and a thinker influenced by Schleiermacher and Husserl, Rudolf Otto displayed a profound interest in sacred sound and music. He established his famous theory of the numinous, the inner core of religion as "the Holy," in the landmark study *The Idea of the Holy* (1958 [German 1917, English 1923]). The numinous experience was universal and *a priori* in authentic religious experience and could be a basis for comparative study across cultures. As a signature element in his theory of the holy, Rudolf Otto (1958: 190) recognized the importance of sound and its connection to the primordial experience of the numinous: "Feelings and emotions, as states of mental tension, find their natural relaxation in uttered sounds. It is evident that the numinous feeling also, in its first outbreak in consciousness, must have found sounds for its expression, and at first inarticulate sounds rather than words." Furthermore, Otto (49) highlighted musical experience as synonymous with the numinous, or "wholly other." "Musical feeling is rather (like numinous feeling) something 'wholly other.'"

Accordingly, Dutch phenomenologist of religion Gerardus van der Leeuw, in *Religion in Essence and Manifestation* (1938), recognized the ubiquitous nature of music and its importance for the study of religious worship. And in *Sacred and Profane Beauty: The Holy in Art* (1963: 225), he stated that "Almost all worship uses music . . . Religion can no more do without singing that it can without the word."

After Otto and van der Leeuw, however, scholars in the phenomenology of religion and history of religions appear to have lessened their interest in music, as it is conspicuously absent in the work of Joachim Wach, Mircea Eliade, Joseph M. Kitagawa, Geo Widengren, Raffaele Pettazzoni, and

Ninian Smart, among others. Despite the significance of sound and music, these categories have remained neglected as areas of inquiry in the academic fields of religious studies and phenomenology of religion. Systematic studies of texts, communities, social issues, artifacts, tools, architecture, verbal testimony, clothing, utensils, and other objects associated with a religion are routinely carried out, often at a distance from the actual practices of living religions, which are rarely silent and almost always sound-full, musical, and frequently noisy. And while the visual dimension of religion has received plentiful attention from art historians, iconographers, mythographers, and anthropologists, complementary studies in the audible or sonic realm of religion are only recently forthcoming. Reasons for this neglect have arisen due to specific challenges within the academy.

Challenges

During the research for this book, and while investigating the problem of the separation of religion and music, I came across theoretical tendencies, old and new, that have posed serious challenges to their combined study. In fact, there are factors, both internal to the discipline of religious studies and outside it, that have hampered, and may continue to hamper, the successful investigation into the cross-cultural phenomena of religion and music. One easy assumption for the distance is that music is thought by non-musicians to be "not my area of expertise." A subtler reason in religious studies may be the prevalence of Protestant attitudes that favor quietude in relation to the study of scripture and religious texts. Isabel Laack (2015: 221) has identified a more compelling reason for their separation among religious studies scholars: "After the phenomenology of religion had fallen into disgrace, scholars of religion hesitated to focus on religious experience and thus on the role of music in religions." Indeed, the turn away from religious experience and phenomenology of religion, while having negative consequences for the comparative study of religion, is indicative of a growing trend within religious studies.

One of the most important "internal" challenges to the comparative study of religion in recent decades has been the critical questioning by religious studies scholars themselves of the ideas and terminologies of "religion" and the "sacred." To provide context for this development, we note that, explicitly or implicitly, the skeptical perspective on religion deriving from Feuerbach persisted through the nineteenth century under the influence of

Marx, Nietzsche, Durkheim, and Freud, influencing the social sciences and religious studies. And surprisingly, certain forms of Christian theology have also utilized Feuerbach's radical skepticism that delimits religion as a general category. One such form in the early twentieth century was the "dialectical theology" of Karl Barth, which rejected all historical religions in favor of the special revelation of Christ. Barth also rejected the liberal theology of Schleiermacher that emphasized the possibility of universal religious experiences. Preferring the concept of individual faith instead of religion, Wilfrid Cantwell Smith, in *The Meaning and End of Religion: A New Approach to the Religious Traditions of Mankind* (1963: 21), nonetheless took note of Barth and famously proclaimed the "end of religion": "The sustained inability to clarify what the word 'religion' signifies, in itself suggests that the term ought to be dropped; that it is a distorted concept not really corresponding to anything definite or distinctive in the objective world." He (1963: 48) later reiterated this view: "My own suggestion is that the word [religion], and the concepts, should be dropped." This position seems to have been impacted by the neo-orthodoxy of Karl Barth, who denied the substance of "religion" and the credibility of the study of religion. This is supported in that, in this same work, Cantwell Smith (1963: 114, 306) pays homage to Karl Barth and his rejection of "religion" as "unbelief," by citing "The Revelation of God as the Abolition of Religion" (Section 17, Part II of Barth's *Church Dogmatics* 1948). Smith's argument also rested on statements gathered from informants from selected world religions that denied that their tradition was a "religion." Smith gives examples (1963: 115): "A modern Jewish thinker: 'The attempt to reduce Judaism to a religion is a betrayal of its true nature' . . . A prominent Buddhist religious leader: 'Buddhism is not a religion in the sense in which that word is commonly understood.' A Muslim: 'Islam is not merely a "religion" in the sense in which this term is understood in the West.'" Yet while Smith remained a theist, successive religious studies scholars influenced by Feuerbach and the Mirror Theory have gone to extremes and called for the unequivocal abolition of religion and the sacred as academic categories worthy of study.

Originally a member of the Chicago School of the History of religions, Jonathan Z. Smith, in *Imagining Religion: From Babylon to Jonestown* (1982: xi), famously proclaimed that "religion" is an academic construction: "Religion is solely the creation of the scholar's study. It is created for the scholar's analytic purposes by his imaginative acts of comparison and generalization. Religion has no independent existence apart from the academy." Smith's book was fully endorsed at the time by religion scholar Donald Wiebe:

"This book ought to be an influential force in the study of religion and in the discussion of the academic study of religion." Following this lead, many universities have produced and sheltered scholars who debunked "religion" and the legacy of the discipline of religious studies, including especially theology and phenomenology of religion, in favor of a reified "scientific study of religion." This trend is characteristic of Wiebe, who later in *The Politics of Religious Studies: The Continuing Conflict with Theology in the Academy* (1999) rebuked the work of Max Muller and Ninian Smart and called for the removal of "theology" from teaching and researching religion, instead reintroducing a scientific approach based on the evolutionary model of Darwin.

Russell T. McCutcheon, in his thesis under Donald Wiebe at University of Toronto, became one of the most severe critics of the work of Mircea Eliade, the History of Religions, and the Chicago School, dismissing the reality of the sacred as an autonomous entity (*sui generis*). In *Manufacturing Religion: The Discourse on Sui Generis Religion and the Politics of Nostalgia* (1997: 3), McCutcheon reinforced the view of Jonathan Z. Smith above: "The common assertion that religion per se or private religious experience in particular, is *sui generis*, unique, and sociohistorically autonomous, is itself a scholarly representation that operates within, and assists in maintaining, a very specific set of discursive practices along with the institutions in which these discourses are articulated and reproduced." Wiebe, however, doubted this assertion of McCutcheon:

> There are a number of scholars who take a constructivist view of religion, arguing that religion is the product of the scholar's attention rather than an independent or autonomous reality. Russell McCutcheon (1997), for example, argues such a case against Eliade and his followers who claim religion to be a *sui generis* reality. Although I agree with McCutcheon's critique of the notion of religion as wholly autonomous with respect to other aspects of our social and cultural existence, it seems to me unwarranted to claim that religion is therefore the product of the scholar's study. Surely it is the product of human activity long before scholarly attention is focused upon it; indeed, only if that were so, could we pay such attention to it. (Wiebe 1999: 295)

McCutcheon had also greatly enlarged the target group of *sui generis* scholars, as indicated in the author's description: "Surveying the textbooks available for introductory courses in comparative religion, the author finds that they uniformly adopt the *sui generis* line and all that comes with it." And although he recognized the influence of Wilfrid Cantwell Smith on scholars who critiqued "religion," McCutcheon unfairly placed him alongside Otto and Eliade in being advocates of *sui generis* religion (or faith) and opposed to naturalistic explanations. The overall impact of McCutcheon in dividing the field in this way appears mitigated in a statement by Ivan Strenski (2015: 157), one of the early critics of Eliade: "McCutcheon's reaction is to indict the entire religious studies community of buying into Eliade's idea of the autonomy of religion. While McCutcheon's jabs at Eliade land serious blows, his attempt to knock out the modern study of religion is well wide of the mark."

Extending the critique of "religion" beyond the scholar's study, McCutcheon (1997) endorsed the view that the study of religion has dangerous geo-political ramifications. As stated in the description, "on the geo-political scale, he contends, the study of religion as an ahistorical category participates in a larger system of political domination and economic and cultural imperialism." Continuing this line of dismissing "religion" as part of a broader postcolonial critique of Western culture, Timothy Fitzgerald, in *The Ideology of Religious Studies* (2000), once again attacked Max Muller and Ninian Smart and called for not only the abandonment of the concept of "religion" from public discourse but also the elimination of religious studies departments and religion publishers due to their being an accessory to imperialist agendas. As for McCutcheon, "religion" for Fitzgerald is no longer merely the innocent creation of the scholar but is now part of an ideology by which religious studies and those who profess it (as "religionists") are complicit in Western imperialism and its oppression of non-Western people: "Instead of studying religion as though it were some objective feature of societies, it should instead be studied as an ideological category, an aspect of modern western ideology, with a specific location in history, including the nineteenth-century period of European colonialism" (Fitzgerald 2000: 4). Two other studies that have followed the postcolonial critique of religion include Daniel Dubuisson's *The Western Construction of Religion: Myths, Knowledge, and Ideology* (2003) and Brent Nongbri's *Before Religion: A History of a Modern Concept* (2013).

There are counter arguments to the above claims and assertions, some of them, cited above, coming from within the discipline. But as these debates fall outside the scope of this book, we take note of only a few responses. The main point for our purposes is that none of the new critics of "religion" and religious studies mention music or chant in their works. This observation suggests that, although music is a formative factor in world religions, its de-emphasis in religious studies has given the discipline a certain vulnerability that can be remedied through meretricious work in the Musicology of Religion. Additionally, the most misunderstood aspect of Eliade's thought is the mistaken idea of the sacred and profane existing as separate ontological realities. Against the claim of McCutcheon and others that the sacred in Eliade refers to a *sui generis* or autonomous reality beyond human existence, Bryan S. Rennie (1996: 30), a prominent interpreter of Eliade, replies: "The opposition of the sacred and the profane lie within the human existential condition and not outside it in some ontological dichotomy." And when Eliade speaks of a dialectic of the sacred and profane, these are not mutually exclusive realities as claimed by his critics but are interconnected in complex ways (Rennie 1996: 31): "Although the starting point for an understanding of Eliade's sacred is its dialectical opposition to the profane, it becomes apparent that the conclusion is not one of simple opposition but one of complex interdependence." Further discussion of the similarities in Eliade and Schleiermacher appears in the next chapter.

Countering the critique of religion as a mere "social construct," Kevin Schilbrack, in "Religions: Are There Any?" (2010: 1121), presents examples in defense of the very idea of a concept: "To show that a concept is a social construction says nothing about whether or not that concept identifies something real. The concept of 'molecule' and 'magnetic field' are social constructs, but this alone does not show that the entities so labelled are chimerical." Schilbrack includes the categories of gender, sexism, colonialism, and imperialism to demonstrate that concepts are not "unreal" simply because they are concepts. Indeed, religion is still the most useful category in which to gather distinct examples or manifestations. Without a precise definition of beauty, for example, scholars of aesthetics continue to discuss "beauty" in diverse contexts. A thought experiment may apply here: just as there is no such thing as a generic automobile, only specific brands like Mazda and Buick, there is no generic "religion" as such. Yet we continue to talk about the reality of automobiles, and religion, and need to do so. Kenneth Rose cites the example of the concept of "cat" to validate the search for the otherwise generic or universal features of religion:

> Against the charge, certain to be raised by many religious studies scholars, that a return to an interest in the generic religious features of religion *as religion* will undercut the scholarly focus on

particular religious traditions, I would suggest that the preference of many scholars for the singular in religion no more invalidates the search for the shared in religion than the preference for one's own cat over a neighbor's cat invalidates the use of the concept of "cat." (Rose 2016: 111)

Taking note of all these critical trends, religious studies scholar Kenneth Rose (2016: 110) has noted their threat to the study of comparative religion: "With the same sweeping gesture of dismissal that recent religious studies scholars pushed Eliade aside, they also rejected comparative work of other great comparativists of the last century such as Joachim Wach, Gerardus van der Leeuw and Rudolf Otto." Consequently, instead of pursuing comparative religion in the direction of the Chicago School, the discipline of religious studies has questioned the very usefulness of the term "religion," embraced the cultural relativism of anthropology, and rejected typological categories involving the sacred and the profane. Rose (2016: 111–112) has explained: "Taking its cues from Wilfrid Cantwell Smith, Clifford Geertz and Jonathan Z. Smith, contemporary academic religious studies set out boldly over a generation ago to overturn and render obsolete and passe the typological imagination of the old Chicago School and its projects of tracing the morphology and typology of religion, of which Wach and Eliade were masters."

In response, the discipline of religious studies needs to reconsider the consequences and reclaim its legacy. Rose has advised:

Although these foundational masters of religious studies have been relegated to the sidelines in recent decades, it may be time for the discipline of religious studies once again to examine itself, to see whether its ultimate vocation is not merely mimicking the methodologies of the sciences and the other humanities but, rather, in taking up once again the search for the universal elements of human religiosity and spirituality while avoiding a crudely reductionistic and dehumanizing worldview, on the one hand, and religious particularism, extremism and fundamentalism, on the other. (2016: 122)

Despite the skepticism regarding categorical thinking, typologies that include universal factors like the sacred or the holy have indeed proven efficacious in the comparative study of religion and are necessary in terms of the study of religion and music. Certain questions need to be repeated, as recommended by Rose:

> Contemporary religious studies might understandably ask, after so long an absence from its own proper subject matter, what is the sacred? To answer this question, religious studies needs once again to turn its attention to religious universals, or the general features of religious experience that mark religious experience as *religious* and not as aesthetic, ethical, philosophical, political, biological, cultural, or psychological. This shift towards religious universals represents a return to the concerns of the older comparative religion of figures such as Joachim Wach, Mircea Eliade and Joseph Kitagawa, who were the founding figures of what is sometimes called the Chicago School of the history of religions. (2016: 114–115)

Without the concept of religion or the sacred in the sense of a universal factor for comparison among the world's religious traditions, the discipline is left hollow and irrelevant (2016: 116–117): "Since the sacred can empirically be shown to have been a pervasive aspect of human existence and its religiosity since the beginning of human awareness, to refuse to study it or to dissolve it away into other factors can be seen as an extreme instance of negative theology or as an expression of a dogmatic materialistic atheism."

While there has been the underlying assumption that the use of the term "religion" is questionable, and that it is an academic construct, scholars and educators continue to teach and discuss "world religions" and "new religions." In fact, both religious studies and ethnomusicology frequently employ the plural use of the terms "religion" (religions) and of "music" (musics). This gives fuel to the perception that the singular is inadequate and must somehow be gradually effaced in the discourse. While the proponents in both disciplines sometimes utilize similar arguments against the singular expression, the preference in ethnomusicology most often suggests a nod to cultural relativism. Since scholars question the reality and utility of the term "music" in the singular, ethnomusicologists frequently talk of "musics" rather than music, implying that there is no general consensus of what constitutes music, but only culture-specific manifestations. A visible example of this trend is the title of Elizabeth May's longstanding popular world music textbook, *Musics of Many Cultures: An Introduction* (1983). As the title of this book is "Musicology of Religion," there is obviously a preference for "musicology" rather than "ethnomusicology." A simple reason for this is that it coincides better with the commonly understood idea of "music" in the singular that is universal, or at least near universal. Peter Fletcher (2001: 41) substantiates this view: "The study of any style of music, other than study directed to proficiency in performance, is a form of musicology. To deny this is to deny even the possibility of a common musical language."

Arising outside the field of religious studies, though seemingly ingrown at times, the other challenges are ideological. Beside cultural relativism, there is Neo-Marxism, Postmodernism, and Deconstruction, as well as the theories of Freud. While a useful approach in social science research that often enables scholars to focus on one tradition alone, cultural relativism has tended to work against human universalism and comparative study. Cultural relativism, to varying degrees, considers all cultures as unique in themselves without overarching connections or possessing universal characteristics. Cultural relativism also views religion and music as individual "cases of culture," unique in their cultural context and thus culture-specific—implying that comparisons are fruitless and even undesirable. The version of cultural relativism found in ethnomusicology is referred to here as "musical relativism," the view that all forms of music are culture-specific.

Cultural relativism occupies a place within the larger context of a long-running debate about whether there are such things as universals upon which scholars can rely on to interpret and compare specific musical and religious cultures. Such universals were widely accepted in the nineteenth to mid–twentieth century through the work of philosophers, theologians, and scholars such as Kant, Schleiermacher, Dilthey, Husserl, Rudolf Otto, Carl Jung, Mircea Eliade, Gerardus van der Leeuw, and Viktor Zuckerkandl. In more recent times, however, musicologists and religionists with social science training have shifted to a more historicized and relativized view in which music and religion are seen as products of unique cultural determinants that defy meaningful comparison.

In addition to cultural relativism, the intellectual movements of Neo-Marxism, Postmodernism, and Deconstruction in the twentieth century have inhibited the study of religion and music. These movements and their ideas have permeated the social sciences and humanities over the past few decades, including the fields of religious studies and musicology. While some critiques are insightful, the comparative study of music and religion has been impacted negatively simply because these movements and thinkers have generally avoided discussion of music. Neo-Marxism is best represented in the modern world by the "Frankfurt School," first in 1920s Germany and later in the United States. Combining the theories of Karl Marx and Sigmund Freud to form "Cultural Marxism" (Neo-Marxism or the "New Left"), this group of intellectuals offered critiques of capitalism and Western "bourgeois culture" that included art, literature, and music. The Frankfurt

School was first established in 1923 as the Institute for Social Research, affiliated with the Goethe University in Frankfurt, Germany. It was also affiliated with the Marx-Engels Institute in Moscow. After the rise of the Nazis to power, the institute moved to Switzerland in 1933, and then to New York in 1934. Assisted by philosopher John Dewey and members of the progressive movement, the Frankfurt School was set up next to Columbia University. Here, it ostensibly conducted empirical research into "prejudice" and "anti-Semitism," yet also pursued analyses of Western culture and the arts that reflected, in their view, symptoms of "late capitalism." The names of Frankfurt School faculty include several widely published scholars and authors: Ernst Bloch, Erich Fromm, Herbert Marcuse, Theodor W. Adorno, Max Horkheimer, Walter Benjamin, and Jurgen Habermas. By the early 1950s, most of the Frankfurt faculty had returned to Germany, except for, principally, Herbert Marcuse, who became an icon of the 1960s counter-culture in the West. Under the banner of "Critical Theory," however, the Neo-Marxism espoused by the Frankfurt philosophers spread very quickly to colleges and universities across Europe and America.

According to Marxist thought, capitalism, as well as the religion and arts that accompany it, are "ideologies" that reflect the debased status of human existence under class struggle. As oppressive and undesirable products of historical circumstances, they are claimed to naturally fade away in a future utopia. While Karl Marx dismissed religion as "the opiate of the people," in the minds of Frankfurt thinkers, capitalism itself is identified as a "religion." Walter Benjamin, in his essay "Capitalism as Religion," claimed that capitalism is a religious cult, a parasitic transformation of Christianity (Mendietta 2005: 260–261): "Capitalism is a purely cultic religion, without dogma. Capitalism itself developed parasitically on Christianity in the West . . . Christianity in the time of the Reformation did not encourage the emergence of capitalism, but rather changed itself into capitalism." "Religion" here is not the creation of the scholar's study but allegedly thrives outside the academy as an entire economic system of oppression. And, ironically, although Freudian thought is part of Neo-Marxism, Walter Benjamin considered Freud a capitalist (Caputo 1997: 260): "Freudian theory also belongs to the priestly rule of this cult. It is thoroughly capitalistic in thought." Nonetheless, the later postcolonial critiques of "religion" and religious studies as a form of Western imperialism owe their origin and impetus to Neo-Marxist thought.

Among the Frankfurt School academics, Ernst Bloch and Theodor W. Adorno wrote about music, primarily in the context of Marxism. While

Bloch wrote historical essays on music in anticipation of a future socialist utopia, Adorno leveled criticism upon popular music as mirroring decadence in capitalist societies. Adorno's contribution to the sociology of music will be discussed in chapter 2. Ernst Bloch (1885–1977), in *Essays on the Philosophy of Music* (1985: 97), defended the view that musical forms were essentially historical, and were easily dissolved and replaced by other forms: "Just as the ancient Church modes have dissolved, so the minor and major scales left over from them will also dissolve one day." Anticipating the inevitability of atonal music, Bloch (1985: 209) described the historical and social context of all music: "So-called atonal music would not have been possible in any other era that that of the late bourgeois decline . . . Hence each musical form itself and not just its expression depends on the given relationship of men to other men and is a reflex of this."

The egalitarianism of Marxism is evidenced in Theodor W. Adorno. In his view, all tonal music should be condemned for its commodification and association with class oppression, ideally to be replaced by non-tonal or "atonal" music, which will spawn a "musical revolution." For this reason, Adorno allied himself with the twelve-tone, "atonal," musical system of Arnold Schoenberg, whereby all twelve notes of the scale must be played before repeating a note a second time—equality of notes! British philosopher and musicologist Roger Scruton (1999) has dismissed Adorno and explained how the history of tonal music has no relation to class struggle or commodity fetishism. Adorno's aim of a musical revolution via non-tonal music is also unfeasible, then, as his approach to music obfuscates the reality of traditional religious music, which is largely "tonal" and comparable across cultures.

As in Neo-Marxism, the ideological trends associated with Deconstruction and Postmodernism have offered significant but surmountable challenges in recent decades to the comparative study of religion and music. All three have attacked the very foundations of reason and rational thought deriving from the Enlightenment. Logocentrism, the notion of the metaphysics of presence that gives priority of speech over writing, as well as situations of "power," have been a target of the Deconstruction project, especially in the work of Jacques Derrida and Michel Foucault. Along with its tenet of *différance* (radical difference, and deferral), Deconstruction attempts to subvert the very possibility of cross-cultural comparison of knowledge, including that of religion or music. The arguments presented by Deconstructionists, however, are refuted by John M. Ellis in *Against*

Deconstruction (1989), which presents its inherent logical fallacies and inconsistencies. Postmodernism, which also rejects universals and the possibility of objective truth, has been contextualized and rebuffed by Stephen R. C. Hicks (2011), who has revealed the limitations of its skeptical and relativistic arguments.

A candid response to Postmodernism and Deconstruction and their rejection of universals in religion is offered by Martin Riesebrodt, in *The Promise of Salvation: A Theory of Religion* (2010: xii): "I reject the postmodern critique of a universal concept of religion and offer a historico-sociological justification for the latter. In all ages people have distinguished interaction with superhuman powers from other forms of action. In different times and cultures, religious actors and institutions have seen each other as similar, no matter whether this perception was expressed in competition and polemics or in cooperation, assimilation, and identification." More recently, British scholar Gavin Flood, in "Religious Practice and the Nature of the Human" (2016: 130–131), has reiterated the position of Riesebrodt and endorsed the comparative enterprise in religion "The post-structuralist emphasis on text and the hermeneutical enterprise of deconstruction has, in the end, proved inadequate to the task of understanding or explaining religion . . . Comparison is at the heart of religious studies and has not been abandoned even in the face of these challenges."

But while the radical ideas of the movements known as Postmodernism and Deconstruction appear to reflect a very reasoned form of atheism and even nihilism, some of the underlying evidence suggests otherwise, especially when examining the thought of Jacques Derrida, a principal founder. John D. Caputo, in *The Prayers and Tears of Jacques Derrida: Religion without Religion* (1997), has revealed a different side to this controversial figure. Caputo (1997: xviii) uncovered the religiosity of Derrida as something very private and indeterminate: "Jacques Derrida has religion, a certain religion, his religion, and he speaks of God all the time. The point of view of Derrida's work as an author is religious—but without religion and without religion's God—and no one understands a thing about this alliance." The religion of Derrida strives for a level of spiritual awareness that very few can attain (1997: 333): "Over and beyond, beneath and before any determinate purpose, there is in Derrida, in deconstruction, a longing and sighing, a weeping and praying, a dream and a desire, for something non-determinable, un-foreseeable, beyond the actual and the possible, beyond the horizon of possibility, beyond the scope of what we can sensibly imagine." There is also a messianic thread in Derrida that leads to a "no-place" of Jewish Augustinianism (1997: 333): "Far from landing us into a place of dissipation, despondency, and enervation, as its most thoughtless critics contend, *différance* leads us by the hand into a quasi-messianic place, a quasi-transcendental messianic no-place. There, in that desert no-where, charged with a passion for the impossible, grows the flower of a certain Jewish Augustinianism." Unfortunately, there is little in the way of music in this "no-place," or in the entire Deconstruction portfolio.

In a sweeping response to the challenges of Postmodernism and Deconstruction for religious studies, the articles in Kimberley C. Patton and Benjamin C. Ray (2000) have presented cogent cases for the continuation of the comparative study of religion. In this volume, historian of religions Wendy Doniger (2000: 63) is optimistic such that while Postmodernism poses a problem for comparative studies, it also offers a solution: "For the comparativist, postmodernism is both a problem (to the extent that the monolithic emphasis of difference would rule out any comparison) and a solution (to the extent that the open-ended approach to texts encourages a wider range of comparisons than had hitherto fore been imagined)." And responding to the impending challenge of Postcolonialism, the view that colonial histories have oppressed marginalized cultures, thus making comparisons problematic, Doniger (2000: 63) also waxes optimistic: "The postcolonial critique is both a problem (in inspiring a guilt that, again, when monolithic, excludes European scholars from the study of postcolonial areas) and a solution (in inspiring new areas of awareness, new consciousness, in the comparative enterprise)." In sum, each challenge is double-edged: "Each of these schools has its own double fronts, one, the earlier wave, harmful and the other, the later wave, helpful in the comparative enterprise" (63). This excellent volume is well supplemented by the collection of articles in Perry Schmidt-Leukel and Andreas Nehring (2016). William E. Paden (2016) has also revitalized comparative studies by taking account of recent developments in the sciences, humanities, and cognitive studies.

As certain claims of Neo-Marxism, Deconstruction, and Postmodernism, as well as works relating to gender, race, and social identity, are important and impact the future of the study of religion as well as music, we take note of the fact that these movements and their authors almost never discuss the topic of music and religion. Hence their influence has fostered the perception that "religion and music" is not relevant as an area of inquiry in the study of religion.

Propitious New Directions

Despite challenges posed by the ideological trends outlined above, the combined topic of "religion and music" is gathering a critical mass of information and beginning to receive proper attention in the study of religion. Moreover, work in theology, liturgical studies, philosophy, cognitive studies, and aesthetics continues to advance the case for the comparative study of music and religion, gradually surmounting the hindrances. As a portent, Bryce Rytting has reawakened the larger public to the multifaceted topography of our study:

> From the beginning religion has communicated through music. Sacred music serves monotheistic, polytheistic, and totemic religions; it served the early high civilizations of China, India, and the near East as well as the New Guinea tribes almost completely secluded from the modern world. In Western culture, most musicians depicted in early Mesopotamian and Egyptian art participate in sacred rites. In the Bible, music is the third profession to be listed (after animal husbandry and agriculture; Genesis 4:2 and 21), and song accompanies the creation of the earth (Job 38:7). Music has always resonated with the magical, the seasonal, and the mysterious essence of things. (Rytting 2010: 275)

The tide had already begun shifting in 1987 with the publication of a sixteen-volume encyclopedia, *The Encyclopedia of Religion,* with Mircea Eliade as editor-in-chief. After the publication of James Hastings's twelve-volume *Encyclopedia of Religion and Ethics* (1908–1921), which included music, most general encyclopedias and dictionaries of religion have omitted music. This new reference work of Eliade signaled the importance of religion and music with a comprehensive set of articles (vol. 10, 163–215). Following the introductory article by Ter Ellingson, "Music and Religion" (Ellingson 1987: 163–172), ten articles covered music and religion in separate geographic areas: Sub-Saharan Africa; Australia and Oceania; the Americas; the Middle East; India and Southeast Asia; China, Korea, Tibet, and Japan; Greece, Rome, and Byzantium, as well as Religious Music in the West. Ellingson (1987: 163) opened this project with the caveat informing us that religion and music occupy a universal and pervasive phenomenon despite modern sensibilities toward music: "Seldom a neutral phenomenon, music has a high positive value that reflects its near-universal importance in the religious sphere. This importance—perhaps difficult to appreciate for post-industrial-revolution Westerners accustomed to reducing music to the secondary realm of 'art,' 'entertainment,' and occasional 'religious' music isolated behind sanctuary walls—has nonetheless been pervasive."

As additional beacons of hope, new anthologies for classroom use have appeared that introduce music as a significant feature in the study of world religions (Irwin 1983; Sullivan 1997; Beck 2006). In the preface to *Sacred Sound: Music in Religious Thought and Practice* (1983: vi), Joyce Irwin waxed prophetic for the *Musicology of Religion*: "The present volume is only a first step in the direction of a phenomenology of religious music." Lawrence E. Sullivan, in *Enchanting Powers: Music in the World's Religions* (1997), has advanced the topic of religion and music with important questions set out in the book description: "What is religious about music? What is intrinsically musical about religion? Why does music evoke religious experience in a way no other expression can?" My own volume, *Sacred Sound: Experiencing Music in World Religions* (Beck 2006), has served the immediate need, in part, for a textbook on music and chant in six world religions, including a CD of selections for student use. See Appendix A for details on all three anthologies, and on the encyclopedias mentioned.

After a long hiatus, professional academic meetings devoted to religion and music have begun to appear (see Appendix A). Moreover, provocative articles also display the rise in attention to the religious side of music. Within the span of thirty years, much progress can be observed. For example, while historian of religion Lawrence E. Sullivan had introduced the sacred music of several indigenous peoples in his pioneering essay, "Sacred Music and Sacred Time" (1984), Martin Hoondert, in "Musical Religiosity" (2015: 128), very nearly equates religious and musical experience: "I want to defend the thesis that music is by its nature religious, or rather, that it has qualities that correspond well with what religion aspires to be. If we listen intensely, we participate in the movement and in the 'now' of the music."

The growing abundance of original research and publication in the separate areas of religious studies and musicology also warrants and supports a new discipline. Scholarly surveys of current research on sound and music in religion, such as Rosalind J. Hackett (2012) and Isabel Laack (2015), are useful tools moving forward. Hackett (2012: 11), after reviewing the work of "authors who have overcome what Isaac Weiner calls our 'disciplinary deafness' and made the sound of the sacred a centerpiece of their research and publication," evoked optimism for the study of music and religion: "In sum, we have greater opportunities than ever before to compare musical and non-musical sound within and across cultures and religious traditions" (2012: 21). Pressing the issue further, Laack (2015: 221) made an urgent call for major change: "Regardless of the reasons for the neglect of sound and music in the academic study of religion, a wide gap in the research remains. Too many experiences of religiosity have been overlooked, too many forms of religious experience have been ignored, too many religious aspects in music have been left unseen and too many factors in identity negotiations and political conflicts have been left undetected."

The future indeed depends on innovative and ambitious scholars to answer the challenges posed here by Laack (2015: 235): "Apart from the sound and music that are used in religious practices and religious references in secular music cultures, many more forms of relationships exist between sound, music and religion that have gone virtually unnoticed to date." In terms of method, Frank Burch Brown, in "Musical Ways of Being Religious" (2014), offered a composite picture of how the academic disciplines of religious studies and theology can be successfully coordinated for the study of religion and music. In fact, Brown (2014: 109) enunciates the methodological position explored and expanded in the present book: "The music that is most easily identified as religious is usually combined with words or with ritual action."

Overall, the general direction indicated by the recent studies in religion and music is that a basic understanding of the role of music in the cultic life of religious communities worldwide is not only desirable but in fact indispensable for the most accurate and authentic portrait of religion. Let us recall the salient points. The historical record speaks for itself and reminds us of the overwhelming importance of music and chant in religion. In fact, the sonic dimension of religious experience, including the phenomena of chant and music, simply cannot be ignored by the academy when one approaches the study of religion or sacred traditions. In the process of rendering sacred texts, devout prophets, chazzans, cantors, tzaddikim, priests, friars, ministers, mullahs, imams, pundits, gurus, swamis, rāgīs, bhikkhus, kīrtanīyas, roshis, monks, and countless others chant and sing Jewish Psalms, Hassidic Niggunim, Christian Hymns, Qur'anic verses, Islamic Calls to Prayer, Vedic Mantras, Hindu Ślokas, Kīrtans and Bhajans, Jain Stavans, Sikh Shabads, Buddhist Sūtras, and Zen Koans. The oral delivery of scripture is often upheld by tradition as statutory, such as in Judaism where Jewish law requires it. The Qur'an is not considered authentic by orthodoxy if studied in translation or read silently. For thousands of years Hindu law forbade the writing down of sacred texts, with serious penalties for violation. Buddhist Sūtras are always chanted, as are Sikh, Zoroastrian, Jain, Taoist, and Confucian prayers. Despite this, hermeneutical and exegetical studies of scriptural texts have often neglected their oral or sound-full dimension.

Chanted scripture in religion is of critical importance due to its sonic origin and the fact that it is received or "heard." Believed to have a "transcendent origin," such sacred sound is "set apart" from other natural sounds ("profane sounds"). Examples include the notion of "the Word of God," the sounds of angels and heavenly chariots, voices in dreams, and communications of ancestors or ghosts. Priests, saints, and religious communities of yore understood the significance of such sound events as they consecrated spaces and marked calendars for events. Ancient cultures like Vedic India revered the power of sound to such a degree that the universe was understood by intelligentsia to have been created from it. Sacred syllables such as OM in Hinduism have represented this cosmic sound and are safeguarded by religious law against contamination through misuse or neglect. Western monotheistic traditions, while containing episodes of divine visions, have preferred hearing rather than seeing God: for example, instead of seeing the divine, Abraham and other Patriarchs hear God, and Paul has a vision of Jesus who speaks profound messages, giving a preeminent status to sound. And whether associated with monotheism, polytheism, pantheism, monism, goddess worship, or animism, the elements of music and chant reflect a deeply significant network of similitude among diverse religious communities. Music is usually associated in religion with notions of the self as a real entity, temporary or immortal, yet Ter Ellingson (1987: 164) notes how Buddhism understands music in reference to the absence of self: "One group of Buddhist texts takes music as the archetypal embodiment of impermanence and conditioned causality, dependent on external sources and conditions, in order to show that there can be no such thing as an individual self." And while most traditions revere "sounded scripture," pristine silence is also valued by tradition, as in Zen Buddhism, the Society of Friends (Quakers), modern Indian movements like the Sri Aurobindo Ashram and the Ramakrishna Mission, and Catholic religious orders such as the Trappists.

In Western culture, music is the only art named after a divinity. The Bible recounts in Genesis 4:21 that the patriarch Jubal was the ancestor of all musicians and instrument makers. In Islam, Arab instruments such as the Ud are attributed to this same patriarchal family. Sacred stories and narratives around the world, while frequently embedded in literature, are often expressed in performance, combining vocal and instrumental music and dance. Hence musical instruments of various kinds also have sacred or transcendent value. In every culture, musical instruments are believed to have a divine origin. In India, as in ancient Greece and other cultures, the gods themselves play musical instruments. Revealed or "produced," musical instruments are a vital part of multiple religious observances. Most religious traditions embrace and elevate the unique sounds emanating from instruments. Though comprising material elements, bells, chimes, gongs, rattles, cymbals, drums, horns, flutes, and strings transform into sacred artifacts when employed in religious services or as part of ritual. Yet other traditions minimize musical instruments to allow for full attention to the verbal chant, psalm, or recitation, as in Rabbinic Judaism, Orthodox Islam, Theravada Buddhism, and Calvinist Christianity.

In his pioneer work *The Presence of the Word* (1967), Walter Ong emphasized how the sonic dimension of reality functions in special ways different from the other sense experiences. For him, sound conveys or reveals presence more than the tactile or the visual sense. Since sound expresses the interiority of people more than other sense experience, including movement and gesture, it best serves to bind people together in a religious community. David Burrows, in *Sound, Speech, and Music* (1990), built on this premise by arguing that, since song originates deeper in the human body than speech, and as there is less semantic intention in singing as opposed to speaking, it is the musical or tonal dimension of sound, rather than mere speech, that more fully unites people instead of dividing them. In terms of religion, the goal of uniting believers of any persuasion into a unified community is achieved when a commonly understood frame of reference is shared by all members. Within the context of a sacred text or teaching, the tonal dimension of language serves to bring that text or teaching more effectively into a common symbolic realm. Accordingly, key religious texts in all the world's religious traditions are sung or chanted in some form of tonal performance rather than merely read aloud.

Religious studies scholar Harold Coward has been an auspicious harbinger of the present book in several ways through his consistent emphasis on the sonic dimension of language. His breakthrough work, *Sacred Word and Sacred Text: Scripture in World Religions* (1988), attracted scholarly attention with his theoretical analysis of the oral dimension of scripture in world religions. In a subsequent edited volume, *Experiencing Scripture in World Religions* (2000), scholars of Judaism, Christianity, Islam, Hinduism,

Sikhism, and Buddhism confirm the importance of the oral rendition of scripture in their respective traditions. The basic premise of the volume is stated clearly at the outset (2000: 1): "In all religions the scriptural word is seen as a means of revealing or realizing the Divine. However, this spiritual power of the word is most often located in the oral rather than the written form of scripture. It is the spoken sound that effectively evokes the Divine."

In a later work, *Word, Chant and Song: Spiritual Transformation in Hinduism, Buddhism, Islam, and Sikhism* (2019), Coward establishes that the spoken or sung expressions of sacred texts in world religions transform the self and directly reach the heart, a theme that resonates cross-culturally: "It is the heard music, not the written score, that is the real thing, Similarly, it is the spoken word in scripture reading, sermon, chanting, or hymn singing that has transforming power. Unlike the merely written text, the oral speaking, chanting, or singing enters the hearts of individuals and joins speakers and hearers together into a fellowship of the word—a logos of giving and receiving. The obstacle to faith is a defective sense of hearing. It is through hearing and oral confession that salvation is realized" (2019: 5). Since scholars of the sacred texts of world religions often characterize them as symbolizing or expressing the "wholly other" of religious experience, their sonic manifestation as chant or music is "transcendental," forming a bridge between word and rite within communities.

Accordingly, the immense historical record of data collected on the relation of music and religion, along with the rising current of discussions of the role of music in various religious traditions, points to the growing need to identify religion and music as a singular unit of study and research. The principal objects of study for the Musicology of Religion are the visible and/or invisible connections between religion and music in the broadest sense, utilizing the methods necessarily geared toward finding cross-cultural patterns and insights about religion that may be concealed or less obvious. The successful pursuit of Musicology of Religion thus requires a refined approach that nonetheless draws on a variety of disciplines representing both the Window Theory and the Mirror Theory, including, but not limited to, history of religions, theology, philosophy, aesthetics, phenomenology, anthropology, sociology, psychology, linguistics, neuroscience, and cognitive studies. As a proper academic response, this book presents the case for a new field, Musicology of Religion, by outlining useful theories, methods, and directions as part of the task of organizing an important and emerging area of scholarship.

Plan of the Book

Following this Introduction, in which I have laid out the landscape for the study of religion and music and the need for Musicology of Religion, Part I surveys the position and presence, or absence, of music in traditional disciplines of the modern university, including religious studies, anthropology, psychology, sociology, and musicology (including ethnomusicology). The discussion in Part I, Theories and Methods, presents evidence and reasons for the lack of attention to religion and music, including theoretical challenges that have prevented their comparative study across disciplines. This is followed by new directions within these fields, as indicated by recent scholarship. As the proposed "Musicology of Religion" is built on the feasibility of comparative studies, issues of universalism versus relativism, supernaturalism versus naturalism, and insider (emic) versus outsider (etic) with respect to music and religion are entertained as a broader set of concerns in each of the disciplines discussed.

Chapter 1 discusses the development of the discipline of religious studies and its relation music. As representative of the "religionist position" and the Window Theory, the focus is on religious experience, including phenomenology of religion and history of religions, areas in which music has played a formative role. Chapter 2 on the social sciences contrasts the two theories, namely the Window Theory of scholars in religious studies and theology, and the Mirror Theory representing the social science approach to religion, culture, and music. Several issues regarding music are also discussed in the subsections on psychology and sociology. Chapter 3 on musicology discusses the rise of "ethnomusicology" and its indebtedness to anthropology, and the methods associated with cultural relativism, or "musical relativism."

Part II, New Directions and Paradigms, outlines areas of positive reassessment as well as promising research that most directly influence the creation and development of the new field of Musicology of Religion. These include philosophy, theology, liturgical studies, and cognitive studies. Chapter 4 on philosophy and music recounts the Pythagorean concept of harmony as a useful philosophical construct bridging the universal with the particular across cultures and religions, countering to a degree the claims of musical relativism. Chapter 5 on theology and music describes the viewpoints of theology and natural theology in terms of the universality of music, music as Divine Gift, the presence of musical angels, and music in the afterlife, both in the West and in Eastern traditions. A focus on Protestant, specifically Lutheran theology, assists in understanding the enormous output of religious music as part of the Western classical tradition. The chapter closes with discussion of Hindu theology and music to provide a balance to the Western emphasis in the first part of the chapter. As an area of theological studies, liturgical studies is the subject of chapter 6, which begins with a brief outline of ritual studies, and follows by recounting some of the interesting cross-cultural work in the study of liturgy, especially with reference to "sound events" in Hinduism, Buddhism, Jainism, and Sikhism. In chapter 7, discussions of research in cognitive studies and neuroscience regarding the prominent place of religiosity and musicality in human evolution and as permanent features of civilization support the premises for establishing the Musicology of Religion.

Part III, Homo Religiosus and Homo Musicus, presents the closing arguments for Musicology of Religion by reiterating and reassessing the foundational dimensions of both religion and music as essential components of human nature. As such, the main points and issues from the previous chapters are reviewed and enlarged in chapter 8 to present the total case for the creation of this new field of study, with suggested methods and approaches that foster growth, including new research in comparative religion, theology, and aesthetics. This is followed by useful appendices of resources and current outlook, with a helpful glossary of terms for the Musicology of Religion. Although much of the data and content for this new field are already well established, the reality of connecting all the data points to create a place for the combined study of religion and music is incumbent on necessity and rapidly growing interest.

I
Theories and Methods

Chapter One

Religious Studies and Music

> Almost all worship uses music . . . Religion can no more do without the singing than it can without the word . . . Music represents the great struggle of reaching the wholly other.
>
> —Gerardus van der Leeuw,
> *Sacred and Profane Beauty: The Holy in Art*

> Across time and geography people have known the power of music for evoking gods and acquiring spiritual insight, whether arising as a textless chant by a single voice or a percussive auditory event for ritual dance, music in its various modes is a virtually ubiquitous companion to religious and spiritual practices.
>
> —Edward Foley, *Music and Spirituality*

> Around the world, music and sound play a vital role in many people's lives and often lie at the heart of their cultural and religious identities. Music, sound, and silence form important parts of religious rituals, and many creation myths including them in their narratives. Complex musical styles have been created within the diverse religious traditions in human history.
>
> —Isabel Laack, "Sound, Music and Religion"

The words "religion" and "music," as primary signifiers of the proposed "Musicology of Religion," require a fresh look at their meaning. We begin in this chapter with the term "religion," followed by a brief synopsis of how religious studies has evolved to the point where the inclusion of music becomes unavoidable.

One of my religion professors at Syracuse University used to say, "when beginning a topic, do an etymology." In that spirit, our context for understanding religion begins with the ancient Greeks and Romans. Historian of religions Eric J. Sharpe, in *Understanding Religion* (1983: 39), sets down the definitional parameters for the term "religion" by reminding us that the Latin term *religio*, from which the word religion is derived, "has strong overtones of a political and moral nature. When the Roman writers used it, they were not describing something, but rather setting bounds to something." Two reputed authors of Antiquity, Cicero and Lactantius, may be consulted here for clarification. Cicero traced the term "religion" from *relegere*, "to re-read" (as in chant), which is passed on from generation to generation. This resonates with the notion of oral transmission and music, since the academic consensus affirms that religious texts in the ancient world were chanted or sung by practitioners. Lactantius, on the other hand, traces *religio* from *religare*, "to bind fast" that which binds people to one another and to the gods. This is the more commonly understood definition. However, according to Sharpe, there is no way of knowing which was right. It seems that either or both are satisfactory.

In a broader context, the ancient Romans distinguished between *religio* and *superstitio*, religion and superstition. According to Sharpe (1983: 40), "*religio* contained *deorum cultu pio* [the pious worship of the gods]." In this regard, "To worship is to revere, not necessarily the maker of the world, but the acknowledged maker of the tribe, city, state or community." The difference between religion and superstition was determined by custom and political authority: "The dividing line passed between what was officially acceptable within the bounds of a particular social and political organization, and what was not."

On the other hand, *superstitio* involved *timor inanis deorum* ("the unreasoning fear of the gods"), and as such was unhelpful to the individual and harmful to the body politic. As explained by Sharpe (1983: 40), "The 'supernaturals' who were acknowledged on the individual level of 'superstition' were not unimportant on the local level: but they had 'made' nothing, least of all the state. Superstition is therefore political, as well as religious, nonconformity, in which the solemn assembly is replaced by unnecessary and unreasoning feat." In this way, the Romans considered as superstition "all that did not conform to the formal, legalistic and conservative state orthodoxy and orthopraxy." For comparison, one may note the Hellenes versus the Barbarians, the Christians against the heathens, and even the Jews over the Gentiles.

Providing a sense of context, Sharpe (1983: 41) further elucidates: "Inside the circle there is order, and there is the gift of life, given by the supernaturals and shaped by law: outside there are only (literally) 'the lesser breeds without the law. They may regulate their lives as they please. They cannot regulate them perfectly. Unreasoning superstition is regulated only by fear: religion (or more properly, *religio*) is regulated by reverence for a divinely established, and therefore 'true,' order of things."

Applying biological categories, the term "religion" would ideally refer to a genus or universal phenomena, and "a religion" a specific species or type. Yet Sharpe (1983: 41) notes that in modern usage the universal aspect seems to retreat in favor of the particular manifestation: "In modern terms, *religio* expressed not 'religion' as a universal form of human behavior related to the sacred, but a religion—a circumscribed form of belief and social organization related to the ethics and structure of a particular culture or group of cultures." Wilfrid Cantwell Smith (1963: 26) has presented two sides of the ancient understanding of religion; one of which goes outward to external realities, and the other toward inner realities, anticipating Schleiermacher and his emphasis on religious experience: "While Lucretius fortified the strand that used the term [*religio*] to refer to something 'out there' impinging on man, Cicero's designation was usually of something interior to persons."

In our own time, the use of the name of "religious studies" raises interesting issues. According to Sharpe (1983: viii), "The trouble with 'religious studies' is the adjectival use of the word 'religious.' We speak of religious drama and religious music, religious behavior and religious ritual, and mean that each is shaped by a quality of devotion or by religious experience." The concept of studies that are "religious" suggests preparation for a vocation. But in the academy, it means, rather, "studies in and around the phenomena associated with religion."

The question of the truth value of religion or of a specific religion also continues to emerge in the discourse. One effective way of viewing religion, and religious music, is to compare it to the category of language—one language is not necessarily true or false, or the correct one. The word "religion" may also function in ways that are similar to "art" and "music," by which there is no "correct" art or music.

The modern rise of religious studies is the product of several phases and developments beginning with the Age of Reason or the Enlightenment of the eighteenth century. The Enlightenment perspective on natural religion (Deism) had sought a rational order to the universe as "proof" for the existence of intelligent design and thus a Creator God external to human consciousness. Enlightenment thinkers had posited that through careful observation and reflection on nature, all human beings could acquire religious truths independently of supernatural revelation. Furthermore, the rise of scientific discoveries removed the sense of mystery to the cosmos, which grew to be viewed by the public in mechanical fashion following fixed physical laws. As it were, the natural was reasonable and reason wedded to nature.

In response to the "dry intellectualism" and speculation of the Enlightenment, an undercurrent of aesthetic approaches to the phenomena of religion began to infuse the minds of theologians, philosophers, and musicians of the Romantic Period. Rather than syllogistic reasoning, ineffable emotional and artistic experiences became the hallmark of religion. In addition to pious devotion and worship of God, most significant for this new turn in religion (and music) was the experience of "the infinite in the finite," as well as the fear and sense of dependence upon the unseen powers that inhabited nature and the universe. As such, autonomous reason was not enough to account for religion, which must now incorporate feeling and inner experience. In effect, what was the "external" natural theology of the Enlightenment had been transformed into the "internal" natural theology of Romanticism, which for the Romantics had supernatural overtones because of its alleged universality. The universality of religion was based on the idea that all human beings could experience the "supernatural," later termed the "numinous" by Rudolf Otto, within their minds and hearts. Sharpe (1983: 54) explained how this switch had occurred: "In a word, what was central, essential, universal in religion—and thus that which was therefore the most capable of being studied on a world map—seemed now to be not its natural and rational, but its supernatural and irrational component." One may go further and say, with Sharpe, that "in Roman terms, where *religio* and *superstitio* come into contention, on this view it is *superstitio* which is the more universal of the two, as well as being the more deserving of being called natural religion" (1983: 54).

Thus, the most prominent definitions of "religion" in the modern world incorporate the sense of mystery, the ineffable, the supernatural, as fundamental elements of human consciousness. Accordingly, Sharpe (1983: 48) has defined religion as belief in, "the actual existence of a supernatural, suprasensory order of being, and of the actual or potential interplay, through a network of sacred symbols, of that order of being with the world." In similar fashion, Oxford professor Keith Ward, in *Religion and Revelation: A Theology of Revelation in the World's Religions* (1994: 51) offered a working definition of religion as, "beliefs and practices concerning non-human spirits, beings with consciousness and will, which can affect humans for good or ill." Yet there is a qualifier, according to Sharpe (1983: 48): "The idea of a suprasensory order of being does not commit one to the existence of individual spirits, but more broadly to the existence of a supersensory dimension which underlies the perceived world and gives it meaning, purpose, and value."

Two Theories of Religion

As we proceed with this discussion, we offer much-needed clarification regarding the various positions involving theories of religion and the sacred as found in religious studies and beyond. In utilizing concepts of the sacred, the numinous, God, religious experience, and the like, one is discussing what amounts to the "religionist" position, namely, the view that takes the existence of religion and the sacred as largely self-evident, autonomous, and formative in human history. This position has been one of the mainsprings in the development of religious studies and theology as separate disciplines but is by no means dominant in the academy if one includes the broader spectrum of the social sciences and humanities. The alternate perspective is the "non-religionist" view, namely, the position that religion and the sacred are products of historical and social forces, or the result of human projection, and have no essence or enduring reality of their own. This domain includes several schools of thought as well, and scholars and students are often confused as to the arguments on each side and how each side might relate, or not, to the comparative study of religion and music. To provide a convenient method of categorization, historian of religions Eric J. Sharpe, in *Understanding Religion* (1983: 56–58), has described the diverse theories of religion as belonging to one side or the other in a grand dichotomy: either the Window Theory or the Mirror Theory. With the same data, two different interpretations are possible leading to two different senses of what is true and dependable.

The Window Theory in its pristine form reflects the religionist position, which views the basic data of religion as evidence of the existence of a Deity, the transcendent, or simply the Infinite. That which sets "religion" apart from "non-religion" is the experience of the sacred, the holy, or the

Infinite. From Numen (Latin for Deity or God) comes "Numinous," that which makes the inner experience of the holy or the sacred possible, just as the term "ominous" derives from omen. This viewpoint has a long history that, influenced by Kant, includes Schleiermacher, Dilthey, Max Muller, Rudolf Otto, Gerardus van der Leeuw, and Mircea Eliade. As an example of the Window Theory, Sharpe (1983: 57) cites Otto asking us to think of an experience we have had of an inexplicable 'Something' that frightened us and attracted us at one and the same time: "This Something is not a reflection of yourself, and the experience it produces in you is totally and qualitatively different from anything else you may have felt in any other situation." Otto was convinced that experiences of this peculiar, "numinous" kind are clear enough evidence of the Numen (God) who produced them. This notion developed as a useful comparative category to include religious experiences as well as musical experiences across all cultures and traditions.

Considered a pioneer in establishing the field of comparative religion or the "Science of Religion," the Orientalist and religion scholar Friedrich Max Muller was an important link between Kant, Schleiermacher, and Otto, and has summarily articulated the religionist position of the Window Theory. In his *Lectures on the Science of Religion* (1870), Max Muller revealed how the religionist position went beyond the philosophy of Kant. Although Kant had proved that knowledge requires the admission of two independent faculties, the perceptions of the senses, and the categories embedded *a priori* in human consciousness, he did not go far enough, according to Max Muller (Jon R. Stone 2002: 114): "Satisfied with having established the independent faculty of reason, . . . [and] with having proved the possibility of apodictic judgments *a priori*, Kant declined to go further, and denied to the intellect the power of transcending the finite, the faculty of approaching the Divine. He closed the ancient gates through which man had gazed into Infinity." As such, Max Muller posited that a third faculty for apprehending the Infinite needed to be identified: "If philosophy is to explain what is, not what ought to be, there will be and can be no rest till we admit, what cannot be denied, that there is in man a third faculty, which I call simply the faculty of apprehending the Infinite, not only in religion, but in all things; a power in a certain contradicted by sense and reason, but yet, I suppose, a very real power, if we see how it has held its own from the beginning of the world, how neither sense nor reason have been able to overcome it, while it alone is able to overcome both reason and sense."

In a later lecture, "The Perception of the Infinite," from *Lectures on the Origin and Growth of Religion* (1878), Max Muller explicated this third faculty and its association with feeling, a theme reminiscent of Schleiermacher and German Romanticism:

> If I differ from Kant, it is only in going a step beyond him. With him the supersensuous of the Infinite would be a mere *Nooumenon* [transcendent reality] not a *Phainomenon* [empirical reality]. I maintain that before it becomes a *Nooumenon*, it is an *Aistheton* [aesthetic reality] though not a *Phainomenon*; it is felt, though not yet represented. I maintain that we, as sentient beings, are in constant contact with the Infinite, and that this constant contact is the only legitimate basis on which the Infinite can and does exist for us afterwards, whether as a *Nooumenon* or as a *Phainomenon*. I maintain that, here as elsewhere, no legitimate concept is possible without a previous percept, and that that previous percept is as clear as daylight to all who are not blinded by traditional terminologies. (Stone 2002: 187)

This is the Window Theory par excellence, explained by one of the most learned scholars of world religions at that time. The "third faculty" described by Max Muller is theoretically a "missing-link" between the realms of the human and the Divine across cultures. Further, the idea that the Window Theory may be explicitly related to aesthetics and feeling, and thus to the perception of music, is of fundamental interest to the Musicology of Religion.

The Mirror Theory, on the other hand, claims that the same data can "mirror" or reflect human self-understanding, whether as individual or as community. Rather than real entities or representatives of the sacred or the Infinite, they are instead "projections" of the needs of the individual human being and the social order. Although influenced by the skepticism of Hume and Comte, it was Ludwig Feuerbach and his initial theory of projection that gave momentum to the Mirror Theory. The Mirror Theory includes the historical materialism of Karl Marx, the psychological theories of Sigmund Freud, and the sociological theories of Emile Durkheim, considered the founder of sociology and an icon in the rise of the social sciences. Religion scholar Rodney Stark (2021: 30–31) describes the genesis of sociology and how Durkheim's view is indebted to Feuerbach: "During the nineteenth century August Comte (1798–1857) coined the word 'sociology' to identify a new field that would replace religious 'hallucination' as the guide to morals. Then Ludwig Feuerbach (1804–1872) 'discovered' that humans create Gods in their own image. That thesis was appropriated (without acknowledgement) by Emile Durkheim (1858–1917), who taught that society itself is always the true object of religious worship." Accordingly, while Durkheim gave us the distinction of sacred and profane (*pro fanum*—outside the sanctuary), these distinctions meant by him that they were made by social consensus and not by the actual or real presence of the sacred or God. In Durkheim's view, the sacred amounts to a reflection of the self-understanding of a human community. That which is sacred becomes so by human consensus and is preserved by custom. The formation of "religion" is simply that such concepts are combined into a unity.

Sharpe (1983: 58) has acknowledged that the current discipline of religious studies operates between these two theories, the Window Theory and the Mirror Theory: "If we take Otto's and Durkheim's positions as types and patterns, then it would not be too much to claim that they represent the two opposite poles of religious studies today—Otto pious, individual-centered, taking the data of religious experience as proof that God has never left himself without a witness. Durkheim rationalist, community-centered, taking precisely the same data as evidence that mankind's religiosity stems from his own and (particularly) his community's needs." In simple terms, the dilemma is that the transcendent realm either exists or it does not.

A new perspective on this dichotomy of theories was introduced by Paul Ricoeur in *Freud and Philosophy: An Essay on Interpretation* (1970). In terms of hermeneutics or theories of interpretation, he described two ways of interpreting religion: "hermeneutics of recollection" (cf. Window Theory) and "hermeneutics of suspicion" (cf. Mirror Theory). Van A. Harvey, in *Feuerbach and the Interpretation of Religion* (1995), presents both hermeneutical theories and how they have impacted the study of religion. As described by Harvey (1995: 1), the hermeneutics of recollection is, "basically sympathetic to religion because it assumes that the religious consciousness is in touch with something real and contains, therefore, a message that can be retrieved or 'recollected' . . . The interpreter of religion must take the religious consciousness and its object, the sacred, with the utmost seriousness; so much so, that he/she must be willing to accept the possibility not only that there is a message imbedded in the symbolic utterances of religion but that this message may even have relevance for the interpreter himself/herself." On the other hand, the hermeneutics of suspicion is skeptical about religion. The practitioners of this method "regard the religious consciousness as a false consciousness; therefore, they do not regard the aim of interpretation to be the retrieval of a message but the discovery of a latent and hidden meaning lying behind the conscious expression. Their aim is [not to recollect, but] to explain and demystify . . . they have devised various sorts of psychological and sociological theories that explain the way in which the manifest or expressed meaning is a function of an unconscious, hidden meaning."

Just as the hermeneutics of recollection is traceable to Schleiermacher, the hermeneutics of suspicion can be traced back to the philosopher of religion Ludwig Feuerbach (1804–1872), a one-time theology student of Hegel and Schleiermacher who later rejected the very foundations of religion including the traditional teachings of Christianity. Feuerbach's principal work, *The Essence of Christianity* (1841), caused a major stir among intelligentsia in Europe. Harvey (1995: 4) confirmed the seminal status of Feuerbach: "Feuerbach was the first to employ the concept [projection] as the basis for a systematic critique of religion." Garrett Green (2010: 420) then corroborated Harvey regarding the hermeneutics of suspicion: "The true father of the hermeneutics of suspicion, the one from who the 'masters' first learned to identify false consciousness, is the philosopher Ludwig Feuerbach." Who are these masters? According to Harvey (1995: 2), Feuerbach's influence was significant, especially upon those figures who are celebrated as the three great "masters of suspicion"—Marx, Nietzsche, and Freud:

> Each of them believed that the religious consciousness should not be taken at face value because it has been influenced or determined by powerful forces of which the believers themselves are unaware . . . at the core of these three suspicious theories of religion is the notion that religion is a "projection," that is to say that the gods are regarded as objectifications or externalizations or "reifications"—the language varies—of some internal or subjective trait or attribute that has been (mistakenly) taken to be real. The gods, as it were, are internally generated superhuman "others," and religion is the attempt to cajole, appease, mollify, and worship these "others."

Harvey (1995: 5) then explained how each of the "masters" was indebted to Feuerbach: "For Marx, religion was 'false consciousness,' an expression of an estranged social existence. For Nietzsche, it was a disorder of the instincts, a reaction to suffering and the longing for another, morally better, world. For Freud, religion was a collective neurosis. For Feuerbach, religion is the 'alienation' produced when the self, in the process of differentiation from others, makes its own essential nature another objectified being." Yet Feuerbach remains less well known and not considered one of the great "masters of suspicion" because, unlike Marx, Nietzsche, and Freud, who found religion negative and detrimental to humanity, Feuerbach had a slightly positive interpretation of religion. For Feuerbach, although religion was projection and illusory, it held value if the projected good qualities of God and the divine were taken back to where they originated, to humankind, in which case humanity would be richer and wiser. That was the "essence of Christianity."

The skeptical tradition known as naturalism, characteristic of Hume and Enlightenment thinkers, overlaps with the Mirror Theory in several ways. J. Samuel Preus, in *Explaining Religion: Criticism and Theory from Bodin to Freud* (1987), has provided a useful historical synopsis of the critical tradition of naturalism in religion. His book discusses the non-theological explanations of religion in the thought of Jean Bodin, Herbert of Cherbury, Bernard Fontenelle, Giambattista Vico, David Hume, Auguste Comte, Edward Burnett Tylor, Emile Durkheim, and Sigmund Freud, as conveyed in the description: "Examining the work of nine seminal figures spanning three centuries, Preus traces the movement away from traditional theological explanations toward the idea that religion could be accounted for without benefit of clergy."

As an important theory with adherents in both religious studies and the social sciences, the Mirror Theory will be further discussed in the next chapter. As stated, these theories should not be viewed as competitors for dominance but should complement each other to advance intellectual understanding and appreciation.

Whether or not one ascribes to either theory of religion, questions remain: How can the universal dimension of religion, if there is such a thing, be studied and researched if one is not a believer? What does it mean to study religion without commitment? In what ways are religion and music connected? For answers, and much more, we now examine the rise of the current field of religious studies in terms of religious experience, and one of its core approaches, the phenomenology of religion.

Religious Experience

The modern study of religion reserves a special place for "religious experience," encompassing emotional and affective aspects associated with nonrational factors of the religious life. This has opened the way for the inclusion of music as a universal element in religion. One of the great twentieth-century historians of religion, Joachim Wach, in *Types of Religious Experience: Christian and Non-Christian* (1951: 35), outlined a broad interpretation of religious experience for the modern study of religion: "Religious experience may be characterized as the total response of man's total being to what he experiences as ultimate reality. In it he confronts a *power* greater than any power which he controls by his own wit or strength." Wach, in *Sociology of Religion* (1944), discussed a "sociology of religion" with a stress on religious experience.

The continuing importance of "religious experience" in religious studies is reaffirmed by Wayne Proudfoot, in *Religious Experience* (1985: xi): "For the past two centuries, the issue of religious experience has been central in the work of religious thinkers and of those how have contributed to the development of the study of religion as an academic discipline. Religion has always been an experiential matter. It is not just a set of creedal statements or a collection of rites. A religious life is one in which beliefs and practices cohere in a pattern that expresses a character or way of life that seems more deeply entrenched in the life of that person or community than any of the beliefs and practices." Yet Proudfoot (1985: xv) provides a caveat: "Both *religious* and *experience* are relatively recent concepts, whose provenance is in the modern West. Though that need not detract from their usefulness in describing or analyzing the religious life of other cultures, it does mean that members of those cultures did not employ these terms in their own attempts to understand their experience and behavior." But as the recognition of the importance of religious experience was set in preference to the earlier emphases on reason and the rational comprehension of the divine as outlined by Enlightenment thinkers in Europe, Proudfoot (1985: xiii) has provided further context: "The turn to religious experience was motivated in large measure by an interest in freeing religious doctrine and practice from dependence on metaphysical beliefs and ecclesiastical institutions and grounding it in human experience."

It was in the late eighteenth century that intellectuals presented religious experience in response to the Enlightenment emphasis on reason as the highest approach in religion. The principal architect of this radical shift toward religious experience, and considered the "father of modern theology," was the Protestant theologian and philosopher Friedrich Schleiermacher (1768–1834). Schleiermacher was descended from a family of Reformed preachers, raised in the pietistic Lutheran tradition of the

Moravian Brethren, served as a pastor his entire life, and was also professor of theology and co-founder of the University of Berlin. Students in religious studies cite Schleiermacher's definition of religion as a "feeling of absolute dependence," ideally understood in relation to the real "object" or source of the feeling, God. His monumental work of 1799, *On Religion: Speeches to its Cultured Despisers,* advanced this view in terms of the experiences of the individual as well as self-consciousness in relation to others and to the infinite. Schleiermacher scholar and historian Terrence N. Tice (Schleiermacher 1969: 9), in the Introduction to his translation of *On Religion*, described the intention of this work: "Schleiermacher's aim in these addresses is to penetrate the excrescences and the corruptions of so-called religion to reach its vital heart so as to clarify what religion essentially is, to suggest how it is to be found, to consider how it may be cultivated, and perhaps also to stimulate a responding chord of sensitivity and devotion among his hears." For Schleiermacher (1969: 10), religion is "essentially a vital inner perspective on the whole scheme of things which is centered in the process of attaining true humanity and is sustained in deeply personal feeling." In praise of the work, Tice (Schleiermacher 1969: 9) noted, "These addresses are the first great modern work on religion as a whole . . . The addresses remain virtually unsurpassed in their presentation of the groundwork for an adequate theory of religion."

A more recent translator of *On Religion*, Richard Crouter (Schleiermacher 2010: 25) described how, for Schleiermacher, religion was defined as a unifying experience of the infinite within the finite: "The universe exists in uninterrupted activity and reveals itself to us every moment. Every form that it brings forth, every being to which it gives a separate existence according to the fullness of life, every occurrence that spills forth from its rich, ever-fruitful womb, is an action of the same upon us. Thus, to accept everything individual as a part of the whole and everything limited as a representation of the infinite is religion."

Seen in context, Schleiermacher's approach to religion and the divine was formed in response to the critical philosophy of Kant, who had postulated a dualism between cognitive reality (*phenomenon*) which could be known, and noncognitive reality (*noumenon*) which could not be known. Religious belief for Kant consisted of either knowing God through "pure reason," an impossibility, or doing good in terms of moral acts through "practical reason." Schleiermacher understood the context of Kant's dualism as a dialectic going back to the ancient Greek philosophers, and had especially recognized the problems associated with it from Descartes to

Kant, as recounted well by C. W. Christian (1979: 50): "This dialectic of life to which Schleiermacher points is the basis of the dualism that has characterized epistemology from the Eleatics to the present day, and that had assumed the proportions of a crisis in the century and a half from Descartes to Kant." The dialectic has existed in several ways (1979: 50): "Most of the dualities characterizing western thought reflect this dialectic: objectivity and subjectivity, isolation and involvement, the individual and the social nexus, knowing and doing, science and art, pure reason and practical reason, metaphysics and ethics." Schleiermacher understood that the true place of religion was not in either side of these dichotomies, but in a sphere or dimension that unifies them (1979: 53): "To assign religion to either of these spheres—knowing or doing—in exclusion of the other, would compromise its relation to the whole of existence, and would perpetuate the tragic separation of the world of fact from the world of value begun with Descartes and continued by Kant. It is a measure of Schleiermacher's creativity that he refused the dualism of fact and value." In the face of this dualism or "splitness," Schleiermacher hoped to heal the divisions and establish the foundation of religion as the unifying element (1979: 57): "Kant had bequeathed to the modern age his bifurcated world, split hopelessly between pure and practical reason, between the scientist and the poet. Thus, the ancient vision of the wholeness of life had been lost, and Schleiermacher's age found itself banished from the land of unity . . . True religion supplies the principle of unity which alone can heal the splitness of the modern world."

Critical of Kant for neglecting the importance of religious experience, Schleiermacher posited a third realm of feeling (*Gefuhl*) that unified knowing and doing and made the unknown realm accessible since the source of the noumenon is God. According to Robert R. Williams (1978: 4), "Schleiermacher is sharply critical of the dualism of the critical philosophy and the apparent metaphysical favoritism that Kant bestows on practical reason. There is no dualism for Schleiermacher, because religion—a modification of feeling—is the underlying foundation and unity of both knowing and doing." Religion was not only about the true and the good, as the Enlightenment thinkers had argued, but also about the beautiful, which Kant had introduced but not sufficiently developed to include its source and inspiration. Williams continued:

> According to Schleiermacher, feeling is neither knowing nor doing, but immediate consciousness; as such it is not simply

noncognitive as in Kant, but rather it is the original, pre-theoretical consciousness of reality . . . Schleiermacher contends that religious belief in God is pre-theoretical: it is not the result of proofs and demonstrations but is conditioned solely by the religious modification of feeling, namely, the feeling of utter dependence. Belief in God is not acquired through intellectual acts of which the traditional proofs for God are examples, but rather from the thing itself, the "object" of religious experience.

The real enemy of religion is the analytical spirit that fragments the universe in order to explain it. The universe can only be interpreted through the intuitive feelings of the individual.

In what would become hugely significant for the comparative study of religion and music, Schleiermacher's approach to religion lent itself to broader cross-cultural perspectives beyond Christianity or Western understandings. He was the first modern thinker to posit the possibility of a universal divine element within all human beings, recognized by scholars in the notion of *homo religiosus*, "religious man." Christian (1979: 58) identified this aspect of Schleiermacher: "Schleiermacher's argument seems to assume the awareness of the divine, however muted, in all men, at least insofar as they are capable of wholeness as selves. Since all men are equally creations of the 'World Spirit,' it is difficult to imagine a human being without at least a dim awareness of the givenness of his being . . . Man then is *homo religious*—religious man." In other words, since every human being is potentially a devout soul, by looking within our own soul we discover a feeling for unity underlying finite multiplicity. The infinite reveals itself to feeling.

As a result of Schleiermacher's "Copernican Revolution in theology," as noted by Christian (1979: 46), successive philosophers like Wilhelm Dilthey compared Schleiermacher to Kant (Makkreel 1975: 262): "In discussing Schleiermacher's contribution to religion, Dilthey calls him the 'Kant of theology' because he used the 'transcendental perspective' in defining both the grounds and limits of religious knowledge." Building upon Kant's epistemological categories for perceiving objective reality, Schleiermacher paved the way for the *a priori* capacity for religious experience that was later championed by Rudolf Otto and other phenomenologists of religion.

A century after Schleiermacher's work, in 1901, the American religion scholar Morris Jastrow Jr., in *The Study of Religion* (1981: 151–153), described the significance of Schleiermacher for religious studies: for Schleiermacher, "Only by direct experience, by an introspective process, can we reach religious truth. Religion is neither metaphysics nor morality but arises at the moment that we become conscious of a contact between ourselves and the universe. This contact he more particularly defines as a feeling of dependence. In this specific feeling, in the recognition that we cannot accomplish our ends through our own efforts alone, Schleiermacher recognizes at once the source and essence of religion." As the great unifier and believer in universalism, Schleiermacher placed all religion and all people in the same sphere of being: "Schleiermacher takes as his starting point a condition which may well be regarded as common to the most ignorant and to the most highly developed intellect. Religion thus becomes a purely subjective process . . . Schleiermacher broadly assumes that every religion is true in its kind, but the sphere being an infinite one, the feeling of dependence may manifest itself in various ways. Indeed, one might expect infinite variations, but since the religious feelings have an inner connection with another, they manifest a natural tendency to be united into a system, and the number of such systems is naturally limited." Thus, the role of feeling has permeated most studies of religion up until the present, though manifest in different ways: "His insistence upon feeling as the essential factor in religion marks his great contribution to the investigation of the subject. Others, since Schleiermacher's time, have defined religion and religious feeling differently, but the definite assumption of a religious instinct . . . forms part of almost every definition of religion proposed since the appearance of Schleiermacher's discourses."

In recent decades, Proudfoot (1985: xiii) lauded the status of Schleiermacher and explained his overall purpose: "This was the explicit aim of Schleiermacher's *On Religion*, the most influential statement and defense of the autonomy of religious experience. Religion had its own integrity, and religious belief and practice were properly viewed as expressions of the religious dimension or moment." The unique position of Schleiermacher in the overall study of religion has also been affirmed by Daniel L. Pals (1987: 267): "One might argue that there is a definably distinctive set of experiences, a singular form of consciousness, which deserves to be called 'religious.' The classic formulation of this view is to be found in Friedrich Schleiermacher. In both the early *Speeches on Religion* (1799), where he centers our attention on human feeling, on 'the sense and taste of the infinite,' and in the more mature *Christian Faith* (1821–1822), where the argument begins from our 'feeling of absolute dependence,' Schleiermacher takes it as his mission to fence off that unique realm of human experience where the true roots of religion are planted." Pals (1987: 267) continues this line of explanation:

He carefully separates the domain of emotion from those other provinces of mind which tradition-mistakenly-supposes to be the sources of religion: the reason and the will. For Schleiermacher, the irreducible core of the religious in man is a matter neither of knowledge nor action; it rests, logically prior to both, in what may be called our elemental human self-awareness. In discovering that we are selves among others, we discern our relative dependence; in discovering ourselves as fragments of a cosmic whole we register a dependence that is absolute. The second of these discoveries is crucial. For the feeling of absolute dependence is by definition unique, and it is here that the secure and *sui generis* home of religion is to be found. Religion is safe from alien explanations because the religious consciousness is unique.

Richard Crouter (2010: xxxii–xxxiii), in the Introduction to his translation of *On Religion*, affirmed the positive and resilient legacy of "religious experience" for the study of religion, crediting Schleiermacher and his supporters Rudolf Otto and Mircea Eliade for establishing the foundations: "The experiential path to religious insight has a continual appeal. Its early twentieth-century champion, Rudolf Otto, acknowledged a considerable debt to the present book [*On Religion*]. Through Otto the legacy of Schleiermacher is also linked to Mircea Eliade and the study of the history of religions. Recent work by philosophers and theologians has defended the experiential and relational aspects of his thought against charges of subjectivism and emotivism [see note 59 of Crouter's Introduction for references]. Indeed, it is difficult to see how a religious argument which seeks to demonstrate its cogency can escape the need to join issue with the nature of experience in pressing its claims."

Noting his continuing relevance for theology and philosophy of religion, Keith Ward, in *Religion and Human Nature* (1998: 26) has assessed Schleiermacher's overall contribution in terms of intuition: "He claimed to find an essence of religion, underlying all its many forms, doctrines and rituals, that was distinctive to religion and irreducible to anything else. This essence he found in experience, in what he called the 'feeling of piety' or 'the sense and taste for the infinite.' To have religion, he says, means to intuit the universe.'"

In response to critics who claim that Schleiermacher's influence is limited to Christianity and to theological issues among the faithful, one needs to see the broader context of the climate of the Enlightenment and his ability to generate a kind of "sea change" within the entire fabric of intellectual life in Western civilization. This is especially relevant while taking stock of the trajectory of the phenomenology of religion and its importance for the study of religion and music. Paul E. Capetz, in *God: A Brief History* (2003: 119), explains how Schleiermacher brought attention to individual experience and its consequence: "In contrast to the disdain with which most Enlightenment thinkers held the historically given (or 'positive') religious traditions, Schleiermacher argued that each one is an individual formation of the common essence of religion. A genuine feeling for individuality will not lead to rejection of what history has produced; rather, the appropriate attitude is the desire to cultivate each individual in its unique relation to the universe and to celebrate the diversity which the various individuals represent. In this fashion, Schleiermacher was a pioneer in appreciating religious plurality." In accounting for the broad approach of Schleiermacher, Capetz (2003: 116) has noted the influence of the philosophy of Spinoza: "Schleiermacher found in Spinoza a nonanthropomorphic alternative to both traditional theism and deism." In *The Living God: Schleiermacher's Theological Appropriation of Spinoza* (1996), Julia A. Lamm presented the case for Spinoza's philosophy and its influence on Schleiermacher. Yet, although Schleiermacher was accused by critics of pantheism during his lifetime, he denied any major impact of Spinoza in his work.

The legacy of Schleiermacher is nonetheless of continued significance in the study of religion. Pals (1987: 269) has noted the enduring but often unnoticed influence of Schleiermacher upon historians of religion and the phenomenology of religion: "Pure and avowed disciples of Schleiermacher are no longer a common sight. But indirectly his influence can be discerned in the loosely associated group of scholars which came to prominence in the first half of this century as advocates of the phenomenology of religion. These include such figures as Eliade (after his fashion), Gerardus van der Leeuw, William Brede Kristensen, Joachim Wach, and C. J. Bleeker, among others."

History of Religions and Comparative Religion

While this chapter is focused on the field of religious studies, what is often overlooked is the considerable overlap between comparative religion, history of religions, and theology, especially in the formation of "religious studies." As an extension of the widened approach of nineteenth-century liberal theology inaugurated by Schleiermacher, whereby the divine is conceived as both transcendent and immanent, the fields of theology and history of religions became closely intertwined. In fact, the academic pursuit of "history of religions" had associations with what was known as the History of Religions School (*religionsgeschichtliche schule*), referring to a coterie of German biblical scholars active between 1880 and 1920. As theologians, primarily Lutheran, they were associated with the University of Gottingen and included the names of Bernhard Duhm, Albert Eichhorn, Hermann Gunkel, Johannes Weiss, Wilhelm Bousset, Ernst Troeltsch, William Wrede, and Rudolf Otto. Rudolf Bultmann is considered a third-generation member. This school advocated for the methods of comparative religion and phenomenology in the interpretation of Christianity. Employing techniques of "higher criticism," they sought to investigate the sociohistorical origins of scriptural texts to understand "the world behind the text." The techniques included the famous "Documentary Hypothesis" of Lutheran biblical scholar and member, Julius Wellhausen.

The leading figure in the History of Religions School was Lutheran theologian Ernst Troeltsch (1865–1923). In "The Dogmatics of the Religionsgeshichtliche Schule" (1913: 1–2), Troeltsch outlined the school's perspective:

> The movement signifies, in general, simply the recognition of the universally accepted scientific conclusion that human religion exists only in manifold specific religious cults which develop in very complex relations of mutual contact and influence, and that in this religious development it is impossible to make the older dogmatic distinction between a natural and a supernatural revelation . . . It becomes impossible as soon as one's horizon is theoretically enlarged to include the totality of human religions, and as soon as it is discovered that in the warfare between religions exclusive claims to revelation conflict with one another. When one attains this broader outlook, the limited horizon of belief in the supernatural, universal validity of one's own religion is widened to include all historical religious movements, with their mutual conflicts and similar claims to truth . . . [Thus], [f]rom the scientific point of view one's attitude toward the religious life of men can no longer be that of a supernatural or philosophical defense of one's own religion, but must rather be that of a comparative, historical study of religions everywhere.

The comparative religion approach to Christianity, however, was often greeted with mixed reception by traditional theologians, as noted by Sharpe (1986: 119): "In those places where traditional theological studies were strong, the impression was usually current that comparative religion was out to corrupt the faithful by relativizing a rightful absolute, [hence] it was difficult to introduce comparative religion on a par with other academic subjects." Despite criticism, advocates for comparative religion championed the view that studying comparative religion was not necessarily inimical to faith or commitment to Christian teachings. In defense of the History of Religions School, Troeltsch (1913: 3) gave the assurance that the intentions were not anti-religious or secular but sought the deeper truths of religion: "Since we are here concerned with the *religionsgeschichtliche* attitude only in so far as it has been appropriated, or can be appropriated, by theology, it is, of course, understood that we shall deal with it only in so far as it is compatible with a personal affirmation of the religious life, and with the affirmation of the Christian thought-world. We therefore exclude all purely skeptical, positivistic, and illusionistic theories which may have adopted the *religionsgeschichtliche* point of view, and we deal only with those interpretations which see in religion the revelation of deepest truth and recognize in the development of religion the advance to clear, religious knowledge."

In a more strident reaction to the liberal theology of the History of Religions School, including especially its emphasis on general revelation and natural theology, some modern theologians have rejected Schleiermacher and his cohorts. These include Karl Barth, Emil Brunner, and others of the neo-orthodox tradition of dialectical theology. For them, any talk of universal religious experiences negates the uniqueness of the Christion revelation. For Schleiermacher and others, special revelation requires the presence of at least a modicum of general revelation or natural theology, some inherent "point-of-contact" between humanity and the divine. In Schleiermacher's defense, Proudfoot (1985: xv) observed: "Schleiermacher's approach continues to inform much contemporary religious thought and philosophy of religion, even among those who think of themselves as having broken with that tradition."

One example of Schleiermacher's influence in contemporary theology is in "Contemporary Affect Theology." This school of thought is influenced by Schleiermacher's *Affekt Theologie*, which was in turn based on a series of lectures delivered in Berlin from 1811 to 1831, published posthumously as *Dialektik* (see Schleiermacher 1996). Theologian and religion scholar Thandeka, in *The Embodied Self: Friedrich Schleiermacher's Solution to Kant's*

Problem of the Empirical Self (1995), explains how a revival of Schleiermacher's dialectic reveals the proper understanding of his religion of "feeling" (*affectus*), which has healed the gap in Kantian thought and restored the full concept of embodied "Self-consciousness" in the modern world. As stated by Thandeka (1995: 1): "Kant lost the embodied self, the self that is an inextricable part of the natural world, because of a gap in his critical philosophy. This gap is the absence of a necessary link between the noumenal and empirical self in Kant's theory of self-consciousness." Thandeka then argues that "religious experience" for Schleiermacher was primordial and preceded the formation of reason (1995: 12): "For Schleiermacher, the gap was a pre-religious, pre-philosophic stage of human nature, which must be experienced in order to be resolved." And, for Schleiermacher, music is a direct expression of that pre-rational stage.

Another example of how the influence of Schleiermacher continues unabated in comparative theology is Jon Paul Sydnor's *Ramanuja and Schleiermacher: Toward a Constructive Comparative Theology* (2011). Sydnor (2011: 3) clearly states the book's purpose in comparing Schleiermacher and famed Hindu theologian Ramanuja: "It will delineate the salient similarities and differences between Ramanuja and Schleiermacher on one shared theme—the doctrine of absolute dependence."

In their assessment of non-Christian religions, the History of Religions School in theology had welcomed the extensive data from the world religious traditions as collected and interpreted by scholars like F. Max Müller, C. P. Tiele, P. D. Chantepie de la Saussaye, and James G. Frazer. As a result of his extensive research into comparative philology and comparative mythology as the foundation for a comparative study of religion, Friedrich Max Muller (1823–1900) is considered the founder of comparative religion. Joachim Wach, in *The Comparative Study of Religions* (1958: 3), has reaffirmed Max Muller's eminent status: "There can be little doubt that the modern comparative study of religions began with Max Muller, about a century ago. His *Comparative Mythology* appeared in 1856, and in 1870 the *Introduction to the Science of Religions* was published." While Max Muller is normally associated with Vedic and Indian studies, especially his translations of ancient Sanskrit texts and his series, *Sacred Books of the East* (1879–1894), often overlooked in scholarly accounts of his work is how Max Muller, a Lutheran, was aligned with the theological ideas of Schleiermacher. Eric F. Sharpe, in *Comparative Religion: A History* (1986: 38–39), explains Max Muller's theory of the infinite as the origin of religion: "Max Muller held that all human knowledge begins with perceptions of finite entities, capable of being registered by the senses. However, such perceptions he considered always to imply something beyond themselves. To perceive any object it is necessary at the same time to perceive that which is not the object in question, that against which the object outlines itself, as it were; hence, in effect . . . in perceiving the finite we always perceive the infinite also . . . This, then, is the origin of religion: the perception of the infinite . . . When the moral sense enters into an alliance with the sense of the infinite, religion is born." John Bowker (1997: 665) has recently stated: "He [Max Muller] held that religion is the human capacity to perceive the infinite, and that all religions consequently contain to some degree the eternal truths of belief in God, in the immortality of the soul, and in a future retribution."

Max Muller's influence has also extended to the formation of the history of religions. In fact, Mircea Eliade (1959: 229) attributes the rise of history of religions as an independent academic field to Max Muller: "As a result of the discoveries made in all branches of oriental studies during the first half of the nineteenth century, as well as of the establishment of Indo-European philology and comparative linguistics, the history of religions first really entered into its own with Max Muller." Eliade (1959: 229–230) further explains Max Muller's theory of language and the genesis of religion: "Max Muller found the genesis of myths in natural phenomena, especially in solar epiphanies, and explained the birth of the gods as a 'disease of language'—what had originally been but a name, *nomen*, became a divinity, *numen*." Later, for theologian and phenomenologist of religion Rudolf Otto, the idea of the holy or "numinous" (from *numen*) became the basis for his theory of the human capacity for religious experience being a fundamentally *a priori* dimension of consciousness.

Eric Sharpe (1983: 56) has emphasized the importance of Rudolf Otto in holding fast to the legacy of Schleiermacher: "Modestly at first, but with growing force, Schleiermacher's vision of religion as consisting essentially not in creeds and codes, not in rational conclusions about the nature of God, but in immediate experience of the Other, was launched by Otto and others into the world of scholarship, and increasingly into the world of religion on both the academic and the practical levels." Historian of religions Mircea Eliade, in *The Quest: History and Meaning in Religion*, has also described Otto's contribution in relation to Schleiermacher:

> With great psychological subtlety, Otto describes and analyzes the different modalities of the numinous experience. His terminology—*mysterium tremendom, majestas, mysterium fascinans,*

> etc.—has become part of our language. In *Das Heilige*, Otto insists almost exclusively on the nonrational character of religious experience. Because of the great popularity of this book there is a tendency to regard him as an "emotionalist"—a direct descendent of Schleiermacher. But Otto's works are more complex, and it would be better to think of him as a philosopher of religion working first-hand with documents of the history of religions and of mysticism. (1969: 23)

Rudolf Otto's reliance on Kant and Schleiermacher has been noted by John Bowker (1995: 168): "There is a religious way of experiencing the universe, just as there is a scientific, or a moral, or an aesthetic. They cannot be collapsed into each other. The religious way of experiencing as a basis of a Kantian category of judgment is already foreshadowed in Schleiermacher, but it received its most thoroughgoing and culminating expression in Rudolf Otto's *The Idea of the Holy*. When one considers the impact of that book when it appeared in 1917, and its subsequent influence for a time, one can see how effectively Kant could be deployed for the defense of religious belief over against the empiricists who had insisted that worthwhile knowledge must be built up from sense experience without appeal to anything *a priori*."

The widespread impact of Otto is further elucidated by Oxford theologian Keith Ward (1998: 27): "Through Rudolf Otto's '*Das Heilige*,' and Martin Buber's '*Ich und Du*,' the idea that some form of personal experience—whether of the Numinous, the 'Thou' which addresses one in and through historical experiences, or of the Cosmic Whole—is the essence of religion became widespread. Revelation becomes, not the verbal utterances of God or particular causal manifestations of the Divine in nature, but the occurrence of a particularly intense or prolonged form of experience, which may be passed on to others by personal influence."

As part of his comparative perspective, Otto was among the first to inaugurate a practical non-sectarian approach to the study of religious experience across religious borders. Joachim Wach (1951: 36), Mircea Eliade's predecessor at the University of Chicago, affirmed the comparative utility of Otto's interpretation of the holy across religions: "It was one of the great insights of the author of *The Idea of the Holy*, Rudolf Otto, that he caught the double notion of the *mysterium magnum* in the twin ideas of its terrifying and its alluring aspect. These *two aspects* are known to the theologians of all religions as Divine Wrath and Divine Love or Grace. Though their natural roles and relationships are differently conceived in different faiths, these two aspects of power are universally recognized." Noting both non-universal and universal aspects of religion, Wach (1951: 217) defined the vocation of the historian of religions: "The task of the historian or religions, requiring much sensitivity, is to weigh carefully both similarities and differences."

Summarizing Otto's contribution to the study of religion, Mircea Eliade (1959: 8–9) echoed Wach in noting his background in Lutheran theology: "Instead of studying the ideas of God and religion, Otto undertook to analyze the modalities of the religious experience. Gifted with great psychological subtlety, and thoroughly prepared by his twofold training as theologian and historian of religions, he succeeded in determining the content and specific characteristics of religious experience. Passing over the rational and speculative side of religion, he concentrated chiefly on its irrational aspect. For Otto had read Luther and had understood what the "living God" meant to the believer. It was not the God of the philosophers—of Erasmus, for example, it was not an idea, an abstract notion, a mere moral allegory."

Current studies in the work of Rudolf Otto continue to reflect favorably on his numerous achievements, but they also reveal criticism. George D. Alles, in *Rudolf Otto: Autobiographical and Social Essays* (1996: 1), began his Introduction with this accolade: "These books [Otto's] are widely regarded as making up one of the most significant influences on the academic study of religions in the twentieth century. Indeed, some rank Otto as one of the founders of that study." But as he proceeds, Alles (1996: 27) gives an account of the critiques of Otto over the years: "Criticisms that address Otto's conceptual apparatus, his claim that the experience he describes is universal, his claim that religious experience is independent and primary, and, in the most general terms, the claim that it is worthwhile or even possible to describe another person's internal experiences and feelings." While some detractors have found disfavor with his subjectivism and universalism as well as his alleged Christian bias, ironically some of the most trenchant criticisms of Otto have been leveled from fellow theologians. For example, Karl Barth's criticism of Otto was based on his own rejection of Schleiermacher, natural theology, and the sense of a general human religious experience. Rudolf Bultmann critiqued Otto for his idea of the numinous as a category for the enterprise of comparative religion.

Even though scholars, noted above, accept a kind of similitude between Otto and Eliade, there are notable differences between them. In fact, Mircea Eliade, in *The Sacred and the Profane* (1959: 10), admits a principal distinction: "After forty years, Otto's analyses have not lost their value; readers of this book will profit by reading and reflecting on them.

But in the following pages we adopt a different perspective. We propose to present the phenomenon of the sacred in all its complexity, and not only in so far as it is irrational. What will concern us is not the relation between the rational and nonrational elements of religion but the sacred in its entirety." After careful evaluation of each thinker, Alles (1996: 25) clarified the differences between Otto and Eliade, as well as between Eliade and Wach, in terms of internal versus external realities: "In Eliade the loose association of experience and expression became a complete divorce. Eliade freed the sacred from any dependence upon internal processes of human experience and talked about it as an object, indeed, as an independent agent. He did not use [Joachim] Wach's language of religious experience and its expression. He used the language of the sacred and its manifestations. True, he claimed that the sacred erupted into the world of profane existence as an element of consciousness, but this claim never required him to reflect much on the experiential content of that consciousness. He was content instead to identify the basic forms in which the sacred manifested itself."

The thought of Eliade regarding the sacred and the profane has been misunderstood in the study of religion. Critics claim that Eliade promotes the concept of the sacred as *sui generis* or an autonomous reality that has ontological standing. In response, Bryan S. Rennie, in *Reconstructing Eliade: Making Sense of Religion* (1996: 30), explains how for Eliade the sacred and the profane operate within human consciousness and not as separate ontological realities: "The opposition of the sacred and the profane lie within the human existential condition and not outside it in some ontological dichotomy. We cannot be completely closed to the sacred, we can only fail to recognize the sacred in some particular form." For additional clarification, it is helpful to recall the basic premise of Schleiermacher regarding religious experience: sensing the infinite in the finite. Rennie (1996: 29) illustrates this in Eliade in terms of sensing the sacred in the profane: "Meaning and reality are not sought *beyond* actual, empirical, historical experience, granted; they are sought *in* these 'profane' categories. Thus the sacred does not *transcend* the profane . . . (30) The ability to recognize the sacred in the radically profane is precisely the central feature of *all* religion according to Eliade's analysis of the sacred as the real . . . (31) The revelation of the sacred is always in and through the specifically profane . . . [and] while all things *can* reveal the sacred, not all things do." Thus, according to Eliade the sacred and the profane are modes of being in the world that rely on the consciousness persons who confront the world and perceive the sacred in the profane. In simpler terms, as one informant confided, "it is not the cow that the scholar sees, but the cow that the Hindu sees."

Despite criticism and misunderstanding, the basic premises of comparative religion have withstood the test of time. Andreas Nehring (2016: 95–96) first recounts the principal challenge that was given by Jonathan Z. Smith: "Jonathan Z. Smith triggered a debate that continues until this day by fundamentally criticizing the comparative method in religious studies. Smith argues that the comparison of religion, as it has been developed by the phenomenologists and is prominent in the writings of Rudolf Otto, Gerardus van der Leeuw, Friedrich Heiler and Mircea Eliade, has predominantly emphasized the commonalities of the *comparativa*, through which differences have been more or less neglected." Smith even considered comparative studies a form of "magic": "Smith makes the criticism that the methodology of comparison developed in religious studies so far resembles a form of magic and is therefore not adequate for systematic research in the field of religions." Despite the challenges posed, Nehring (2016: 98) explains: "Religious studies discourse today has still not managed to leave Eliade behind, although the necessity of distancing oneself from Eliade remains explicit in most recent publications." In fact, "Eliade's concepts, terms and ideas, and even his diffused differentiation of sacred and profane, are adopted, extended, praised and almost taken for granted in many areas of academia, such as ethnology, literary studies or history, and even more so in popular culture."

Eliade's unique style of comparison is often misunderstood since it is linked in several ways to established notions of religious experience rather than to raw empirical data. Nehring (2016: 98–99) has clarified this aspect of Eliade's comparative methodology: "Eliade's contribution to comparative religions and his few reflections on comparative methodology indicate that it is not comparison of religious phenomena of different cultural contexts that is the focus of his interest, but, rather, a comparison of two different modes of being in the world: the sacred and the profane." Consequently, "the point of departure in Eliade's approach is the historical data that express religious experiences. These data have to be described and interpreted by the historian of religion; further, they have to be deciphered as expressions of the life experience of *homo religiosus*." One must understand the idea of a dialectic between the sacred and the profane that functions within the enterprise of the comparison of religious experiences (Nehring 2016: 99): "Since Eliade argues that it depends first of all on the perspective of whether an experience is considered as sacred or profane, his comparative approach as a historian of religion, as he prefers to call himself, is more concerned with the dialectic of the sacred and the profane than with the comparison of religious elements from various cultures."

Music and Religious Experience

> Were I to compare religion with anything it would be with music, which indeed is otherwise closely connected with it. Music is one great whole; it is a special, a self-contained revelation of the world.
>
> —Friedrich Schleiermacher, *On Religion: Speeches to its Cultured Despisers*

> The real content of music is not drawn from the ordinary human emotions at all, and is in no way merely a second language, alongside the usual one, by which these emotions find expression. Musical feeling is rather (like numinous feeling) something "wholly other."
>
> —Rudolf Otto, *The Idea of the Holy*

In addition to his enormous influence in shaping the direction of both theology and the study of religion up to the present, Schleiermacher opened the way for the experience of music to be taken seriously by scholars of religion. Having recognized his critical importance for understanding religion, we now cite Schleiermacher's relation to music and his insistence on music as being close to religious experience. In *On Religion: Speeches to its Cultured Despisers* of 1799, Schleiermacher (1958: 51), with his rare literary gift, compares religion to music in important ways:

> Religion . . . fashions itself with endless variety, down even to the single personality. Each form again is a whole and capable of an endless number of characteristic manifestations . . . Were I to compare religion in this respect with anything it would be with music, which indeed is otherwise closely connected with it. Music is one great whole; it is a special, a self-contained revelation of the world. Yet the music of each people is a whole by itself, which again is divided into different characteristic forms, till we come to the genius and style of the individual.

Each actual instance of this inner revelation in the individual contains all these unities.

Schleiermacher had a marvelous way of bringing subtle nuance to his expression (1958: 152): "The muse of harmony, the intimate relation of which to religion has been long known, though acknowledged by few, has from of old laid on the altars of religion the most gorgeous and perfect works of her most devoted scholars. In sacred hymns and choruses to which the words of the poet are but loosely and airily appended, there are breathed out things that definite speech cannot grasp. The melodies of thought and feeling interchange and give mutual support, till all is satiated and full of the sacred and the infinite."

In the early nineteenth century, one of the most interesting developments relevant to religion and music was the idea of a "religion of art," which also has ties to Schleiermacher. Apart from the metaphysical associations of music (i.e., Pythagorean *harmonia*), this idea or movement was inspired by the search, primarily in German Romanticism, for a truly transcendent dimension of pure music as it relates to inner feeling or contemplation. In ancient times, *harmonia* was inevitably bound to *rhythmos* (rhythm and the dance) and to *logos* (i.e., words of praise to the gods). However, due to the aesthetic theories of Kant and Schiller, as well as the influence of writers like Ludwig Tieck, E.T.A. Hoffman, and Wilhelm Wackenroder, many thinkers embraced the notion of the reality of conscious reflection on beauty as something autonomous and "in itself." In this notion, music was to be ideally stripped of its association with language and programmatic imagery, such that purely instrumental music was elevated to the status of "absolute music," and understood as a viable means to contemplate the "Absolute." Musicologist Carl Dahlhaus, in *The Idea of Absolute Music* (1989), has explained this concept: "The idea, which has its roots in German Romanticism, is that 'absolute' instrumental music (music lacking text and extramusical reference) is the purest, most sublime form of music, and that, unlike any other art form, it allows the listener to experience the 'absolute' in a quasi-religious way." As Dahlhaus (1989: 3) affirmed, "The concept of absolute music was the leading idea of the classical and romantic era in music esthetics." Inspired by this trend, Arthur Schopenhauer (1788–1860) identified the object of absolute music as "the Will" (the universal essence behind all phenomena in the world), claiming he had discovered philosopher Kant's "thing-in-itself," behind appearances. As interpreted by Dahlhaus (1989: 73), "Music never expresses appearances but solely the inner nature, the of-itself of all manifestations, the will itself." Interestingly, the concept of "absolute music" appears to have been prefigured by Schleiermacher (1969: 212), who in *On Religion* envisions the beauty and depth of music without words: "Just as such address is a kind of music without notes or singing, so there is also a kind of music among the saints which speaks, as it were, without words though it is offering the most definite and understandable expression of what lies deep within."

An interesting corollary to the idea of "absolute music" in Europe is the rise of Hasidism, a Jewish movement founded by the saintly figure of Israel Ba'al Shem Tov (1700–1760). Rather than worry about fulfilling all the provisions of Jewish law, he taught a method of singing and dancing to achieve joy and ecstasy through *niggunim*, or wordless songs. This is explained by Cantor Joseph A. Levine (2006: 49): "Music provided the medium by which joy and ecstasy was to be aroused. One of Hasidism's more innovative dispensations was to permit singing melodies without words, Niggunim, as an acceptable form of prayer when worshippers could not read the liturgy. Filler syllables (e.g., ai-di-di-di dai) were sung and danced to steadily accelerating tempos—and rising volumes and pitches—until a crescendo was reached."

Another theme associated with German Romanticism was the concept of religion as art, or *kunst religion*. This was the belief that art, though created by humans, was nonetheless a revelation. In a sense, then, the essence of religion was synonymous with the essence of music (Dahlhaus 1989: 86): "The ineffable—the objective correlative to the subjective 'inner state' in which religion constitutes itself—can be enciphered through music, which is a language above language . . . [In other words] The fact that music expresses the feeling of infinity that is the substance of religion was sufficient to allow esthetic contemplation and religious devotion to flow into one another . . . [such that] the theologian of feeling—feeling that was 'immediate self-awareness' on the one hand and the perception of 'simple dependency' on the other—was simultaneously, if implicitly, the theologian of the art religion." Dahlhaus (1989: 88–89) has indicated Schleiermacher's role in the religion of art, and the signature position of art and music in his thought: "In his 1799 *Lectures on Religion*, Schleiermacher, who seems to be the source of the term 'art religion,' distinguished three paths that allow one to go from the finite to the infinite: self-absorption, absent-minded contemplation of a piece of the world, and finally the devotional contemplation of works of art." Thus, with Schleiermacher, music and holiness are virtually interchangeable (Dahlhaus 1989: 86): "Music can be 'holy' because, inversely, holiness as Schleiermacher understands it is capable of manifesting itself in music."

Wilhelm Dilthey (1833–1911), renowned German historian, hermeneutic philosopher, and biographer of Schleiermacher, also lauded music as a significant factor in religious experience. In fact, the line of continuity regarding music between Luther, Schleiermacher, and Dilthey has been documented in the words of Dilthey biographer Rudolf A. Makkreel (1975: 366): "As early as 1853, in a letter to his father, Dilthey referred to a bond between music and religion, when he wrote, 'Luther and Schleiermacher, our two greatest theologians, realized that music is the closest sister of religion and that listening to music, when this is true music, is a religious act." Dilthey's realization of the importance of music in religious consciousness is especially evident here in his love for Bach (1975: 367): "So seriously does Dilthey take the musical nature of the religious *Erlebnis* [experience] that he sees the supreme embodiment of Protestant consciousness not in Luther's writings, but in J.S. Bach's music."

The significant role of music in the thought of Schleiermacher and Dilthey finds its twentieth-century successor in Rudolf Otto (1869–1937), a systematic theologian as well as one of the pioneers in the phenomenology of religion and the modern field of religious studies. The Centenary Introduction to Schleiermacher's work by Rudolf Otto in 1899 reaffirmed the essential link between the two thinkers. This connection is further underscored by their mutual recognition of the importance of music in religious experience.

The views of Otto regarding religion and music were remarkably close to those of Schleiermacher. These observations hold great significance for the Musicology of Religion, as Eliade and others in his camp rarely touched on music. Thus in the wake of Schleiermacher's views on religious and musical experiences, Rudolf Otto provided a few well-chosen remarks on the feelings associated with music, which in his view were very similar to feelings of the holy itself, the numinous, the "wholly other": "Music, in short, arouses in us an experience and vibrations of mood that are quite specific in kind. . . . The resultant complex mood is, as it were, a fabric, in which the general human feelings and emotional states constitute the warp, and the non-rational music-feelings the woof. . . . The real content of music is not drawn from the ordinary human emotions at all, and . . . is in no way merely a second language, alongside the usual one, by which these emotions find expression. Musical feeling is rather (like numinous feeling) something 'wholly other'" (1923: 49). The human response to music thus comprises similar feelings and experiences as toward the numinous, such as *mysterium tremendum* (mystery and awe) and *fascinans* (attraction).

Within the corpus of his writings, Otto's favorite analogy was indeed music, which he developed more than others and returned to often. Christopher I. Lehrich, in "The Unanswered Question: Music in Theory of Religion" (2014: 27), reflected on the nature of music for Otto with a salient thought experiment: "Suppose you listen to a musical masterpiece—say, a Beethoven symphony. You find yourself caught, enraptured by an extraordinary power that transports you beyond yourself, into a transcendental realm. Numinous experience is like this, only more so." Lehrich (2014: 28) explained how Otto viewed music as different from the graphic and plastic arts as well as poetry: "Otto points to musical experience as 'wholly other.' Music is not mimetic, representational, expressive, or communicative in any plausible sense of these terms." Formulating the connection offered by Otto into a reasonable hypothesis, Lehrich (2014: 29) then suggested the possibility of music being on par with religion as a human universal: "If Otto's parallel between music and the numinous experience, music and religion could be sustained as homology rather than analogy, one would have to wonder whether numinous experience were not a human norm, presumably processed in definable neurological systems." Lehrich states that his musical analogy demands thoughtful consideration: "We cannot dismiss this out-of-hand: at least on the musical end Otto's argument is strong, and after all the majority of the book [*The Idea of the Holy*] reveals evidence to sustain the parallel with religion."

Building on the work of Schleiermacher and Rudolf Otto, Gerardus van der Leeuw (1890–1950), in his classic *Religion in Essence and Manifestation* (1938: 453), broadened the scope by attesting that "musical expression of the holy occupies an extensive domain in worship. There is hardly any worship without music." In a subsequent work, *Sacred and Profane Beauty: The Holy in Art* (1963), there is an entire section on "Music and Religion" (1963, Part Six, 211–262) that includes subsections on "Holy Sound" and the "Theological Aesthetics of Music." In this work (1963: 225–227), van der Leeuw confided that "Almost all worship uses music . . . religion can no more do without the singing than it can without the word . . . Music represents the great struggle of reaching the wholly other, which it can never express."

Further studies in the relation between religion and music along the lines of Schleiermacher, Otto, and van der Leeuw are disappointingly few, however, and the detailed study of music as part of religious experience appears to have played a relatively minor role in the subsequent history of the disciplines of phenomenology of religion, comparative religion, or the history of religions. Nonetheless, we next provide discussion of phenomenology of religion and phenomenology of music as fruitful disciplines that approach religion and music from the perspectives of the world's religions.

Phenomenology of Religion

While music and religion are researched from several angles, one of the most effective means of integrating the variety of disciplines into an effective Musicology of Religion is the phenomenology of religion. As an introduction to phenomenology of religion, Sumner B. Twiss and Walter H. Conser Jr., in *Experience of the Sacred: Readings in the Phenomenology of Religion* (1992: 1), described its focus and value in the study of religion: "Phenomenology typically brackets or lays aside metaphysical questions of the real existence of the sacred or the divine. In this way it, too, distances itself from traditional theological inquiry and demonstrates the fruitfulness of an academic approach to the study of religion." As a distinctive method of philosophy, phenomenology originated with Edmund Husserl, but owing much to the twentieth-century work of Rudolf Otto, Gerardus van der Leeuw, and Mircea Eliade, the phenomenology of religion has developed as a unique method of studying religion. This point is summed up by Ninian Smart, in *The Phenomenon of Religion* (1973: 53): "Talk of religion as phenomenon has sprung from the tradition of philosophical phenomenology (from Husserl onward), whose methods, with variations, have been applied to the study of religion."

Yet preceding Husserl was a line of influence going back to the nineteenth century, from Schleiermacher to Wilhelm Dilthey. Robert R. Williams (1978: 27) noted the liberal theologian Schleiermacher's influence on Husserl via Dilthey's work: "There is an historical and intellectual lineage between Schleiermacher and Husserl; the mediating figure is Wilhelm Dilthey, one of Schleiermacher's leading interpreters. In his delineation of the human sciences (*Geisteswissenschaften*), Dilthey both continues Schleiermacher's fundamental distinction between the ethical and physical sciences and is influential on Husserl's development of phenomenology. Husserl's work after his *Logical Investigations* can be viewed as a refinement and continuation of Dilthey's program of *Geisteswissenschaften,* and consequently as an indirect refinement and continuation of Schleiermacher's."

Schleiermacher indeed provided groundwork for later theorists in phenomenology, including Husserl and Otto. In his work *Friedrich*

Schleiermacher, C. W. Christian explained the phenomenological continuity between Schleiermacher and modern thinkers:

> The phenomenological methodology of the *Speeches*, is, of course, not identical with that of twentieth-century phenomenology derived from the thought of Edmund Husserl. It could, however, be said to anticipate Husserl and the later phenomenologists in significant respects, for example, in its attempt to circumvent a narrow positivism by carefully circumscribing its own goals and truth claims. In common with the phenomenologists, Schleiermacher asks the hearer to pay attention to the phenomena as experienced, without prior ontological commitment, before judging how they can be interpreted in the larger scheme of things. Insofar as Schleiermacher is the first major theologian consciously to adopt a phenomenological methodology, he clearly points out the path to be followed by Otto, Sabatier, Bergson, and, more recently, Tillich and Hartshorne. (Christian 1979: 146)

Edmund Husserl (1859–1938), the German founder of the philosophical school of phenomenology, influenced important twentieth-century philosophers including Heidegger, Sartre, and Merleau-Ponty. Rudolf Otto, whose important contributions in terms of locating the "essence" of religion in the experience of the "holy" or the "numinous," owes a great deal to Husserl and his phenomenological investigations. Phenomenology is also important for the Musicology of Religion, as Husserl's thought was influenced by musicology through his association with renowned German musicologist Carl Stumpf, one of his principal academic advisors (see Husserl 1964). We will briefly outline here some of the significant aspects of phenomenology in relation to religion, and then discuss its importance for understanding music.

The philosophy of Husserl known as phenomenology has many complexities and avenues of thought, including the writings of numerous philosophers who were influenced by him. Husserl argued for the pure realm of consciousness as the primary field of inquiry. Our attention here is on how his method or process of thinking relates to the domain of "religious consciousness," and how phenomenology becomes a useful tool for understanding religion as a special area of human experience. By way of introduction, John Bowker (1971: xiv) described how Husserl's phenomenology operates on two distinct levels: "Phenomenology at the first level makes an attempt to map and describe those appearances in consciousness without commenting on whether they have any reality in existence." The second level is ontological: "But Husserl insisted that those appearances are so different in kind and quality that one is entitled and indeed required to infer a sufficient ground in reality for at least some of them, given the way they constitute themselves in consciousness. This is the second level of phenomenology, which is at once, and necessarily, an engagement with issues of ontology: what may we, and sometimes what must we, infer as a sufficient ground in reality to account for the appearances in consciousness having the nature and consistency that some of them have?" In response, Bowker (1971: xv) explained: "Husserl felt entitled to infer a sufficient existence in reality to account for the appearances in consciousness appearing with the sort of persistence and reliability that they do." Bowker (1971: xvi) then observed that at the end of life Husserl realized that the consistent appearance of "one which extends across space and time" is God. The consistent appearance of music in consciousness across space and time also becomes pertinent to this discussion.

We now refer to relevant points made in the writings of Husserl. Husserl's writings cover decades of teaching and research at German universities where he held positions. Both Husserl and Rudolf Otto taught at Gottingen University. In *The Essential Husserl: Basic Writings in Transcendental Phenomenology* (Welton 1999: 60–85), there is a section, "III. Phenomenology as Transcendental Philosophy. 5. The Basic Approach of Phenomenology," which reveals aspects of Husserl's thought relevant to the study of religion. To arrive at a new and deeper perspective on existence, Husserl devised the *epoché*, a process or "operation" of separating out, "bracketing" or "parenthesizing," what he called the "natural attitude" or the scientific view of reality. Charting out a different path from the radical dualism of Descartes with its method of doubt, the empiricism of Locke and Hume, and the idealism of Berkeley, Husserl argued for "opening up for scrutiny" the entire realm of pure consciousness. Regarding the procedure for opening up pure consciousness, in what he called the phenomenological *epoché*, Husserl explains:

> We put out of action the general positing which belongs to the essence of the natural attitude; we parenthesize everything which that positing encompasses with respect to being: thus the whole natural world which is continually "there for us," "on hand," and which will always remain there according to consciousness as an "actuality" even if we choose to parenthesize it. If I do

that, as I can with complete freedom, then I am not negating this world as though I were a sophist; I am not doubting its factual being as though I were a skeptic; rather I am exercising the phenomenological *epoché* which also completely shuts me off from any judgment about spatiotemporal factual being. Thus, I exclude all sciences relating to this natural world no matter how firmly they stand there for me, no matter how much I admire them; I make absolutely no use of the things posited in them. (Welton 1999: 65)

The critical importance of *epoché* for phenomenology is enunciated by Husserl (Welton 1999: 66–67), as he states that delimiting and accessing this new realm of "pure consciousness" by means of *epoché* is the comprehensive goal of phenomenology: "Our goal is the acquisition of a new region of being never before delimited in its own particularity—a region which, like any other genuine region, is a region of individual being . . . The phenomenological *epoché* will deserve its name only by means of this insight; the fully conscious effecting of that *epoché* will prove itself to be the operation necessary to make 'pure consciousness,' and subsequently the whole phenomenological region, accessible to us." Husserl (Welton 1999: 66–67) then presents more details about this new unique realm called by him the "phenomenological residuum": "What we absolutely need is a certain universal insight into the essence of any consciousness whatever and also, quite particularly, of consciousness in so far as it is, in itself, by its essence consciousness of 'natural' actuality. In these studies, we shall go as far as necessary to effect the insight that, consciousness has, in itself, a being of its own which in its own absolute essence, is not touched by the phenomenological exclusion. It therefore remains as the phenomenological residuum, as a region of being which is of essential necessity quite unique, and which can indeed become the field of a science of a novel kind: phenomenology." Husserl (Welton 1999: 67) thus claims to have discovered uncharted territory for the study of humanity: "As long as the possibility of the phenomenological attitude had not been recognized, and the method for bringing about an originary seizing upon the objectivities that arise with that attitude had not been developed, the phenomenological world had to remain unknown, indeed, hardly even suspected." Accordingly, Husserl (Welton 1999: 67) elevates the concept of "'pure consciousness' into the category of 'transcendental consciousness,' attained by a gradual process of 'phenomenological reduction': Important motives . . . justify our designating 'pure' consciousness, . . . as transcendental consciousness and the operation by which it is reached the transcendental *epoché*. As a method this operation will be divided into different steps of 'excluding,' parenthesizing,' and thus our method will assume the characteristic of a step-by-step reduction."

Adopting the methods and terminology of Husserl's phenomenology, including *epoché*, the phenomenology of religion as an academic enterprise within the field of religious studies has aimed to understand religion as a universal human phenomenon, both in a broad sense and in its specialized expressions. While we have discussed the phenomenology of religion presented by Otto in terms of the "holy" and the numinous, the name of Gerardus van der Leeuw is pivotal for phenomenology of religion after Otto. In his most famous work, *Religion in Essence and Manifestation* (1967: v. 2, 671), van der Leeuw very clearly lays out the basic principle of phenomenology as it will relate to religion: "Phenomenology seeks the phenomenon, as such; the phenomenon, again, is what 'appears.' The principle has a threefold implication: (1) Something exists. (2) This something 'appears.' (3) Precisely because it 'appears' it is a phenomenon." The phenomenon is not a phenomenon unless there are two parties: "But 'appearance' refers equally to what appears and to the person to whom it appears; the phenomenon, therefore, is neither pure object, nor the object, that is to say, the actual reality, whose essential being is merely concealed by the 'appearing' of the appearances; with this a specific metaphysics deals . . . The 'phenomenon' as such, therefore, is an object related to a subject, and a subject related to an object . . . The phenomenon, still further, is not produced by the subject, and still less substantiated or demonstrated by it; its entire essence is given in its 'appearance,' and its appearance to 'someone.' If (finally) this 'someone' begins to discuss what 'appears,' then phenomenology arises."

Drawing on the principles of phenomenology, historian of religion C. J. Bleeker has explained how specific aspects of Husserl's system have entered the phenomenology of religion. In *The Sacred Bridge: Researches into the Nature and Structure of Religion* (1963: 3), Bleeker describes this process: "The Husserlian phenomenology is a theory of knowledge, i.e. a so called science of pure consciousness . . . Full attention should only be paid to the method, by which Husserl tried to detect pure consciousness, because this method has been taken over by many students of the phenomenology of religion. It comprises two principles, namely the *epoché* and the eidetic vision. The first principle means the suspension of judgment. In using the *epoché* one puts oneself into the position of the listener, who does not judge according to preconceived notions. Applied to the phenomenology of religion, this means that this science cannot concern itself with the question of the truth of religion." There is consequently an openness to all things "religious," along with the development of critical faculties: "Phenomenology must begin by accepting as proper objects of study all phenomena that are professed to be religious. Subsequently the attempt may come to distinguish what is genuinely religious from what is spurious. The second principle, that of the eidetic vision, can easily be understood. It has its aim the search for the *eidos*, that is the essentials of religious phenomena."

John Bowker (1971: xiii–xiv) further emphasized the key role of phenomenology for the study of religion, especially in its ability to avoid theological affirmations and at the same time employ a variety of methods: "Phenomenology is concerned (as the underlying Greek words imply) with reflection on the way things appear . . . Applied to the study of religion, phenomenology offered the opportunity of avoiding issues of value-judgment and truth—as though, for example, one religion can be regarded as true and others evaluated from its own point of view." There was value in the phenomenological reduction: "*Epoché* was invoked. It came to mean, in effect, the 'bracketing out' of presuppositions about truth and value, so that a detached account could be given of what people say and do as descriptively as possible." Consequently, phenomenology "offered an escape route from confessional teaching or instruction (or indoctrination, as it was more often put); and it thus offered also a chance to make the study of religion genuinely educational, according to the prevailing paradigms of educational propriety: it could be value-free, not advocating without question the beliefs or opinions of the teacher, and it could be poly-methodical (availing itself of many different methods of human enquiry)."

Another basic premise of the phenomenology of religion, one that distinguishes it from other disciplines like the social sciences, is the awareness that understanding a religion, especially one that is foreign to the student or scholar, is best undertaken with the recognition of its absolute value for the believers. While the existence and true nature of God, the divine, or the Supreme Being, are debated in disciplines such as theology and philosophy of religion, these issues are set aside so that the phenomenologist or historian of religions is free to explore and interpret the various religions of the world in ways that are intelligible to the larger human community. This necessarily involves developing a distinct symbolic language with which to describe, classify, and reflect upon the multitude of religious expressions found around the world. Technical terms such as "the sacred," "profane," "numinous," "hierophany," *axis mundi, illo tempore*, "rites of passage," and "eschatology" have tended to have a more-or-less stable meaning throughout the discipline, in addition to more generally accepted categories like myth, ritual, scripture, deity, community, initiation, priesthood, and liturgy. None of these terms are limited to a specific religion or context, and thus they serve to enhance the universality of the discipline, which, by its very nature, is comparative.

In distinguishing the phenomenology of religion from other endeavors within the field of religious studies, S.G.F. Brandon (1970: 494) defined the phenomenology of religion as distinct from history of religions and theology: "Phenomenology of Religion is distinguished from Theology (which assumes existence of God) and History of Religion, in being concerned not with validity or origin of religious belief and practice, but with their existential significance as evidence of man's thought and action. It is basically a humanistic, not a theological, discipline; it is inevitably concerned with the historical data of religion, but it does not seek to study religion in its historical development."

One of the important aspects of the phenomenology of religion is that it endorses comparative studies across a broad spectrum. According to philosopher Douglas Allen (2010: 214), "There is widespread agreement that phenomenology of religion is a very general, comparative approach concerned with classifying and systematizing religious phenomena." Regarding the comparative method, Allen (2010: 209, 214) declares it to be searching for essential structures across a wide spectrum of data: "The central aim of the phenomenological method is to disclose the essential structure embodied in the particular data. After assembling a variety of phenomena, the phenomenologist searches for the invariant core that constitutes their essential meaning. Phenomenologists are able to gain insight into essential structures and meanings only after comparing a large number of documents expressing a great diversity of religious phenomena." As understood by religionist scholars, Allen (2010: 211) explains how the relevant terms and categories used by Rudolf Otto are utilized by them when describing the essential structures sought in the phenomenology of religion: "Otto describes the universal 'numinous' element as a unique a priori category of meaning and value. By numen and numinous, Otto means the concept of 'the holy' minus its moral and rational aspects. This constitutes the universal essence of religious experience." His experiential approach thus involves the phenomenological description of the universal, essential structure of religious experience.

Maintaining the presence of the numinous or the holy as an autonomous category, the phenomenology of religion does not evaluate or pass judgment upon a specific religion, much less tries to prove, or disprove, the truth of its claims or practices. Allen (2010: 205) has discussed this point: "Phenomenology of religion attempts to describe religious experiences with their religious phenomena as accurately as possible. In its descriptions, analysis, and interpretation of meaning, it attempts to suspend value judgments about what is real or unreal in experiences of others. It attempts to describe, understand, and do justice to the religious phenomena as they appear in religious experiences of others."

In line with Schleiermacher and Otto, Allen (2010: 203) has reaffirmed its strong emphasis on religious experience: "Phenomenology of religion starts with the view that religion is based on religious experience. Human beings have experiences that they describe as religious. These may be traditional or nontraditional. They may focus on inner feelings or outward forms and relations. They may be institutional and involve organized religion, or they may be highly personal and outside any institutional framework. They may involve prayer, worship, rituals, nature, or cosmic experiences." To embrace and encompass other approaches and disciplines such as musicology, Allen (220) explains that phenomenology of religion will be able to face the inevitable challenges that lay ahead through its ability to embrace a diversity of approaches: "If phenomenology of religion is to deal adequately with controversial issues, the following are several of its future tasks. First, it must become more aware of historical, philological, and other specialized approaches to, and different aspects of, its religious data."

The methods employed in the phenomenology of religion are enumerated by Thomas Ryba (2009: 97): "Phenomenology is a method of pure description concerned not with material causation but with the logic of parts and wholes, logical dependence and independence. It looks for the essential structures that lie behind religious phenomena not because it wants to explain them in terms of simpler causes or in terms of a more scientific theory but because it wants to understand how the world view of the believer logically coheres." According to Ryba (2009: 111–112), "Phenomenology is a method of entry into the inner, historically conditioned, self-understanding of religions in order to provide structural descriptions and explanations of religious experiences, concepts, doctrines, myths, ethics, rituals, and institutions . . . Its method consists of empathetic entry (interpolation) into phenomena that involves bracketing religious truth, demands, and values to produce (relatively) unprejudiced essential descriptions [and] continually tests this meaning against data from cognate fields."

As distinct from the social sciences and humanities, the phenomenology of religion aligns itself with the "religionist" position, the view which, true or not, relies on the assumption that religion itself or the sacred is *sui generis* and the basis for all explanations of the origin and function of religion. To provide context for this assessment, Robert A. Segal (2010: 77) has explained the distinction in theories of religion between religious studies and other disciplines in the humanities and social sciences: "The key divide in theories of religion is between those theories that hail from the social sciences and those that hail from religious studies itself." Regarding the social sciences, Segal (2010: 77) explains that "Social scientific theories deem the origin and function of religion nonreligious. Social scientists account for religion by showing secular needs, such as crops, prosperity, social unity, and meaningfulness, anything not directly connected to religious experience." Sometimes referred to as "functionalism," the social sciences are able to observe how religions "function" within the social context by measuring outcomes through statistical analysis of metrics like demographics, gender, race, logistics, geographic concerns, and political pressures.

Elsewhere, Robert A. Segal (2009: xiv) clarified the religionist position, such that according to religionists (defenders of religious studies as an autonomous discipline), the "defense of religious studies as a discipline is that the field does in fact explain religion 'religiously' rather than anthropologically, sociologically, psychologically, or economically . . . Religious studies accounts for religion not as a case of anything else [i.e., culture, society, childhood fantasy, class struggle] but in its own right—as religion." Segal (2009: xiv) explains that, while the underlying methodological assumption is that religion is a human construct, religion is generated from the deepest needs within the human psyche: "Now for religionists, no less than for anthropologists, sociologists, psychologists, and economists, religion is a human, not a divine, creation. Religious beliefs and practices are concocted by humans, not revealed from on high. But humans purportedly concoct them in order to make contact with God. That is the irreducibly religious origin and function of religion. Humans do not happen to seek contact with God. They need to do so. Just as they came into this world with a need for food and for love, so they come into this world with a need for God. That need, like the need for food or love, is innate. Religion arises and serves to fulfill it."

As a way of validating how humans produce religion to fulfill the need for contact with the divine, Segal (2009: xiv) cites the example of Mircea

Eliade: "For Mircea Eliade, the most influential contemporary religionist, religion provides contact with God through myths and rituals. Myths carry one back to the time when, so it is believed, God was closest to humans. Rituals offer a place where God has once appeared to humans and so, it is believed, is likeliest to appear anew." Taking this further, one may simply reflect on the enormous data on how music and chant figure in virtually all religious rituals (and many myths) to recognize the need for a specific area of expertise involving music and religion.

Nonetheless, phenomenology of religion has been the target of a variety of critiques. The principal objection by critics is that the field is overly apologetic to religion or the sacred and is thus "theological." At the same time, there are tendencies in postmodern discussions to dismiss the existence of religion or "the sacred" altogether. And yet the relation between phenomenology and religious studies continues to inspire new theoretical developments, as found for example in Gavin Flood, *Beyond Phenomenology: Rethinking the Study of Religion* (1999). Responding to its critics, Thomas Ryba (2009: 117) reaffirms that, "Phenomenology of religion does not require the Transcendent or the Holy to do its work. Phenomenological method may be turned to any phenomenon relevant to religious studies, supernatural or otherwise." And despite being on the defensive, the phenomenology of religion still has "skin in the game," according to Ryba (2009: 119): "No critique thus far has proven fatal to the phenomenological project, and some critics have even shown the way to its improvement."

Douglas Allen (2010: 222) also responds to critics and qualifies the phenomenological approach by placing its method as both general and contextual: "Often criticized for claiming to uncover nonhistorical, nontemporal, noncontextualized, essential structures and meanings, phenomenologists of religion tend to be more sensitive to the perspectival and contextual constraints of their approach and more modest in their claims. There is a value in uncovering religious essences and structures, but as embodied and contextualized, not as fixed, absolute, ahistorical, eternal truths and meanings." One also needs to maintain critical distance: "Phenomenologists of religion, emphasizing religious experience, recognize that being religious is not identical with studying religion. There is the first, foundational level of experience for the religious believer. Phenomenology and other scholarly approaches always involve some distance between the scholar and the subject matter necessary for critical reflection, analysis, interpretation, and verification of findings. While disagreeing on the relation between being religious and studying religion, scholars agree that scholarly study is not identical with being religious or having religious experience" (2010: 206–207). Despite controversy, Allen (2010: 223) has encouraged an optimistic view toward the future of phenomenology of religion as it holds its ground and adjusts to the various critiques: "Within its specific discipline and approach, a more self-critical and modest phenomenology of religion has much to contribute to the study of religion. In providing descriptions and interpretations of phenomena, it will include awareness of its presuppositions, its historical and contextualized situatedness, and its limited perspectival knowledge claims."

As a recent example of the resilience of the phenomenology of religion and its ability to rebound after criticism, Jason N. Blum (2012) presents a moderate phenomenology that is a "middle way" between the extremes of crypto-theology and naturalism. Contending that "religion" and the "sacred" need to be in place as heuristic categories to produce new knowledge, he keeps the door wide open for musicological analysis of religious experience. Blum (2012: 1025) recognizes the "disrepair" in the field and offers ways to revive the methodology: "I suggest three ways in which phenomenology of religion may be reinterpreted and thereby retrieved as a viable method for the study of religion. I characterize phenomenology of religion as a distinctly interpretive approach to the study of religious experience and consciousness, which makes no claims concerning the sui generis or essential nature of religion, and which uses historical evidence as a guide to interpretation of religious consciousness. Understood in this fashion, phenomenology of religion has a necessary, but not exclusive, role to play in religious studies."

While not discussing music in their work, current phenomenologists of religion have provided a suitable framework for incorporating music into the study of religion. As such, one can readily envisage a pivotal place for music within the theory and method of phenomenology of religion due to its emphasis on religious experience.

Phenomenology of Music

While the phenomenology of religion forms a benchmark in the field of religious studies, its affiliation with music reinforces our interest in phenomenology. The mere fact of the consistent appearance of music in consciousness across space and time elevates it to a prominent place in phenomenology. The founder of the philosophical school of phenomenology, Edmund Husserl (1859–1938), had associations with musicologists and was influenced by music theory in establishing his philosophical thought. Carl Stumpf

(1848–1936), one of the pioneer founders of musicology and a teacher of famed musicologist Erich von Hornbostel (1877–1935) who later worked with Curt Sachs (1881–1959), was an academic advisor to Husserl. Stumpf had conducted groundbreaking studies in tonal psychology, especially on the sensation and perception of musical tones, which was published as *Tonpsychologie* (*Tone Psychology*) in 1875. Many insights and conclusions from these studies helped to form the foundation for phenomenology. Combining theoretical analysis and empirical observations, Stumpf had explored intervals and tone sequences along with single tones. Distinguishing phenomena and mental functions, he suggested that phenomena such as tones, colors, and images may be either sensory or imaginary. Naming the study of such phenomena as phenomenology, he also conducted a wide range of experimental studies of the characteristic sounds of different instruments, the determinants of melody, tonal fusion, and the consonance and dissonance of tones. Husserl presented many of his findings related to tone and time-consciousness in *The Phenomenology of Internal Time-Consciousness* (Husserl 1964), originally published in 1928. But despite only sparse references to music in the other writings of Husserl, philosopher F. Joseph Smith (1979: 92) has identified how Husserl's thought was influenced by musicology: "For, it is clear, that in his treatment of both time and of synthesis the musical model is central to his thought, for he deals with the single tone, the musical phrase, the melody, and even with the extended symphonic form."

The term and idea of "phenomenology" is well established in the humanities and philosophy, yet if phenomenology is to focus on sound and music, it behooves one to recall that the word itself raises questions as to its suitability. Since the original Greek root, *phanein*, is associated primarily with the visual field, additional vocabulary will fulfill the need of the audible dimension. In *The Experiencing of Musical Sound: Prelude to a Phenomenology of Music* (1979), F. Joseph Smith addressed these issues and laid out the guidelines for a phenomenology of music. Smith (1979: 148) first distinguishes visual phenomena from audial phenomena by introducing the term *akumena* for sonic or musical "phenomena": "Traditional esthetics has described music as a phenomenon and has brought to the task the whole visually oriented vocabulary bequeathed on it since Kant. Yet music is not something to be studied with the mind's eye; it is an akumenal and not a phenomenal experience." Applying Husserl's method of eidetic reduction or *epoché* (bracketing) of "seen" phenomena to sound as *akumena* that is heard, as Smith further explains: "This reduction means simply cutting through the sedimentation of history and theory and returning to the primordial experience itself. In the case of music, it would mean laying bare the fundamental musical experience that has been covered over by too much history and theorization. With regard to esthetics, it would connote 'bracketing' the intellectualism of so much esthetic theory so that we can get through to the 'inner meaning' of music as an akumenal phenomenon" (1979: 151). Phenomenology thus serves as a corrective to the tendency to over-intellectualize the musical experience.

The entire history of the primacy of visual expression is challenged by the phenomenology of music. Smith (1979: 148) confronts the history of esthetics (aesthetics), which he ascribes primarily to visual arts and intellectual comprehension, and which falls short when dealing with the immediacy of the sonic and musical encounter. He prescribes a transition from esthetics to *esthesis*, described as, "a return to the musical experience itself, which implies an overcoming of the merely theoretical and abstract approach to things."

To support this new direction in phenomenology, Smith (1979: 161) drew on early Greek culture that had combined philosophy and music: "Music and philosophy, both creations of the Greeks, were originally conceived as basically one phenomenon." This combination was gradually severed, however, leading to centuries of viewing sight as the primary venue for epistemic knowledge or logos. In juxtaposition to the primal *eidos* (idea or form) discussed by Plato in visual format, primal sound in its raw state was conceived as *echos* that manifest as *tonos*, music that is structured by notes and intervals. Smith (1979: 194) explains: "Musical *tonos* is the echo of a primal *echos*, which is accessible in phenomenology, as the study of *logos*, but only if it becomes an akumenal phenomenology, i.e., one of primordial sound."

How is music approached through the method of phenomenology? As in the search for the "essence" of religion in the phenomenology of religion, Smith (1979: 17) contends that music should be allowed to sound for itself in the phenomenology of music: "Phenomenology is not merely a standpoint or a perspective but a radical attempt to let reality speak (or sound) for itself. . . . We let things—including other humans—speak for themselves instead of dictating to them from prefabricated cultural and metaphysical categories. Thus, instead of trying to cast music in a spatial form, which is visually oriented, we let it speak in its own form. And above all, we stop dictating western forms into music, as such. We allow reality its own language and voice. We allow it to 'sing' in its own modalities and forms. For when we study it, we do not force it into our own scientific categories.

That is why the truly phenomenological attitude is one of listening. It is a musical attitude, if indeed listening is important in the musical world."

The understanding of the "primordial musical experience," as described by Smith (1979: 149), is based on the totality of human experience, including all of the physical and mental faculties: "By 'bodily' perception we mean that we are aware of things not just intellectually but as they give themselves to us 'in person' in the living context of primordial experience. The primordial musical experience is that which arises out of our 'first' encounter with musical sound before any 'esthetic' judgment." Neither an art-for-art's-sake form of entertainment nor a purely speculative exercise, music must be understood always to embody both performance and its underlying philosophical and intellectual formulations. According to Smith (1979: 160), "The musical experience is something the musician knows in his fingers and arms, in the movement of his whole body. Any description, which is not based on this total involvement of the musician in the tonal world, leaves out a crucial part of the musical experience or describes it insufficiently." Furthermore, Smith claims that, "For musical sound does not exist except in and through the musician . . . Musical tone does not exist at all unless I give it its bodily musical existence as composer or performer. Unlike the classic cogito, musical tone is not the product of mentalistic efforts" (1979: 161). His method here thus combines the role of the musician and the musical theorist, in that both are necessary to arrive at the nature of the primordial musical experience.

The approach we have been discussing here also involves something referred to as the "inner meaning of music." Smith (1979: 151) explains this phenomenon: "The inner meaning of music is thus music itself, stripped of the accoutrements of mere history of scientism, music appearing as the creative Muse of the creative subject, as the very source of history and theory . . . It is not a question of peeling the rings off an onion, so to say, and expecting to find the 'essence' after the last ring has been removed and nothing remains. The inner meaning of music is thus revealed as a primordial bodily experience. Music is thus experienced by the subject, but not intellectually." The essence of music, or the "inner meaning" of music ascribed to a "primordial musical experience," thus appears to resemble the experience of the numinous in religion as referred to by Rudolf Otto and other phenomenologists of religion.

After the work of F. Joseph Smith, interest in the phenomenology of music began to rise. Influenced by Husserl as well as Martin Buber

("I-Thou"), Thomas Clifton, in *Music as Heard: A Study in Applied Phenomenology* (1983), affirmed the central axiom of phenomenology as it relates to music, such that music must be defined in terms of the source of sound as well as the receiver of the sound. In his initial statement, Clifton (1983: 1) equates music with meaning: "Music is the actualization of the possibility of any sound whatever to present to some human being a meaning which he experiences with his body." In context, "body" refers to the totality of mind, feelings, senses, and will. Elsewhere (1983: 281), he states: "There is no music without the presence of the music-ing self." As the essence of his thesis, Clifton (1983: 297) announces: "Music is what I am when I experience it." What this says is that it is essentially the human reception and interpretation of the meaning of sound, the separation of musical meaning from non-music, that "creates" the reality of music (1983: 5): "Music is not a fact or thing in the world, but a meaning constituted by human beings." In other words (1983: 36–37), "The sounds, the techniques, and the notation are all vastly important aspects of music, but *they are not music itself.*" Clifton develops his phenomenology of music around four basic features of musical experience: musical experience includes the essence of time; musical experience includes the essence of musical space; musical experience includes the element of play; musical experience includes the element of feeling. In her study of Clifton, Doreen B. Rao (Reimar 1983: 59), explains that, for him, musicality or musical experience must include the personal investment of participation on some level: "Musical experience is dependent on the ability to identify the world of music and refer to it—to participate and be involved in the musical activity of time, space, play, and feeling."

Returning to the study of religion, we still encounter methodological challenges in the comparative study of religion and music. In the next chapter we will discuss the role of music in the social sciences, including anthropology, psychology, and sociology. These areas, with exceptions, subscribe to the Mirror Theory that considers religion and music as cases of culture. We will examine the rise of culture as the principal currency in the study of humanity and how changes have occurred that open the way for deeper realizations of the abiding connections between religion and music across these disciplines. A principal theme will be the debate regarding universals and the view of cultural relativism, the position that each culture is unique and cannot, or should not, be compared to another culture. This notion regarding music, musical relativism, has influenced ethnomusicology, which took its cue from anthropology.

Chapter Two

Social Sciences and Music

The universal people know how to dance and have music.
—Donald E. Brown, *Human Universals*

There is evidence that music is universal. In all cultures we find singing and the production of specific rhythms by drumming and hand clapping.
—Christoph Antweiler, *Our Common Denominator: Human Universals Revisited*

No culture so far discovered lacks music. Making music appears to be one of the fundamental activities of humankind.
—Anthony Storr, *Music and the Mind*

The previous chapter outlined the history and approach of religious studies, developing as it were out of history of religions, comparative religion, and theological study. This focused on the "religionist" position in terms of phenomenology and how these disciplines understood music. The general "religionist" position, also known as the Window Theory, takes the holy or the sacred as a near universal, autonomous *a priori* phenomenon that is experienced and recognized through empathetic understanding. There is, however, an opposing side to this view in the study of religion represented by the Mirror Theory, which has many subscribers and brings new and alternative perspectives to balance out the dichotomy. This is the, let us say, "non-religionist" position that does not accept at face value the premises of either "religionist" religious studies or theology. The label of "naturalism" is often applied to this view but also that of "functionalism." This book's Introduction introduced the challenges to religious studies posed by the approaches of the social sciences and the developments of Postmodernism and Neo-Marxism. Discussing the social sciences of anthropology, psychology, and sociology, this chapter will provide a synopsis and analysis of the two positions, "religionist" and "non-religionist," in terms of history and methodology, with new developments in the social sciences that bode well for the Musicology of Religion and the study of religion and music.

The dichotomy of perspectives, "religionist and non-religionist," is not new. In fact, they are represented in modernity by different angles of vision. As noted in chapter 1, historian of religions Eric J. Sharpe, in *Understanding Religion* (1983: 56–58), distinguished this pair of perspectives in terms of theories: the Window Theory and the Mirror Theory. The Window Theory in its modern form may be traced back in Germany to Kant, Hegel, and Schleiermacher, with representatives in the phenomenology of religion like Rudolf Otto and other historians of religion. The second theory, the Mirror Theory, is traceable to Ludwig Feuerbach, Emile Durkheim, and the radical skepticism of Marx, Freud, and Nietzsche. According to each theory, the same data leads to two different results. In the Window Theory, the data of religion is evidence enough for the existence of the sacred or God; that which sets "religion" apart from "non-religion" are the experiences of the sacred. Otto and others were convinced that experiences of this kind validated the sacred or the God who produced them.

In contrast, in the Mirror Theory, the data of religion "mirror" or reflect the conscious, self-understanding of human beings in society and community. Rather than real entities, God and the supernatural are mere "projections" of the needs of the individual human being and the social order. Ludwig Feuerbach (1804–1872) established these ideas in his work, *The Essence of Christianity* (1841), which soon influenced the young Karl Marx, Engels, Freud, and Durkheim. Feuerbach had studied philosophy and theology under Hegel and Schleiermacher, but at some juncture became a leader of the "Young Hegelians," a group of radical disciples of Hegel formed after his death in 1831. Members included David F. Strauss and later Karl Marx. Although originally adhering to Lutheran theology, Feuerbach rejected the reality of God and the Absolute that Hegel had posited, and instead developed his own theory of projection. This was done through a process of clever inversion, sometimes referred to as "standing Hegel on his head." Theology had become anthropology. Van A. Harvey, in *Feuerbach and the Interpretation of Religion* (1995: 11), explained this process through a compelling example: "If Hegel had argued that the cosmos is the 'objectification' of the Absolute Spirit, then Feuerbach and his friends could argue that God could be shown to be the objectification of human spirit. And if Hegel had argued that the Absolute Spirit comes to self-consciousness by taking the objectified and alienated cosmos back into itself, then they could claim that human beings come to full consciousness by realizing that God is their own objectified activity." Thus, although the logical methods of Hegel were accepted, in their inverted form they did not lead to the theism of Hegel but to atheism and eventually to many of the secular approaches in the study of religion.

Influenced by the Mirror Theory and its early adherents, scholars and researchers in the social sciences have preferred to observe and describe the elements of religion from a distance as "outsiders," using the distinction of etic (outsider) versus emic (insider) to arrive at credible data that could be reliably tested to form generalizations about human behavior in isolation or in social groups. For those adhering to the Mirror Theory, this has developed to the point that there is no reason to accept such things as "religion," the "sacred," the divine, or "God" because they are viewed as mere social constructs at best, and symbols of privilege and oppression at worst.

One interesting way to further understand the dichotomy of the two theoretical models is to present a kind of thought experiment in the form of a challenge. Instead of entertaining the issue of whether God exists, one may simply request an account for the near-universal "sense of God" in human experience, and how that sense is manifest within a tradition. This challenge was posed as a question to the social sciences by John Bowker in *The Sense of God: Sociological, Anthropological and Psychological Approaches to the Origin of the Sense of God* (1995: 8–9): "How does a sense of God originate in human consciousness, and what light do sociology, anthropology, psychology throw on that question?" Continuing along this line, one can observe how that very question reveals the weaknesses of the social scientific method and outlook when it comes to religion and its relationship with music. As such, Bowker (1995: 9) revealed that, "If we had asked those questions about the origins of the sense of God at any point from a hundred and fifty years ago, we would have received confidant and unhesitating answers. Sociology and anthropology (which in that period were just becoming established as disciplines) both provided crystal-clear answers; so also did psychology, at least after the arrival of Freud. The majority of those who were working to establish those disciplines as disciplines had no doubt that the origin of the sense of God could be identified, and that all subsequent theistic phenomena could be explained as derivations, through the mechanism of cause and effect, from whatever was claimed to have been the origin or point of departure." We now recount Bowker's assessment of the "sense of God" according to three founders of the social sciences: Durkheim, Tylor, and Freud.

Emile Durkheim (1858–1917), hailed as the founder of sociology and the sociological method, approached religion as a social fact in his major work on religion, *The Elementary Forms of Religious Life* (1912). Bowker (1995: 9) described Durkheim's basic position regarding God: "For Durkheim, the origin of the sense of God lay in the endeavors of men to objectify (that is to say, give an objectivity to) the social forces which constrain their individual lives." For Durkheim, the most sacred item was the totem, but instead of containing divine or sacred elements, a totem is to be viewed as merely an emblem or symbol of the original ancestor that lives on in the members of the community who ritually "eat" the sacrificial animal. Sharpe (1983: 38) cites Durkheim himself on the formation of the idea of "religion" as a unified system of concepts: "When a certain number of sacred things sustain relations of coordination or subordination with each other in such a way as to form a system, having a certain unity, but which is not comprised within any other system of the same sort, the totality of these beliefs and their corresponding rites constitutes a religion."

E. B. Tylor (1832–1917), widely recognized as the founder of anthropology while working under the influence of Darwinian evolution, maintained that all religions originate in the belief in spirits (animism) and evolve through polytheism into monotheism. Bowker (1995: 9–10) summarized the main points regarding his understanding of God: "For Tylor, . . . the origin of the sense of God lay in the endeavors of men to account for phenomena which are common in experience but difficult to explain—in particular, the experience of dreams, in which one's 'self' seems to wander out of the body, but also the experience of visions and trances, even to the extent of seeing someone, or the impression of someone, whom one knows to be absent or dead." According to Tylor, then, "the origin of the sense of God lay in animism, in the attempts of primitive men to explain the 'animation' of their bodies, as also of trees, animals, clouds, rivers, and all other moving (and eventually even immobile) objects."

As the founder of psychoanalysis and the psychological approach to religion, Sigmund Freud (1856–1939) was less optimistic about religion, viewing it as a form of dependency. Bowker (1995: 10) explained his position this way: "For Freud, the origin of the sense of God lay in the projection on to the universe at large of the situation in which every human being learns that it cannot continue its life without dependence on others; and that is the situation in which infant is dependent on its parents. Those who cannot face the fact of ultimate non-continuity (that is, oblivion in death) project into the universe a father figure on whom they can be dependent, and live *as if* this comforting illusion is true, and *as if* there will be continuity of some personal existence in relation to that figure, even through and after death."

While for generations students and scholars in the social sciences have basked in the critical approaches inaugurated and sustained by Durkheim, Tylor, and Freud, some able detractors have resisted these approaches. Bowker (1995: 16) joins these detractors in rejecting their conclusions and raises enough doubt to re-envision their entire purpose and perspective: "What has made us more cautious in defining, with absolute certainty, the origin of the sense of God, is the realization that *a priori*, in behavioral terms alone, the possibility cannot be excluded that God is the origin of the sense of God—a possibility which to Tylor, Durkheim, and Freud was simply inadmissible." Bowker (1995: 46) thus takes issue with the social science (anthropological) premise that there are no universal essences outside of history, especially the sacred: "No matter how much anthropology may contribute to the anti-essentialist argument, this does not in itself dissolve the problem of the reality of the objects of human attention, including the objects of belief—not simply the actual sacral objects which serve to deliberate cues of the transcendent or of the paranatural, but the possible realities in existence to which those beliefs approximate . . . There is nothing in the current stance of anthropological research, despite the enormous light it throws on the effects of cultural relativity, to rule out an analogous possibility in the characterization of the sense of God." Pondering this conundrum, we continue to explore the Mirror Theory as well as the issue of universalism versus relativism.

Cultural Relativism

One of the principal issues within the social sciences has been that of human universals. Since their inception, the social sciences have largely challenged the universalist position and endorsed cultural relativism. To frame this debate, one begins by asking the question: is each culture, including religion or music as part of culture, completely unique and noncomparable with other cultures, or are there commonalities worth acknowledging and developing into theoretical models or patterns? According to the Window Theory, the foundation of a proposed Musicology of Religion rests on the reality of human universals and thus the efficacy of comparative studies. Yet, following the Mirror Theory, the social sciences have tended to endorse the non-universalist approach of cultural relativism, which views each separate culture as unique and incomparable. Historian of religion Wendy Doniger (2000: 65) has warned of the extremes of cultural relativism: "This emphasis tends to generate a smaller and smaller focus until it is impossible to generalize even from one moment to the next: nothing has enough in common with anything else to be compared with it even for the purpose of illuminating its distinctiveness. The radical particularizing of much recent theory in cultural anthropology, for instance, seems to deny any shared base to members of the same culture, much less to humanity as a whole." In the modern context, Doniger (2000: 65) recommends a balance, however difficult, between the extremes of relativism and universalism: "Maintaining this balance is particularly difficult in an age like ours when the extremes of globalization and diversification have come to power simultaneously and continue to egg one another on."

Cultural relativism is most prominent in twentieth-century anthropology, particularly in the works of anthropologists Ruth Benedict, Margaret Mead, and Clifford Geertz. For example, Clifford Geertz, in "Anti-Anti-Relativism" (1984: 264), argues for cultural relativism and rejects comparative models or universalizing tendencies in favor of paradigms upholding the uniqueness and incomparability of specific ethnic groups, cultures, and nations: "The relativist bent, or more accurately the relativist bent of anthropology, so often induces in those who have much traffic with its materials, is thus in some sense implicit in the field as such; in cultural anthropology perhaps particularly, but in much of archaeology, anthropological linguistics, and physical anthropology as well."

In his critique of the methods of the social sciences, Gopāla Śaraṇa, in *The Methodology of Anthropological Comparisons: An Analysis of Comparative Methods in Social and Cultural Anthropology* (1975: 75), described how the position of cultural relativism may have arisen in the course of conducting fieldwork: "An anthropologist's exclusive concern with a single people at a certain period of time of their existence may give rise to a viewpoint opposing all comparisons. In such case it is contended that every culture is unique and possesses a set of values which is not easy to define. But an anthropologist, with his long and close association with the people, may experience and understand it. The uniqueness of each culture is inviolable. So there can be no comparison of cultures or parts of cultures." Śaraṇa (1975: 76) counters this view and explains how it is nonscientific, how it hinders the search for knowledge, and yet in modified form remains the hallmark of cultural anthropology: "Extreme or arch-relativism, if accepted and practiced generally, becomes an impediment in the development of any scientific discipline. In its reasonably restricted form cultural relativism is one of anthropology's notable contributions."

The approach of cultural relativism has also included preferences for the separation of "culture," an infinite variable, from biology, a finite variable that tends toward fixed and thus universalist interpretations: the classic nature versus nurture debate. Standing on the side of nurture, social scientists have defined the core of humanity as culture rather than "nature" and sustained this majority position in the social sciences. Ian Cross (2009: 4) has reaffirmed the non-universalist position of cultural anthropology and how it has been at loggerheads with the developing biological view of human existence: "Within Anthropology, an increasing tendency to focus on the cultural specifics of societies rather than on pancultural universalities or on any necessary concept of cultural progress diminished the apparent explanatory role of any biological foundation for culture and mind." However, the evolving status of culture in the social sciences and the study of music does not unilaterally reflect this view. And while cultural relativism seems to have enveloped the discipline of anthropology for years, this perspective has been occasionally overturned. We may cite the case of George Murdock.

As early as the 1930s, a separate realm of "culture" was designated by anthropologist George Murdock (1932: 207): "Cultural phenomena, from their independence of the laws of biology and psychology, may be said to operate in a distinct realm, the 'superorganic' . . . According to this concept, the phenomena of nature fall into three great realms: (1) the inorganic, where the chemical and physical sciences study the phenomena of matter and energy: (2) the organic, where the sciences of biology and psychology study living organisms and their organic behavior; and (3) the superorganic, where the social sciences study culture and historical phenomena."

Murdock (1932: 200) understood the uniqueness of individual cultures to be the prevailing view among social scientists in his day: "That culture, a uniquely human phenomenon independent of the laws of biology and psychology, constitutes the proper subject of the social sciences, is a proposition accepted with practical unanimity by social anthropologists today. A large and increasing proportion of sociologists hold substantially the same position." Murdock (1932: 201) based his view on the edges of controversy: "There is, in the first place, universal agreement—if we except the racialists, eugenists, and instinctivists—that cultural behavior is socially rather than biologically determined; that it is acquired not innate; habitual in character rather than instinctive. Culture rests, in short, not on man's specific germinal inheritance, but on his capacity to form habits under the influences of his social environment." His fourfold analysis of human culture and behavior as separate from biology revealed his mode of thought:

> Four factors, as we have now seen, have been advanced by various writers, and have received wide recognition, as explanations of the fact that man alone of all living creatures possesses culture-namely, habit-forming capacity, social life, intelligence, and language. These factors may be likened to the four legs of a stool, raising human behavior from the floor, the organic level or hereditary basis of all behavior, to the super-organic level, represented by the seat of the stool. No other animal is securely seated on such a four-legged stool. Many live in societies. Some manifest no mean intelligence and habit-forming capacity. None, however, possesses language. Just as no one or two of these factors alone can suffice to explain culture, so no animal can maintain an equilibrium on a stool with but one or two legs. All four legs seem necessary to attain the level of the superorganic, and man alone possesses all. (1932: 213)

However, after years of teaching and ethnographic research, Murdock (1971: 20) repudiated this view as "mythology," and opined that culture, never a reified abstraction, always results from the interaction of individual human beings in historical context: "I therefore feel no hesitation in rejecting the validity and utility of the entire body of anthropological theory, including the bulk of my own work, which derives from the reified concepts of either culture or social system, and in consigning it to the realm of mythology rather than science." This pivoting of Murdock foretold the gradual rise of cognitive studies that recognizes that both human biology and human culture are interacting factors in an evolutionary context.

Cultural Universalism

The debate in the social sciences regarding cultural relativism versus universalism has been fueled by another burning issue—the origin of religion. Rodney Stark, in *Discovering God: The Origins of the Great Religions and the Evolution of Belief* (2007: 24–38), opens the discussion by describing four approaches of schools of thought regarding primitive religions: Naturism (Max Muller—the personification of natural forces lead to myths), Animism (Tylor, a critic of Naturism, believed that everything is inhabited by a spirit, animate and inanimate), Ghost Theory (Spencer, also a critic of Naturism, believed that spirits were capable of detached movement, as in dreams and afterlife, belief in which leads to ancestor worship and invention of gods), and Totemism (Tylor, W. Robertson Smith, whereby a clan of tribe identifies with an animal which is sacred but sacrificed and eaten at times, leads to all religions). The latter also include Durkheim, whereby all rites involved the worship of societies themselves, and Freud, whereby blood sacrifices on the altar are central to all religions, such as the slaying of the ancestral father.

The Mirror Theory regarding the sacred and religion, as portrayed in the four approaches listed above, was upheld by the concept of evolution and historical materialism. However, Tylor's evolutionary thesis about the origin of religion in animism or belief in spirits received considerable backlash. Tylor had held that all religion developed in a series of stages from animism to ancestor worship, to polytheism, and to monotheism.

One theory that emerged, even if partially conclusive, presented a formidable obstacle to the theory of evolution and to an entire host of advocates of the Mirror Theory, and thus to widespread forms of cultural relativism. The discovery of "High Gods" among large segments of primitive peoples raised fundamental questions about the primacy of lower forms of cult worship, including animism, totems, spirits, fetishes, and magic, as argued by several contemporary anthropologists. Andrew Lang (1844–1912), trained at Oxford under Tylor, was the first to reject Tylor's theory of animism, as described by Stark (2007: 55): "In *The Making of Religion* [1898], Lang broke with Tylor and overturned all previous studies of primitive religions, which were unanimous in claiming that groups in the earliest stages of cultural development had no Gods and that belief in a moral Supreme Being is a very late result of evolution." Stark continued: "Not content to note the prevalence of High Gods, Lang proposed that because they were so often found among the least advanced peoples, High

Gods would seem to represent the earliest form of religion and that 'lower' religions, such as animism and crude idolatry, probably devolved from these more ethical religious beginnings" (2007: 58–59).

Because of Andrew Lang's rebuttal of the esteemed Tylor, he is all but ignored in history of anthropology. Yet the basic theory that Lang proposed, what came to be called "primitive monotheism," was a bold rejection of evolution as understood by anthropologists and ethnologists at the time. Lang received his greatest champion in Wilhelm Schmidt (1868–1954), whose work *The Origin and Growth of Religion* (1931) was a massive contribution to ethnology. In the current edition, Schmidt (2014: 8) stated: "The fact that ethnology in general is at present in a state of transition makes its unwelcome presence felt in the history of religion in particular. In the whole domain of ethnology, the old Evolutionary school is bankrupt." Schmidt (2014: 15) placed the theory of evolution in historical context as an attack against the nascent conservative and religious spirit associated with the history of religion: "So it came about that the second half of the nineteenth century was marked by the intrusion, first of Liberalism, then of Socialism, both more or less associated with materialism, which, in both these movements, turned with ever-increasing strength against religion and tradition. This materialism was strengthened by a doctrine of progressive Evolution, the fruit of Darwinism in natural science, which was opposed to the idealistic Evolutionism of Hegel, this having already appeared in the previous epoch."

In advancing the theory of primal monotheism, the theory of progressive evolution of religion was explained and thus debunked by Schmidt (2014: 176): "From the idea of the soul, according to it, is developed on the one hand the concept and the worship of nature-spirits, and on the other the cult of ancestral ghosts. Then came polytheism, and from some form of this monotheism was at last developed. But it is just the most primitive peoples, . . . the Australians, the Andamanese, who do not possess any tendance of the dead, at least no religious tendance, no ancestor-worship. But where no ancestor-worship exists, no monotheism can develop out of it." The very pillars of animism were broken, as Schmidt concluded: "Thus the fundamental idea of the animistic theory, the origin of the idea of God from the idea of spirit, misses its mark. The former concept need not have been developed out of the notion of a soul at all."

Rodney Stark (2007: 62) has recently expanded Schmidt's theory of original monotheism and described it in terms of universal revelation: "The many similarities of religions around the world are not evidence that they all are human inventions but reflect a 'universal revelation' dating from earliest times. Schmidt proposed that at the dawn of humanity all religions were alike; everyone knew the name of God. It is the variations from one religion to another that reveal the insertion of human inventions, of misunderstanding, and of faulty transitions across generations—an additional source of variation being subsequent revelations as humans became capable of better comprehending God. In this way, Schmidt showed how snugly the huge ethnographic literature of primitive religions fits with the account in Genesis of the Creation and the Fall." But since Schmidt was a Catholic cleric, his work was dismissed as apologetics.

Decades after Schmidt, Mircea Eliade, in *The Quest: History and Meaning in Religion* (1969: 24), gave this positive assessment: "Whatever one may think of Schmidt's theories on the origin and growth of religion, one must admire his stupendous learning and industry. Wilhelm Schmidt was certainly one of the greatest linguists and ethnologists of this century. To him, the *Ur-religion* consisted in the belief in an eternal, creator, omniscient, and beneficent High God, supposed to live in the sky. He concluded that in the beginning a sort of *Ur-monotheismus* existed everywhere, but that the later development of human societies degraded, and in many cases almost obliterated the original beliefs." In his *Patterns in Comparative Religion* (1958: 25), Eliade all but embraced the primacy of belief in a Supreme Being: "But though they may not appear there as very important, Supreme Beings do belong to the religious patrimony of 'primitives' and cannot therefore be left out of any worldwide study of early mankind's experience of the sacred." Eliade (1958: 24) clearly develops this idea as an important aspect of the history of religions: "No religion, however 'primitive' is capable of being reduced to an elementary level of hierophanies (mana, totemism, or animism). Alongside these wholly simple religious theories and experiences we continually find more or less marked traces of other experiences and theories, traces, for instance, of worship of a Supreme Being . . . Belief in a Supreme Being, creator, omnipotent, dwelling in the heavens and manifesting himself by epiphanies of the sky, appears to some extent among almost all primitives; but this Supreme Being has almost no place in the cult—his place is taken there by other religious forces (totemism, ancestor-worship, mythologies of sun and moon, epiphanies of fertility, and so on)."

British historian of religions E. O. James, in *Comparative Religion* (1961: 199–200), though initially hesitant, agreed substantially with Eliade on the importance of Schmidt's theory as a counterpart to Rudolf Otto: "So far as the evidence available can be taken as a guide, it seems that while there are no adequate grounds for the assumption that monotheism was the primeval religion of mankind, a universal monotheistic tendency is probably more fundamental than any final product of an evolutionary system, being the emotional evaluation of the *mysterium tremendum* in the intuitive realization of a Power awful and mysterious as the transcendent ground of the visible order, though not to the exclusion of other lesser supernatural beings in their respective spheres."

In his earlier Wilde Lectures at Oxford, published as *The Concept of Deity: A Comparative and Historical Study* (1950: 15–16), E. O. James stressed that much rational theory in anthropology is speculation when confronting the deeply mystical nature of religious experience: "In the matter of belief in God, all that he [the anthropologist] can affirm is that religion is apparently a universal phenomenon in human society as it is known under existing conditions. To go beyond this is speculation and conjecture, but, nevertheless, the principle of continuity suggests that all the more important kinds of vital activity have been present from the beginning . . . The religious consciousness being so essentially an emotional experience of the external world—of beneficence, harmony, and orderly creation in conflict with their opposites—it has acquired a very deeply laid traditional and mystical significance which tends to make authority and 'feeling' rather than critical reason the ground of belief and practice." Thus, for James (1950: 18) the entire world in primitive society is enveloped in the sacred: "In primitive society every object or event which arrests attention, or is inexplicable in terms of the normal, is assigned to the sacred order and given a transcendent significance, so that the whole phenomenal world is regarded as permeated with forces and influences which, though imperceptible to sense, are thought to be real and tremendously powerful in the control of natural processes and human destinies."

Recent years have seen a resurgence of interest in the work of Wilhelm Schmidt and his theory of primal monotheism. Winfried Corduan, in *In the Beginning God: A Fresh Look at the Case for Original Monotheism* (2013: 3), offered this conclusion: "My contention is that regardless of how one explains the origin of human beings, one cannot get around the fact that the first religion of human beings was monotheism, the recognition and worship of one God." We leave it as an open question—the truth of monotheism or primal revelation as the reality behind the universe. But a growing tendency is to consider the possibility of some form of primal revelation to account for both universalism and relativism regarding religiosity and musicality in human societies as attested by a significant consensus in the social sciences.

In one of the most remarkable reversals in the social sciences, sociologist Peter L. Berger has shown that cultural relativism cannot be the definitive answer, and instead has turned toward cultural universalism. For many years, Berger was the "sociologists' sociologist," a scholar of renown who espoused the social science critique of all things essential, universal, and "religious." In standard Marxist fashion and labeled as cultural relativism, this meant that the work of sociology is the documenting of all human behavior in terms of historical and cultural forces. John Bowker (1995: 31) described Berger's early position as the antithesis of the religionist stance: "It is part of the task of sociology to . . . map the boundaries of the behaviour which is likely to occur in the identified contents of constraint. This is what made Berger suggest that sociology poses a greater threat to any 'absolute truth-claims' in religion than perhaps any other discipline, because it can always specify the cultural relativity of any particular belief." On this basis, Berger, in *Sacred Canopy: Elements of a Sociological Theory of Religion* (1967), offered a "rigorously sociological account of how human beings arrive at a sense of God."

However, within a few years Peter L Berger reversed his earlier thinking and began to recognize that the entire notion of the supernatural had been obfuscated due to the influence of Feuerbach. In *A Rumor of Angels: Modern Society and the Rediscovery of the Supernatural* (1970: 20), Berger states: "The supernatural elements of the religious traditions are more or less completely liquidated, and the traditional language is transferred from other-worldly to this-worldly referents. The traditional lore, and in most cases the religious institution in charge of this lore as well, can then be presented as still or again 'relevant' to modern man." How did this happen? Berger (1970: 45–46) surmised that the process of "liquidating the supernatural" arose due to the Hegelian dialectic and its perversion in the work of Ludwig Feuerbach:

> Feuerbach regarded religion as a gigantic projection of man's own being, that is, as essentially man writ large. He therefore proposed reducing theology to anthropology, that is, explaining religion in terms of its underlying human reality. In doing this, Feuerbach took over Hegel's notion of dialectics, but profoundly changed its significance. The concept of dialectics, in Hegel as elsewhere, refers to a reciprocal relation between a subject and its object, a 'conversation' between consciousness and whatever is outside consciousness . . . Hegel's notion of this [conversation

or dialectic] was first developed in a theological context, the 'conversation' was ultimately one between man and God. With Feuerbach, it was a 'conversation' between man and man's own productions. Put differently, instead of a dialogue between man and a superhuman reality, religion became a sort of human monologue. A good case could be made that not only Marx's and Freud's treatment of religion, but the entire historical-psychological-sociological analysis of religious phenomena since Feuerbach has been primarily a vast elaboration of the same conception and the same procedure.

This realization appeared to have been a "game changer" for Berger (1970: 52–53), who henceforth desired to "rescue the supernatural" in all its complexity through the possibility of confronting the supernatural through what he called "signals of transcendence": "I would suggest that theological thought seek out what might be called signals of transcendence within the empirically given human situation . . . By signals of transcendence, I mean phenomena that are to be found within the domain of our 'natural' reality but that appear to point beyond that reality." For Berger, the supernatural was not beyond the real world as we know it but found in the world through a remarkable skill of vision. He cited examples of how through what he calls "inductive faith" we may perceive universal "signals of transcendence" in ordinary life: the tendency to place order over chaos, to play (or make music) as something above ordinary time, the infectious joy of laughter, the reassurance of a mother to her child, and the automatic avoidance of incest and violence toward children. Peter Berger's act of opening the door to the reality of transcendence has implications, in sociology and in all the social sciences, for a greater balance between universalism and relativism in the comparative study of religion and music.

A more recent example of the positive recognition of cultural universalism in the social sciences is the work of anthropologist Roy A. Rappaport. Rappaport, in *Ritual and Religion in the Making of Humanity* (1999: 1), announced his intention to focus on the "universal elements" of religion in the form of the numinous and the sacred: "The most general aim of this book is to enlarge, if only a little, our understanding of the nature of religion and of religion in nature . . . It will be centrally concerned with religion's most general and universal elements, 'The Sacred,' 'The Numinous,' 'The Occult,' and 'The Divine" and with their fusion into The Holy' in ritual." Moreover, in chapter 12 of this work, entitled "The numinous, the Holy, and the divine," Rappaport (1999: 371) analyzes the nature of the Holy: "The Holy has two fundamental constituents: the sacred, its discursive, logical component, those of its aspects that can be expressed in language; and the numinous, its non-discursive, non-logical, affective component; its ineffable constituent, that of its aspects which cannot be expressed in words but is, rather, experienced inarticulately." Here he also presents an insightful comparative discussion of the works of Rudolf Otto and William James regarding individual religious experiences, and Emile Durkheim on collective or societal religious experiences. The implications of this type of approach in the social sciences are significant for the comparative study of religion and music.

Anthropology and Music

A long-standing connection between anthropology and music was made by the field of ethnomusicology. Historically, from about 1880 until the 1950s, the comparative study of diverse types of music flourished in the field known as "comparative musicology." During the early 1950s, "comparative musicology" suddenly receded in favor of the more culturally based study of "musics," that is, music within specific cultural contexts. This approach formed the content of ethnomusicology, established by the founding of the Society for Ethnomusicology (SEM) in 1955. Scholars in ethnomusicology have since focused primarily on non-Western music with an ethnographic component and have mostly followed the lead of cultural anthropology such that music, outside of its cultural context, offers little basis for comparison. The early connections between anthropology and ethnomusicology, as found in Alan P. Merriam's groundbreaking *The Anthropology of Music* (1964), form part of the discussion in the next chapter, along with cultural relativism in music, referred to as "musical relativism."

Nonetheless, anthropologists who have recently begun to recognize the similarities across a variety of cultures are prone to include music as a distinct example of universalism. In fact, in a strong rebuke to non-universalism in human culture, anthropologist Donald E. Brown took issue with cultural relativism and identified several hundred universals, including many relating to religion and music. Brown, in *Human Universals* (1991: 140) included music and religion as part of his hypothetical description of "Universal People": "The universal people know how to dance and have music. At least some of their dance (and at least some of their religious activity) is accompanied by music. They include melody, rhythm, repetition, redundancy, and variation in their music, which is always seen as an art, a creation. Their music includes vocals, and the vocals include words."

As a follow-up to Brown, anthropologist Christoph Antweiler, in *Our Common Denominator: Human Universals Revisited* (2016: 178–179), strengthened the case for universals as the basis for any comparative study of culture: "Comparison is central to the study of universals. The relevance of comparison as a method in universal research springs directly from the definition of universals as features that occur in all cultures. This definition implies the broadest possible comparison of societies. In contrast to the daily use of the word, 'compare' does not mean here 'equate.' Comparisons have a more open-ended meaning depending on whether sameness, likenesses, or differences in cultures have been uncovered. But any type of comparison must be based on something, must be considered from a particular time or place." In likewise fashion, Antweiler discussed music as a universal part of culture, with examples: "As with representational art, there is evidence that music is universal. In all cultures we find singing and the production of specific rhythms by drumming and hand clapping. Many universals regarding tones, melodies, and rhythms are of a very specific type. Tonal or musical scales in all cultures contain only a few ranges, mostly of five or six tones" (2016: 106).

Antweiler also recognized the contested issue of nomenclature, namely, the use of "music" versus "musics" in both anthropology and its musical offshoot, ethnomusicology. Music, seen as an underlying unified phenomenon with accompanying notions of universal aesthetics, is opposed by the moniker "musics," which signifies separate identifiable musical traditions in a multicultural world: "An open question today in music research asks whether music is in fact a phenomenon from a transcultural point-of-view, or whether one can speak here only of music in the plural form [musics] . . . If there are universal patterns in art and music, then we can venture toward a concept of aesthetics that has as its core the notion that certain things are perceived as especially attractive" (2016: 106–107).

Recent work in anthropology has fully recognized sound and music as critical dimensions warranting further study. For example, Judith Becker, in "Anthropological Perspectives on Music and Emotion" (2001), offers valuable insights, followed by her penetrating study, *Deep Listeners: Music, Emotion, and Trancing* (2004). A recent article summarizes a wide range of research on the role of sound in anthropology: "Soundscapes: Toward a Sounded Anthropology" (2010), by David W. Samuels, Louise Meintjes, Ana Maria Ochoa, and Thomas Porcello.

Psychology and Music

This section outlines ongoing themes and challenges regarding the place of music in psychology as it relates to religion, its presence or absence in the work of James, Freud, and Jung, and current debates regarding music and emotion. While the objective is to demonstrate how music must be viewed as a key component in the field of psychology of religion, it will be handled with a kind of double-layer approach. The first is to underscore the case for the importance of religion within the field of psychology. This is initially self-evident since "psychology of religion" is already an established discipline, becoming an official division of the American Psychological Association in 1976. The second layer explores important research that has been undertaken in music and psychology, a far more challenging task but one that is gaining momentum. In the field of music psychology, the standard view is that music is a product of the human mind. But so far, the description of music as a human art and acquired skill in the field of psychology has been developed to the extent that it inadvertently sidesteps religious consciousness, focusing exclusively on scientific experiments in acoustics, tone and rhythm perception, music disorders, brain research, and secular music therapy. Yet these advances, and the conclusions reached, are imminently and potentially capable of impacting the study of religion and music in innovative ways. Since it can be demonstrated that music is central and formative within the history of religions, it follows that music, as a fundamental aspect of human consciousness development according to recent scientific research, is more firmly embedded within psychology by virtue of its deep presence in the psychology of religion.

When the topic of music and religion arises within psychology, there are new challenges coupled with conceptual issues. Jacob Belzen, in "Music and Religion: Psychological Perspectives and their Limits" (2013: 1–2) affirmed the vastness of the field while at the same time provided a cautionary message: "Anyone trying to give an account of the relation between music and religion by means of psychology will find . . . that she has taken on an enormous task. The problem lies not just in the unimaginable number of connections between music and religion but in the more problematic fact that the terms 'music,' 'religion,' and 'psychology' address utterly heterogeneous realities, each of which resist efforts at conceptualization." The important themes, challenges, and issues form the ensuing discussion.

The relation between religion and psychology has a checkered history, with each side exhibiting reservations since the nineteenth century. Psychologist of religion Dan Merkur (2010: 186) has aptly summarized the tension between religion and the psychological approach to religion: "The Psychology of Religion studies the phenomena of religion in so far as they may be understood psychologically. Religions and their denominations differ regarding the extent of the psychologizing that they each embrace, tolerate, and reject. For many religious devotees, psychological understanding is inherently antagonistic to religion because it ascribes to the human mind what those devotees credit to more-than-human agencies. They view the psychology of religion as a program that reduces religion to psychology." Yet members of other types of religious organizations view psychology of religion more sympathetically: "They value critical research as an irreplaceable means for the purification of religion from idolatry of the merely human."

In recent times the task of defining religion and spirituality continues to be challenged by an enormously wide spectrum of factors, both within the field of religious studies and outside it to satisfy various subgroups within both religion and psychology. In the popular imagination, religion tends to be associated with traditional or institutional forms of worship, ritual, and devotion to sacred realities, whereas spirituality encompasses a broader format for individualized approaches and practices. A useful discussion of the meaning of religion and spirituality within psychology of religion is K. I. Pargament's "The Psychology of Religion *and* Spirituality? Yes and No" (1999). While acknowledging the lack of an agreed-upon definition, Pargament (1999: 12) contends that the understanding contained in the phrase "a search for the sacred" is "the most central function of religion. It deals with however people think, feel, act, or interrelate in their efforts to find, conserve, and, if necessary, transform the sacred in their lives." Pargament then warns against common stereotypes associated with the extremes of religion and spirituality in people's lives, a polarization between religion (dogmatic, legalistic, fixed, conservative, institutional, i.e., bad) and spirituality (open, humanistic, changing, liberal, individual, i.e., good) that ignores the good and the negative of each category.

Mary Whitehouse and Rick Hollings, in "Psychology of Religion" (2008), provide a concise summary of the history and development of the psychology of religion, which is augmented in Dan Merkur's "Psychology of Religion" (2010). For more extensive treatment, including lesser-known figures and movements, we might consult David Wulff's comprehensive work, *Psychology of Religion: Classic and Contemporary Views* (1991). Unlike other works of this nature, Wulff incorporates phenomenology of religion, including the work of Rudolf Otto and his successors, as well as discussion of the ritual context of music and dance.

From the perspective of psychology, the pairing of religion and psychology in the modern sense begins with William James (1842–1910). James recognized, like Schleiermacher a century before, the importance of religious experience in understanding religion. As a psychologist, James also stressed the positive role of a variety of religious experiences on the healthy or "reality-minded" person, as opposed to the despair and frustration of the "sick soul" who is without those experiences. According to Hillary Rodrigues (2009: 91), "James focused on 'immediate personal experience' of religion rather than doctrine, origins, texts, or ritual. He declared these other aspects to be secondary developments, and he asserted that the religious experiences, feelings, urges, and propensities form a compelling subject for psychological study." While not explicitly discussing music at length in his principal work, *Varieties of Religious Experience* (1902), James (1982: 420–421) included brief comments about music and its relation to mystical truth beyond language and concepts: "Not conceptual speech, but music rather, is the element through which we are best spoken to by mystical truth. Many mystical scriptures are indeed little more than musical compositions . . . Music gives us ontological messages which non-musical criticism is unable to contradict." As an example, he referred to the Hindu concept of transcendental sound known as Nāda-Brahman, discussed in chapter 5, "Theology and Music."

For Jung and analytical psychology, religion also held a positive status as a legitimate way to wholeness, such that one's religious outlook could impact mental health. However, the tables were already turned with Freud and his compatriots in psychoanalysis, for whom religion was viewed as sublimated wish-fulfillment and a sign of neurosis and repression of the unconscious mind. Since religious experience, like musical experience, could not be measured, it was dismissed by Freud as irrelevant and confusing. Hence psychoanalysis proceeded toward a scientific model along the lines of logical positivism. The subsequent embrace of behaviorism (B. F. Skinner) led to further denouncement of religion and reinforced the empirical worldview. At universities, as psychology separated from its former home in philosophy departments, it divorced itself from both philosophy and theology. Religion also distanced itself from the secular health profession, including clinical psychology.

Despite the traumas of two world wars and the Holocaust, making people wary of religion, the belief in God and morality associated with religion and spirituality continued to grow. In fact, the growing rate of religious belief in America, as measured by Gallup polls, has ensured the place of religion within the field of psychology, according to Davis and Buskist (2008: 476): "The 1990 Gallup poll on Religion in America reported 94 percent believe in God or a Universal Spirit, 84 percent believe in God as a Heavenly Father who can be reached by prayer, and the same number reported trying to practice what they believe . . . In essence, the continued, consistently high percentage of persons believing in God was one factor that caused the field of psychology to rethink the significance of religion in human behavior and thought." These statistics can be corroborated at this site: https://news.gallup.com/poll/1690/religion.aspx.

In recent decades, the status of religion has undergone a kind of sea-change in the field of psychiatry. For years, the consensus was influenced by Freud and his negative accounts of religion, such that until 1994 the American Psychiatric Association officially classified "strong religious belief" as a mental disorder. However, neuroscientist Andrew Newberg, Eugene d'Aquili, and Vince Rause, in *Why God Won't Go Away: Brain Science and the Biology of Belief* (2001: 129–130) quickly dispelled these notions with scientific research: "Studies have shown that men and women who practice any mainstream faith live longer, have fewer strokes, less heart disease, better immune system function, and lower blood pressure than the population at large . . . New data indicates that religious beliefs and practices can improve mental and emotional health in several significant ways. For example, research shows that rates of drug abuse, alcoholism, divorce, and suicide are much lower among religious individuals than among the population at large."

Other factors indicating a sustained interest in religion among psychologists are the rising acceptance of holistic medicine, the success of Alcoholics Anonymous with its emphasis on spiritual healing, the successes of best-selling Christian, New Age, and self-help authors, and the inclusion of religion in university doctoral programs in psychology. Moreover, mental health counselors find it beneficial, and even necessary, to offer guidance that is faith-based (Davis and Buskist 2008: 479–480): "There is an increasing desire on the part of the consumer to receive counseling that is faith-based . . . The majority of Americans seeking counseling prefer to see a counselor who is religious." In summary, there has been a steady positive change in thought and practical attitudes about the mingling of psychology and religion, and this has accompanying ramifications for the study of music, which is gaining more recognition as a formative element in human evolution and central to religious experience from ancient times to the present.

The endorsement of music as a legitimate concern of psychological inquiry is evident in the number of monographs and anthologies that have appeared in recent decades. *The Oxford Handbook of Music Psychology*, edited by Susan Hallam, Ian Cross, I., and Michael Thaut (2008), contains fifty-two articles by renowned experts that cover topics including the origins of music, music perception, performance, learning skills, music and the brain, improvisation, and music therapy. This work is followed by the more easily accessible text by William Forde Thompson, *Music, Thought, and Feeling: Understanding the Psychology of Music* (2009). The anthology edited by Diana Deutsch, *The Psychology of Music* (2012), furnished the results of contemporary scientific studies on acoustics and sound perception. A barrage of shorter monographs found in their bibliographies fills out this burgeoning field with exhaustive research and analyses.

However, religion and religious experiences have often slipped through the cracks in works on music psychology. For example, the Thompson work has no mention of religion in its index, and there is no separate article or discussion of religion as an important subject in either the *Oxford Handbook* or the Deutsch anthology. In the *Oxford Handbook*, out of 585 pages of theoretical and practical concerns, all one finds on religion is the comment that "Music as expression of religious faith is a worldwide phenomenon" (Hallam 2008: 147). In general, these works, and others, reveal a lack of attention to traditional religious music as well as to the entire dimension of spirituality as a motivating force in shaping human engagement with music. Instead, following a secular or scientific approach, the tendency is to concentrate solely on the acoustical aspects of sound, note, scale, and rhythm, with additional attention given to hearing disorders and the effects of music therapy on mental illness. In the popular book by Robert Jourdain, *Music, the Brain, and Ecstasy: How Music Captures Our Imagination* (1997), religious experience is not mentioned as a factor in musical ecstasy. Moreover, the more recent work of D. A. Hodges and D. C. Sebald, *Music in the Human Experience: An Introduction to Music Psychology* (2011), offers scant treatment of religion as a factor in musical experience. The large anthology of 975 pages known as *The Oxford Handbook of Music and Emotion* (2010), edited by Patrick N. Juslin and John A. Sloboda, is an extremely impressive array of scholarly essays on a variety of secular topics yet does little to address the topic of religious experience, including "oceanic feeling," spiritual ecstasy, or various trance states associated with melody or rhythm. On only one page of Juslin and Sloboda (2010: 727) is there a token reference to ancient Greek theories of music and the Islamic, Hebrew, and Christian suspicions about music.

Despite the burgeoning rise of interest in music psychology, which has in fact created its own niche, a random search of principal reference works and monographs in the general field of psychology revealed a lack of proportionate treatment of music as part of psychological theory or practice. The large (620 pages) reference work edited by Raymond J. Corsini, *The Dictionary of Psychology* (1999), contains only one short entry on "music therapy." Likewise, the *APA Dictionary of Psychology*, with Gary R. VandenBos as editor-in-chief (2007), follows in the same direction with a brief mention of musical intelligence and ability. The eight-volume work edited by Alan E. Kazdin, *Encyclopedia of Psychology* (2000), selectively covers the areas of music perception and music therapy: the main article here on "Music" by Diana Deutsch (2000, v. 5: 360–363) focuses exclusively on acoustical issues and pitch perception in human beings. There are no discussions of specific musical traditions, much less religious songs or hymns and their status as objects of psychological inquiry. A two-volume work edited by Stephen F. Davis and William Buskist, *21st Century Psychology: A Reference Handbook* (2008), contains a short section on "Audition" (v.1, 226–236) dealing with acoustic aspects of pitch and neural coding. Throughout the work, music appears to be enshrined as primarily a special skillset of gifted human beings and not a key feature in the overall development of world cultures and societies. Musical intelligence is therein defined as "[t]he ability to appreciate music and to demonstrate talent regarding the discrimination of tones in terms of melody, intensity, and rhythmic patterns. Groups with musical intelligence include singers, composers, and musicians" (v. 2, 416). With additional sections on developmental psychology, autism, schizophrenia, sport psychology, the environment, and law, the topic of music and religion is all but nonexistent. Recently, while the enticing volume edited by Raymond F. Paloutzian and Crystal L. Park, *Handbook of The Psychology of Religion and Spirituality* (2013), does not contain information on music, the situation turns optimistic in Lawrence De Rosen's article, "Music and Religion," in the *Encyclopedia of Psychology and Religion* (2014).

The current state of affairs in the psychology of music is laid out in the very readable, compact book, *The Psychology of Music: A Very Short Introduction* (2019) by Elizabeth Hellmuth Margulis. Margulis (2019: 1) first indicates the two major camps in the history of musical inquiry: "Since at least the age of Pythagoras, people have attempted to understand musical structures in terms of mathematics. Musicologists and ethnomusicologists, alternatively, think about music as a product of human history and culture." In the latter camp, there is resonance with the Mirror theory discussed above. Yet the field of psychology of music is meant to be integrative among several disciplines, all the way to including current research in neuroscience, according to Margulis (2019: 2): "The cognitive science of music integrates ideas from philosophy, music theory, experimental psychology, neuroscience, anthropology, and computer modeling to answer the big (and little) questions about music's role in human lives . . . The art of music psychology is to bring rigorous scientific methodologies to questions about the human musical capacity, while applying sophisticated humanistic approaches to framing and interpreting the science." Basic philosophical questions entertained in this field should lead to scientific experimentation. What does it mean to be musical? What aspects of music stem from biology and what aspects are from culture? Why do people like music so much? Why does music make people dance? Is music like language? Later developments in science and the humanities continued to assist in the development of music as part of the study of psychology.

Breaking away from the tradition of Pythagoras (sixth century BCE), which taught the consonance of divinely ordained numerical and musical relationships and the "harmony of the spheres," musical psychology as a distinct perspective took its point of origin from Aristoxenus (fourth century BCE) who, according to Margulis (2019: 4), "adopted a more empirical approach that shifted the focus from numerical relationships to human sensory and perceptual systems . . . One fundamental contribution of the psychology of music is [thus] to place human music makers and listeners at the center of research questions on this topic." In support, Margulis (2019: 20–21) cites a salient example of an exception to Pythagorean consonance as the norm: "In the west, people have attributed consonance—the perception that certain notes sound good together—to such universal forces as mathematics or the physics of the inner ear. Yet the Tsimane, an isolated Amazonian society with little exposure to western culture, were shown to rate consonance and dissonance as equally pleasant."

While tending to delimit Pythagorean tuning as a universal standard, Margulis (2019: 21) nonetheless shares the universal features of music that are observed and accepted in the psychology of music: "Certain characteristics are broadly or universally shared among musical cultures throughout the world. Cultures tend to recognize pitches an octave apart as equivalent, and they divide the space between them into scales. Scales tend to apportion the octave unevenly, making it easier to build rich hierarchic musical structures. The most common interval between pitches tends to be small—about the size of the interval formed by two adjacent keys on a piano. At least some of the music in every known culture is metric—based on the regular pattern of a beat—and these beats often group into twos and threes. Music usually takes place in discrete, repeatable acts, such as the performance of a song, and repetition tends to play a major role at multiple levels of musical structure." In a nod to phenomenology, which takes seriously the insiders' view of "phenomena," Margulis (2019: 20) cited a compelling example of musical universalism that has implications for cognitive studies: "As an entry point to the debate about music and biology, it can be useful to identify what musical features tend to be shared across cultures. One fascinating—paradoxical—shared characteristic is a tendency for people to view their own musical system as 'natural' rather than culturally constructed." She concluded that music is an essential part of human nature: "The fundamental role that music plays in people's earliest social experiences tends to support a vision of humans as essentially musical" (2019: 22).

Although music thus appears to have been a concern in psychology for generations, the relation of music to the work of Freud and Jung, two of the most important psychologists of the twentieth century who have impacted the study of religion in myriad ways, is minimal. Freud appears to have had a dislike for music, and Jung simply ignored music as outside of his area of expertise.

Sigmund Freud (1856–1939), the father of psychoanalysis, began his career in Vienna studying the anatomy of the human brain. He then switched to the medical practice of neuropathology whence he began his journey toward psychoanalysis by dealing with patients with hysteria and various forms of neurosis through the monitored use of cocaine, electrotherapy, and hypnosis, especially during his stay in Paris. Instead of continuing to focus on physical abnormalities or injuries as causes of hysteria, Freud came to discover that the true sources were found in the psychological experiences and emotional traumas of early childhood that had been repressed. To explore the ways in which the conscious mind worked, he developed new techniques of therapy to tap into the unconscious mind, including free association and dream interpretation, which were seen to relieve the neurotic symptoms of patients. His research on dreams was published in his famous work *The Interpretation of Dreams* (1899).

Freud was attentive to religion in his writings, especially toward the end of his life. Though often complicated, these assessments were mostly negative, as he described religion as a projection of the conscious mind (cf. Feuerbach and the Mirror Theory), an obstacle to emotional stability and maturity, and at worst a mental pathology like neurosis in the form of wish-fulfillment. In turn, Freud viewed religion as well as art and aesthetic fulfillment as forms of sublimation of the sex drive. Hence, devotion to the arts was a substitute for sexual gratification, which was normally restricted in civilized society. For example, the overt attachment to religious practice or the arts was a neurotic strategy to postpone or avoid the inevitable inner conflict of the ego arising from the disconnect between the inborn drives (id), including the sexual cravings (libido), and the sense of conscience due to the restraints of civilized society (super-ego).

The references to music in Freud's works are equally derogatory though less frequent. It is noted by Freud's biographers that Freud had a particular dislike for music because it invoked sets of emotions and feelings that were abstract and beyond the reach of measurement and analysis. Anthony Storr, in *Music and the Mind* (1992: 89–90), stated, "Freud acknowledged that he was almost incapable of obtaining any pleasure from music," and cites a less charitable assessment by Harry Freud, his nephew: "He despised music and considered it solely as an intrusion. For that matter, the whole Freud family was very unmusical." More information is in Harry Freud, "My Uncle Sigmund,' in Ruitenbeck (1973: 313). Furthermore, Jerome D. Levin (1992: 87–88) recalled Freud's early dislike of music and gave examples of musical works that were appreciated for nonmusical reasons: "Freud's secondary school career was spectacular; always at the top of his class, he was the adored darling of his family. He alone had his own room, and when his sisters played their piano, he complained that the noise distracted him, and the piano went. Throughout his life, Freud remained unresponsive to music, with the exception of the operas of Mozart, which appealed to him with their crystalline clarity, knowing insight into the vicissitudes of sexuality, and embodiment of enlightenment values, and Wagner's Meistersinger von Nurnberg with its middle-class craftsman artist hero."

Overall, Freud concluded that music, in and of itself, was irrelevant to his program of psychoanalysis because it was intangible and difficult to measure in terms of emotional reaction. Since the manner in which music could move people emotionally was not well comprehended, it brought

Freud a degree of anxiety, as he feared music as a rival to psychoanalysis. From his perspective, performing and listening to music was an obsessive-compulsive disorder that needed treatment or therapy, just like religion. Yet given the link between music and emotion, especially that of songs, lullabies, and musical experiences heard in early childhood, it is surprising that music did not form part of the discussion as a point of entry into the unconscious mind.

Freud's negative attitude toward music was contrasted by some early psychoanalysts who discussed it freely in their own work. After 1950, "psychoanalytical musicology" began to flourish with studies by Andre Michel, Ernst Kris, Anton Ehrenzweig, and Theodor Reik. Reik (1888–1969), one of Freud's earliest and brightest pupils, seriously took up the issue of music, as suggested in Freud's *Introductory Lectures on Psychoanalysis* (1915–1917), to demonstrate that melody can convey emotion better than speech. Reik's monumental work *The Haunting Melody: Psychoanalytic Experiences in Life and Music* (1953) is the first successful attempt to bring music into psychoanalysis. While Freud neglected music in so much as he was unconcerned with its value in diagnosis or therapy, Reik provided a valuable exploration of the role of melody in the psychic life of human beings: for example, how a tune or a "haunting melody" moves the unconscious mind, sometimes obsessively, in specific directions unknown to the conscious mind. As Reik states in his operating premise, "Music expresses what all men feel much more than what they think. Its language is an *esperanto* of emotions rather than of ideas. It does not emerge from the flow of conscious thought, but from the stream of pre-consciousness" (1953: 15). The idea of the "preconscious mind" for Freud was not technically the repressed unconscious mind but a third area of mental activity on the verge of emerging into consciousness. In this work, Reik located anecdotes of doctor–patient interaction regarding melodies and refrains that have guided people's lives, with specific instances of how melodies conjure up memories more readily than mere word association. He even presents some rare glimpses of Gustav Mahler's association with Freud. While his insights are supported primarily by Western musical examples, this study has wide and provocative implications for the study of the unconscious impact of religious music on followers of all types of cult worship and liturgical structures that employ chant and music. Continuing this line, a resource containing later studies in music and psychoanalysis is the two-volume essay collection edited by Stuart Feder and colleagues, *Psychoanalytic Explorations in Music* (1990, 1993). More recently, Gilbert J.

Rose (2004), Oliver Sacks (2007), Paul Cantz (2013), and Julie Jaffee Nagel (2013) apply psychoanalysis to various musical idioms.

One of Freud's most advanced colleagues and rivals, Carl Jung (1875–1961), took a more positive interest in religion than did Freud. Accepting the notion of the unconscious mind, Jung enlarged it to encompass a much broader collectivity across generational and ethnic barriers, calling it the "collective unconscious." This larger entity contained information, images, and patterns called archetypes that reached back to ancient times but could resurface in the present. The purpose of human life is to recognize the archetypes as they emerge in dreams, poetry, religion, and the arts, and to reconcile opposing factors in life which would gradually shape the complete unitary Self through a process that he called individuation. But while Jung was not averse to music, he, like Freud, left it unattended in his lectures and writings. The reason for this was not that he was confused about the effects of music like Freud, but simply that he was not a musician and did not feel it appropriate to deal with musical subjects. In a rare article by Gunter Pulvermacher, "Carl Gustav Jung and Musical Art," in *Jung in Modern Perspective: The Master and His Legacy* (1991), we find glimpses of Jung's personal attitudes toward music and its relation to archetypal psychology. In reaction to a request to draft an article on the role of music in the collective unconscious, Jung, while declining to write the article, wrote the following response to this issue in a letter to Serge Moreaux, dated January 20, 1950 (Pulvermacher 1991: 257): "Music certainly has to do with the collective unconscious. Music expresses, in some way, the movements of the feelings (or emotional values) that cling to the unconscious processes. The nature of what happens in the collective unconscious is archetypal, and archetypes always have a numinous quality that expresses itself in emotional stress. Music expresses in sounds what fantasies and visions express in visual images. I am not a musician and would not be able to develop these ideas for you in detail. I can only draw your attention to the fact that music represents the movement, development, and transformation of motifs of the Collective Unconscious." Possibly influenced by Otto, Jung used the term "numinous" when referring to the qualities of archetypes.

Victor Zuckerkandl (1896–1965) was an important Jewish-Austrian musicologist and music critic who taught music theory in Vienna from 1934 to 1938. Immigrating to the United States in 1940, he taught at Wellesley College, The New School in New York, and St. John's College in Annapolis. His explanations of the importance of music in human life reflect a creative blend of Gestalt psychology and phenomenology. Believing music to be a central underlying dimension of human existence, he sought to explain its presence in all cultures as a mystical, universal phenomenon. He is most well-known for the works *Sound and Symbol: Music and the External World* (1956) and *Man the Musician* (1973). In the latter work, echoing the idea of *homo religiosus* (religious man) in the study of religion as part of human nature, he advanced the notion of *homo musicus*, suggested by Plato, as a kind of paradigm shift in the study of humanity (1973: 3): "The notion to which the *Phaedo* gives expression is that of *homo musicus*, of man the musician, the being that requires music to realize itself fully. This dimension of our humanity has largely been in shadow over the course of Western thought. It is time to bring it into the light."

At the beginning of the twentieth century, J. W. Slaughter, in "Music and Religion: A Psychological Rivalry" (1905), made prescient remarks on the relation between music and religion that remain relevant today. Slaughter (1905: 354) observed: "If we grant the conclusion of the general consciousness that there is a real difference between the attitudes which characterize music and religion, it becomes highly necessary to account for the constant confusion and intermixture in practice. We may say in general that this results from their exceedingly close kinship, as both find their psychological origin in that part of human nature which we denominate the mystical." He concluded that "since music and religion are rivals for the same claim in human nature, and so long as music occupies its present place in the general consciousness, we can look for no widespread revival in religion." Music thus becomes a "religion" in the sense of its intimate connection to the inner self and to the higher consciousness of ultimate reality. For a perspective, a century later, on the psychology of music in Christian worship, see John Sloboda, "Music and Worship: A Psychologist's Perspective" (2000).

Sociology and Music

While psychology of music deals with the mind, consciousness, and the inner meaning of music, the sociological study of music conforms best to the social scientific approach discussed above as the Mirror Theory. The sociological study of music, also called music sociology or the sociology of music, refers to both an academic subfield of sociology that is concerned with music (often in combination with other arts), as well as a subfield of musicology that focuses on social aspects of musical behavior and the role of music in society. The scholarship and research in sociology of music resembles ethnomusicology in terms of its exploration of the sociocultural context of music yet contains less of an emphasis on ethnic and national identity and is not limited to ethnographic methods. Though regarded as outside the field of musicology proper, due to the increased popularity of ethnomusicology in recent decades the sociological study of music is becoming more well-established. Herein the values and meanings associated with music are constructed outside the individual self, as they are assembled collectively by music audiences and performers. This resembles Durkheim's account of religion as the construction of the larger social collective. Accordingly, the sociology of music looks specifically at the social context and connections among composers, performers, and listeners. In this approach, the various steps in the creation of music make all music a combined "social production" as well as a "social activity," bringing issues of economics into the conversation about the overall "business" of music production that also includes distribution of music as a social act. Among the most notable intellectuals to examine the social aspects and effects of music are Georg Simmel, Max Weber, Ernst Bloch, and Theodor W. Adorno.

A preeminent pioneer in the field of sociology, German sociologist Max Weber (1864–1920) wrote on a vast number of topics, including religion and music. While he worked in an atmosphere infused with Marxist thought, whereby all spheres of life are interpreted exclusively in terms of economics, he rejected the Marxist dictum that religion was "the opium of the masses." His most important work, *The Protestant Ethic and the Spirit of Capitalism* (1904–1905), argued just the opposite: religious attitudes determine economic systems, in this case that the Protestant religion has established the system of capitalism. Weber's work on music, while not Marxist in approach, demonstrates how social elements shape musical structure and performance according to time and place. In his major work on music, *The Rational and Social Foundations of Music* (1921), Weber shows how rationalism was most fully evident in Western music. According to the Introduction to the English translation of this work (Weber 1958: xii), "Weber attempted to trace the influence of social factors on the very creative core and technical basis of music. In its broadest sense, Weber's thesis was that western music has peculiar rational properties produced by social factors in Occidental development." Discussing the relevant role of religion, historians have produced studies of the social history of Western music, such as Henry Raynor, *A Social History of Music: From the Middle Ages to Beethoven*, Vol. 1 (1978), and *Music and Society: Since 1815*, Vol. 2 (1978).

The most important name in the twentieth century associated with the sociological study of music is Theodor W. Adorno (1903–1969). As a celebrated member of the Frankfurt School of Neo-Marxist criticism also known as "Critical Theory," Adorno held two doctorates in philosophy from the University of Frankfurt, one on the philosophy of Husserl and the other on Kierkegaard. Though trained as a philosopher and not a performing musician, Adorno was an avid student of aesthetics, sociology, and music, and attempted in novel ways to blend the three in a series of influential works that bear the impact of Marxist and existential thought. Thus, his writing on music is heavily laden with philosophic insight and sociological determinations. For Adorno, all music has a cognitive character that reflects certain truths about the changes in society and the individual. Lucia Sziborsky (2010: 238–239) characterized his contribution regarding the sociology of music: "Adorno does not conceive of musical material as a natural, quasi-substantial thing that remains the same through various tones, sounds, rhythms, musical forms, and so on, and is available to the composer at all times. Rather, he sees it as historically and socially mediated spiritual or intellectual material that is repeatedly pre-formed in the consciousness of the artist. Thus, it exists in a state of constant change." Composing music thus becomes a dialectical process between what is socially sedimented in the musical material available to the composer and the contemporary zeitgeist influencing individual consciousness: "Artworks [act] as 'congealed' or 'unconscious' history, in which the truth of social reality is made manifest and thus rendered accessible to interpretation." The process of aesthetic theorization is a negative dialectic or negative metaphysics in the attempt to express the inexpressible: "Its longing aims at annihilation in the object whose mystery it wants to decipher. In this refusal to let go, a process in which it consumes itself, it holds fast to the possibility of the 'salvation of the hopeless,' like the work of art, like authentic music."

In *Introduction to the Sociology of Music* (1976: 221), Adorno explained the complex nature of music and its relation to society: "Musical forms, even constitutive modes of musical reaction, are internalizations of social forms. Like all art, music is as much a social fact as an inner self-shaping, a self-liberation from immediate social desiderata. Even its socially unintegrated side is social, confirming that emancipation of the subject whose idea was once envisioned by the bourgeois libertarians. The freedom of art, its independence of the demands made on it, is founded on the idea of a free society and in a sense anticipates its realization." He then proceeded, in purely Marxist fashion, to affirm the crucial importance of economics and the social context for the study of music: "Extremely crucial for any musical sociology is a task now being undertaken in several places: the exploration and analysis of the economic basis of music, the element in which its relation to society is actualized. This concerns primarily questions of musical life: the extent and the effects of its determination, not only by economic motives but, more deeply and importantly, by economic legalities and structural changes . . . Something to be vigorously scrutinized is how the economic base, the social setup, and the production and reproduction of music are specifically linked. Musical sociology must not be content to state some structural congruence; it has to show how social circumstances are concretely expressed in types of music, and how they determine the music, that wordless and concept-less art" (1976: 222–223).

In this work, Adorno (1976: 223–224) described music in relation to ideology by virtue of its ability to generate what he and other Marxists refer to as "false consciousness" by virtue of its role as a commodity: "Music is ideological where the circumstances of production in it gain primacy over the productive forces. What should be shown is what can make it ideological: engendering false consciousness; transfiguring so as to divert from the banality of existence; duplicating and only reinforcing that existence . . . Music is unthinkingly accepted as a proffered consumer commodity, like the cultural sphere as a whole." The truth value of music is relevant to sociological inquiry regarding the historical context, according to Adorno (1976: 224): "As far as musical sociology concerns itself with the ideological content and the ideological effect of music it becomes part of a theoretical critique of society. This imposes an obligation on it: to pursue the truth of music. Sociologically that amounts to the question of music as a socially right or wrong consciousness. Musical sociology would have to illuminate what it means to pursue the manifestations and criteria of such consciousness in music . . . Also to be researched are the historical, social, intramusical conditions of musical consciousness." While Adorno (1976: 224) recognized the religious origin (magic!) of music, this element of music is diminished in favor of the contextual form of musical consciousness that is evaluated through his critique: "The affirmative moment of all art, and that of music in particular, is inherited from the ancient magic; the very tone with which all music begins has a touch of it. It is Utopia as well as the lie that Utopia is here now. It would take an explication of the idea of truth to lend theoretical dignity to the sociology of music."

Now that popular music around the world is receiving proper academic attention and respect in the work of Sylvan (2002), Gilmour (2005), and Partridge (2014), the radical denouncements of popular music by Adorno seem anachronistic and reveal the inherent bias of his critique: "A critical sociology of music will have to find out in detail why—unlike a hundred years ago—popular music is bad, bound to be bad, without exception . . . Entertainment music no longer does anything but confirm, repeat, and reinforce the psychological debasement ultimately wrought in people by the way society is set up. The masses are swamped with that music, and in it they unwittingly enjoy the depth of their debasement. The proximity in which popular music besets them violates human dignity along with esthetic distance. It would be up to empirical research to develop methods subtle enough to track down such enjoyments and to describe their course" (Adorno 1976: 225).

Postmodern critiques of music influenced by Adorno have made headway, nonetheless. Feminist musicology, while interesting on its own merits, draws heavily on Adorno and Marxist evaluations of the alleged banality and oppressiveness of male-dominated musical forms and histories. While their analyses are useful, the dismissal of large segments of music and music history by postmodernists and neo-Marxists tend to inhibit balanced research and development in the musicology of religion. However, new research on Adorno and Bloch holds promise, as in Michael Gallope's *Deep Refrains: Music, Philosophy, and the Ineffable* (2017).

Chapter Three

Musicology and Ethnomusicology

All informants thought that universals did exist in the music, and in fact, universals were seen as embedded within the concept of music itself.

—Ellen Koskoff, "Thoughts on Universals in Music"

There is some kind of universal grammar or syntax of music, perhaps somewhat like that of language. Surely significant among them must be the association of music with the supernatural. All known cultures accompany religious activity with music.

—Bruno Nettl, *The Study of Ethnomusicology*

Many if not most writers on musical experience believe that the ability to experience music is so widespread that it must be considered an inborn capacity for all humans.

—Bennett Reimar and Jeffrey E. Wright,
On the Nature of Musical Experience

As discussed in the previous chapter, the prevailing view in the social sciences, and especially cultural anthropology, is to consider music, like religion, as a case of culture. This has often complicated the pursuit of comparative studies in religion and music, which normally seeks to collect data, make comparisons by noting similarities and differences, observe general patterns, and posit theories. Without the possibility of universality or near-universality, and thus allowing for fruitful comparison, none of these activities are feasible or even desirable. We have discussed the issue of "universalism" in the social sciences and will now observe how the "comparative study of music" has fared in this regard within the field of musicology, and especially in the more recent discipline of ethnomusicology, a field indebted to anthropological method and perspective. As scholars in ethnomusicology have focused primarily on non-Western music with an ethnographic component, they have followed the lead of cultural anthropology, whereby musics, like cultures and religions, are in the plural, offering little basis for comparison beyond their context and function. Ethnomusicologist Bruno Nettl (2000: 466) has concurred: "The typical anthropological approach to universals involves the concept of musics, societies, cultures, all definitely plural." In cultural anthropology, this position is called cultural relativism. In ethnomusicology, we will refer to it as "musical relativism." These issues pose interesting challenges for the possibility and success of Musicology of Religion.

Musicology

The term "musicology" derives from the Greek *mousikē* ("music") and *logos* ("area of study"). In ancient Greek culture, *mousikē* referred to music, poetry, and bodily movement, but has since been limited to music alone. As the modern academic study of music, musicology has three main divisions: historical, systematic, and ethnomusicology. Historical musicology studies European traditions, while systematic musicology conducts research in aesthetics, music theory, instrument classification, acoustics, and scientific aspects of musical perception and cognition related to the social sciences. Ethnomusicology is closely aligned with the field of anthropology in its methods for the study of world cultures and music-making in non-European contexts. While our attention here is on ethnomusicology, a few words about its predecessor, comparative musicology, are relevant for context.

Before ethnomusicology, the comparative study of world music developed within the field known as "comparative musicology" from around 1885 until the 1950s. A principal center was the International Musical Society in Berlin, which contained leading pioneers of the field. But while comparative musicology, and later ethnomusicology, originally gave primary attention to non-European music, ethnomusicology has more recently applied its ethnographic methods to European or Western music. The greatest names in early comparative musicology were associated with the "Berlin School," including Carl Stumpf (1848–1936) and his student Erich von Hornbostel (1877–1935). Curt Sachs (1881–1959), who worked with Hornbostel, was one of the most widely read historians of music, dance, and musical instruments. Sachs echoed the general "scientistic" and empirical position of early musicology in his statement at the beginning of *A Short History of World Music* (1949: 1): "Mythology is wrong. Music is not the merciful gift of benevolent gods or heroes . . . not even the earliest civilizations that have left their traces in the depths of the earth are old enough to reveal the secret of the origins of music."

In addition to writing *The Beginnings of Music* (1911), Stumpf had conducted groundbreaking studies in tonal psychology, especially on the sensation and perception of musical tones, published as *Tonpsychologie* (*Tone Psychology*), in 1875. It is highly significant for the study of religion and music that the founder of the philosophical school known as phenomenology, Edmund Husserl, studied music under these musicologists. Albrecht Schneider (1991: 294), in his discussion of Carl Stumpf and his work in psychology of music, *Tonpsychologie*, notes Stumpf's influence on the thought of Husserl: "Stumpf, a disciple of the philosopher and psychologist Franz Brentano, postulated a complex theory of tone sensation with a primarily phenomenological basis. The theory focused on the cognitive functions, such as judgment and comparison, mental analysis by means of similarity or difference, attention, and memory . . . The work of Edmund Husserl also contains parallels, especially his *Readings on the Phenomenology of Internal Time-Consciousness* [1928] and his investigations of 'experience and judgment, both of which relate to the thinking of Brentano and Stumpf" (see Husserl 1964). We repeat here that Rudolf Otto, one of the founders of the phenomenology of religion, was a colleague of Husserl at the University of Gottingen and was influenced by his thought.

The term "musicology" first appeared in a famous article by Guido Adler (1855–1941) entitled "The Scope, Method, and Aim of Musicology" (1885). Adler was an Austrian musicologist who had just founded the first journal of musicology in 1884, *Musical Quarterly*. According to Adler, the aim of musicology was "the discovery of Truth and the advancement of the beautiful" by applying the inductive method of science in which the gathering of facts leads to generalized laws. As a follower of evolution and the idea of the survival of the fittest, Adler viewed music as a set of evolving forms rather than a series of famous composers. Music was the supreme "tonal art," a sister to visual art, and musicology a "tonal science," or means toward knowledge. While he does not mention theology or religion when discussing origins, Adler (see Mugglestone 1981: 5) interprets both music and musicology—reflection on music—as simultaneous products deeply embedded in diverse cultures: as such, musicology originated simultaneously with the art of organizing tones. As long as song breaks forth from the throat freely and without reflection, as long as the tonal products merely well up, unclear and unorganized, there can be no tonal art:

> Only in the moment when a tone is compared and measured according to its pitch . . . at that moment when one takes account of the organic relationships between several tones and tonal phrases bound into a unified whole, and the imagination organizes their product in such a way that they may be assumed to be based on primitive-aesthetic norms, only then can one speak of a musical knowledge as well as an art of working with tonal material. All peoples of whom it can be said that they have a tonal art, also have a tonal science, even if not always a developed musicological system. The more advanced the first, the more developed is the second. The tasks of musicology vary according to the state of development of the tonal art. In the beginning the science endeavors especially to determine, define and explain the tonal material.

In this article, Adler (Mugglestone 1981: 13) introduces "comparative musicology" as a fruitful type of inquiry: "A new and very rewarding adjacent field of study to the systematic subdivision is 'musicology,' that is, comparative musicology. This takes as its task the comparing of tonal products, in particular the folk songs of various peoples, countries, and territories, with an ethnographic purpose in mind, grouping and ordering these according to the variety of [differences] in their characteristics." As a result of the efforts of Adler and others, including Sachs and Hornbostel, comparative musicology became established in a scientific sense.

Ethnomusicology

In the 1950s, however, the name "comparative musicology" receded in favor of the more culturally based study of "musics" (music in specific cultural contexts) that formed the content of ethnomusicology. The academic study known as ethnomusicology became officially established with the founding of the Society for Ethnomusicology (SEM) in 1955. The person who originally coined the term "ethnomusicology" was Jaap Kunst, a Dutch musicologist, in his landmark book *Ethnomusicology: A Study of its Nature, its Problems, Methods and Representative Personalities to which is Added a Bibliography* (1950). At the outset of this work, Kunst (1950: 1) defined ethnomusicology: "The study-object of ethnomusicology, or, as it was originally called: comparative musicology, is the traditional music and musical instruments of all cultural strata of mankind, from the so-called primitive peoples to the civilized nations. Our science, therefore, investigates all tribal and folk music and every kind of non-Western art music. Besides, it studies . . . the sociological aspects of music." In his explanation of the change in terminology, Kunst downplays the comparative component: "The original term 'comparative musicology' fell into disuse, because it promised more—for instance, the study of mutual influences in Western art-music—than it intended to comprise, and moreover, our science does not 'compare' any more than any other science."

While music and musicology continue as subjects within the humanities at many academic institutions, ethnomusicology retained its strong ties to the social sciences, especially anthropology. According to Nettl and Bohlman (1991: xii), "Although the majority of the ethnomusicological population comes from formal training in the world of music, the intellectual leadership in ethnomusicology has always drawn heavily on its anthropological component." Their historical connection is confirmed in a candid statement from one of the classic works in ethnomusicology, Alan P. Merriam's *The Anthropology of Music* (1964: 4–5): "Because anthropology and ethnomusicology grew up at the almost precisely the same time, each influenced the other, although the impact of the former upon the latter was the greater. Ethnomusicology tended to be shaped by the same theoretical currents which shaped anthropology." Here, Merriam outlined the four goals of ethnomusicology: to help protect and explain non-Western music, to save "folk" music before it vanishes away in the modern world, to study music as communication in furthering world understanding, and to provide a means for exploration and reflection for those interested in primitive studies.

The professional relationship between ethnomusicology and anthropology becomes more transparent when one considers how ethnomusicologists began as anthropologists. In fact, a long-standing connection exists between anthropology and music, especially in the United States, where the founder of American-style anthropology, Franz Boas, was also interested in music. The renowned ethnomusicologist Bruno Nettl (2001: 300–301) has revealed the close affiliation on a person-by-person basis: "A considerable number of the leaders in ethnomusicology in the twentieth century came from anthropological backgrounds. Alice C. Fletcher, whose work began well back in the nineteenth century, was an outright anthropologist; George Herzog, first a music student, received a PhD in anthropology; so too did Richard Waterman, David P. McAllester, Alan P. Merriam, John Blacking, Charlotte J. Frisbie, Anthony Seeger, Steven Feld, Daniel Neuman, Christopher Waterman, Adrienne Kaeppler, Norma McLeod, Marcia Herndon, and others. A good many also received their degrees in folkloristics, whose assumptions and methods approximate those of anthropology. All in all, ethnomusicologists of all sorts have a substantial background in anthropology." As mentioned earlier, my first training in ethnomusicology was under Professor Patricia Waterman, an anthropologist.

In the spirit of cultural anthropology, Merriam (1964: 7) referred to ethnomusicology as the study of "music as culture," and hence confined music to the realm of human thought and invention, without reference to the sacred: "Music is a product of man and has structure, but its structure cannot have an existence of its own divorced from the behavior which produces it. In order to understand why a music structure exists as it does, we must also understand how and why the behavior which produces it is as it is, and how and why the concepts which underlie that behavior are ordered in such a way as to produce the particularly desired form of organized sound." Merriam (1964: 27) then explained that all music is culture-specific and determined by the cultural context: "The sounds of music are shaped by the culture of which they are a part. And culture, in turn, is carried by individuals and groups of individuals who learn what it is to be considered proper and improper in respect to music. Each culture decides what it will and will not call music; and sound patterns, as well as behavior, which fall outside these norms are either unacceptable or are simply defined as something other than music. Thus, all music is patterned behavior; indeed, if it were random, there could be no music. Music depends upon pitch and rhythm, but only as these are agreed upon by members of the particular society involved."

Apart from cultural relativism, the above view also reflects the "consensus approach" characteristic of the social sciences and the Mirror Theory previously described, namely, that what is considered "religion" or "music" in a single society or community arises purely by self-understanding and human consensus, by agreement stipulated within that human group. What is left out in this approach, of course, is the frequent view among communities that music is believed to be a gift of the gods, the result of a primal revelation (*hierophany*) or somehow embedded in the natural order. Psychologist Margulis (2019: 20) acknowledged this trait: "One fascinating—paradoxical—shared characteristic is a tendency for people to view their own musical system as 'natural' rather than culturally constructed." While recognizing the perspectives afforded by ethnomusicology to account for music, Merriam (1964: 31) neglected to mention religious studies or theology: "Music can and must be studied from many standpoints, for its aspects include the historical, social psychological, structural, cultural, functional, physical, psychological, aesthetic, symbolic, and others. If an understanding of music is to be reached, it is clear that no single kind of study can successfully be substituted for the whole."

Beholden to the social scientific approach, Merriam (1964: 25) articulated the objective standpoint of the ethnomusicologist: "His position is always that of the outsider who seeks to understand what he hears through analysis of structure and behavior, and to reduce this understanding to terms which will allow him to compare and generalize his results for music as a universal phenomenon of man's existence. The ethnomusicologist is sciencing about music." Interestingly, by the mention of music as a "universal phenomenon" here, he suddenly appears to lower the bar of contention and briefly distance himself from the cultural relativism of the social sciences, as also suggested in a later statement (1964: 33): "Our attitude is not exclusively that of the social science or the humanities, of the cultural and social or the structural, of the folk or of the analytic, but rather a combination of them all."

Musical Relativism

As we have discussed universalism versus relativism in anthropology, we will now address the issue in ethnomusicology. As in anthropology regarding culture and religion, the issue of the "universality of music" has sustained a lively debate in ethnomusicology: is music universal across cultures or only relative to specific cultures? For clarification, we introduce here the term and concept of "musical relativism," which is the view that nothing about music is "natural" to the human species but is completely the idiosyncratic product of separate ethnic groups or cultures. There are distinct origins of this idea and specific reasons why this position receives support by ethnomusicologists up to the present. The musical relativism of ethnomusicologists has even been recognized outside of the field itself, as seen in this statement by Nicholas Bannan, in *Music, Language, and Human Evolution* (2012: 5): "Ethnomusicology has tended to present cultures as so individually different that detecting universals has been taken to betray a prejudicial viewpoint, especially given the religious and ritual purposes associated with music in many cultures and matters of taboo and researcher sensitivity that these determined."

What is the rationale for musical relativism? Timothy Rice, in *Ethnomusicology: A Very Short Introduction* (2014: 19), revealed the rise of musical relativism in ethnomusicology by tracing its source to the work of British philologist Alexander John Ellis (1814–1890): "He [Ellis] divided the octave into 1200 units so that each equal-tempered half-step was 100 units or cents. Comparing music from all over the world with this new tool, Ellis discovered that tuning systems were far too varied to be explained by a mathematical theory such as numerical ratios or a natural phenomenon such as the harmonic series, the complex set of pitches that sound when a musical tone is sung or played." Ellis began to distance himself from earlier Greek theories that placed music as part of the natural order: "His new measuring tool allowed him to contradict Pythagoras and all the others after him who claimed that musical scales can be explained mathematically or naturally as opposed to culturally. Although Ellis did not employ a theory of culture, he demonstrated that musical scales are 'very diverse, very artificial, and very capricious.' They must result from human intervention and choice rather than from nature, a position modern ethnomusicologists share."

The musical relativism of Ellis had also been noted by Bruno Nettl (1983: 96): "The classic seminal publication of ethnomusicology, A. J. Ellis's relativistic statement about the coexistence of many musical scales (1885), established the primacy of melodic considerations in the early history of the field." The publication that Nettl refers to is an 1885 article by Alexander J. Ellis, "On the Musical Scales of Various Nations." In this article, Ellis (1885: 26), after examining a host of musical scales from Greece, Europe, Arabia, India, Java, China, and Japan, presented his conclusion: "The final conclusion is that the musical scale is not one, not 'natural,' nor even founded necessarily on the laws of the constitution of musical sound, so beautifully worked out by Helmholtz, but very diverse, very artificial, and very capricious." Ellis, said by his contemporaries to be "tone deaf" and not a musician, worked out his system of vibrational "cents" to scientifically distinguish the musical scales of various cultures and hence disprove the natural theory of Pythagoras, which had posited among the ancient Greeks that musical intervals coincide with string lengths determined by the relation of prime integers like 1, 2, 3, 4, and so on, as fractions. To his own admission, Ellis recognized the universality of the octave (1/2), though sometimes imperfectly tuned. Yet after discovering the system of quartertones of the Arabs and the semitones of Japan, he rejected the fourth (3/4) and fifth (2/3) found in Pythagorean tuning to be the universal foundations for scales. This "discovery" by Ellis had severed for him the connection with the Pythagorean tradition of European music (this also includes musical theory in Judaism and Islam, which will be discussed in a later chapter), and led to musical relativism such that, according to Ellis and his successors, musical scales are each relative to the native culture where they exist, and there can be no overriding structure or system of tone, interval, or scale that can account for the diversity of music across history and the globe. Whereas Pythagoras established a natural and universal connection between mathematics, music, and consciousness, Ellis argued that musical structure is arrived at purely by individual cases of consensus, design, and habitual custom. Yet Ellis, a non-musician, failed to account for the possibility that tunings in other cultures may not be rendered perfectly, such that the ordinarily pure fourth and fifth intervals sounding "out of tune" may not necessarily establish an entirely new tuning system that would "disprove" Pythagorean harmonic laws. If the goal of ethnomusicology is to radically distance the study of "ethnic" music from European and hence Pythagorean models, it may not be a stretch to understand the current race to cultural relativism in other fields. For example, a trend toward so-called "ethno-mathematics" argues for the relativism of mathematics and thus of science. Although accepted as a universal standard of measurement for centuries, mathematics is claimed to represent European hegemony.

Since Ellis was a famous philologist, the comparison between music and language became a factor in ethnomusicology. Was music a universal language? Pioneer ethnomusicologist Charles Seeger (1941: 122) appeared to have laid this position to rest: "We must, of course, be careful to avoid the fallacy that music is a 'universal language.' There are many music-communities in the world, though not, probably, as many as there are speech communities. Many of them are mutually unintelligible." Musicologist Leonard B. Meyer, in *Emotion and Meaning in Music* (1956: 62–63), followed suit, but with a qualification: "Music is not a 'universal language.' The languages and dialects of music are many. They vary from culture to culture, from epoch to epoch within the same culture, and even within a single epoch and culture . . . Yet, while recognizing the diversity of musical languages, we must also admit that these languages have important characteristics in common." Meyer provided examples for comparison that move beyond the concept of scales (Ellis), and nonetheless seem to fit well with the approach of Musicology of Religion: "The most important of these [possible universal characteristics], and the one to which least attention has been paid, is the syntactical nature of different musical styles. The organization of sound terms into a system of probability relationships, the limitations imposed upon the combining of sounds, and so forth, are all common characteristics of musical language. It is to these that comparative musicology must turn if it is to make further progress in studying the music of different cultures. In this respect musical languages are like spoken or written languages which also exhibit common structural principles . . . But different musical languages may also have certain sounds in common." Meyer also discussed intervals, notes, and scales and their relationship: "Certain musical relationships appear to be well-nigh universal. In almost all cultures, for example, the octave and the fifth or fourth are treated as stable, focal tones toward which other terms of the system tend to move. Similarly, many systems have organized tonal progressions, scales, thought the relationships between these sound stimuli will vary greatly from system to system." Meyer later summarized his views in "Universalism and Relativism in the Study of Ethnic Music" (1960).

In the 1960s, Alan P. Merriam (1964: 28) joined the universalist debate: "Music is also a universal in human culture, though not an absolute, and the fact that it is found everywhere is of great importance in reaching an understanding of what it is and does for men." Yet later, ethnomusicologist David McAllester pondered the universality of music by any other name: "Any student of man must know that somewhere, someone is doing something that he calls music but nobody else would give it that name. That one exception would be enough to eliminate the possibility of a universal." But the entire context of this statement by McAllester, published in his article "Some Thoughts on 'Universals' in World Music" (1971: 379), suggests that he might accept "near-universals" as a mediating point: "Let me venture the opinion, first, that there are probably no absolute "universals" in music. I say this simply on the grounds of human variability and complexity. Any student of man must know that somewhere, someone is doing something that he calls music but nobody else would give it that name. That one exception would be enough to eliminate the possibility of a real universal. But I think there are plenty of near-universals and, even though such a term contradicts itself, a near-universal is near enough for our purposes. I will be satisfied if nearly everybody does it." He even provided examples: "Almost everywhere there is some sense of the tonic, some kind of a tonal center in music. Almost everywhere music establishes a tendency. It seems to be going somewhere, whatever its terms are, and the joy that the performers of that music feel has to do with the way in which that tendency is realized . . . Music in almost every tradition seems to have a beginning and an end. Everywhere there is the development of some kind and form of some kind. There is pattern, there are formulae, there are special signs that all the practitioners of a particular music recognize."

McAllester (1971: 379–380) then discussed music in relation to culture and social communication, adding nuance: "Music is both an individual and a cultural phenomenon, yet 'culture' is something individuals learn about themselves and their world, a learning which is shared with others. We should expect, if this be so, that some aspects of musical behavior will be universal if only because some learning processes are universal to human beings. But other aspects of musical behavior will be universal because, as part of a social community, human beings must communicate experiences to each other, establish a 'universe of discourse' which make the world more understandable, and thus more manageable. While the nature of a musical universe of discourse varies from society to society, its presence is common to all."

British ethnomusicologist John Blacking, in his classic work, *How Musical Is Man?* (1973: 7), significantly enlarged the issue of musical universalism by observing it as something germane to all human existence and pointed toward the cognitive studies of the future: "There is so much music in the world that it is reasonable to suppose that music, like language and possibly religion, is a species-specific trait of man. Essential physiological and cognitive processes that generate musical composition and performance may even be genetically inherited, and therefore present in almost every human being."

Musical Universalism

In an attempt to document the rapidly developing debates surrounding the universalist theme, the journal *The World of Music* (1977, vol. 19.1; 1984, vol. 26.2) devoted two volumes to musical universals, still a volatile issue today among ethnomusicologists. In the first volume, Bruno Nettl

(1977: 2), in "On the Question of Universals," sets out the parameters of the debate and provides needed insight into the polarity of the issue: "In a certain sense, the history of ethnomusicology is one of tension between the conviction that each culture has its own music, distinct from all others, derived from its own history, value structure, and types of social relationships, and, on the other hand, the search for musical universals. To attempt to define music is to recognize both its diversity and its unity." For Nettl (1977: 3), universals were to be found in the identifiable features of music across cultures: "When all is said and done, there is no doubt in my mind that there is such a phenomenon as music in the world, that all cultures have music, and that except in the most unusual cases, it can be recognized (though not necessarily understood) by persons from other cultures. And it is the features, whatever they are, that makes music thus recognizable that are in a sense its universals." Nettl (1977: 4–5) even identified "universal" features in world music: "All cultures have singing. In all vocal musics, the chief melodic interval appears to be something in the general area of the major second (we are not speaking, of course, about accuracy in tuning, distinguishing a tempered second from other types). But intervals roughly in that area and including anything up to five-quarter tones and down to three-quarters, surely make up the bulk of the world's melodic progressions. And there are no cultures, to my knowledge, in which many pieces progress exclusively by half or quarter tones, or, for that matter, by thirds and fourths." These also include rhythm:

> In all cultures, musical utterances tend to descend at the end although they are not similarly uniform at their beginnings. All cultures make some use of internal repetition in their musical utterances . . . All have a rhythmic structure which depends on distinction among note lengths and among dynamic stresses. These are universals in the sense that they exist everywhere, but also in another sense: they would not have to be present in order for music to exist, and thus are not simply a part of the definition of music. In other words, it is conceivable for a music to come into existence using only major thirds or having all of its notes of equal length. Evidently, then, mankind has not only decided to make music, but to make it in a particular way, and this despite the vast amount of variation among the musics of the world. (1977: 5)

In a later article, Bruno Nettl provided some early context for the issue of universals in "An Ethnomusicologist Contemplates Universals in Musical Sound and in Musical Culture" (2000: 463–464), with a personal anecdote: "When I was a student, I was taught that any attempt to generalize about the music of the world should be countered by an example falsifying that generalization. I was taught to reject the notion that all of the world's music had anything in common. But by the 1970s all this had changed." In another piece, Nettl (2000: 468) explained that "[a]s graduate students of ethnomusicology, we learn early, when faced with generalizations based essentially on Western music, to shout, 'Hold on! There is nothing that is universal, and nothing that doesn't occur somewhere.' Our profession began with a firm belief in the incredible variety of the world's musics. Universals, as a serious object of discussion, did not surface until the 1960s." After naming several prominent scholars in the field, including David McAllester, Klaus Wachsmann, Charles Seeger, and George List, John Blacking, Frank Harrison, Gertrude Kurath, Mantle Hood, Tran Van Khe, Jean-Jacques Nattiez, and Alan Lomax, Nettl (2000: 464) remarked: "It may be no surprise that virtually all of these authors looked with considerable skepticism at the possibility that universals can be defined, identified, and described." Despite the widespread skepticism, Nettl held out hope for the future in the search for universals: "One possible approach is to throw up one's hands and just admit that we will never know whether there are really universals, or whether we can ever learn about the earliest human music and the moment of invention, as it were . . . The question is too interesting, and in a sense too important . . . I suggest that it should continue to be of interest to ethnomusicologists, despite what appears to be their temporary abandonment of it" (2000: 471).

Mantle Hood and George List have upheld the other end of the universalist-relativist spectrum. Hood, in "Universal Attributes of Music" (1977), rejected specific universals about music based on ethnographic data collection, yet admitted that as universals three basic assumptions about music could not be contradicted: (1) music is heard and not seen; (2) music evolves in time, not space; and (3) music is directed at the emotions rather than the intellect. And while he can provide an exception for each one, he does not concede their validity: (1) composer Arnold Schoenberg had said that his music was written to be seen; (2) some medieval antiphonal choirs were designed to project spatially; and (3) some music may stimulate the intellect. Hood (1977: 65) concluded: "I believe the three assumptions can stand as universals in music. The exceptions, considered in worldwide perspective, seem to prove the rule."

In "Concerning the Concept of the Universal in Music" (1984: 40), George List was more strident and relegated universals to religionists and philosophers: "The belief in universals is of course proper to priests and philosophers. The first deals with faith, the second with pure speculation. But why should workers in other fields also believe in universals?" List (1984: 47) believed that universals, like Buddhist nirvana, was beyond the reach of scholars: "On the basis of a wealth of data already available it is reasonably clear that we shall be unable to establish any absolute universals. There are always exceptions to undermine any postulates. The precept that the exceptions prove the rule is hardly applicable to a universal. What we can arrive at with sufficient labor, are norms, means, and majority practices, but no more. The nirvana of the universal in music is, alas, unattainable."

Ethnomusicologist Ellen Koskoff, in "Thoughts on Universals in Music" (1984: 72), however, took an empathetic approach and suggested that universalism may be built into the very nature of music: "All informants thought that universals did exist in the music, and in fact, universals were seen as embedded within the concept of music itself." As a point of reference, she conveyed a "universalist" definition of music based on her vast range of experience and fieldwork: "Music is a system of sound structures given and received (i.e., communicated with intention) by all humans (although in different ways by different societies but nonetheless found universally) where emotions and experiences which are part of our universal 'human-ness' are manifested through the universal medium of performance."

Alan Merriam later rejoined the universalist debate with his 1982 article that argued for the integrity of comparative study. In "On Objections to Comparison in Ethnomusicology," Merriam (1982: 174) took issue with some of the common reservations about comparative study: "The subject is important because objections seem to me to be either half-truths or simply vague statements of the views of their proponents. Further, these anti-comparativist views have gained increasingly wide credence and influence among ethnomusicologists and by no means always with demonstrably positive results . . . We are in danger of throwing the baby of comparativism out of the bath we are filling with the water of increasingly sophisticated methodologies." For his argument, Merriam (1982: 175) characterized the extreme form of musical relativism of renowned ethnomusicologist Mantle Hood: "A denial of all possibility of the usefulness, or even the comprehensibility, of comparison." Merriam appears to have decided in favor of comparativism: "The basic argument . . . then, is that we should not abandon comparativism in favor of ideographic studies, no matter how great the methodological advances. Rather, we need to focus considerable attention and energy directly on comparativism in order to search for more feasible ways of making it a useful research tool in ethnomusicology." Merriam nonetheless recognized the tension within the debate as something that remained unresolved: "My assumption is that ethnomusicologists attempt to operate under a combination of methods borrowed from those used in both the humanities and the social sciences. Indeed, it is this mixture of borrowings, never reconciled with each other, that has led to so much of the confusion that marks ethnomusicology. The borrowings from the social sciences are at prime issue here since comparison is at the root of many kinds of generalization and generalization is widely assumed to be the end result of scientific methodology" (1982: 176).

But a larger question looms large about universals: what does it mean that such phenomena exist? Bruno Nettl waxed prophetic in his analysis of how ethnomusicology began in search of universals, moved to the study of separate musics, and has since resumed its quest for universals, now and into the future:

> Our search for universals is still in a very unsophisticated state. Ethnomusicologists began their work, decades ago, with the implicit assumption that there were universals; and they concentrated on the task of showing the infinite variety of human musics. This devotion to the description and explanation of variety has been a hallmark of the ethnomusicological research everywhere, and it has served, I venture to say, as the emotional motivation for many who have entered this field. Only in recent years, intimidated, perhaps, by the variety they have helped to uncover, and stimulated also by the resurgence of faith in the role of genetics in human behavior, have they reasserted the interest in universals. Is it possible that the search for universals will someday become the central task of the ethnomusicologist? (1977: 7)

The issue of universals has certainly continued to be of interest to Nettl (2000: 468), who has more recently laid down the standard universals according to his understanding of ethnomusicology: "All societies have vocal music. Virtually all have instruments of some sort, although a few tribal societies may not, but even they have some kind of percussion. Vocal music is carried out by both men and women, although singing together in octaves is not a cultural universal, perhaps for social reasons. All societies have at least some music that conforms to a meter or contains a pulse. The intervallic structure of almost all music involves, as the principal interval, something close to the major second but to be sure, not with precision; I am talking about anything, say from a three-quarter tone to five quarters. All societies have some music that uses only three or four pitches, usually combining major seconds and minor thirds."

In *The World of Music* ("Can Musical Universals be Heard?"), John Blacking (1977: 17) expressed some qualified reservations in the view that despite similarities in musical structure, the presence of music as "universal" lies more in the innate feelings shared among human beings: "If human beings can never share feelings, the discovery of universal musical traits would not reveal much about the nature of music: the octave, certain patterns of rhythm and melody, and any other structures that might be found universally, could not be given musical significance, since without evidence that feelings can be and are shared, two people could not even be said to share a sentiment through their common attitude to the same music, let alone be affected similarly by the same patterns of sound . . . Thus, musical universals would be arbitrary and accidental, as music, and interesting only for reasons that are not specifically concerned with their musical characteristics." But then Blacking (1977: 19) admitted the reality of universals on a higher mental platform that are accessible to special composers or performers: "Musicians reared in mutually incomprehensible cultural traditions may use a common device which, because it is based on a universal mental structure, may resonate with listeners unfamiliar with the cultural or musical idiom. To do this, they must reach beyond the conventions of their particular society to the universal mental processes of the species; . . . This is how the most individual composer can have the most universal appeal: he communicates to others at the level of the innate; he begins with cultural conventions but transcends them by reorganizing his sound structures in a personal, but basically universal, way, rather than slavishly following culturally given rules." Blacking's insights have informed later cognitive studies that highlight the role of music in the cultural evolution of the human species, corroborating the ongoing perspectives in the Musicology of Religion.

Following Blacking in the same volume, Frank Harrison, in "Universals in Music: Towards a Methodology of Comparative Research" (1977: 32–33), brought the discussion of musical universals into the practical sphere by outlining their utility and function as points of comparison: "It is perhaps in the spheres of use and function that the most fruitful researches and those most likely to contribute to understanding about music 'universals' remain to be accomplished." Harrison (1977: 35) then outlined functional types of universals fruitful for comparative study, including religion or the supernatural: "Certain categories of use, some of which, or some aspects of some of which may possibly be universals, may be proposed, while maintaining the methodological distinction between use and function. These could be: (1) reservation; (2) communication-heightening; (3) invocation of the supernatural; (4) multiple participation; and (5) message sending." The function of each is shown through the pairing of columns: "Use/Function 1. Reserved to one or relatively few socially distinct persons/One indicator of social distinction, and a reinforcement of social prestige 2. Communication by one or a few to relatively many/Intensifying a presentation so as few to achieve more potent communication 3. As an element in a ritual that appears to call upon supernatural powers/To help to open the avenue to those powers; to avert natural sanctions; to prevent social disintegration 4. Situations of multiple participation/To help to co-ordinate the projection activity of a relatively large number of persons 5. Communication of distinctive semantically precise rhythms/To transfer a specific word-message over a relatively long distance."

As part of *The World of Music* (1977) series of essays on universalism mentioned above, Alan Lomax revealed innovative methods of discovering universals in vocal music through his method of "canto-metrics," which was designed by him to investigate cross-cultural ethnographic data on singing. Drawing on his careful analysis of 4,000 songs among 400 societies of human culture and observing that human song is a social act, Lomax (1977: 129) concluded: "I am, therefore, encouraged to believe that in the search for the basics of music we have found the underlying patterning elements of cultural communication systems. Here Plato preceded us, but with far different results. Whereas he located his universals in the heaven of absolute ideas, we find them in the warm busy streets and alleys of everyday social communications." Also in this volume Tran Van Khe, in "Is the Pentatonic Scale [five note scale] Universal? A Few Reflections on Pentatonicism" (1977: 83), after giving dozens of examples, states: "Don't you believe, as I do, after all of this, that the pentatonic phenomenon is truly universal?"

Although pondering the issue of universals, the ethnomusicologists mentioned thus far have side-stepped the prominent role of music in religious activity. Nettl (1977: 5), however, stands out in his bold observation that all musical traditions share in their association with the supernatural: "Are there similar universals in the conceptualization of music, in musical behavior? They are harder to isolate but let us attempt to name a few. Surely first among them must be the association of music with the supernatural. All known cultures accompany religious activity with music." In his popular textbook *Excursions in World Music,* Nettl (2001: 9) later reaffirmed this observation: "In all societies, music is found in religious ritual—it is almost everywhere a mainstay of sacred ceremonies—leading some scholars to suggest that perhaps music was actually invented for humans to have a special way of communicating with the supernatural." And more recently, Nettl (2005: 46) repeated this conclusion with insight into a possible universal grammar of music: "There is some kind of universal grammar or syntax of music, perhaps somewhat like that of language. Surely significant among them must be the association of music with the supernatural. All known cultures accompany religious activity with music." All these statements are highly significant in terms of the Musicology of Religion.

An additional question remains regarding the possible universal relationship between the sacred and musical instruments. In this regard, Sue Carole DeVale (1988: 126) has investigated the sacred power and meaning in musical instruments throughout the world as they are central to rituals: "Ritual is a worldwide phenomenon in which music and musical instruments play an essential role." She also analyzed the role of instruments in ritual through twelve stages. Building on this research, DeVale (1989: 94) demonstrated how musical instruments are invested with spirits in many diverse cultures: "Power and meaning are invested in musical instruments throughout the world. They are ascribed to musical instruments essential to the efficacy of rituals of all kinds, from those ensuring fertility to those of royal courts. Power in music instruments resides in the spirits believed to be embodied within them or working through them; it often emanates from their music, their very sound." For a description of sacred musical instruments in the Hindu and Indian traditions, see "Divine Musical Instruments" (Beck 2013).

While anthropologists have made ample contributions to ethnomusicology, one of the most compelling for the Musicology of Religion is that of Oxford scholar Rodney Needham. Needham, in "Percussion and Transition" (1967: 607), makes a remarkably bold assertion regarding the widespread association between percussive sound (drums, rattles, cymbals, noise makers, etc.) and rites of passage, including other rituals involving the world of the spirits and gods: "All over the world it is found that percussion, by any means whatever that will produce it, permits or accompanies communication with the other world," followed by his conclusion (1967: 611) that, "There is a constant and incredibly recognizable association between the type of sound and the type of rite . . . there is a significant connection between percussion and transition." In support of this ubiquitous connection, Needham (1967: 607) cites Mircea Eliade, whose *Shamanism: Archaic Techniques of Ecstasy* (1964: 179) revealed this ("curious fact"): "There is always some instrument that, in one way or another, is able to establish contact with the world of the spirits. This last expression must be taken in its broadest sense, embracing not only gods, spirits, and demons, but also the souls of ancestors, the dead, and mythical animals. This contact with the suprasensible world necessarily implies a previous concentration, facilitated by the shaman's or magician's 'entering' his ceremonial costume and hastened by ritual music." These evidentiary claims, corroborating the statements of Nettl above, provide more solid ground for research in music and religion.

The domain of world music has also elicited scholarly approaches that coincide with other current academic trends focusing on race and economic class. In *Music and the Racial Imagination* (2000), Ronald Radano and Philip V. Bohlman assembled a formidable set of articles that illuminate how racial prejudice has been involved in the formation and support (or suppression) of various musics, including those of China, Chicano culture, Indonesia, Trinidad, Yugoslavia, and the Blues, as well as of composers Bela Bartok and Duke Ellington. An ominous mood is visible on the first page: "A Specter lurks in the house of music, and it goes by the name of race." Meanwhile, the volume edited by Regula Burckhardt Qureshi, *Music and Marx: Ideas, Practices, Politics* (2002), portrays social and economic impulses and constraints in the production of various musics. One takes note that the singular "music" rather than "musics" is in vogue when discussing ideology. These works, and others, undoubtedly pose challenges for the current study of religion and music in that attention is diverted by the authors from religious experiences, underlying beliefs, ritual practice, and shared states of consciousness of the performers and listeners of music.

Lastly, attempts by contemporary musicians have strengthened the case for the study of chant and music as part of religious "soundscapes," a terminology that now enjoys wide adoption in research on sound and music in religion. Canadian composer R. Murray Schafer coined the term "soundscape" in *The Soundscape: Our Sonic Environment and the Tuning of the World* (1977) to indicate the sonic environment as, paraphrasing, the sum total of all sounds within any definitive area which surround us as a result of certain historical, technological, and demographic processes. Schafer's soundscape, comprising keynote sounds, sound signals, and soundmarks, has been used effectively to describe the "auditory environment" of religious communities, as in Edward Foley (1995), chapter 2, "The Auditory Environment of Emerging Christian Worship," and in Charles Hirschkind, *The Ethical Soundscape: Cassette Sermons and Islamic Counterpublics* (2006), which describes the Islamic "pious soundscape." Steven Feld, in *Senses of Place* (1996), advanced the notion of "acoustemology" (acoustic epistemology), whereby the bodily experience of sound is a unique way of knowing. As a method of examination of how subjects know the world in and through sound, acoustemology has wide applications in the Musicology of Religion.

In Part II, we assume the challenge of investigating the formative systems of philosophy and theology behind the widespread creation and performance of music.

II

New Directions and Paradigms

Chapter Four

Philosophy and Music

> The same dream came to me often in my past life, sometimes in one form and sometimes in another, but always saying the same thing: "Socrates," it said; "make music and work at it."
>
> —Plato, *Phaedo*

> Not all music is heard with the ears. There is another music of the soul and of the spheres which gives to the actual music that is sung by voices and played on instruments its reason for existence.
>
> —Joscelyn Godwin, "The Golden Chain of Orpheus"

> Not only did Pythagoras first employ the term *philosophy*, and define the discipline thereof in the classic sense, but that he bequeathed to his followers, and to the whole of Western civilization, many important studies and sciences.
>
> —David R. Fideler, *The Pythagorean Sourcebook*

While music is the object of empirical study in the social sciences and ethnomusicology, the field of Musicology of Religion cannot ignore the multiple traditions engaged in the search for music as a philosophical truth or metaphysical reality that transcends ordinary consciousness. Arising in the minds of the ancients, speculative music or *musica speculativa*, ("music as mirror," from Latin: *speculum*) was the idea that music reflected the cosmos and higher metaphysical truth. Joscelyn Godwin (1989: 13) explained that in this view the universe first existed in the form of sound: "The first postulate of speculative music immediately sifts the believers from the profane. It is that sound (or tone, or music) is ontologically prior to material existence. One way of giving assent to this is through recognizing that underlying the apparent solidarity of matter there is nothing but a network of vibrations, which may be allegorized—as no doubt they have been since time immemorial—as 'sound,' the name given to vibrations in the human audible frequency range." Godwin continues with reference to mystics able to see and hear visions and sounds beyond the capacity of ordinary people: "Speculative music often goes further and asserts that the whole cosmos is audible in its superior modes of existence, just as heaven and its inhabitants are visible to certain mystics, even when there are no light vibrations striking the eye." As such, "The priority of the sounding cosmos over the visible or material may be due to the fact that this was its first form of existence."

As an introduction to this topic, Julius Portnoy, in *The Philosopher and Music: A Historical Outline* (1954: ix), describes the perennial philosophical quest relating to music: "The ancient philosopher viewed music as something more than an expression of feeling. He was not content to accept music as an artistic form of communication through which the musical poet of antiquity conveyed his emotional moods and ideas to others. The Greek philosopher attempted instead to find out if music had its origin in some 'higher source' which transcended human understanding. He believed that he detected moral overtones in melody and ethical significance in rhythms. He observed the effects of music on human behavior and decided that music could improve or degrade character. Since he was ill-equipped to understand the actual music itself, he attributed mystical qualities to the origin and powers of music." The purport here is that melody and rhythm are connected to the movements of nature and thus to nature itself (Portnoy 1954: ix–x): "He deduced that rhythm and melody were an imitation of the movements of the celestial bodies which moved through the heavens emitting a divine music which was imperceptible to human ears. On the basis of this assumption, he concluded that the art of music was imitative of the laws of nature and since a moral order pervaded the universe, then music had moral value."

To understand and explain the moral and spiritual value of music, it is necessary to view music-making as placed in divine hands. Portnoy (1954: 4) describes how the word "music" was linked by ancient authors with the higher powers of nature and with spiritual beings: "The word music itself is of Greek origin and was in myth-like fashion originally considered an art which was directly inspired by and descended from a Muse. The early Greeks had three Muses to begin with: study, memory, and song, but with the passing of time each art medium came to have a Mother Muse. Pre-Homeric legend has it that Orpheus the sweet singer and bard servant of Apollo, was himself the son of a Muse. The magic quality of his voice could heal the sick and engender religious devotion at the temple rites." Yet music does not remain in a purely mythical world but forms a link with the very nature of human consciousness and rational thought.

Music continued to play a prominent role in the life of ancient Greece, especially in education. Two works by Warren D. Anderson focus on this topic, *Ethos and Education in Greek Music: The Evidence of Poetry and Philosophy* (1966) and *Music and Musicians in Ancient Greece* (1994). Music also became firmly ensconced in medieval education as part of the quadrivium. Theodore C. Karp, in his chapter on "Music" in *The Seven Liberal Arts in the Middle Ages* (1983), described how music remained a critical element in the formation of rational and philosophical thought throughout the Middle Ages. The central pillar behind the attention to music was the Pythagorean tradition of numbers and their cosmic corollaries (*harmonia*), the subject of the next section.

Pythagoras and Harmony

The name of the Greek mathematician Pythagoras (570–495 BCE) is well known to young students of geometry, especially for his "Pythagorean Theorem"—the square of each of two sides of a right triangle added together equals the square of the hypotenuse. Yet there is much more to his life and thought beyond rudimentary mathematics and geometry. He was also a mystical philosopher—the first to use the term "philosophy"—and, although born in Greece, he set up a school in Croton in Italy that appears to have been a religious society centered on the Muses, the goddesses of learning and culture, and their leader Apollo. Julius Portnoy (1954: 7–8) has provided an introduction: "Pythagoras evolved the metaphysical belief that numbers were the true realities. His disciples became even more mystical and added that numbers were the very essences which constituted and governed all nature. Since man was part of nature, he was the embodiment of a combination of numbers and was numerically related to nature as a part is to the whole. He was what he was because of his numerical components. In nature, as in the arts which man created for his needs, proportion, symmetry, harmony, and dissonance were born of mathematical relationships." At this point music becomes "moral": "Music was therefore a unity composed of numerical relationships and since numbers inherently possessed moral attributes; because nature was intrinsically good, music must be evaluated in moral terms. If the components of music had moral attributes, argued the Pythagoreans, then music itself had moral value. This moral conception of music tinged the Greek writings on the aesthetics of music with a doctrine of ethos which reached its fullest development and theoretical application in Plato."

Musicians and students of music history often hear the story of Pythagoras and his experiments with the monochord, a rectangular wooden box that serves as a sounding board for the one string stretching over it. Yet some people do not fully comprehend the monumental significance of his discoveries regardless of their philosophical or religious persuasion. Despite ongoing debate about the source of Pythagorean ideas—Egypt? Asia?—the widespread importance of these ideas remains undiminished. Among authors who have described the story of Pythagorean tuning, Portnoy (1954: 10) captures it succinctly:

> Legend has it that Pythagoras discovered the octave and then deduced the intervals in the octave through a unique series of experiments in which he applied the knowledge he had gathered in his travels to fertile ideas of his own. Pythagoras found that in (1) stretching a taut string over a piece of wood; (2) placing his finger in the exact center of this monochord; (3) plucking it; each half of the string vibrated twice as fast as the whole string, thus producing a tone which sounded like the original one emitted from the full string but on a higher level of pitch. He then applied this method to strings of the same thickness and tension and found that the lengths of the strings governed the tone but that the physical properties of the octave could be explained through the exact division of the string, be it of whatever length or thickness. But then how to fill in the upper and lower tones of the octave? Pythagoras further learned that if he held the string at a point representing the ratio of 3:4, he would get the interval of a musical fourth; and that through the ratio of 2:3 he would get the musical fifth. He regarded the octave, fourth, and fifth as consonant tonalities and the third and sixth as dissonant tonalities.

To further understand the metaphysical context and profound implications of Pythagorean musical thought, we turn to David R. Fideler and the reissue of the classic work, *The Pythagorean Sourcebook and Library: An Anthology of Ancient Writings* (1987), which relates to Pythagoras and Pythagorean philosophy, translated by Kenneth Sylvan Guthrie. In the Introduction, Fideler (1987: 43) explains the context of the notion of *harmonia* ("harmony"): "The central focus of Pythagorean thought is in many respects placed on the principle of harmonia. The universe is One, but the phenomenal realm is a differentiated image of this unity—the world is a unity in multiplicity. What maintains the unity of the whole, even though it consists of many parts, is the hierarchical principle of harmony, the logos of relation, which enables every part to have its place in the fabric of the All." The position of the human being is one that straddles two realms, the temporal and the eternal, in an endless dialectic (1987: 47):

> Rather than being a worthless speck meaninglessly situated in the infinite expanse of space, each person, according to the Pythagorean view, is a microcosm, a complete image of the entire cosmos, with one foot located in the realm of eternal principles and the other foot rooted in the particular world of manifestation. Poised as he is between time and eternity, matter and spirit, man possesses an incredible freedom to learn, create and know, limited only by those principles on which creation is based. From this vantage point, humanity is engaged in a never-ceasing dialectic between time and eternity, possessing the ability to incarnate eternal principles in time (and in this sense mirror the creative work of Nature), yet also possessing the ability to elevate the particular to the universal through conscious understanding.

As the first person in history to use the term, Pythagoras viewed "philosophy" as part of the human condition and its ongoing and compelling search for truth on several levels. The essence of the Pythagorean system revolved around his understanding of "Number" as a cosmic element. This understanding was basic to his whole approach. According to Fideler (1987: 21), Number for Pythagoras was much more than mere calculation or quantification: "The Pythagorean understanding of Number is quite different from the predominantly quantitative understanding of today. For the Pythagoreans, Number is a living, qualitative reality which must be approached in an experiential manner . . . Number is not something used; rather, its nature is to be discovered. In other words, we use numbers as tokens to represent things, but for Pythagoreans Number is a universal principle, as real as light (electromagnetism) or sound. As modern physics has demonstrated, it is precisely the numeric, vibrational frequency of electromagnetic energy—the 'wavelength'—which determines its particular manifestation. Pythagoras, of course, had already determined this in the case of sound."

In terms of pure metaphysics, Number is the underlying principle and the genesis of the cosmic process. The universe is first an undifferentiated unity or Monad, which is not a regular number but the principle underlying Number. Diversity manifests first as the Dyad, which represents Duality, followed by the Triad or connecting link between the Duality. The Dyad, according to Fideler (1987: 21–22), is "the beginning of multiplicity, the beginning of strife, yet also the possibility of logos, the relation of one thing to another . . . With the Dyad arises the duality of subject and object, the knower and the known. With the advent of the Triad, however, the gulf of dualism is bridged, for it is through the third term that a Relation of Harmonia ('joining together') is obtained between the two extremes." In short, the formula is as follows: (1) There is an undifferentiated unity; (2) from this unity two opposing powers are separated out to form the world order; and (3) the two opposites unite again to generate life. In a broader sense, it is explained thusly: "The idea of order is intimately connected with Limit (*peras*), the opposite of which is the Unlimited (*apeiron*), and these are the two most basic, and hence most universal, principles of Pythagorean cosmology."

To facilitate understanding, we present a convenient "Table of Opposites" with the following polarities: Odd–Even, Right–Left, Light–Darkness, Straight–Crooked, Good–Bad, One–Plurality, Male–Female, Resting–Moving, Square–Oblong (see Fideler 1987: 22). As it relates to music, the string represents the Unlimited continuum of tonal flux, which may be limited by being infinitely divided. The limiting power of Number creates the scale, beginning with the halving of the length of the string (1:2), which doubles the vibrational frequency that can be heard. Using 6:12 as the octave, one arrives at (1) the arithmetic mediation; just add the two extremes 6 + 12 (= 18) and divide by 2 (= 9). The arithmetic mean is 9, which in relation to 6 (6:9) is in the ratio of 2:3, the perfect fifth, the most powerful musical relationship; (2) the harmonic mediation: just multiply the two extremes 6 x 12 (= 72), double the sum (= 144), and divide the result by the sum of 6

+ 12 (144 divided by 18 = 8). The harmonic mean is 8, which in relation to 6 (6:8) is in the ratio of 3:4, the perfect fourth, which is the inverse of the perfect fifth. With these two operations we have the foundation of the musical scale, which is universal. To fill out the scale with notes, the ratio of 8:9 defines the whole tone: "The tone having been defined, the final creation of the scale is quite simple. The vibration of the tonic C is increased by the ratio of 8:9 to arrive at D. [Then] D is increased by 8:9 to arrive at E . . . The ratio between E and F ends up being 243:256, called in Greek the *leimma*, or 'left over,' corresponding to our semitone" (Fideler 1987: 25–27). The same system applies to G, A, B, and upper C. These two four-note groups are tetrachords.

While the above may appear overly technical, the most important point is that the purest notes that are also pleasing to the ear correspond to string lengths measured in simple numbers of one, two, three, and four. This is not a contingent or random phenomenon, invented by human ingenuity or based on choice, but is waiting to be discovered by anyone who investigates the issue. It is one of the pillars of natural theology, the process of thought that recognizes the reality of the Divine without specific revelation. To grant this discovery, Fideler (1987: 27) advised: "This arrangement of the perfect consonances of the octave, fifth and fourth needs to be played out, preferably on the monochord, in order to fully appreciate its significance."

For the many who find these discussions overly complex, Philip E. Stoltzfus (2006: 19–21) simplified the Pythagorean contribution and explained its relation to the developing coordination between mathematics and religious ideas of God: "He [Pythagoras] taught that four musical intervals—the unison, octave, perfect fifth, and perfect fourth—correspond to simple ratios based upon the first four natural numbers, as follows: 1:1, 1:2, 2:3, and 3:4. Using a simple vibrating string, he would have been able to show how each ratio marks the string length necessary to sound the corresponding interval . . . The symmetry, simplicity, and aural delight associated with these simple consonantal relations provided the inspiration for Pythagorean speculation upon points, lines, surfaces, planets, bodies, societies, emotive and cognitive states, and concepts of God . . . This musical metaphysic naturally went hand in glove with a distinctive religious worldview . . . [Indeed, the] Pythagorean *harmonia* may have been a pivotal concept for facilitating the theological move among some Greek thinkers from polytheism to a critical monotheism." In the geometrical model of the triangle, the same simple integers are used in the ten dots of the Tetraktys, Fideler (1987: 29) explained: "The Tetraktys [Decad, comprising 10 dots in a perfect triangle with one at the top and four at the bottom] also contains the symphonic ratios which underlie the mathematical harmony of the musical scale: 1:2, the octave; 2:3, the perfect fifth; and 3:4, the perfect fourth." Stoltzfus then notes the influence of Pythagorean thought (2006: 30): "The Pythagoreans, then, were the first to use numerical and geometrical diagrams as models of cosmic wholeness and the celestial order. This use of arithmetic and geometrical paradigms of whole systems has a long and interesting history, extending from antiquity through Medieval times, through the Renaissance, up until the modern era."

The Pythagorean concept of the soul and its ascent to immortality also had a profound basis in musical intervals, according to Stoltzfus (2006: 20): "Harmonic theory facilitated in the construction of a concept of the spiritual life, featuring rational movement of the soul or intellect toward apprehension of the ideal proportions of the cosmos. The soul must also become aware of its own 'harmonic' origin, structure, and content in order to realize its analogia with the whole." Because the soul is originally in harmony with perfect intervals and tones, its salvation and peace are dependent on hearing the consonant notes and avoiding dissonant ones (2006: 22–23): "Human souls, as well, are designed to 'perceive ideas or species of certain nature or number.' An added difficulty for the soul, however, is that it is by nature 'diluted' by dissonant tones in the second and third octaves, thus making it susceptible to the 'terrible and irresistible' sensations and affections. Knowledge of the proper *harmonia*, however, helps the soul regain its balance." Thus, the souls have an intimate connection to the cosmos. Fideler (1987: 48) illustrates this point by noting the correspondence or equity between quantity and quality in the natural world: "It is precisely through the Pythagorean approach that quantity (number) and quality are discovered to be integrally related." In other words, what is measured through reason (i.e., number) also has value in terms of beauty or aesthetic pleasure; there is equal reality and equal importance to each.

A misleading perception of Pythagoreanism is that it forms a branch of Western esotericism. This is no doubt a fact, but the true picture is that Pythagorean ideas had enormous influence on subsequent Greek philosophy as well as on currents of mainstream Western thought and culture. Indeed, great philosophers and thinkers were influenced by Pythagorean thought, the most famous being Plato, who made it central to his philosophy. Portnoy (1954: xi) has noted the significant legacy of Pythagoras throughout the Western hemisphere as part of the influence of Plato (428–348 BCE): "The similarities of musical concepts in ancient, medieval and modern aesthetics are variations on the original theme which Plato included as a necessary prerequisite for the creation of an ideal society and the beginning of the ideal man." This transmission is attributed to Socrates (469–399 BCE): "Just as society could be fashioned after a pattern in the heavens, Socrates believed, so music could attune the human soul to synchronize with this very pattern which permeated the behavior and activity of the heavenly bodies" (1954: 13). Accordingly, Portnoy (1954: 21) summarized the view of Plato on music as tied to morality: "The essence of Plato's philosophy of music is that music as an educational and cultural discipline should be used for the attainment of a sound morality. In the *Timaeus*, Plato propounded an ontology which envisioned the world as created out of geometric elements. While in the process of reducing nature to a mystical pattern of numerical relationships, he expressed the view that music was bestowed upon man for the purpose of helping him live a harmonious and judicious life. Music thereby took on a teleological function which should help in the attainment of a sound morality." As stated by Plato (1963: 65) in the *Timaeus* 47c7–e2, "All audible musical sound is given us for the sake of harmony, which has motions akin to the orbits in our soul, and which, as anyone who makes intelligent use of the arts knows, is not to be used, as is commonly thought, to give irrational pleasure, but as a heaven-sent ally in reducing to order and harmony any disharmony in the revolutions within us."

Classicist Leo Spitzer (1944: 419) expanded on Plato's notion of the world-soul and its influence on Neo-Platonism: "In *Gorgias* 507 E, Socrates makes his own the Pythagorean theory that heaven and earth, God and man, are bound together by a geometrical proportion and 'therefore' the universe is called a cosmos. In the *Republic* 616 B, we find the poetic explanation of the harmony of the spheres by their revolving on the spindle of Necessity. On each of the spheres there is a siren who utters her own sound; and by the voices of the eight sirens singing together harmony is produced. Plato assumes a world-soul as a general principle, outside of the particular corporeal beings, and having its seat in the midst of the universe which it pervades and embraces; this world-soul is also identifiable with light and with the good—hence later the emanationist theories of the Neo-Platonists." For those inclined toward complex mathematical analysis, Ernest G. McClain, in *The Pythagorean Plato: Prelude to the Song Itself* (1978), has thoroughly delineated the underlying numerical structures in Platonic thought.

Initially established by Pythagoras, music's role in the formation of human character and morality continued after Plato, as taught by Aristotle: "Aristotle (384–322 BCE) borrowed generously from Plato. He agreed with his teacher that music was an imitative art which was modelled after the cosmic harmonies. Aristotle further regarded music as the Greeks did generally, to be the most personally imitative and representative of the arts since it was thought of as a direct image or copy of character . . . Not only states of feeling but ethical qualities and mental dispositions were reproduced by musical imitation. The music which man made could mold the character of his listener for good or bad. Music was a reflection of its maker. It was not only that his character was depicted in what he created, but those who came in contact with his music were strongly influenced by it" (Portnoy 1954: 23). But while Aristotle transmitted the Pythagorean philosophy to future generations, he did not embrace it.

What are the principal sources of information on Pythagoras and his teachings? Besides the fragments attributed to Philolaus and Archytas, contemporaries of Plato, four biographies serve as primary sources: Iamblichus of Chalcis (c.250–325 CE), *The Life of Pythagoras*; Porphyry of Tyre (c.233–305 CE), *Life of Pythagoras*; Diogenes Laertius (third century CE), *The Life of Pythagoras*; and Photius (c. 820–891 CE) *Anonymous Life of Pythagoras Preserved by Photius*. Subsequently, the greatest thinkers and philosophers in Western civilization absorbed elements of the Pythagorean tradition, including Cicero, Pliny the Elder, Nicomachus of Gerasa, Theon of Smyrna, Ptolemy, Censorinus, Philo of Alexandria, Apollonius of Tyana, Plutarch (equates Apollo with the One; a = not, pollon = of many), Macrobius, Proclus, Plotinus, and Boethius. For many more details, one may consult James Haar's "Musica Mundana: Variations on a Pythagorean Theme" (1960), which provides a thorough historical account of the Pythagorean tradition, its appearance in Plato's *Timeaus* and *Republic*, and many later commentators.

Apart from his influence on philosophers in the intellectual realm, Pythagoras left his mark on the religions of Judaism, Christianity, and Islam. And while it may be convenient, even commonplace, in music history to separate "Jewish music," "Christian music, and "Islamic music," a less-traveled approach in terms of the Musicology of Religion is to explore their common underpinnings, one of which is certainly the Pythagorean metaphysical tradition. Accordingly, early church fathers held Pythagoras and his teachings in high esteem, including Justin Martyr, Saint Athanasius, Clement of Alexandria, and especially Saint Augustine. According to Fideler (1987: 43), "Pythagorean ideas continued to be transmitted in the work of Christian thinkers and applied in the realm of sacred architecture by groups of medieval masons. Insofar as Pythagorean thought had been Christianized, it had been changed, yet nonetheless many important conceptions—such as the ideas of celestial harmony and the significance of Number as a cosmic paradigm—remained unaltered."

In reference to the bond between the soul and the cosmos, Leo Spitzer (1944: 419) explained how the harmony of the spheres had a strong appeal to Christianity:

> The order introduced into the soul by music, an order which re-establishes the order of the universe; *harmonia* is the result of being well-joined, well fitted together and the soul which really understands music, does not 'enjoy' hedonistically alone, but understands the Nous of the Muses, the beauty of order. The whole cosmos is based on numbers: the four elements are bound together in friendship by numbers ordained by God— the forms are connected with numbers, since the four elements originate from triangles numerically determined: the corporality characteristic of matter is based on limitations of planes; from the triangles originate the geometrical forms which correspond to the elements (the cube to the earth, the pyramid to the fire, etc.). The numerical beauty of the Creation, and its origin, could not fail to appeal to Christians.

One important form of Pythagorean influence on Christianity concerns the concept of God. This is with reference to Plato's *Timaeus*, which is heavily imbued with Pythagorean thought (Stoltzfus 2006: 23): "In *Timaeus*, the concept 'God' stands for the source of ideal cosmological harmony." Stoltzfus gives the example of the Church Father, Clement of Alexandria: "Clement of Alexandria (c.150–215) quoted extensively from the *Timaeus*, finding in the action of the Demiurge the creating Logos of Gen 1 and John 1 . . . Clement identifies Christ as the primordial 'song,' which 'composed the entire creation into melodious order, and tuned into concert the discord of the elements, that the whole universe might be in harmony with it . . . [Citing Clement's *Protepticus* "Exhortation to the Greeks"] . . . The Lord made man a beautiful breathing instrument after his own image; certainly, he is himself an all-harmonious instrument of God, well-tuned and holy, the transcendental wisdom, the heavenly Logos" (Stoltzfus 2006: 24–25).

The influence of Pythagorean concepts of harmony is not limited to Christianity. Musicologist Joscelyn Godwin, in *The Harmony of the Spheres:*

A Sourcebook of the Pythagorean Tradition in Music (1992), presented primary sources along with discussion of important medieval Jewish and Islamic thinkers who absorbed ideas of Pythagorean harmony of the spheres. The Muslims include The Ikhwān Al-Safā (Brethren of Purity, tenth century) and Al-Hasan Al-Katib. For Jewish, he includes Isaac Ben Abraham Ibn Latif (Kabbalist) and Isaac Ben Haim. Godwin then displays the remarkable influence of Pythagoras on key Renaissance figures like Marcilio Ficino, Pico Della Mirandola, Francesco Giorgi, Heinrich Glarean, Gioseffo Zarlino, and Jean Bodin. Godwin then examines scientists and occultists from the Baroque era, such as Johannes Kepler, Robert Fludd, Marin Mersenne, and Athanasius Kircher, followed by the Enlightenment period: Isaac Newton, Jean-Philippe Rameau, Giuseppe Tartini, Louis-Claude de Saint-Martin, Arthur Schopenhauer, and Fabre D'Olivet,

At certain points, especially in Protestant Christianity, there were subtle shifts away from Pythagorean concepts to the notion of music as a Divine Gift of God. Julius Portnoy (1954: x) has described this change in emphasis: "The fanciful imagery and moralistic tenets which the ancient philosopher ascribed to music were embellished in the writings of the Christians. The fathers of the Church, and the leaders of the reformation after them, gave up the picturesque theory of the harmony of the spheres as the divine source of music for the belief that music was bestowed upon man by a benevolent Being for the purpose of enhancing the Word of God." These ideas in theology form the discussion of the next chapter on theology and music.

However, one must resist the temptation to restrict Pythagoras to the humanities and literary domains, and to acquiesce in the notion that Pythagoreanism faded out as a major influence in world culture. While one cannot overestimate the significance of Pythagoras for music and esotericism, he was also pivotal for the rise of science, as seen in the inclusion of Kepler and Newton above. The German scholar and musician Hans Kayser was a pioneer in reaffirming the Pythagorean tradition of *harmonia* and its importance for science and the modern world. In his *Akroasis: The Theory of World Harmonics* (1970), Kayser outlined the basic features of world harmonics, from the Greek *harmonikos*, pertaining to music. The term *akroasis*, from the Greek "hearing," stands in contrast to *aesthesis*, seeing or perceiving. Kayser (1970: 28) stressed the pivotal role that the reality of musical harmony played in the birth of science: "Pythagoreanism became of basic importance to present day scientific thought: with the discovery of the relation between pitch and string length, which could be established numerically, western science was born. Qualities (tones) were derived from quantities (string or wave lengths) in an exact way. Thus, harmonics stands at the very beginning of European scientific thought."

In addition to the influence of Pythagorean harmony on the rise of science, Kayser (1970: 29) interprets this tradition further, anticipating one of the key themes of the Musicology of Religion, the role of music in transcendence and religious experience:

> Although Pythagoras, undoubtedly following very much older traditions, transformed the audible (qualities) into numbers (quantities), for him and for those who thought and worked as he did, the reverse was at least of equal importance: quantities, material things measurable by means of number (string lengths, monochord) acquired a spiritual meaning, a psychic value (intervals, tones), for one could in fact hear the numerical ratios. Did not the essence of matter reveal itself to us and did not the relations of numbers of the string show a deep inner correspondence between the 'I' and the 'you'? The principles of measure and value here entered into a miraculous union: each recognized itself in the other, the measure of the string saw itself reflected in the value of the experienced, sensed tone, and the value of this tone saw itself reflected in the measured length of the string.

The effects of the ancient Pythagorean contribution thus cannot be overestimated: "Through this experience of sounding numbers, the world began to sound. Matter acquired a structural counterpart in the psyche, and the spiritual, the realm of ideas, became anchored in harmonical shapes and forms. A bridge between being and value, world and soul, matter and spirit, was found" (1970: 29).

A convenient summation of these views is found in the work of modern musician and theorist Brian Capleton (2015: 101), who states unequivocally what the ancients affirmed centuries ago: "In the context of the harmony of the spheres tradition, the essence of music in all its forms, is *harmonia*. Whether it is as practical music, *musica practica*, or as human music, *musica humana*, or as the music of the spheres, *musica mundana*. *Harmonia* is all about bringing the limited, that exists, into harmony with the infinite, or the One, the Divine behind the appearance of existence."

Recent studies by mathematicians have confirmed the abiding influence of music on the rise of the "hard" sciences. Eli Maor, in *Music by the*

Numbers: From Pythagoras to Schoenberg (2018), explains how music has influenced mathematics, physics, and astronomy from ancient Greece to the twentieth century. While composers were influenced by mathematical relations, the mutual interchange between music and mathematics over the years is expressed in the description: "Music is filled with mathematical elements, the works of Bach are often said to possess a math-like logic, and Igor Stravinsky said 'musical form is close to mathematics,' while Arnold Schoenberg, Iannis Xenakis, and Karlheinz Stockhausen went further, writing music explicitly based on mathematical principles." Yet music has influenced math at least as much as math has influenced music: "Starting with Pythagoras, proceeding through the work of Schoenberg, and ending with contemporary string theory, *Music by the Numbers* tells a fascinating story of composers, scientists, inventors, and eccentrics who played a role in the age-old relationship between music, mathematics, and the sciences, especially physics and astronomy."

Comparative Philosophy

While we have focused thus far on ancient Greece and Pythagorean harmony in our discussion of philosophy and music, we note here that an upsurge in interest in comparative philosophy has brought ancient Indian thought into conversation with the philosophers of ancient Greece. Beginning with some valuable information on the ancient world of Pythagoras, much remarkable comparative spadework has been achieved by Thomas McEvilley in *The Shape of Ancient Thought: Comparative Studies in Greek and Indian Philosophies* (2002), which correlates aspects of Platonic thought with the metaphysics of the Upanishads, with Indian theories of karma and transmigration, and with the monistic philosophy of Vedanta. In ways that parallel a principal theme in the Upanishads and Vedanta philosophy—the soul within is identical to the cosmic soul without—Pythagoras taught that the inner self is consonant with the outer cosmos. Stoltzfus (2006: 32) describes this state of being: "Man realizes the divine by knowing the universal and divine principles which constitute the cosmos—i.e., for the Pythagoreans, Number. To know the cosmos is to seek and know the divine element within, and one must become divine and harmonized since only like can know like. From this perspective it also becomes obvious that philosophy is nothing other, at least in one respect, than the care of the soul." Mathematics is thus not simply a calculative operation but is in fact a path, like music, to self-realization (2006: 34): "If, as the Pythagoreans held, man is a microcosm, and the soul is a harmony, perhaps it is through a form of resonance that we relate so intensely to the archetypal ratios of musical proportion. Moreover, by experientially investigating and employing the principles of harmony in the external world, one comes to understand and activate those same principles within. This idea in fact underlies the Pythagorean approach to mathematical study." That is why Pythagorean teachings, like Vedanta, emphasize unity between the upper and lower dimensions of reality, and integrate both of them within consciousness, as explained by Stoltzfus (2006: 35): "Rather than focusing exclusively on either the immanent or transcendent levels of being, the Pythagoreans were intent on unifying all levels of human experience through the principles of harmony. . . . By means of *theoria* or contemplation the universal and abstract principles of harmony may be perceived, but through *praxis* they may be felt in the soul, itself a harmonic entity. Yet there is another level, that of *therapeia,* where harmonic principles can be used to effect changes in the psychic disposition." Thus, there is a positive attitude toward the world since all levels of being are represented in harmony: "The Pythagorean goal is not to leave the divinely beautiful cosmos behind for a realm of transcendent harmony, but rather to become aware of, and enhance the function of, transcendent harmony *in* the natural, psychological, and social orders" (2006: 36).

Concerning metaphysics, the edited collection by Richard Seaford, *Universe and Inner Self in Early Indian and early Greek Thought* (2016), contains noteworthy discussions of comparative interest—Indian and Greek—regarding concepts of the universe and the self. In this volume, John Bussanich (2016) highlights patterns of comparison between the experiences of Socrates and Yoga meditation in "Plato and Yoga."[1] More recently, Richard Seaford, in *The Origin of Philosophy in Ancient Greece and Ancient India: A Historical Comparison* (2020), continues this fertile direction with socioeconomic theories that help explain the origins of philosophy in a cross-cultural context. While music is not developed in these works, there remains an enormous scope for comparative study of the role of music in philosophical thought between these two civilizations.

There is an interesting parallel between Greek and Indian thought that is directly related to music. Complementing the "unheard" harmony

---

1. Thanks to Sanskrit scholar Paul H. Sherbow for this reference (personal communication, November 7, 2022).

of the spheres in Pythagorean tradition, the concept of Nāda-Brahman as the "unmanifest" sound absolute is described in the Indian philosophical and musical texts. Described in the next chapter, and discussed more fully in Beck (1993), the concept of Nāda-Brahman encompassed, in addition to linguistic sounds and utterances, all musical and other nonlinguistic sounds. Since Brahman is described in the Upanishads as pervading the exterior cosmos as well as the interior human soul, sacred sound as Nāda-Brahman provided a veritable thread binding the human realm to the divine. Nāda-Brahman is hence involved in the salvific process to attain final liberation or release from rebirth, known as Moksha. Musical treatises discuss Nāda-Brahman as the foundation of musical sound, and Yoga texts use the term Nāda-Brahman to refer to the musical sounds heard during deep meditation (i.e., Nāda Yoga). The most important musical text is the thirteenth-century *Saṅgīta Ratnākara* (1.2.1–2), which describes Nāda-Brahman as the source of all kinds of musical sound as well as dance and language (1978: 21–23): "*Nāda* is the very essence of vocal music. Instrumental music is enjoyable, as it manifests *nāda*. *Nṛtta* (dance) follows both (i.e., vocal and instrumental music); therefore, all the three together depend on *nāda*. *Nāda* manifests the letters (of alphabet), letters constitute the word, and words make a sentence; so, the entire business of life is carried on, through language; and therefore, the whole phenomenon (i.e., the world) is based on *nāda*." Nāda-Brahman may be either unmanifest (*anāhata*, "unstruck," existing in the divine realm) or manifest (*āhata*, "struck," existing in the human realm, i.e., music), as stated in the text (1978: 23): "*Nāda* is said to be twofold, viz., produced and unproduced. Since it manifests itself in the human body, the (process of) embodiment is being described." A corollary to the unmanifest and manifest Nāda-Brahman is found in the practical worship of Deity, wherein two sides of Brahman may be addressed: Nirguṇa (unmanifest Deity, without attributes) and/or Saguṇa (manifest Deity, with attributes). We now proceed with the modern European tradition of philosophy and music, which has interesting parallels.

Modern Philosophy and Music

> Supposing it were possible to give a perfectly accurate, complete, even detailed, explanation of music . . . it would be the true philosophy.
>
> —Arthur Schopenhauer, *The World as Will and Idea*

Music continued to draw the attention of philosophers in the Renaissance and Enlightenment periods. Warren Dwight Allen, in *Philosophies of Music History: A Study of General Histories of Music 1600–1960* (1962), was among the first to outline the history of musical philosophy in the Baroque era, the Reformation, the Enlightenment, the Romantic era, in revolution and evolution, and in the early twentieth century. One finds, for example, that great philosophers like Descartes were much engaged with musical theory. Following this theme, Downing A. Thomas, in *Music and the Origins of Language: Theories from the French Enlightenment* (1995), carefully examines the musical thought of the French philosophes, especially Condillac and Rousseau.

German philosophers of the nineteenth century were engaged with aesthetics and the concept of beauty, including music, according to the outlook of the Romantic movement. Yet many biographical accounts of these philosophers have omitted the role of music in their overall philosophical systems. For example, in the standard biography of Schleiermacher by Martin Redeker (1971), little to nothing is mentioned about the role of music in his life and thought. A welcome reversal of this trend is *Music in German Philosophy: An Introduction* (Sorgner 2010), which examines music in the thought of Kant, Schleiermacher, Hegel, Schelling, and Nietzsche.

A compelling research prerogative in the Musicology of Religion is the further study of music, or lack thereof, in the thought of the great philosophers, many of whom were born or raised in the Lutheran Church. Some questions may be raised as to why Kant and Hegel preferred vocal music while others subscribed to the emerging notion of the superiority of instrumental or "absolute music." And while the Lutheran provenance of Kant, Fichte, Hegel, Kierkegaard, Nietzsche, and Husserl is well known, others like Leibniz, Herder, Lessing, Feuerbach, Dilthey, and Schopenhauer either practiced their faith or rejected Lutheranism in various degrees. What is also noteworthy is the Lutheran connection to the rise of modern atheism and its critique of religious culture, including music. Karl Marx became a Lutheran in 1824, but by the 1830s he rejected his religious roots, both Jewish and Christian, and became an ardent atheist and critic of the arts as "bourgeois." Marx and his Lutheran compatriots, the Young Hegelian philosophers Ludwig Feuerbach and Bruno Bauer, were radical critics of traditional religion and culture, laying the basis for the Mirror Theory discussed in chapter 2.

While modern philosophers included discussions of music in their work, the name of Arthur Schopenhauer (1788–1860) stands out as one who elevated music to superior heights. Born in present-day Poland to a wealthy German family, Schopenhauer switched from science and medicine to the study of Plato and Kant, earning his doctorate at the University of Jena in 1813. He attended lectures in theology at the University of Berlin (from Schleiermacher and others), yet this led to a growing dislike of Christianity and theism. Moreover, his introduction to Eastern philosophy from a follower of Herder, especially the Upanishads and Buddhism, helped to shape his ascetic and increasingly pessimistic worldview. His principal work of 1819, *The World as Will and Idea,* brought aesthetics into full parity with philosophy. Aligning the Platonic Ideas with Kant's transcendental idealism, Schopenhauer claimed to have discovered the essence of reality, the noumenon or "thing-in-itself" of Kant, in his understanding of the Will, the all-devouring and encompassing desire for existence of everything in the universe. His pessimism came into play with his rejection of a compassionate God in favor of a dark vision whereby humankind is forever trapped within a continuous cycle of suffering relieved only by the cessation of desire, and thus of normal sensate existence (cf., Buddhist Nirvana). For the depths of his thought, Schopenhauer is significant for his influence on such figures as Nietzsche, Freud, Jung, Wittgenstein, Einstein, Sartre, and Thomas Mann.

Despite his pessimism, important and interesting ideas regarding music appear in Schopenhauer's philosophy. For example, why does he elevate music, especially instrumental music, above all the other arts to represent the essence of reality? In his discussion of music in *The World as Will and Idea* (book 3, section 52, 1995: 164), he explained: "So music is by no means (as are the other arts) the copy of the Ideas, but the copy of the Will itself, whose objectivity the Ideas are. Therefore, the effect of music is so much more powerful and penetrating than that of the other arts, for they speak only of the shadow while music speaks of the essence." Music is thus not related to any specific feeling or phenomenon in the real world but to the inner core or essence of the Will, the "things-in-themselves" (1995: 168): "Music . . . never expresses the phenomenon, but only the inner nature, the in-itself of all phenomena, the Will itself. Thus it expresses not this or that particular and definite joy, this or that sorrow, or pain, or horror, or delight, or merriment, or peace of mind; but it expresses, joy, sorrow, pain, horror, delight, merriment, peace of mind *themselves,* to a certain extent in the abstract, their essential nature, without incidentals and so also without the motives for these emotions." He even went so far as to relate specific melodies to phenomena in the real world (1995: 168): "The inexhaustible variety of possible melodies corresponds to nature's inexhaustible variety of individuals, physiognomies, and ways of life." Despite infinite melodies of music, they all coalesce into the universal Will (1995: 169): "All the will's possible expressions, its endeavors and excitements, all that goes on in the human heart . . . may be expressed by the infinite possible number of melodies, but always in the universality of mere form, without the material, always according to the thing-in-itself, not according to the phenomenon, but as the inmost soul, as it were, of the phenomenon, without the body." He goes on to explain that the myriad of life experiences are essentially incomplete without music (1995: 169): "The deep relationship which music has to the true nature of all things also explains the fact that suitable music played to any scene, activity, event or circumstance seems to divulge the most secret meaning of that occasion, and to play the part of its most accurate and clearest commentator." For Schopenhauer, the world is what he called "embodied music" (1995: 170): "For music . . . is a direct copy of the will itself, and therefore it presents the metaphysical, and to all phenomenon it presents the thing-in-itself. So, we might just as well call the world 'embodied music' as 'embodied will;' this explains why music makes every picture, indeed every scene of real life and of the world, at once appear more intensely meaningful, and the closer the melody is to the inner spirit of the given phenomenon, the more this is so." In effect, Schopenhauer described music as a perfect universal language (1995: 171): "In the whole of this exposition of music I have been trying to bring out clearly that it expresses in a perfectly universal language, in a homogenous material (that is, in mere tones), and with the greatest distinctness and truth, the inner nature, the in-itself, of the world, which we think of under the concept of will, because will is its clearest manifestation."

As Schleiermacher and Schopenhauer were near contemporaries and each held music in high esteem, it might be useful to make comparisons. Regarding differences, Schleiermacher was a steadfast Christian believer in an all-powerful Deity and in the optimistic prospect of redemption. Schopenhauer, on the other hand, though not directly identifying as an atheist, discarded Christian ideas of sin and redemption in favor of the pessimistic Buddhist worldview of the everlasting miserable plight of humankind. Aside from this, both philosophers were raised in Lutheran surroundings, made extensive study and use of the works of Plato and Kant, made valuable critiques of Kantian thought, were intensely critical of Hegel, and were to a degree influenced by Spinoza. Regarding music, Schleiermacher held that music was a Divine Gift, close to religious experience and the "taste of the Infinite," and something of permanent value in life. For Schopenhauer, music was the "embodiment of the Will," the driving impulse of existence, and something not necessarily subject to Kant's principle of sufficient reason. Yet for both, music was the highest of the arts, timeless, a "universal language," and something that provided relief from the throes of universal suffering in the balance between self and universe. As discussed, the views of Schleiermacher tend toward the Window Theory, whereby music is evidence of the sacred or divine creation. Yet the views of Schopenhauer, while contrary to the Window Theory, do not fit with the Mirror Theory either, since for him music was not a projection of the human condition but a metaphysical reality in itself, albeit independent and not derived from God. A third "theory" may be necessary. Nonetheless, the significance of music in both thinkers is provocative, and lends itself to comparative study in the Musicology of Religion.

While the name of Schleiermacher has continued to be an originating nexus in our discussions of modern theology, religious studies, and the role of music in religious experience, this nexus expands when one considers his important status as a philosopher. Andrew Bowie presents, in *Aesthetics and Subjectivity: from Kant to Nietzsche* (2003: 183–220), a lengthy elaboration of Schleiermacher's contribution to hermeneutics and aesthetics, including his relevance to modern continental philosophy. Bowie (2003: 183) introduces Schleiermacher the philosopher with these words: "Despite his lack of influence on mainstream philosophy, Schleiermacher is of major philosophical importance, being the first to combine the sort of ideas concerning the mind–world relationship we have encountered in the early Romantics, Schelling, and Hegel with sustained attention to the role of language in philosophy. Most people are aware that Schleiermacher formulated the first modern account of hermeneutics but too few people seem aware that this was only part of a wider philosophical project, some of which has now turned out to prefigure central ideas of key thinkers in contemporary philosophy, such as Brandom, Davidson, Gadamer, Habermas, McDowell, and Rorty." In retrospect, "Most of his philosophy can stand without his theology, and this was something upon which Schleiermacher himself often insisted." Recently, Bowie, in "Music, Transcendence, and Philosophy" (2020), has discussed Schleiermacher as part of his analysis of music and modern philosophies of language and transcendence.

The discussion of religion in philosophical terms is known as the philosophy of religion, and important developments have occurred in this area, primarily among British and American philosophers. As such, within the corridors of analytical philosophy, a recent turn in attention toward theism has occurred by reviving interest in the traditional proofs for the existence of God, whether ontological or cosmological. Since Kant rejected these arguments, they no longer attract philosophical discussion—until now. While there are levels of scholarship in this fold, mostly in the Christian context, we mention the most prominent philosophers so that the inquiring reader can pursue this topic in greater depth. J. L. Mackie, in *The Miracle of Theism: Arguments for and against the Existence of God* (1982), provides a through overview of the various arguments in their original context. For new developments and methods applied to the cosmological argument, Oxford philosopher Richard Swinburne has produced a trilogy of compelling works raising the level of certainty for some degree of truth in the reality of God: *The Coherence of Theism* (1993), *The Existence of God* (2004), and *Faith and Reason* (2005). Alvin Plantinga, in *God and Other Minds: A Study of the Rational Justification of Belief in God* (1990), presents new and insightful perspectives on the ontological argument. And last, William P. Alston, in *Perceiving God: The Epistemology of Religious Experience* (1991), carries forth the area of religious experience in new directions after Schleiermacher and William James. But while treatment of music is minimal in analytical philosophy, the developments contained here offer promise of more solid ground in Musicology of Religion that cannot be ignored. For research related to music in philosophy, see *The Routledge Companion to Philosophy and Music* (Gracyk 2011).

In the next chapter, we explore the ancient roots of theology, natural theology, the role of Pythagorean ideas of harmony in combination with theistic religions, "musical angels" in heaven, music in the afterlife, and music as Divine Gift. As prominent examples of music as Divine Gift, the chapter will specifically discuss Lutheran and Hindu theologies of music.

Chapter Five

Theology and Music

Music is the way we should like life to be, a glimpse of that world where all strife ends. It takes us towards that world . . . music is useful in as much as it takes us toward our Final End—God.

—Alfred Pike, *A Theology of Music*

In the final analysis, music and theology may require one another . . . Music is the language of the soul made audible especially as music is the performative mode of the prayer and ritual engagement of a community.

—Don E. Saliers, *Music and Theology*

Music, sound arts, and practices are not merely decorative: they also function as modes of "doing" theology.

—Richard David Williams, "Sounding Out the Divine,"
The Oxford History of Hinduism: Hindu Practice

The previous chapter on philosophy and music discussed the Pythagorean tradition of harmony and music as a "science," or *musica speculativa*, which had enormous impact on Plato and the whole of Western philosophy. While universalist in its formulation, the theistic content of a personal God and spiritual beings was often undeveloped in Pythagoreanism. Yet in several religions, especially Judaism, Christianity, and Islam, we find a blend of

Pythagorean ideas with theistic beliefs. As in philosophy, the perspective of universalism is germane to the study of music and theology, as most theological traditions envision a unitary cosmos. After discussing the origin and meaning of theology, including natural theology, this chapter examines how theology relates to music in the world's religions. The traditions discussed, whether ancient Greek, Judaism, Christianity, Islam, Hermeticism, Zoroastrianism, or Hinduism, all share basic features that accord with theism: a personal God, messengers of God (angels), and survival in the afterlife. In each, we find that music is integrated with these aspects in some capacity, whether as a Divine Gift (*musica creatura*), as an art performed by "musical angels," or as an accompaniment to life in the hereafter.

Theology provides equitable balance in our presentation because it furnishes a key factor in the search for the "why" of music. Many of the social sciences, including ethnomusicology, avoid this question and utilize the inductive method in search of empirical evidence and facts regarding what music is, how it is produced, when and where it is performed or created, and how it functions in society or upon the mind. Theology, resting on the deductive method of first postulating a premise such as the existence of God or the supernatural realm, raises the issue of "why" there is such a thing as music and how it originated. Theological thought also provides a useful corollary to the social scientist's observation of the tendency of most human societies to view their musical systems as "natural" rather than culturally constructed.

At the outset, we recognize that the general postulate of theological thinking is simply that the divine or God exists, that the divine or God is inseparable from nature and/or the creation of the universe, and that the divine or God may manifest in the world of phenomena. All succeeding statements and conclusions issue from these basic premises, though varieties of interpretation have occurred along the way. As a general field of study, theology also takes the reality of the sacred and God as axiomatic and not as human projections, such as found in the Mirror Theory of several of the social sciences and ethnomusicology. To frame the discussion, we cite the etymology given by Ian Markham (2009: 152): "Theology comes from two Greek words. *Theos* means God; *logos* means word. Literally, then theology means 'words about God,' or perhaps more helpfully, 'study' of God." Geoffrey Wainwright, in *Doxology: The Praise of God in Worship, Doctrine and Life. A Systematic Theology* (1980: 1), has defined the scope of theology: "Theology is intellectual reflection on all the dealings between God and humanity." Religious historian Rodney Stark elaborates further in

Discovering God: The Origins of the Great Religions and the Evolution of Belief (2007: 5): "Theology involves formal reasoning about God. The emphasis is on discovery of God's nature, intentions, and demands, and on understanding how these define the relationship between human beings and God."

In theology, scholars across the world's religions recognize two forms of human access to knowledge of God or the divine. One is general revelation, sometimes called natural revelation, which refers to knowledge about God or the divine through natural means, which is available to all humankind, and which is enabled by reason and the observation of nature. This may extend to include the human mind. The other type is special revelation, which refers to knowledge of God or the divine that is discoverable through supernatural means such as miracles and revealed scriptures. Other forms of special revelation include voices and messages from angels, prophets, saints, shamans, visions, dreams, and divine inspiration variously defined. When these two viewpoints, general revelation and special revelation, are each developed methodologically, they are known as natural theology (*theologia naturalis*), and revealed theology (*theologia revelata*)—the former encompassing the universal apprehension of the divine and the latter oriented toward specific revelations in time and space.

Theology in common usage, however, is frequently associated with a specific denomination or religion separated from others; for example, in Christianity there is Roman Catholic theology, Lutheran theology, Reformed theology, and beyond there is Hindu theology, Islamic theology, and others. The distinction that separates natural theology from revealed theology has not always been so pronounced and may be unnecessary within the broader spectrum of theology. In fact, traditions of revealed theology often have natural theology as a foundation. Drawing on ancient models of thought, theologian John Baillie, in *The Interpretation of Religion: An Introductory Study of Theological Principles* (1928: 3), explained how theology might be understood as a kind of unified "science" that focuses on all aspects of religion: "Theology may be defined as *the science of religion*—the science, that is, which selects religion as its special object of study." The plural notion of "religions," however, is indicated in the simple definition of theology by David F. Ford, in *Theology: A Very Short Introduction* (2013: 3): "Theology at its broadest is thinking about questions raised by and about the religions."

As to the impression in the modern academy that there is no such thing as "religion in general" but only a vast number of different "religions," Baillie (1928: 63) offered this response: "What the modern theologian must conceive of himself as setting out to study is not one particular variety of religion, but rather religion itself . . . There was a time when the history of religion read like the record of an almost infinite succession of wild, haphazard guesses at truth. Gradually that has been changed until the vast panorama is coming to look more and more like a single scene. As we better learn to understand where the real heart of religion lies, we become increasingly aware of elements of identity, such as we had never-before suspected, which unite every form of religion known to us. Certain common central characters more and more stand out; and above all we are forced to recognize that it is one impulse which has led all men everywhere to seek God and one insight which has enabled them, in however varying degrees, to find Him."

However, it cannot be denied that every religion is a composite of multiple historical and ideological features and currents of thought going back centuries. On this point, Baillie (1928: 64) concurred: "It is now impossible to mention any 'religion' that is regarded by the historian as a self-contained unit. Every known 'religion' is a complex phenomenon, a synthesis of previous historical entities, many or all of which have entered also as elements not these partially different combinations which are called the other 'religions.'" In other words, just as there are no completely new languages, there are no completely new religions. Yet Baillie (1928: 64–65) reiterated his case for one religion, hence one theology: "The truth is, therefore, that however many competing varieties of religion there may be in the world, however many rival religious institutions, however many successive stages in the progress of religion, yet in any proper and profound sense there is but one religion . . . And if there is only one religion, then there can be only one theology."

While there are several examples of a "unified theology" in the world's religions, Baillie reinforces the foundation of an underlying, universal "natural theology" by citing biblical references (New Revised Standard Version): "Ever since the creation of the world his [God's] eternal power and divine nature, invisible though they are, have been understood and seen through the things he has made" (Romans 1:20); "From one ancestor he made all nations to inhabit the whole earth, and he allotted the times of their existence and the boundaries of the places where they would live, so that they would search for God and perhaps grope for him and find him—though indeed he is not far from each one of us. For in him we live and move and have our being" (Acts 17:26–28), and "The heavens are telling the glory of God; and the firmament proclaims his handiwork" (Psalm 19). This underlying natural theology also has roots in ancient Greece and India.

Theology in Ancient Greece

For the ancient Greeks, philosophy and theology were intertwined, meaning that natural theology and revealed theology were also closely aligned. This combined position has endured for centuries in Greek Orthodox theology yet has become separated in the other Christian communions. Werner Jaeger in *The Theology of the Early Greek Philosophers* (1967) outlined the birth and development of theology and philosophy among the ancient Greeks and how they emerged from a universalist view of reality. Jaeger (1967: 48) first explained the Greek sense of universalism and its impact: "In the western world, universalism began neither with the Christians nor with the prophets of Israel, but with the Greek philosophers." Among the pre-Socratic philosophers, the role of Xenophanes in articulating early Greek universalism and theology is highlighted by Jaeger (1967: 48): "Xenophanes was the first to formulate that religious universalism which, both in later antiquity and more especially in the Christian era, was deemed to be an essential feature in the idea of God, indispensable to any true religion. From his time on, universalism had a place in the theology of all the Greek thinkers as one of the basic assumptions, whether or not they took the trouble to express it." Accordingly, Jaeger (1967: 6) revealed the generally unacknowledged nature of the thought of the pre-Socratics as an early form of universalism or "natural theology": "We shall find that the problem of the Divine occupies a much larger place in the speculations of the early natural philosophers than we are often ready to acknowledge, and that it receives in actuality a much greater share of their attention than we might be led to expect from Aristotle's picture of the development of philosophy in the first book of the *Metaphysics*." Thus (1967: 3), "Greek philosophy is genuine natural theology because it is based on rational insight into the nature of reality itself," a reality that is universal. Jaeger (1967: 8) then argued for the universal approach to reality in theological thinking that included both "philosophy" and religion: "The theology of the early philosophers makes them appear quite as much a part of the history of Greek religion as of the history of philosophy. The usual histories of religion have hardly ever treated their theology seriously in this larger context, presumably because their chief interest has always been more in the cult divinities and the institutions of the religious life than in ideas." These two worlds were indeed originally viewed as inseparable (1967: 2): "Originally, the concept of natural theology did not stand in opposition to supernatural theology, an idea which was unknown to the ancient world."

A universalist view of reality is one that encompasses all aspects of creation and posits a divine presence in everything, gradually leading to the conception of God. This was the background among the Greeks and their formulations of deity. According to Jaeger (1967: 172), "The problem of the origin of all things was so comprehensive and went so far beyond all traditional beliefs and opinions that any answer to it had to involve some new insight into the true nature of those higher powers which the myths revealed as the gods. In the all-creative primal ground of becoming, no matter how much this idea was further particularized, philosophical thought had always discovered the very essence of everything that could be called divine. All the individual features and forms of the gods with which the mythological consciousness had occupied itself became dissolved in it, and a new conception of deity began to take shape." This concept of deity as it was gradually formed took on much more than mere animistic belief or cult worship, and informed the very nature of the idea of God (1967: 172–173): "Even the word 'God' itself, which is used by a number of these thinkers, now takes on the same new ring it had acquired in the Milesian philosophy of nature from the very beginning in the formulation 'the Divine': all the perfections ever attributed to any divine persons of the cult-religion by the epithet 'God' are now collected and transferred to that primal ground which philosophical thought regards as involving the essence of supreme power over all existence, and therefore worthy to possess this predicate (for Greeks always thought of the word 'God' as predicative." In other words (1967: 173), "If we ask upon what this new evaluation is based, we find that the real motive for so radical a change in the form of the godhead lies in the idea of the All. The philosophers are continually speaking of the Divine as all-encompassing, all-governing, and so forth, on the assumption that its claim to the name of God is thereby directly established."

While in Western philosophy the notion of reason was often opposed to nonreason and religious belief, for the Greeks they were of the same fabric whereby one dimension infused the other. Jaeger (1967: 173–174) explained how this process occurred: "Whenever the Greeks experienced the Divine, they always had their eyes on reality, and all their experiences were oriented in that direction. But at the earliest stage of the philosophy of nature they approached reality with entirely new intellectual powers and grasped it in entirely new forms. Accordingly, the achievements of this philosophy strike us at first as no more than the emergence of a radically destructive and fundamentally anti-religious force such as we often attribute to reason and science . . . But Greek religion is much richer and less restricted in its development. It does not consist in any revealed teachings reconcilable with rational thinking only to a limited degree; it springs rather from a lavish profusion of mythical views of the world, the characteristics of which are constantly changed and revised with each new shift of perspective." Therefore, the nature of God must be nondifferent from the human capacity to know or experience the divine as both partake of the same essence (1967: 174–75): "Any type of thinking that derives all existence from nature and its characteristic law and order must come to the point of regarding even the belief in God as a product of human nature in interaction with the world that surrounds it, and therefore as something natural in itself."

While the meaning of terms applied in early Greek philosophy may have their origin in particular thinkers, Jaeger (1967: 4) explained how "Theology is a mental attitude which is characteristically Greek and has something to do with the great importance which the Greek thinkers attribute to the *logos*, for the word *theologia* means the approach to God or the gods (*theoi*) by means of the *logos*." And while the concept is present in the pre-Socratics regarding natural philosophy (natural theology), it was Plato who devised the term "theology" in the way we understand it today, as explained by Jaeger (1967: 4): "Plato was the first who used the word theology, and he evidently was the creator of the idea. He introduced it in the Republic [ii.379a], where he wanted to set up certain philosophical standards and criteria for poetry." In Plato's ideal Republic, theology was set at a higher bar than what was acceptable in the mythic accounts of Homer and the poets (1967: 4): "In his ideal state the poets must avoid the errors of Homer, Hesiod, and the poetic tradition in general, and rise in their representation of the gods to the level of philosophic truth. The mythical deities of early Greek poetry were tinged with all kinds of human weakness; but such an idea of the gods was irreconcilable with Plato's and Socrates' rational conception of the divine. Thus, when Plato set forth 'outlines of theology,' in the Republic, the creation of that new word sprang from the conflict between the mythical tradition and the natural (rational) approach to the problem of God." Jaeger (1967: 4) then affirmed that this sense of "theology" as a universal apprehension of the divine permeated many succeeding schools of thought, including not only Platonic but Aristotelian, Epicurean, Stoic, Neopythagorean, and Neoplatonic theology.

The philosophical nature of theology carried well over into Aristotle's metaphysics, according to Jaeger (1967: 5): "He [Aristotle] understands by 'theology' that fundamental branch of philosophical science which he also calls 'first philosophy' or 'science of first principles'—the branch which later acquires the name of 'metaphysics' among his followers. In this sense theology is the ultimate and highest goal of all philosophical study of Being." Jaeger (1967: 2) describes how the great Christian theologian Augustine drew upon the Roman writer Terentius Varro (116–27 BCE) and his delineation of "natural theology," which Varro opposed to the mythology of the gods and the state religion, to almost single-handedly erect the vast edifice of Christian theology: "According to St. Augustine he [Varro] distinguished three kinds of theology (*genera theologiae*): mythical, political, and natural. Mythical theology had for its domain the world of the gods as described by the poets; political theology included the official state religion and its institution and cults. Natural theology was a field for the philosophers—the theory of the nature of the divine as revealed in the nature of reality. Only natural theology could be called religion in the true sense." In many ways, then, the universalism of the Greco-Roman world laid the foundation for Christian theology, as confirmed by Jaeger (1967: 3): "To St. Augustine it is inconceivable that any true religion should be restricted to a single nation. God is essentially universal and must be worshipped universally." Interestingly, much of Jewish, Islamic, and Hindu theology also rested on the foundations of a universal "natural theology."

Natural Theology

Theology, in the original context of ancient Greece, was dedicated to discovering the essence of divinity in the universe rather than promulgating a specific deity or revelation. In this line of thought, Plato, Aristotle, Plotinus, and the Stoics formulated the early traditions of natural theology as a universal perspective. The field of theology thus contains an approach that is non-denominational and relevant to the cross-cultural study of religion and music. The Christian understanding of natural theology is given in *Baker's Dictionary of Theology* (Harrison 1960: 372): "The basis of natural theology in the church is a supposed quality in man that enables him to know God as Creator if not as Redeemer, or at least to know of his existence and in some respects what he is like, or at any rate what he is not like. This rudimentary knowledge will then form the starting point for a fuller understanding of God and hence of the divine-human relationship."

In his comprehensive historical overview of general revelation and natural theology, Bruce A. Demarest, in *General Revelation: Historical Views and Contemporary Issues* (1982: 14), provides a broader definition: "General revelation, mediated through nature, conscience, and the providential ordering of history, traditionally has been understood as a universal witness to God's existence and character. Through the modalities of general revelation, man at large knows both that there is a God and in broad outline what he is like." The basis for the possibility of knowledge of the divine relied upon a unity or likeness between the knower and the known. This idea came to be known as the "analogy of being" (*analogia entis*), as explained by Demarest (1982: 35): "Aristotle held that all knowledge presupposes an essential likeness between knower and that which is known. From the postulate of a real similarity between created and uncreated being, knowledge of contingent effects leads to knowledge of the divine Reality." Demarest continues with reference to Creator and Creation: "The finite creature can know in part the infinite Creator by virtue of the analogy that exists between God and all created things. In the case of humanity, the analogy rests on man created in the *imago Dei*. God is not totally other than man, nor identical with man's being. God's existence is analogous to man's existence."

While the teachings of natural theology and the "analogy of being" are often associated with medieval scholasticism and Roman Catholic theology, Demarest (1982: 45) reveals how, despite differences in doctrine, this concept formed part of the Protestant Reformation, beginning with Martin Luther (1483–1546 CE): "Luther argues that . . . all people possess an intuitive knowledge of God." Demarest (1982: 51) also shows how general revelation is found in the thought of John Calvin (1509–1564 CE): "Internal knowledge of God, in Calvin's view, is that knowledge with which man created in the *imago Dei* is naturally endowed." In fact, Calvin, while best known for his teachings on Predestination and Redemption within the Biblical context, provides one of the most distinctive statements on general revelation and natural theology in *Institutes of the Christian Religion* (2008: Book First, Chapter 3, 9–10): "Since there never has been, from the very first, any quarter of the globe, any city, any household even, without religion, this amounts to a tacit confession, that a sense of deity is inscribed on every heart . . . All men of sound judgment will therefore hold, that a sense of deity is indelibly engraved on the human heart. And that this belief is naturally engendered in all, and thoroughly fixed as it were in our very bones." In another passage, Calvin (2008: 12) supports his position by applying the physiological process of implanting the "seed of religion": "Experience testifies that a seed of religion [*semen religionis*] is divinely sown in all." These attitudes of course precluded the main emphasis of Luther and Calvin in their works on the singular saving grace of Christ in terms of special revelation and revealed theology.

Following the Protestant Reformation, the greatest support for natural theology came during the Enlightenment. As part of the intellectual movement known as Deism, William Paley (1743–1805) was a major figure through his analogy of the watchmaker in *Natural Theology* (1802). In Deism, special revelation was downplayed in favor of general revelation. The biologist Charles Darwin (1809–1882), under the influence of Paley, was essentially a Deist rather than an atheist as often supposed. Though not embracing the Christian concept of God, Darwin, in *The Descent of Man* (1871), accepted the universality of the human religious impulse: "There is no evidence that man was originally endowed with the ennobling belief in the existence of an omnipotent God . . . If, however, we include under the term 'religion' the belief in unseen or spiritual agencies, the case is wholly different; for this belief seems to be universal" (Darwin 2004: 116–117).

In reaction to the Enlightenment's over-emphasis on reason, however, theologians and philosophers of the Romantic period championed the idea of religion based more on feeling and self-consciousness. As we have discussed, Friedrich Schleiermacher (1763–1834) taught that all people possessed a "taste for the Infinite." Demarest (1982: 96–97) has restated this conclusion: "Since the sense and taste for the Infinite is universal, it follows that all men by nature are religious." This notion has greatly influenced the study of religion and traditions of comparative theology up to the present.

The field of comparative theology, in part resting on the feasibility of natural theology in a wider context, offers a potentially useful type of universal background for understanding religion and music. Providing historical context, we mention here an early work in "comparative theology" by F. Harold Smith who in *The Elements of Comparative Theology* (1937) developed a rubric for comparing the theology of world religions under the following chapter headings: Sacred Literature and Theories of Revelation, Ideas of God and Reality, Cosmogony and Cosmology, Man and the Good Life, Salvation. In each chapter, Shintoism, Confucianism, Buddhism, Taoism, Hinduism, Zoroastrianism, Judaism, and Islam are discussed and compared. However, each chapter concludes with a discussion of the superiority of Christianity in each category. The field has since broadened and become more inclusive, with a much more balanced approach, as conveyed by Oxford professor Keith Ward in *Religion and Revelation: A Theology of Revelation in the World's Religions* (1994). In this work, Ward (1994: 40) defines and distinguishes comparative theology from revealed or confessional theology: "One is confessional theology; the exploration of a given revelation by one who wholly accepts that revelation and lives by it. The other is termed 'comparative theology'—theology not as a form of apologetics for a particular faith but as an intellectual discipline which enquires into ideas of the ultimate value and goal of human life, as they have been perceived and expressed in a variety of religious traditions. It is therefore naturally, though not exclusively, concerned with the concept of 'God' as it arises within many such traditions."

The composite nature of all world religions is supported with references to the historical development of specific aspects regarding deity and religious practice, thus reinforcing the usefulness of natural theology as a foundational approach. In the Western world, for example, the notion of "God" carries a legacy of dependence on both Greek and Hebraic conceptions that have overlapped throughout the history of Europe and beyond. We have discussed the contributions of Pythagoras to philosophy and music in the previous chapter, but it is often overlooked how important they were in the formulation of the theological position of monotheism. Francis Schussler Fiorenza and Gordon D. Kaufman, in *Critical Terms for Religious Studies* (1998: 142–143), locate their definition of God in the Oneness that was inevitable in ancient Greece and that was also the basis of biblical revelation: "The Greek affirmation of the oneness of God goes back to Plato's adoption of the Pythagorean method of seeking explanation in mathematical terms. The ultimate principle of all reality, order, and goodness is to be found in the origin of all numbers, the *One*. God, the originative source of all being, was not dependent upon any other being, and was thus the sole ultimate, without beginning, without change, without parts, existing from all eternity. This Greek understanding was linked with the biblical God of Exodus, 'He Who Is' (cf. 3:14), in both Jewish (Philo of Alexandria [c. 20 BCE to 54 CE]) and Christian theology." Philip E. Stoltzfus, in *Theology as Performance: Music, Aesthetics and God in Modern Theology* (2006: 21), concurs: "Pythagorean *harmonia* may have been a pivotal concept for facilitating the theological move among some Greek thinkers from polytheism to a critical monotheism."

Wesley J. Wildman, in "Comparative Natural Theology" (2013: 376), revisits the case for the study of natural theology through the idea of ultimacy in world religions: "Comparative natural theology seeks to compare numerous compelling accounts of ultimacy in as many different respects as are relevant." Taking note of this direction, we reference the religions of India as an important root of universal natural theology, in which the supreme truth known as Brahman is perceived to be co-substantial with the Ātman, the Self in all created beings. Jessica Frazier, in "Natural Theology in Eastern Religions" (2013: 171), provides cogent illustrations of the utility of this approach when encountering the ultimate metaphysical truth in the Hindu tradition: "Most of the Hindu thinkers agreed that there is *something* eternal lying beyond the finite natural world that is accessible to our routine perceptions." With centuries of exploration of the mind in the Yoga and meditation traditions, Hindu thinkers gave equal importance to both the physical and the mental phenomena in relation to eternal truth underlying the finite world, as explained (Frazier 2013: 175): "Hindu thinkers give systematic empirical consideration to mental phenomena as well as physical ones. This allowed natural theologians to reason causally from mental facts as well as from physical facts (and sometimes in preference to the latter)."

Frazier cites examples of natural theology associated with the concept of Brahman from sacred texts such as the Upanishads (ca. 1000 BCE) and the *Bhagavad Gītā*. In fact, recognition of nonphysical forces in the universe are found in the Upanishads (Frazier 2013: 175): "The *Kena Upanishad* sketches a rough mental-efficient cause argument that would be influential in later reasoning that an underlying source of thought and volition must exist. It asks, 'by what' ('*kena*') do thought, breath, will, and action arise, and implies that the answer is a source which itself does not require a source (1.1–8) . . . The *Aitareya Upaniṣad* speaks of Brahman as that by which one sees, hears, smells, speaks, perceives, and discerns . . . and it summarizes: 'Brahman is knowing.'" This concept is shown by Frazier (2013: 175) to have developed further in the Upanishads as well as in later theistic texts such as the *Bhagavad Gītā* and the philosophical tradition of Vedanta: "The *Kaṭha Upanishad* and, following it, the *Bhagavad Gītā* carry through this idea of Brahman as the first cause not only of the existence of sentient beings, but also of their actions, as the 'inner controller' (*Kaṭha Upanishad* 5.12), 'that by which one perceives,' the 'honey-eating self' (*Bhagavad Gītā* 4.4–5) who enjoys all perceptions but—as it is not seen to be created or destroyed—is thought to be self-existent (4.1) and 'without beginning and end' (3.15) . . . The Brahma Sūtras [Vedanta] try to bring coherence to these ideas, and the notion of the divine as an originary controller recurs in the first section and is repeated in the *Bhagavad Gītā*, in which Arjuna plays the role of a natural theologian, asking 'what is nature? What is mind? What is the field (of experience)? What is the knower of the field?' (13.1). The answer is that the divine is the 'knower of the field,' the experiencer who serves as a substrate for the changing and contingent realm of thought." Thus, the Hindu tradition affirms that the individual Self (Ātman) possesses a unity or likeness to the cosmic Soul (Brahman).

However, despite the apparent efficacy of this approach in the study of world religions, there have been detractors of general revelation and natural theology. During the twentieth century, vigorous debates ensued between natural theology and its opposite, revealed theology, the view that knowledge of God is revealed only at specific times and places or to certain persons in history. These debates in Christendom have often revolved around differing understandings of what is meant by "general revelation" in the Bible. One of the contentions of general revelation is that God created the universe in the beginning for everyone, and that all human beings were made in the image of God (*Imago Dei*, from Genesis 1:26–27, 9:6); hence, all humans can acknowledge the presence of God and know something about God, if only in a fundamental sense. While accepted throughout the Judeo-Christian tradition in varying degrees, this position, in widened form, was viewed as part of liberal theology that informed the History of Religions School and the general academic study of religion. One of the most significant debates occurred between Swiss theologians Karl Barth and Emil Brunner in the 1920s, whereby Barth vehemently rejected liberal theology in all its forms. This included especially natural theology and general revelation in favor of the special revelation of Christ, a position that stemmed from Barth's Neo-Calvinist view, namely, that sin had defiled all humankind and erased any chance to know God except through Christ. The documents of this debate, originally published in 1946, contain essays by both protagonists (Brunner and Barth 2002). The extent of Barth's influence in the form of "crisis theology" ("dialectical theology") cannot be overestimated, as attested by Gary Dorrien in *The Barthian Revolt in Modern Theology* (2000: 3): "The story of how Barth rebelled against his eminent liberal teachers and became the leader of the 'crisis theology' revolt against a liberal theological establishment is the founding narrative of twentieth-century theology."

Karl Barth's exclusivist position has been noted by Catherine Cornille (2020: 47), especially in terms of its effect on the neutral study of world religions: "The modern attitude of exclusivism is generally associated in Christianity with the Protestant theologian Karl Barth. He drew a sharp distinction between Christianity as revelation and all other religions. Christianity is to be regarded as the only true religion . . . As historical realities, all religions, Christianity included, are forms of 'unbelief' as far as they attach importance to their own teachings and practices as means of salvation."

For his rejection of all "religions" as human products, Barth utilized the perspective of Feuerbach and his theory of projection. Harvey (1995: 20), in his study of Feuerbach, noted that "Feuerbach's work for the most part has been taken seriously only by Marxist philosophers and Protestant theologians [e.g., Barth] and has been virtually neglected by scholars in religious studies." In fact, Barth wrote "An Introductory Essay" to Feuerbach's *The Essence of Christianity* (see Feuerbach 1957: x-xxxii), in which he extolled Feuerbach's analysis of religion on those aspects that coincided with Barthian theology. In his foreword to this work of Feuerbach (1957: viii), H. Richard Niebuhr characterized Barth's use of Feuerbach: "Barth recommends Feuerbach to students of theology in order that they may see what the outcome is bound to be of every theology that begins with man's subjective states, be they man's God-consciousness, or his sense of the Holy, or the need for a spiritual victory over nature. The theological statements resulting from such an inquiry are bound to be anthropological statements." The theology of Barth and his followers has served to dismiss other manifestations of religion in the world (including religious music) and has spawned an unfortunate dichotomy in theological studies to this day.

Nonetheless, natural theology has gained more relevance in contemporary theological discourse. As an approach in religious studies, it is now broadened to include the arts, as evidenced by Russell Re Manning in his Introduction to *The Oxford Handbook of Natural Theology* (2013: 2): "What is undeniable is that interest in natural theology—and the issues it is concerned with—is very much at the center of contemporary thought, be it in the retrieval of the complexity of the relations between science and religion in recent historical scholarship, the increasingly prominent place of the arts in theological thinking and research, the rise of science and religion as a field of study, and the particularly vibrant state of philosophical reflection on the question of God, not to mention the wide popular appeal of recent 'new atheist' critiques of natural theology."

As an advocate of this trend, Anthony Monti, in *A Natural Theology of the Arts: Imprint of the Spirit* (2003), introduced and developed the role of the arts in natural theology. Frank Burch Brown, in "Aesthetics and the Arts in Relation to Natural Theology" (2013: 537), agrees and urges more scholarship in this field: "A natural theology that is serious about the very nature of aesthetic experience and its potential religious and Christian significance has every reason to attend to the arts specifically, and in all their diversity." Additionally, Jeremy S. Begbie, in "Natural Theology and Music" (2013: 567), spoke for music: "The contemporary conversation between music and theology is still in its early stages." The important topic of aesthetics in religion, including the emerging field of "theological aesthetics," is discussed in chapter 8.

Having established the foundations of theology, especially in the form of natural theology and the universal apprehension of the divinity of existence, we are in a better position to discuss the role of sound and music in creation and as worldwide aspects of human consciousness. The connections among theology, philosophy, and culture hence point to a tenable "theology of music," as will now be noted in a variety of religious traditions.

Theology of Music

We proceed in our discussion of theology and music by consulting an interesting but early work that, although based within a Christian perspective, speaks to a general understanding of what music means theologically, and develops this in terms of a belief in a Creator God. Alfred John Pike wrote his doctoral thesis, *A Theology of Music*, for the Philadelphia Conservatory of Music in 1953. Grounded in the biblical narrative, Pike (1953: 80) explained that all music has a divine source and existed before the creation: "Archaeology has unearthed evidence that earliest man used music in religious ritual and worship. Our First Parents, and their descendants, used some form of song in their praise of God, and from this it can be inferred that God approved of this method of worship. The Old Testament states that the Creator infused all natural knowledge (including knowledge of artistic principles), into the progenitors of the human race at the time of creation. If this were true, music pre-existed the human race, and is divine." And even though history has torn asunder the close connection between music and religion, vestiges of the divine remain ever present in music: "It is only down through the years that music finally became independent of religion, and developed into pure art, but the underlying feeling of its divine origin is still present in all great music worthy of the heritage."

In terms of diverse cosmogonies or creation myths, Catholic theologian Joseph Gelineau (1989: 136) corroborated Pike by underscoring the common centrality of sound and music in religious traditions: "The vast majority of cosmogonic stories originating from the most diverse cultures call upon acoustic images to explain the origin of things, of animals, of man. Everything happens as if the most intimate relationship which exists between a human being and his creator-parent was first perceived by man as being a resonant one: noise, sound, voice, music." Despite the ubiquity of music in human societies from the beginning, music will always remain a multidimensional phenomenon that provides unending causes for inquiry, as explained by Stoltzfus (2006: 4): "As a location for theological reflection, music provides a fascinating study of the way in which a single phenomenon can generate impulses of deep suspicion and criticism, as well as rapturous attraction and speculative extravagance. In early Christianity, for example, music could represent both an instrument of the devil and fount of all corruption, and at the same time a potent means of spiritual uplift and an image of divine harmony."

As part of the theology of music, the eschatological and soteriological functions of music are fruitful topics for research, either as the role of music in providing a pathway to the divine, or as a component of the blessed afterlife. In many religions and cultures, music acts as a salvific vehicle to reach God in the end because the source of music is considered divine, unlike other arts that imitate nature. While bemoaning humanistic approaches to music that avoid the inclusion of ultimate reality as a possibility, Alfred Pike (1953: 48) stated, "Music may be a better medium than metaphysics as an approach to ultimate reality. The other arts are an imitation of Nature and its laws. It can also be identified with idea and is *a priori* in the sense that potential music governs the actual music." Eventually, Pike (1953: 94) revealed music's ultimate soteriological or teleological purpose: "Music has more undeveloped potentiality for spiritual expression than any other art—in it man finds one of the best approaches to truth. His search for ultimate beauty is like prayer—not having reached perfection nor eternal beatitude, he merely contemplates various aspects of Absolute Beauty in its many manifestations. Music is an attempt to communicate these gleanings. All art in its correct sense is an effort to express the Absolute. Music is the way we should like life to be, a glimpse of that world where all strife ends. It takes us towards that world—we transcend the music. To extend the practical Scholastic view of the arts—music is useful in as much as it takes us toward our Final End—God."

Philip Stoltzfus (2006: 2) has placed Protestant theologian Paul Tillich, author of *Theology of Culture* (1959), at the forefront of the current conversation of theology and music with two basic questions: "In relation to the issue of music, the legacy of Tillich left two fundamental questions wholly unexamined: (1) Is reflection upon musical materials themselves a legitimate resource for constructive theological work? (2) Can theological methods and constructs be thought of in terms of musical performance models?" As a cross-cultural response to the queries of Tillich, John N. Sheveland, in "Solidarity through Polyphony" (2010), discussed the structure of musical polyphony in relation to the thought of St. Paul, the Buddhist Santideva, and the Hindu Vedanta Desika. For further development, see Sheveland's "What has Renaissance Polyphony to offer Theological Method?" (2014). But while the mention of a "theology of music" in secular academia does not invoke a large body of research or published monographs, the works of Oskar Sohngen, Robin A. Leaver, Joyce Irwin, and Miikka E. Antilla, while Lutheran in orientation, have established important foundations. In addition, the late twentieth century experienced a surge in more diverse theological commentary on music and aesthetics, including Albert Blackwell, *The Sacred in Music* (1999), and Jeremy S. Begbie, *Theology, Music, and Time* (2000), which offer Reformed Protestant perspectives, and Heidi Epstein, *Melting the Venusberg: A Feminist Theology of Music* (2004), presenting a broad feminist approach to theology and music.

Music as Divine Gift

> The legends and myths of nearly all pagan peoples have sought to explain the elaborate use of music in their worship by indicating that the art of music was a gift of the gods to men.
>
> —Johannes Quasten

Inasmuch as "theology of music" recognizes general beliefs about the divine origin of music, one might ask: just where and how did music originate? One of the most prominent theological answers to this question involves music as a Divine Gift. The theological position that recognizes music as a Divine Gift appears in many places in the history of religions. As the only art form named after a divinity (Muses), music in ancient Greece and among pagan peoples was perceived as a gift of the gods. Many traditions subscribe to this view in some form or another, from Islamic Sufi traditions like the Turkish Whirling Dervishes and South Asian Qawwali, from Jewish Chasidic Niggun to Javanese Gamelan, or from African American Spirituals to Chinese ceremonial music.

To begin, William Edgar, in *Taking Note of Music* (1986: 24–25), narrates the origin of music among the ancient Greeks: "The Greeks, who gave us the word itself [music], have a myth about the origins of music which attributes it to the gods. Apollo's young brother Hermes had stolen some oxen from him, and he used the guts of the animals to make strings. Tying them to the two ends of a turtle shell, he gave us a primeval lyre. He appeased his brother's anger by letting him use it, and he played it with great skill. Thus, the gods are directly involved in giving us instruments. It was the same for the *aulos*, a kind of pipe which is found in Asia Minor." As a corollary, Edgar (1986: 22) recognized the religious nature of most music: "No-one denies that much of the world's music is religious in its purpose. Many would even see a religious meaning in all music, at least in a very broad sense."

We may recall the general attitude toward music among the Greeks and Romans. In the ancient world of Greece and Rome, music was viewed as a Divine Gift, and was performed to please the gods. Johannes Quasten (1983: 1) explains: "The legends and myths of nearly all pagan peoples have sought to explain the elaborate use of music in their worship by indicating that the art of music was a gift of the gods to men . . . Music is pleasing to the gods, for if it were not pleasing to the gods, then the public games which are intended to placate the gods would not have been instituted; the flutist would not attend prayers of supplication offered sacred shrines; the triumph in honor of Mars would not be celebrated to the accompaniment of flute music or the trumpet's blast; the cithara would not be dedicated to Apollo, nor would flutes and other instruments be dedicated to the Muses; flutists would not be permitted perform in public." Many of these notions filtered into the biblical record. It is no accident that flutes are associated with death and the afterlife at the time of Jesus: see Matthew 9:23.

Referencing the German theologian J. A. Scheibe (1754), Alfred Pike (1953: 4–5) presented a biblical scenario for the origin and rise of music: "Adam and Eve lifted up their voices in song in praise of God, but instrumental music, which was man's invention, came about through the tribe of Cain who were estranged from God, and indulged in secular instrumental music as a pastime. The two branches of the art remained distinct until the time of Moses when instruments were introduced into the religious service and have been used intermittently since then." Furthermore, referring to Pere Martini, the Italian music scholar, Pike continued: "God instructed, or infused knowledge of every art and science in Adam—music being included. Instrumental music did not come into existence until after the Fall."

From the perspective of ethnomusicology, Philip V. Bohlman, in *World Music: A Very Short Introduction* (2020: 8) has placed the origin of music in Hebrew tradition with the invention of instruments by patriarchs in the book of Genesis, noting the connection to the divine only with the "discovery" of the Shofar:

> In Jewish tradition there are two origin myths, both in the first book of the Torah, Genesis. In the fourth chapter, music comes into being associated with two different types of instruments, those made with the bodies of animals and shaped to resemble humans, and those moulded from the elements of the earth. One inventor of music, Yuval, is associated with the first, and another inventor of music, Tubal Cain, is associated with the second. Elsewhere in Genesis we encounter the ontology of music at the symbolic centre of one of the most far-reaching of all biblical stories, the *Akeda*, or "Binding of Isaac." In this story (Genesis 22) Abraham shows himself willing to carry out God's commandment to sacrifice his son, Isaac. As Abraham is about to kill his son, the voice of a messenger from God intervenes, informing Abraham that he may substitute a ram trapped by his horns in the nearby bushes. After Abraham has sacrificed and burned the ram, the animal's horns are left, and he rescues these to use them as the *shofar*, the sounding of which ritually and sonically represents Jewish identity, and which remains traceable even today to the first musicians in Genesis.

Yet one might argue that the mere discovery of instruments does not certify that vocal music appeared contemporaneously with instruments. Peter Gradenwitz, in *The Music of Israel: From the Biblical Era to Modern Times* (1996: 30–32), concluded that singing predated the invention of instruments in both Hebrew and Greek traditions: "That the 'invention of music' was attributed by both Hebrew tradition and Greek historians to artists and theoreticians of music instruments—Jubal, Pythagoras—points to their knowledge that singing surely was an older art than the building of instruments for playing music; this is as true in the history of Greek poetry as in that of ancient Hebrew poetry and music."

The developments of music in the West continued to rely on the sacred foundations of *harmonia* laid by the Greeks as well as the biblical revelation. This included the establishment of the diatonic scale and the eight modes of the church, both of which had divine associations. As noted by musicologist Alec Robertson, in *Sacred Music* (1950: 12), "Greek music provided the basis of the diatonic scale system out of which the theorists, though not before the tenth century, deduced the eight ecclesiastical modes." Further musical elements such as the major and minor scale system and the process known as solmization were also grounded in theology and religious experience. Guido of Arezzo (995–1050 CE), a Benedictine monk in Italy, wrote a theoretical treatise called the *Micrologus* (1025–1026 CE) and created the Solfeggio or solmization scheme: originally Ut, Re, Mi, Fa, Sol, La, Si but later changed to Do Re Mi Fa Sol La Ti in its final form. Utilizing a religious hymn based on the New Testament, this system of note identification has become standard throughout the world in terms of Western music. Julius Portnoy (1954: 65) described the monumental contribution of Guido regarding music: Guido of Arezzo "invented notation and the beginnings of the scale as we know it today . . . Guido devised a system which led to the Solfeggio in which we use syllables to read notation. He took the hymn to St. John the Baptist and incorporated the first syllable of each line to indicate a different step of the scale." The hymn is as follows:

Ut queant laxīs, Resonāre fibrīs, Mīra gestōrum, Famulī tuōrum, Solve pollūtī, Labiī reātum, Sāncte Iōhannēs.

Translation: So that your servants may, with loosened voices, resound the wonders of your deeds, clean the guilt from our stained lips, O Saint John.

To reach its present form, Julius Portnoy (1954: 65) explained how the Sol-Fa system evolved: "A whole tone separated Ut to Re, Re to Mi, Fa to Sol, Sol to La, and from Mi to Fa was a half note. The Ut was later changed to Do and the two initials of the last line in the poem were brought in after Guido as Si to round out the full scale. Guido originally included an extra tone preceding Ut, using the Greek character Gamma, which added to Ut, conceived the term gamut. In subsequent years, the word gamut came to denote the full scale structurally." In the nineteenth century, "Si" was changed to "Ti" so that every syllable might begin with a different letter.

The great Italian musical theorist Gioseffo Zarlino (1517–1590 CE), a Franciscan monk, was the first to delineate the two types of chords, major and minor, based on their formation from a triad of notes. As understood, the idea of three basic notes had its inspiration and reference from the Trinity, which could be expressed in the form of the musical triad. In his monumental work of 1558, *Le Istitutioni Harmoniche*, music is described by Zarlino as fundamentally connected with the divine life since it permeates all of creation, as interpreted by Joyce Irwin (1993: 51): "Zarlino argues that music is necessary for eternal life. In addition to its comforting properties, it leads to contemplation of celestial matters. Not only is heaven itself populated by nine choirs of angelic spirits, but heaven and earth are united through harmony." And since the biblical record includes descriptions of music in the highest spheres of heaven, it behooves human beings to cultivate it for fulfillment in the hereafter: "Because the traditional conception of the activity of saints and angels is that they sing praise to God unceasingly, music is regarded either literally or metaphorically as indispensable in the preparation of the soul for heaven" (Irwin 1993: 43).

There will be more discussion of music as Divine Gift in the sections on Lutheran and Hindu theology below. Meanwhile, with the establishment of the sacred origins of music in the West, we now turn to the various beliefs about musical angels and music in the heavens.

Musical Angels

> Perceiving the "music of the cosmos" becomes listening to the song of the angels.
>
> —Joseph Cardinal Ratzinger

An extremely rich and viable tradition of musical angels or "singing stars" has been documented in Judaism, Christianity, and Islam, pointing to the theological nature of music as not only part of the Creation but as a specific attribute of God or the divine. The biblical tradition of heavenly music represents a long and complicated blend of pre-biblical and pagan elements that were gradually fused together over centuries. Among the myriad of examples of heavenly singing in the Bible (i.e., Psalms), we cite Job 38.4–7, where music appears "scientific" in the Pythagorean sense, as part of the measurement of the cosmos: "Where were you when I laid the foundation of the earth? Tell me if you have understanding. Who determined its measurements—surely you know! Or who stretched the line upon it? On what were its bases sunk, or who laid its cornerstone when the morning stars sang together, and all the heavenly beings shouted for joy?" (New Revised Standard Version 1989: 420). In the New Testament (NRSV 1989: 833), the older tradition of singing angels continues, as Luke 2: 9 reports that a single angel announced Christ's birth. Then, in verses 13 and 14: "And suddenly there was with the angel a multitude of the heavenly host, praising God and saying, 'Glory to God in the highest heaven, and on earth peace among those he favors." Although the text uses the word "saying" rather than "singing" to describe how the angels praised God, most Christians interpret this as "singing."

Eventually, the Pythagorean idea of music of the spheres fully merged with theology and coincided with the rise of angels in the Jewish and Christian traditions. Kathi Meyer-Baer, in *Music of the Spheres and the Dance of Death: Studies in Musical Iconology* (1970: 5), traced this history with documents and artefacts, beginning with this preliminary statement: "The image of angels singing, playing, and dancing to praise the Lord may be traced back to early concepts of the music of the spheres, as well as to the idea of harmony in the universe expressed through music," pointing to, "The transmutation of the early pagan figures of the movers of the spheres into Christian angels, as well as of their association with music."

Paraphrasing this early history as outlined in Meyer-Baer (1970: 7–19), the idea of divine music of the universe began with the Babylonians. The ancient Babylonians developed the science of astronomy as the basis of their religion. In their view, seven was a sacred number; seven heavens corresponded to seven planets, each moving on a sphere ruled by a god, the highest of which was Ashur, the sun god. The fate of individuals was determined by the time and place of their birth, being presided over by winged messengers or *angeloi* (angels). In contrast with the idea of moving planetary spheres as in Babylonia, both the early biblical and early Greek notions of the cosmos held it to be static. In the early biblical accounts, Heaven is depicted like a canopy or bell-like lid, with stars permanently affixed, over the earth. The Lord sits on a throne supported by Cherubim and served by Seraphim. In the later Book of Ezekiel, which reflects Babylonian influence, there are winged spirits with two, four, or six wings that also have four faces (man, eagle, bull, and lion), as in Babylonian iconography. These ideas become fused with the developing Greek tradition of musical harmony. The Greek cosmos of Homer was also viewed as static in that the universe was understood to comprise the earth as a large flat disc surrounded by the river Oceanus. The Gods lived on top of Olympus Mountain and moved about at will. Elysium was a paradise island beyond Oceanus where favored humans were allowed after death.

Everything changed with Plato the Pythagorean, whose works contain two separate descriptions of the cosmos. In *Phaedrus*, the gods hold processions in chariots across the sky drawn by winged horses in which the unborn human souls take part. Eros (inspiration) is the cause of all motion. In the *Republic*, the motion of the planetary spheres corresponds with the notes of the musical scale; on the edge of each of eight discs sits a female siren singing one note of the scale. Their singing forms a harmony, and this harmony is the harmony of the universe. Meyer-Baer (1970: 15) explained further: "As long as the earth was regarded as the stable center of the cosmos, that is, until the time of Pythagoras, the movement of the stars was explained as their movement around the earth. Once their courses were understood to follow certain rules, the stars were thought to move on spheres. Only the Babylonian creed, based on astronomical observation, took motion of the spheres into consideration . . . The heaven of the Bible's early books was stable, and the stars were fixed to the firmament. The idea of motion occurs only later, and through Babylonian influence, in Ezekiel's wheels. In Greek mythology of the Homeric period, the heaven did not move, the gods lived on a stable mountain, Olympus. Nor did the gods move the spheres; they themselves moved about freely, and only Eros and later Helios had prescribed paths." Regarding Plato and his adoption of Pythagorean ideas, Meyer-Baer (1970: 15–16) has attested: "In both of Plato's versions . . . motion is an important factor in the universe. The description of the universe in Plato's *Republic* . . . provides the first reference to music in connection with the motion of the cosmos . . . the narrator of the myth in the *Republic* is supposed to represent Pythagorean ideas, and Pythagoras is credited with having discovered a correlation between the ratios of musical intervals and the ratios of the orbits of the celestial bodies. Part of the Pythagorean creed was based on the belief that this correlation originated from as well as resulted in the harmony of the universe."

The Pythagorean and Platonic traditions of music of the spheres, as well as the biblical tradition of musical angels, both influenced the early Church, as described by Meyer-Baer (1970: 35): "The writings of the Church Fathers reflect all the traditions mentioned so far: the sounding cosmos of pagan ideology, the manifold structure of the heavens from the Neoplatonists and the Gnostics, and the hosts and choirs of singing angels and the blessed from the Bible." For example, "St. Ambrose, quoting Origen, stated that through the motion of the stars, a marvelous sweet harmony is established and that Plato was its discoverer." St. Augustine, an ardent admirer of Plato, described a cosmos with seven, eight, nine, or ten heavens, since "it is not surprising that the Church fathers, many of whom were brought up in the classic tradition, accepted them without debate, though they were strongly opposed to the pagan rites" (1970: 36). Consequently, Pythagorean notions of numerical systems incorporating harmonies between music and the planets continued unabated within scholastic traditions of theological reflection: "The idea of music of the spheres was also the foundation for the semi-mythological theories of music that evolved in the early centuries of the Christian era and became one of the preoccupations of medieval writings on music. During the centuries preceding 1100, considerable intellectual energy was lavished on elaborating systems of musical scales and harmonics with reference to planetary orbits and mythical figures" (1970: 70).

Regarding the acceptance of angelic orders, it was especially the Fathers of the Eastern Church who brought about this change that, after some opposition from the Roman Church, came to be accepted throughout the Christian world. An early example is Cyril of Jerusalem, explained by Meyer-Baer (1970: 36): "Cyril of Jerusalem (third century) mentions nine hosts of singing angels; Ephrem of Edessa (third century) has the seraphim sing and extol the Lord while the cherubim have the duty of carrying the throne of God." Meyer-Baer continued in her description: "In the liturgy of the Eastern Church, Syrian as well as Byzantine, the nine hosts of angels were represented in processions . . . This certainly is evidence that a cult of angels was incorporated into the liturgy of the Eastern Church of the fourth century. Opposition to this cult was reflected in the decisions of the Councils of Laodicea in 375 and 492. It is understandable that adoration of angels would have been forbidden in the early Christian era, because the Fathers were afraid that the sirens and victories, *nikes*, invoked in pagan Greek and Oriental funeral rites, might have too much influence. After the fourth century, the restrictions were eased, and the castes of angels acquired special characteristics" (1970: 37–38).

Dionysius the Areopagite, in his landmark work, *Celestial Hierarchy* (533 CE), lists nine classes of angels. While this work contains little on music theory, Meyer-Baer (1970: 39) described its over-arching theology as informing subsequent descriptions of angels: "The theory that a light mystically emanates from the Lord and is transmitted through the hierarchy, the holy order of the angels, to mankind . . . This treatise on the hierarchy is accepted as the source of the many later descriptions and representations of musician angels and orchestras."

Grounded in a basic requirement of comparative study, the Musicology of Religion does not seek to separate out religious traditions according to notions of "autonomous history." What is significant here is the association of music with each stage in the development of angels, whether in Hinduism, Buddhism Judaism, Christianity, or Islam. Joscelyn Godwin, in *Harmo-*

nies of Heaven and Earth: The Spiritual Dimension of Music from Antiquity to the Avant-Garde (1987: 73), stated this proposition rather succinctly, with examples: "All religious traditions that acknowledge the existence of angels concur to giving them musical attributes. Since it is not clear in visual representations when someone is singing, they are usually given musical instruments to make their function plain. One can see such angels in the courts of heaven as pictured in Iranian manuscripts. They appear in Hindu temple sculptures as the seductive Gandharvas, of whom the Mahabharata has much to tell. In some *tankas* of Mahayana Buddhism they surround the central figure, and in certain meditations on Tantra one is instructed to imagine one's guru attended by beautiful *dakinis* singing, dancing, and playing. One need scarcely mention the musician-angels to be found in the sculpture, wood-carving and stained glass of innumerable European churches, or in the painting of manuscripts and altarpieces."

The presence of musical angels is well documented in religions besides Christianity, including traditions both East and West. Geddes MacGregor, in *Angels: Ministers of Grace* (1988: 112), explained the Indo-Aryan roots of the name and concept of angels going back to ancient India and Iran: "Although the religious development of India and Iran was essentially to proceed along different lines (what we call Hinduism and Zoroastrianism are strikingly different), the ancient, pre-Zoroastrian religion of Iran and the religion of India [called Indo-Iranian] in the early Vedic period had some common features. One of these is the use of the word *deva* [Sanskrit] or *daeva* [Persian] for the gods . . . The word *deva* is taken to mean 'shining one' and from it comes, of course, the Latin word *deus*." The Rig Veda is the most ancient Aryan text in Sanskrit and has key information on "musical devas" as important features of Hindu religion.

While some translators prefer the term "gods" or perhaps "demigods" for devas, MacGregor (1988: 114–116) correlated them with "angels" and noted their counterpart as bodhisattvas in Buddhism. But while the term "angel" comes from the Greek, *angelos*, the idea of a multitude of angels in the Bible, derives from the older Eastern category of devas who were arranged in a hierarchical order, as explained by MacGregor (1988: 112–113): "The Hebrews, after the Babylonian Exile, were much influenced by the religious ideas they encountered among their captors [the Persian Zoroastrians] . . . The devas were among the imports, but before they could be naturalized in a society that had developed along such strongly monotheistic lines, they had to undergo adaptation . . . By the time of Ezekiel, Yahweh had become so lofty and remote that he could be appreciated only through intermediaries. Angels, patterned after the old devas but adapted to the monotheistic system, functioned as such. The Hebrews were already prepared for the idea of angels as divine messengers, but now they could have a new role as heavenly courtiers around a divine throne, arranged in hierarchical order."

The confluence of angels and music reappears in medieval Judaism, as Meyer-Baer (1970: 29) has enumerated the presence of musical angels in the Jewish Talmud: "The Talmud elaborated classes of angels praising the Lord . . . Their number in the Talmud is a thousand times a thousand, alternatively ten thousand times ten thousand, and later ninety thousand myriads. In one place it is said that the angels sing during the night only, to replace the Jewish community, which sings during the day. The Talmud's angels understand and know only Hebrew. Seven spirits appear before the throne of the Lord, and there are seven heavens." For a general introduction to music in Judaism, see Joseph A. Levine (2006).

Regarding Islam, although information on angels and music is not in the Qur'an, it appears in some of the sacred traditions. First, it should be noted that the approach to the chanting of Islamic scripture is that it is a gift of God, not a human invention. Seyyed Hossein Nasr (1997: 221) confirmed the divinely inspired practice of chanting the Qur'an: "There are sciences of chanting of the Qur'an which go back, according to Islamic tradition, to the prophet David and which have continued unabated to this day. The chanting is revealed and of sacred origin; it is not a human creation but divinely inspired." Geddes MacGregor (1988: 116–117) affirmed that the Islamic tradition continued in line with biblical revelation that included prophets and angels: "When Muhammad established his uncompromisingly monotheistic faith, he recognized prophets, including Moses and Jesus among them. He also, however, took account of angels. They were already known entities and were part of the biblical scenario from which he took much of the material he used in the construction of his new religion."

The descriptions of heaven in Islam relied on earlier depictions involving multiple levels, including angels and the application of Pythagorean ideas of harmony. Regarding heaven, Edward J. Wright, in *The Early History of Heaven* (2000: 210), indicates the continuity of the earlier Pythagorean and Platonic (and Pauline) systems of seven heavens in the Qur'an: "Not surprisingly, the heavenly realm is a focal point of Islamic spirituality much as it is in Judaism and Christianity. The Qur'an, betraying the authors' adoption of the Ptolemaic model, states that the heavenly realm consists of seven spheres (Qur'an 17:44, 65:12, 78:12)." Succeeding Islamic philosophers and theologians developed their perspectives by attempting to reconcile all classical knowledge of the natural and harmonious universe with the Divine presence of God through the principle of Unity. One of the most prominent groups of such philosophers was the order known as Brethren of Purity (Ikhwān al-Safā) in Basra in Iraq during the tenth century. They produced a monumental fifty-two-volume encyclopedia in Arabic called *Rasā-il of Ikhwān al-Safā*. A leading scholar in this tradition, Seyyed Hossein Nasr, described their indebtedness to Pythagoras in *An Introduction to Islamic Cosmological Doctrines: Conceptions of Nature and Methods Used for its Study by the Ikhwān al-Safā, al-Bīrūnī, and Ibn Sīnā* (1978: 47): "The Ikhwān believed themselves to be disciples of Pythagoras and of such followers as Nicomachus, especially in considering numbers as the cause of all things and the key to the understanding of the harmony pervading the universe." Nasr cited the stated aims of the work: "One of the aims of our treatise on music consists in demonstrating clearly that the whole world is composed in conformity with arithmetical, geometrical and musical relations. There, we have explained in detail the reality of universal harmony. We understand, therefore, that thus considered, the body of the world resembles an animal or a unique system of a single man or the totality of a city which shows also the Unity of its Maker (*mukhtari*), the Creator of forms (*musawwir*), or of its Composer (*mu'allif*), that is God" (Nasr 1978: 45).

The Prophet Muhammad is believed to have ascended through the heavenly realms in his miraculous Night Journey. Beginning in Mecca he rode to Jerusalem on his winged-horse Buraq. Once in Jerusalem, Muhammad ascended into heaven from the place now commemorated by the Dome of the Rock. This event is explained in context by Wright (2000: 211): "The Prophet was accompanied by a guiding angel as he ascended, and prior to entering the heavenly realm he was stopped by another angel whose job was to protect the divine realm from unwanted or unqualified visitors. In the heavens Muhammad met several notable religious figures (Enoch, Abraham, Aaron, Moses, and Jesus) whose presence in the heavenly realm shows that only the truly religious belong there . . . This narrative follows precisely the format and themes of the earlier Greek, Roman, Jewish, Christian, and Persian ascent texts."

The Qur'an provides an idyllic description of heaven or Jannah, stating that each person is greeted there by angels from every gate with the words, "Peace be with you, that you persevered in patience! Now how excellent is the final home!" (Qur'an 13:24). Paradise is described as surrounded by eight principal gates, each level being divided into a hundred degrees guarded by angels. Both men and women will have beautiful and pure spouses (Qur'an 2:25, 4:57). While not described in the Qur'an, Islamic tradition conveys the notion that the women in heaven sing beautiful melodies in perpetuity. Jannah is described as an eternal dwelling (3:136), with its supreme joy and greatest bliss being God's infinite pleasure (9:72).

The spirituality of music in association with angels in Islamic tradition is found regarding a specific archangel named Israfil. The encyclopedic work *Angels A–Z*, by Lewis and Oliver (2002: 224), contains an entry on Israfil, a master musician amidst a heavenly chorus: "Although not mentioned in the Koran, Israfil, or Israfel (the Burning One) [Raphael] is one of the four archangels of Islam, along with Mikhail, Djibril, and Isra'il. Israfil is known particularly as the angel of Judgment Day, who blows his horn to awaken the dead. According to tradition, he is an extraordinarily tall angel, with his feet below the earth and his head reaching the pillars of God's throne. He is so saddened by the thought of hell that whenever he glances down to the infernal regions, which he is said to do six times a day, his tears would flood the earth if God did not prevent them from flowing. Israfil is also an angel of music. He has four wings and a beautiful face. His body is covered with mouths that constantly praise God in a thousand different tongues. From his breath, God is said to create hundreds of thousands of other angels for the heavenly chorus." Israfil is also well known in mystical traditions and was the subject of a poem by American poet Edgar Allan Poe.

The spirit of Pythagorean thought has also found a home in Roman Catholic theology, which continues to recognize the reality of cosmic music and the musical laws of the universe. Erich Przywara (1889–1972), a Jesuit theologian from Poland influenced by Husserl and phenomenology, developed his theology of "analogy" around the model of Pythagorean musical harmony and rhythm. In his most influential work of 1932, *Analogia Entis: Metaphysics—Original Structure and Universal Rhythm*, Przywara (2014: 314) explained this innovative concept as based on Pythagorean and Platonic precedents: "The 'being'—Sein—which all philosophies take to be the primordial question and primordial datum with respect to everything else, does not (subsequently) 'have' analogy as an attribute or as something developing from it; rather analogy *is* being, and thus thought *is* (noetically) analogy. As this primordial dynamic, analogy is a rhythm—just as, according to Pythagoras, the cosmos vibrates with a 'resonant rhythm,' and just as, according to Plato, God is the 'measure of all things and all actions.' Only in the sense of such a rhythm and such a measure is analogy a principle. Ontically as being and noetically as thought, it is 'principally' the mystery of the primordial music of this rhythm—as with the fugues in Bach's 'Art of Fugue,' which, interweaving one another, pass beyond themselves into 'great silence.' The 'resonant analogy' is fulfilled in this 'silent analogy.'"

Joseph Cardinal Ratzinger, in *The Spirit of the Liturgy* (2000: 152–153), included Pythagorean thought as relevant to modern Catholic understanding: "According to Pythagoras, the cosmos was constructed mathematically, a great edifice of numbers . . . For the Pythagoreans, this mathematical order of the universe ('cosmos' means 'order') was identical with the essence of beauty itself. Beauty comes from meaningful inner order. And for them this beauty was not only optical but musical." Then he affirms that truly beautiful earthly music must reflect the laws of the universe: "The music made by man must . . . be taken from the inner music and order of the universe, be inserted into the 'fraternal song' of the 'fraternity of the spheres.' The beauty of music depends on its conformity to the rhythmic and harmonic laws of the universe. The more that human music adapts itself to the musical laws of the universe, the more beautiful will it be."

Further, the continuing influence of the Pythagorean concept of cosmic harmony in relation to angels is evident in official statements of Roman Catholic theology by Joseph Cardinal Ratzinger (2000: 153): "Perceiving the 'music of the cosmos' thus becomes listening to the song of the angels, and the reference to Isaiah chapter 6 naturally suggests itself. But a further step was taken with the help of the trinitarian faith, faith in the Father, the Logos, and the Pneuma. The mathematics of the universe does not exist by itself, nor, as people now came to see, can it be explained by stellar deities. It has a deeper foundation: the mind of the Creator. It comes from the Logos, in whom, so to speak, the archetypes of the world's order are contained." Art is associated directly with the Logos in the act of creation (2000: 153–154): "The Logos, through the spirit, fashions the material world according to these archetypes. In virtue of his work in creation, the Logos is, therefore, called the 'art of God.' The Logos himself is the great artist, in whom all works of art—the beauty of the universe—have their origin. To sing with the universe means, then, to follow the track of the Logos and to come close to him. All true human art is an assimilation to the artist, to Christ, to the mind of the Creator. The idea of the music of the cosmos, of singing with the angels, leads back again to the relation of art to *logos*, but now it is broadened and deepened in the context of the cosmos." As music permeates the heavens in many religions, are humans able to participle in music after death?

Music in the Afterlife

> All other arts, be they as wonderful as they want, will end with this life, but the art of singing and playing will prevail even in eternal life.
>
> —Georg Albrecht, German theologian

Many traditions of religious belief envision the afterlife in heaven as a setting both pleasing and beautiful. In most cases, music is an essential factor and often forges a connecting link between this world and the next. The Neo-Pythagoreans among the Romans in antiquity, for example, followed in the footsteps of their namesake Pythagoras and used musical harmony as a means toward heavenly delight. According to Franz Cumont, in *After Life in Roman Paganism* (1922: 24), "All the Neo-Pythagoreans agree in stating that the human soul is related to God and therefore immortal . . . Music, which caused it to vibrate in harmony with the universe, and science, which lifted it toward divine things, prepared its ascension to heaven."

The profound significance of music for Christianity is grounded to some degree in the appearance of music (and dance) in the afterlife among the blessed in heaven. According to Meyer-Baer (1970: 40–41), "By the eleventh century, the various traditions of cosmic and angelic orders had merged, and the vision had assumed an aspect familiar today: the blessed sing and dance in the highest heaven, be it Elysium or Empyrean. There are nine spheres or heavens and nine choirs of angels. The spheres are moved by angels or the Muses. Their song results in the harmony of the universe, and this harmony can be transmitted, through music, to the human soul. The idea of correspondence of heavenly and human harmony through music was first formulated by St. Augustine, later by Boethius, and subsequently adopted by many poets and philosophers."

Relying on some of the earliest manuscripts of the New Testament book of Revelation (Beatus manuscripts of seventh-century Spain), Meyer-Baer (1970: 89) revealed the first appearance of celestial musicians, including the blessed in heaven: "The text of Revelation mentions five major groups as singing and making music: the four beasts, the seven spirits, the twenty-four Elders, the hundred and forty-four blessed, and, finally, the multitude of ten thousand times ten thousand angels. Their instruments are said to be harps. They are mentioned in Revelation 4, the vision of the Lord, Revelation 5, the vision of the Lamb, Revelation 7, the adoration of the Lord and of the Lamb, Revelation 14, the Lamb standing on Mount Zion. Various of the manuscripts show angel musicians." Thomas Allen

Seel, in *A Theology of Music for Worship Derived from the Book of Revelation* (1995), presents a practical analysis of how a theology of music approach yields valuable insights into the role of music in the afterlife as found in the New Testament.

In subsequent medieval Christian writings, according to Meyer-Baer (1970: 110), dancing became an integral part of the life of both the Elders and the blessed in heaven: "Dancing in heaven is a primary concern for the history of heavenly music. Dancers appeared in a number of the visions and representations of the cosmos in antiquity, and they begin to re-emerge in the Romanesque period . . . Dancers reappeared first as Elders or as one of the beasts, and then, ultimately, dancing was transferred to the community of the blessed." In various works of art, the chronology of dancing by angels and the blessed is also noted (1970: 130–132): "The angel as a participant in the making of celestial music finally began to be a prevalent figure in works of art in the fourteenth century. Angels first appeared as dancers, joining the dance of the blessed in paradise, and as singers in the heavenly chorus. The angel instrument player, ultimately the most popular image, was the last to join the making of celestial harmony." By the twelfth century, the dance of the blessed in paradise had definitely entered the sphere of Christian iconology, and "[b]y the fifteenth century the figures of the dancing blessed and the dancing angels became quite common." Dancers even formed a ring in a round dance (1970: 130): "Figures of angels or blessed souls dancing a round became a new motif to denote paradise in Christian iconography beginning in the first half of the fourteenth century." An interesting comparison worthy of research in the Musicology of Religion, discussed below, is the famous heavenly round dance (Rāsa Dance) of Lord Krishna and the Gopīs in Indian texts and paintings.

In Western esotericism, the nineteen treatises attributed to Hermes Trismegistus (Thrice-Greatest Hermes) in the collection known as *Corpus Hermeticum* were highly influential during the religious revival of the Renaissance period of 1470–1650 CE. These texts represent ancient Egyptian mystery teachings emerging from first-century Alexandrian philosophy and religious syncretism. Significant here is the inclusion of music in the afterlife of the initiate who attains to Gnosis or knowledge God, and the relation between the human soul and the divine. Joscelyn Godwin (1986: 14) introduces this tradition through its most important text, the Poimandres: "*Poimandres,* the first and most comprehensive treatise, relates a vision of Hermes (representing the initiate) in which he is shown the creation of the Cosmos and of Man, and the destiny of the soul. The image of the Soul ascending through the planetary spheres and hearing the planetary music on the way is one of the most powerful and recurrent in this collection." In the 1924 translation of Walter Scott, *Hermetica: The Ancient Greek and Latin Writings which contain Religious or Philosophic Teachings ascribed to Hermes Trismegistus* (V. 1, 1985: 129), we find the following description of music in the ascent of the Soul to the 8th sphere of the Fixed Stars:

> And thereupon the man mounts upward through the structure of the heavens. And to the first zone of heaven [Moon] he gives up the force which works increase and that which works decrease; to the second zone [Mercury], the machinations of evil cunning; to the third zone [Venus], the lust whereby men are deceived; to the fourth zone [Sun], domineering arrogance; to the fifth zone [Mars], unholy daring and rash audacity; to the sixth zone [Jupiter], evil strivings after wealth; and to the seventh zone [Saturn], the falsehood lies in wait to work harm. And thereupon, having been stripped of all that was wrought upon him by the structure of the heavens, he ascends to the substance of the eighth sphere [sphere of the Fixed Stars], being possessed by his own proper power; and he sings, together with those who dwell there, hymning the Father; and they that are there rejoice with him at his coming. And being made like to those with whom he dwells, he hears the Powers, who are above the substance of the eighth sphere, singing praise to God with a voice that is theirs alone. And thereafter, each in his turn, they mount upward to this Father; they give themselves up to the Powers, and becoming Powers themselves, they enter into God. This is the Good; this is the consummation, for those who have *gnosis* [knowledge of God, and of the relation between man's true self and God].

Another example of the continuing presence of music in the afterlife is in the Celtic religion. Karen Ralls-MacLeod, in *Music and the Celtic Otherworld: From Ireland to Iona* (2000: 1), outlined the central role of music in ancient Celtic traditions: "From the beautiful, enchanting music of the fairy harp to the sacred singing of the choirs of angels, Celtic literature has many references to a spiritual or supernatural dimension of music. This sacred dimension is called the Celtic Otherworld, in which music is often prominently featured." Examples include fairy harpers, songs of mermaids, the power of the saint's bell, the singing of angels in heaven, and musical trees. In earlier times, music provided access to unseen realms: "The mysterious, sacred dimension of a people's culture and experience is most often described in terms of their religious beliefs and rituals, but various art forms can also be used to show this, including music. By a careful examination of the sources, the early Celts believed that music could give access to reality in both every day, mundane and otherworldly contexts" (2000: 5). As confirmed (2000: 15), music for the Celts was the definitive link from this world to the next: "Music is seen as a universal 'connector' to the Otherworld, and as an especially effective link between this world and the Otherworld."

The ancient religion of the prophet Zoroaster (ca. 2000 BCE) provides striking evidence of the presence of music in the afterlife. In the poetic hymns known as the Gathas of the Avesta, the sacred scriptures of ancient Zoroastrianism, the highest heaven is described as a house or abode of music and songs called *garö demāna*, "House of Song." According to the literature, if a person's good thoughts, words, and deeds in life are abundant, the bridge will be wide enough to cross, and the Daena, a spirit representing revelation, will appear and lead the soul into the House of Song. Those souls that successfully cross the bridge are united with God or Ahura Mazda. This is detailed by renowned Zoroastrian scholar Jal Dastur Cursetji Pavry in *The Zoroastrian Doctrine of a Future Life: From Death to the Individual Judgment* (1929: 112): "The fateful crossing of the Bridge [Chinvat Bridge] means either joy or doom. The ascent to felicity rises through the past accumulation of good thoughts (*humata*), good words (*huxta*), and good deeds (*hvarsta*) into the beatitude of Garö-demāna, 'House of Song.'"

The next two sections explore music in two theological traditions, one Western and one Eastern: Lutheran Christianity and Hindu Religion. Yet both traditions hold music as Divine Gift, recognize music as a spiritual practice, and incorporate music in life after death.

Lutheran Theology and Music

> Music is the *donum Dei*, the gift from God, and therefore is only secondarily a human art or science.
>
> —Martin Luther, sixteenth-century Germany

In early Protestant Christianity, we may note the continuity with the ancient world regarding the closeness of music to theology and the idea of music as a gift of God. In this sense, Protestant Reformer Martin Luther (1483–1546

CE) stands out as a pinnacle and major influence for the idea of music as Divine Gift. Drawing much of his thought from Platonism and St. Augustine, Luther has influenced countless theologians and musicians up to the present. Lutheran scholar Robin A. Leaver (2017: 65) states the situation succinctly: "It is this distinctive statement—'music is next to theology'—that distinguishes Luther from his predecessors, as well as from many of his contemporaries, and has therefore been continuously quoted and commented upon." Nonetheless much has been written on Lutheran theology without mention of his monumental contribution to religious music and his reflections on music and the divine. Two examples of otherwise comprehensive treatments are *The Westminster Handbook to Martin Luther* (Denis R. Janz 2010) and *The Oxford Handbook of Martin Luther's Theology* (Robert Kolb 2014). While not discussed herein, the role of music in the thought of John Calvin and Reformed theology is noteworthy, though differing significantly from Luther. For a description and assessment of Calvin and music, see Charles Garside (1979) and Jeremy Begbie (2013: 10–40).

One of the theological debates in the Baroque period regarding music revolved around the question of whether music was truly a gift of God, or *adiaphora*—something given in nature that was neither commanded nor forbidden in Scripture but nevertheless acceptable. As *adiaphora*, music is considered neutral, a part of nature but not a Divine Gift. For example, music as "Harmony of the Spheres" could be viewed as "part of nature" but not necessarily a special gift of God to man. Luther, on the other hand, elevated music as Divine Gift above its place in creation or nature. In some places, Luther combined the two concepts. Many issues regarding music in Lutheran theology are further discussed by Joyce L. Irwin in *Neither Voice nor Heart Alone: German Lutheran Theology of Music in the Age of the Baroque* (1993).

Luther's overall approach to music is determined by his early studies of music and metaphysics. Carl F. Schalk, in *Luther on Music: Paradigms of Praise* (1988: 18), outlined his educational background: "Luther's formal education in the medieval quadrivium had placed significant emphasis on music as a speculative science (*musica speculativa*). Relying largely on an understanding of music derived from such Greek philosophers as Plato, Aristotle, and Boethius, the Middle Ages understood real, performed music to be on a lower level than and a mere shadow of the celestial music of the spheres. It tended to view music as a reflection of the stability and continuity of an ordered universe." Luther's earliest writings exhibit this tendency, such as his lectures on the Psalms, and some of his later works continued in this line. Schalk (1988:18) cited Luther's reference to Pythagoras in his lectures on Genesis in the 1530s: "We do not marvel at the countless other gifts of creation, for we have become deaf toward what Pythagoras aptly terms the wonderful and most lovely music coming from the harmony of the motions that are in the celestial spheres."

Paul Nettl, father of ethnomusicologist Bruno Nettl, revealed in *Luther and Music* (1948: 12) that music brought great comfort to Luther in his darkest hours: "When Luther entered his great struggle on October 31, 1517, by posting his famous Ninety-five Theses on the portals of the Wittenberg church, music became the sweet comforter of his bitterest hours—his solace, inspiration, joy, and balm." Citing Luther, Nettl (1948: 12) translated this passage from *Encomium Musices*: "Music is a beautiful, gracious gift of God. It has often been the inspiration of my sermons. Music rouses all the emotions of the human heart; mothing on earth is so well-suited to make the sad merry, the merry sad, to give courage to the despairing, to make the proud humble, to lessen envy and hate, as music."

The closeness of music to theology for Luther was emphasized by Schalk (1988: 19) in terms of *musica practica*, music as a performed art: "For Luther as a theologian, music was not primarily a matter for mystical or allegorical speculation but a practical art, closely tied to theology and its goal of the praise of the Creator and the proclamation of the Word. This had been the whole thrust of Luther's own personal experience with music." As a practicing musician, Luther played the flute and the lute in small groups and sang polyphonic music.

In establishing Luther's view of music as Divine Gift, Schalk (1988: 33) cited Luther's Preface to Georg Rhau's *Symphoniae iucundae*: "Although Luther did not deny the importance of these earlier models [music as a moral and educational paradigm], he chose instead to point to a more basic and primary paradigm that simultaneously encompassed and superseded them both. For Luther, that paradigm, that glowing center of awareness and comprehension that was for him the basis of understanding music in the life and worship of God's people, was music as creation and gift of God." Furthermore, Schalk (1988: 37) pointed to the fact that for Luther music was meant for more than contemplation; it had the distinct divine purpose of glorifying the Creator in the form of doxology: "Luther's primary paradigm for music in the life of the church was that it is the creation and gift of God. But music, as God's creation and gift, was given to humanity with the intent that it be used for a specific purpose. That purpose was, in Luther's view, the praise and glorifying of the Creator, especially through the proclamation of the Word."

Lutheran scholar Robin A. Leaver, in *Luther's Liturgical Music: Principles and Implications* (2017: 89), further reinforces Luther's notion of music as Divine Gift by aligning it with justification by faith: "That music comes from God as a gift means that it has dimensions of meaning, power and effectiveness that far exceed any human art or science. Music is not an *inventio*, a work of humankind, but a *creatura*, a work of God . . . In the same way as justification is God's gift of grace rather than the reward for human effort, so music is in essence God's gift of creation rather than a human achievement." Yet to reach this conclusion, Luther first had to confront the standard perception that music was a human invention, especially since both the biblical record and the Greek philosophical tradition espoused this position.

In his exposition of the invention of music, Robin A. Leaver (2017: 67) set down the juxtaposition between the biblical and Greek accounts: "On the question of the invention of music there was the fundamental conflict between the Judeo-Christian biblical tradition and Greek philosophic perceptions of history. On the one hand, Genesis 4:21 states, 'Jubal is the father of those who play harp and organ.' On the other hand, according to Greek tradition it was Pythagoras who, on hearing the different pitches made by blacksmiths hammering metal, deduced the basic proportions of music sound . . . Moses says Jubal . . . but the Greeks say Pythagoras." Throughout the Middle Ages, theorists credited each with the invention of music. Yet Luther went beyond both Jubal and Pythagoras in asserting that music was not a human invention at all but a gift of God that they both discovered and developed. According to Leaver (2017: 69), "When thinking about the origins of music Luther had a more fundamental approach compared to that of his medieval predecessors. For him it was beside the point to discuss the primacy of either Jubal or Pythagoras since neither invented music."

As it were, God created music, first vocal, and then instrumental. The scenario envisioned by Luther and other early Lutheran thinkers was that Adam and Eve originally sang praise to God unaccompanied in Eden, but after the Fall and the murder of Abel, languages, culture, and the arts were dispersed. Musical instruments were made by the descendants of Cain (Jubal, etc.), and vocal music was continued by Abel's descendants until both were combined in Abel's "True Church" at the time of Moses and the Temple. Leaver (2017: 69–70) explains: "Luther envisages that music had a fundamental place in the worship of the 'true church' before the Fall, and that it was the simple combination of human voices singing praise to God. After the Fall, the descendants of Abel continued such vocal singing in the true worship of God, whereas the descendants of Cain employed instruments in their misdirected worship. Nevertheless, Luther appears to suggest that instrumental worship was introduced into the 'true church' by some of the descendants of Cain who chose to worship with the descendants of Abel."

For Luther, then, even though music was part of creation, it was a Divine Gift at the time of creation that was meant to be utilized in worship. This is further explained by Leaver (2017: 70): "For Luther the question of the origin of music cannot be answered simply in terms of history, chronology, or human progenitors; indeed, the question cannot be understood, let alone answered, without recourse to theology, since music per se was not invented by humans but rather created by God. Repeatedly in his writings Luther states that music is the *donum Dei*, the gift from God, and is therefore only secondarily a human art or science." Leaver (2017: 70) supports this contention with translations from Luther himself: "The gift of language combined with the gift of song was only given to man to let him know that he should praise God with both word and music[;] Music is an outstanding gift of God and next to theology[;] Music is God's greatest gift[;] Music is an endowment and gift of God, not a gift of men[;] Music, or the notes are a wonderful creation and gift of God." Therefore, the notion of music in its raw form as discovered by Jubal or Pythagoras, for example, is not really a human invention but a Divine Gift, as reaffirmed by Leaver (2017: 70) with this statement: "For Luther, therefore, music is a God-given benefit to humankind: it may be developed and refined in new ways, but the raw material of music—physical vibrations in the air, the proportions and relationships of different pitches and so forth—is absolutely and fundamentally the gift of God in creation."

Martin Luther wrote a beautiful poem, *Frau Musica* ("Lady Music"), that conveyed the notion of music as God's gift but also music as a female songstress (Goddess) or mistress always singing at his side. Leaver (2017: 74–75) has translated this work, from which a few lines are given here: "The best time of the year is mine when all the birds are singing fine. The heavens and the earth are filled with much good singing, clear, and skilled. Above all, the precious nightingale makes all now joyful overall with her delightful songs and lays for which she must be thanked always, but more so to God, our Maker, who carefully created her to be his own beloved songstress and of *musica* a mistress. Thus, day and night she always sings, untiring praise to God she brings. I too will sing my laud and praise, eternal thanks will I thus raise." According to Oskar Sohngen, as cited by Leaver (2017: 89), this poem asserts the reality of music as female in creation: "Oskar Sohngen rightly points out that Luther's personification of music as 'Frau Musica' in his vernacular poem is no mere allegory but rather the expression of the ontological reality that from the beginning of the world has been an essential element within God's creation, and it—"she"—continues to inspire and influence human lives."

Current studies in Lutheran theology continue to emphasize the many ways in which music is integrated within the core of Christian thought. For example, Miikka Antilla, in *Luther's Theology of Music: Spiritual Beauty and Pleasure* (2017: 13), focuses on music as an essential part of theological study: "Theology of music can be practiced in the different branches of theological studies; for example, exegetical studies of music can explain the musical expressions and instruments in the Old Testament and the way singing together was a part of the life of New Testament congregations." She then explains how systematic theology treats Luther's statements about music as theological statements; how systematic theology focuses on the use and meaning of these central concepts in the textual material: "Music is thus something essential, related to central concepts like Word of God, gift of God, or best gift of God."

The "Lutheran spirit" in music, embodying the theological premise that music as inherently a gift of God, has penetrated the European classical tradition to a monumental degree. It is not coincidental that many of the most deeply religious and prolific composers of the past four hundred years were born and raised Lutherans or were practicing Lutherans. While deserving more recognition, the beautiful choral works in the form of passions, masses, motets, Psalms, and oratorios of Lutheran composers Heinrich Schutz, Dietrich Buxtehude, Johann Pachelbel, and Georg Philip Telemann convey deep Christian piety and devotion. The Lutheran Georg Frideric Handel (1685–1759) won wide acclaim for his religious oratorios, including the *Messiah*, and the exceptional Bach family of Lutheran composers and musicians needs little introduction: Johann Sebastian Bach (1685–1750), elder brother Johann Christoph Bach, and sons Wilhelm Friedemann Bach and Carl Philipp Emanuel Bach.

The Lutheran convert Felix Mendelssohn-Bartholdy (1809–1847), influenced by attending the Lutheran philosopher Hegel's lectures on the glories of Bach, was responsible for the Bach revival in the early nineteenth century, while Lutheran-born Johannes Brahms (1833–1897) wrote religious choral works and a *German Requiem*. German opera composer Richard Wagner (1813–1883) and the principal Scandinavian composers, Edvard Grieg (1843–1907) and Jean Sibelius (1865–1957), were born Lutheran. Howard Hanson (1896–1981) was a respected Lutheran composer of the twentieth century. The overall "Lutheran phenomenon" in classical music, however, has not been fully researched. One catches a glimpse of Luther's influence in the confidential statement by Paul Nettl (1948: 37): "Luther restored and revived German song, and we may well say that the songs of Schubert, Brahms, Schumann, and Hugo Wolf would have been impossible without Luther." In addition, many figures associated with German Romanticism, aesthetics, linguistics, and the *Sturm und Drang* movement of literature and the arts were also Lutheran: Hamann, Herder, Goethe, Schiller, Holderlin, Novalis, Tieck, Wackenroder, E.T.A. Hoffman (*The Nutcracker*), Schlegel, and Schelling.

An impressive list of prominent Lutheran theologians over the past two centuries touched on music to varying degrees: Albrecht Ritschl, Adolf von Harnack (teacher of Barth), Wilhelm. Herrmann (teacher of Barth), Franz Overbeck (friend of Nietzsche), Ernst Troeltsch, Albert Schweitzer (musicologist), Rudolf Bultmann, Ernst Fuchs, Dietrich Bonhoeffer, Gerhard Ebeling, Wolfgang Pannenberg, and Paul Tillich (*Theology of Culture*). In addition, the Lutheran identity runs deep through the academic study of religion and is germane to the development of the Window Theory. As we recall from chapter 1, the founder of modern theology, renowned philosopher, aesthetician, and pioneer in the study of religion, Friedrich Schleiermacher (1768–1843), was also involved with music in his life and thought. Although born to a family of Reformed ministers, Schleiermacher was influenced by Moravian Pietism, a movement emerging out of the Lutheran church. He was active musically, singing in religious choirs and attending concerts. He was also influenced by Kant and the Schlegel brothers in his approach to aesthetics and the role of the arts in religious experience. In fact, the present-day study of theology and religion is indebted to Schleiermacher for his emphasis on "religious experience" in preference to earlier rational and moral comprehensions of the divine. He described religion as a "sense and taste for the infinite," and as a "feeling of absolute dependence." His early exposure to Lutheran Pietism paved the way for his deep appreciation of music as part of religious experience. In his work of 1799, *On Religion: Speeches to its Cultured Despisers* (1958: 51),

Schleiermacher compared religion to music: "Were I to compare religion in this respect with anything it would be with music."

Developing the theme of music in Schleiermacher's thought, Jonas Lundblad, in "Theomusical Subjectivity: Schleiermacher and the Transcendence of Immediacy" (2020: 101), aptly interprets Schleiermacher's association of music with an inner religious experience: "In the end Schleiermacher ascribes music (and dance) the potential to provide symbols of the particular 'inner world,' the most intimate manifestations and determinations of immediate self-consciousness." Further, Lundblad (2020: 96–97n34) identifies Pythagorean influences and points to a dialectic between feeling and the arts: "Schleiermacher's early aesthetics is deeply resonant with Pythagorean images of a *harmonia mundi*, a fact that simultaneously establishes a musical preference for harmony over against melody. However, this harmony is no longer pre-critically established through mathematical and rational procedures but through the immediate relations between self and the world, intuition and feeling, mind and body . . . Throughout the gradual development of his mature and comprehensive system of thought, Schleiermacher continued to assert the mutual kinship of music and religion as expressions of feeling (or immediate self-consciousness) . . . Schleiermacher's works suggest that the lasting profoundness of this paradigm lies in its dialectical nature, thus, in an emphasis that subjectivity and art are reciprocally transformative."

Rudolf Otto (1869–1937), the German Lutheran theologian highly influenced by Schleiermacher, also prioritized religious experience over reason and morality, including the experience of music. In terms of theology, Otto had been a member of the History of Religions School (*Religionsgeschichtliche Schule*), a term applied to a group of German Protestant theologians affiliated with Gottingen in the 1890s, including Lutherans Ernst Treoltsch and, later, Rudolf Bultmann. This school utilized the method of higher criticism regarding biblical texts, argued that Christianity was one religion among others, and professed that Christianity shares characteristics and historical features with other religions. In terms of the study of religion, Otto formulated many of the essential themes and ideas of religious phenomenology that further informed the Lutherans Gerardus van der Leeuw, Friedrich Heiler, and Joachim Wach. Other Lutheran scholars in the academic field of the History of Religions include Scandinavians W. Brede Kristensen, Nathan Soderblom, Geo Widingren, and Stig Wikander. Considered the prime instigator of the comparative study of myth and religion, German Orientalist Friedrich Max Muller, also a Lutheran, was influenced by Schelling and the liberal tradition in theology. Müller's concept that the infinite was present in all finite things was evidence of the influence of Schleiermacher's views. What stands out in our account at this point is the abiding connection, though often clandestine, between liberal theology, especially Lutheranism, music, and the modern academic study of religion.

British philosopher Roger Scruton (2020: 81) has encapsulated the various ideas discussed so far regarding the theology of music in his reflections on the musical perspective of Rudolf Otto: "It is an experience whose ineffability is part of what is valued: for it is a visitation from a sphere that cannot be reached by any merely human effort and cannot be known except in this way. It is a kind of gift, for which we cannot ask since we lack words to summon it. Hence, in usual religious parlance, it is identified as one manifestation of the grace of God. Could it be that music can capture this experience and make it imaginatively available to us ordinary mortals? I think this is what people have in mind when they have defended the view that music can reach the transcendental. Music can put us in the presence of something that has no place in this world, and which moves in a world of its own. And it can do this in a way that seems both orderly and personal, moving with a complete necessity that is also a kind of freedom."

Hindu Theology and Music

> Indian music . . . was always held to be but an extension and outward symbolization of the Omnipresent Praṇava Sound—OM—and utilized only for purposes of God attainment—the subject of musical compositions has rarely been anything but God and his glories.
>
> —Swami Śivānanda, *Music as Yoga*

We continue our discussion of the role of music in theology by focusing on the Hindu religious tradition, noting parallels regarding music as Divine Gift, principles of sacred sound, musical angels, and music in the afterlife among the gods. Hindu theology forms an essential part of understanding the nature and history of sacred sound and music in India. The history of Indian sacred music began thousands of years ago when sages contemplated the nature of the universe and discovered profound connections between heaven and earth. Divinely revealed in meditation, music and chant formed part of Vedic religion and extended its influence for millennia in Hindu traditions. The ancient texts of the Vedas and Upanishads (4000–1000 BCE) contain seminal information about chant and vocal utterances in relation to both sacrifices to the gods and metaphysical speculation on the origin of the creation through sound. The Vedas are collections of Mantras and hymns for the purpose of sacrifice, and are believed to be eternal, authorless, and the embodiment of the primeval sound that generated the universe.

The sacred syllable OM in the Vedas is associated with ritual and was a practical tool for invocation and application as a preface to the Mantras that accompanied oblations into the sacrificial fire. Before any ritual act, the intonation of sacred sound in the form of Mantra was necessary. Without Mantra, there was no sacrifice, and without OM there was no Mantra. The potencies of OM were generated from the use of vocal sound or chant in association with fire in Vedic sacrifices and were believed to interact with deities in charge of sectors of the universe. The concept of OM (A + U + M) was later enlarged into the metaphysical notion of sacred sound or Sound Absolute, first as Śabda-Brahman in the Upanishads and later as Nāda-Brahman in medieval Tantric traditions as well as in the theistic traditions of Vaishnavism, Śaivism, and Śaktism. Medieval Tantra and Sanskrit music texts introduced the concept of Nāda-Brahman as the source of music expressed in terms of Rāgas, melodic formulas, forming the basis of Indian music. For a general introduction, see Beck (2014); for more in-depth discussion, see Beck (1993, 2012).

Sacred sound as Nāda-Brahman became established as the primary metaphysical basis and origin of all music in the Hindu tradition. Musical texts discussed Nāda-Brahman as the foundation of musical sound, and Yoga texts used the term Nāda-Brahman for the musical sounds heard during deep meditation, as in Nāda Yoga. The universal concept of Nāda-Brahman thus indicated that God or the Supreme Truth contains the elemental of primal sound that can be approached through chant and music. As the sonic expression of Nāda-Brahman, OM is also the foundation of music. In ancient ritual, OM was chanted in a monotone, followed by verses from the Rig Veda chanted in three distinct tones or accents: Udatta, Anudatta, and Svarita. These notes were expanded to five or seven descending notes in the hymns (Sāmans) from the Sāma Veda (ca. 1000 BCE). As part of the evolution toward the present-day Indian scale, the original descending Sāma Veda scale was recast into a new ascending and descending seven-note structure, corresponding to the standard scale of seven notes known as the Svara-Saptaka ("seven notes")—Sa Re Ga Ma Pa Dha Ni—in the *Nāṭya Śāstra* of Bharata Muni and the *Dattilam*.

The original term used for the seven notes was Svara-Maṇḍala—circle of notes—and is coordinate with the idea of the "Mandala" as the circle of the Gods in the ancient Pūjā rituals of worship. In the *Nāradiya-Śikṣa* (first century BCE), we find how these seven ascending and descending notes were also evolved from the original three Vedic accents: Udatta into Ni and Ga, Anudatta into Re and Dha, and Svarita into Sa, Ma, and Pa. The seven notes are named metaphorically after the sounds of birds and animals: Sa–peacock, Re–bull, Ga-ram, Ma–crane, Pa–cuckoo, Dha–horse, and Ni–elephant. Five of the notes—Re Ga Ma Dha Ni—are also modified with raised or lowered half-notes (like the Western sharp and flat notes) to create multiple variations of scale formulas, while the tonic C (Sa) and the dominant G (Pa) remain fixed. Still employed today, these seven notes roughly correspond to the Western Solfeggio discussed above or simply the diatonic scale of C D E F G A B. Principal differences are that the Western notes do not derive from a single syllable as in OM, and there is no harmony or chord structure in the Indian system of music.

Although traced to the origin of music and chant, the sacred syllable OM continues to have a lasting connection with Indian music performance, in that just as the chanting of OM begins most forms of worship in homes and temples, classical and devotional songs begin with the utterance of the base note or tonic in the form of OM. Whether amateur or professional, Indian musicians consistently begin recitals with OM as a matter of respect for their Guru and tradition. Even singers who do not follow an Indian religion—for example, Muslims—adhere to this custom. OM is uttered in a steady drone-like sound on the tonic note suitable for the singer's vocal range, which is manifest in the subsequent gamut of notes relevant to the Rāga or melodic formula employed in the song or composition. It is understood that all the notes in Indian music—including those produced by instruments—flow out of the initial OM. As the musician serves as the vessel for the manifestation of Nāda-Brahman, the voice acts as an access point for singers, and the hands and fingers for string, flute, and drum players. At the conclusion of the song or composition, the voice or instrument fades away on the drone in recollection of OM.

Indian classical music is known as Saṅgīta, including three divisions of vocal (*gītā*), instrumental (*vādya*), and dance (*nritya*). The oldest surviving texts are the *Nāṭya Śāstra* by Bharata Muni and the *Dattilam* by Dattila (ca. 400–200 BCE), which provide evidence of the music performed in sacred dramas, festivals, courtly ceremonies, and temple rituals. The ancient epics and histories contain descriptions of temple musicians and dancers who performed this music for the pleasure of the deities. First described in the *Nātya Śāstra* (ca. third century BCE), Sangīta is performed by the gods and thus considered divine in origin. Building on earlier scales described in this text, the concept of the Rāga and its relation to the eternal principle of Nāda-Brahman appeared in a ninth-century musical text imbued with Tantra philosophy, the *Brihaddeśī* by Matanga Muni. Gradually, Rāgas as specific melodic patterns of ascending and descending notes were classified and identified with times of the day and seasons. The thirteenth-century treatise *San gīta Ratnākara* of Śārngadeva (1978: 108–109, 115) proclaimed Nāda-Brahman as the source of musical notes, dance, and language, and identified it with the gods Brahmā, Vishnu, and Śiva: "We worship Nāda-Brahman, that incomparable bliss which is immanent in all the creatures as intelligence and is manifest in the phenomenon of this universe. Indeed, through the worship of Nāda are worshipped gods Brahmā, Vishnu, and Śiva, since essentially they are one with it . . . Nāda is differentiated into twenty-two grades which, because of their audibility, are known as Śrutis. From the Śrutis arise the seven musical notes."

Viewed as Divine Gift, Sangīta was similar in kind to the music performed and enjoyed in Lord Indra's court in Svarga or heaven. Viewed as a replica of heavenly archetypes, this ancient religious music was primarily vocal but included instruments such as the Vina (harp or zither), flutes, drums, and cymbals. The original name for music was Gandharva Sangīta, named after the group of heavenly angels, called Gandharvas and led by Nārada Rishi. Music, drama, and worship are described by ancient authors as being received on earth as part of heavenly dramatic performance and worship of the great gods of Brahmā, Vishnu, and Śiva (Trimūrti). Nārada Rishi was the son of Brahmā, who resided in heaven but was capable of journeying throughout the universe. The Gandharvas were accompanied by their wives, the dancing Apsarās, and the Kinnaras on musical instruments. The arts, including vocal music, dance, and instrumental music, were divine, performed by divine beings. Nārada is considered the inventor of the Vina and the sage who instructed human beings in Gandharva Sangīta, having learned it from the Goddess Sarasvatī who had received it from Brahmā himself. In other accounts, Śiva is the original instructor of sacred music to Brahmā.

The Goddess Sarasvatī, depicted with the Vina instrument in hand, is the divine patroness of music and receives the veneration of all students and performers. Brahmā, the creator of the universe, is said to have fashioned

Indian music out of the ingredients of the Sāma Veda and plays the hand cymbals. Vishnu, the Preserver who sounds the conch shell, plays the flute as Krishna. Śiva, as Naṭarāja, plays the Damaru drum during the dance of cosmic dissolution. Each of the above instruments symbolizes Nāda-Brahman and forms an indispensable part of each Deity in veneration. Music is double-edged: a vehicle awarding liberation (Moksha) that also pleases the senses. As a form of religious practice, Sangīta is more efficacious than other forms of observance, including the chanting of the names of God on rosary beads (*japa*). The *Nātya Śāstra* (36.27) confirms: "I have heard from the God of Gods (Indra) and afterwards from Śankara (Śiva) that music vocal as well as instrumental, is in fact a thousand times superior to bath [in holy waters] and to Japa" (Beck 2012: 88–89). Sangīta also had the power to remove evil forces and defilements.

Hindu religious music incorporates a simple aesthetic in the form of the concept of Rasa ("essence," "flavor"), considered part of Indian aesthetics and dramatic theory. Rasa is central to the experience of music and the encounter with the divine and may be traced back to the ancient period. Since the Upanishads describe Brahman (Absolute or God) as full of Rasa or aesthetic delight (*raso vai sah; Taittirīya Upanisad* 2.7.1), the performing arts, including theater and music, are believed to be infused with Rasa and closely aligned with religion. A primary goal of music is hence to experience divine Rasa and is meant for communion with a chosen deity.

Bharata Muni, in *Nātya Śāstra* (ca. 400 BCE), was the first to outline the various aesthetic sentiments (Rasa) associated with drama and the worship of deities. Rasas are the artistic or aesthetic expressions of emotional experiences that are otherwise found to be universal traits of humanity, like love, compassion, and heroism. As explained by Adya Rangacharya (2003: 54, 56, 142), in *Nātya Śāstra* (6.15, 39–45), Bharata Muni enumerates the eight Rasas: Śriṅgāra–erotic, Hāsya–comic, Karuṇā–compassion, Raudra–terror, Vīra–heroic, Bhayānaka–fear, Bibhatsā–disgust, and Adbhuta–wonder. *Nātya Śāstra* 19.38–40 also tied the Rasas with the seven individual notes of the musical scale (Sa Ri Ga Ma Pa Dha Ni). A ninth Rasa, Śānta Rasa (peace) was added by the Kashmiri philosopher Abhinavagupta in the tenth century CE in conformity with the nondual and formless nature of the divine as endorsed by schools of Kashmiri Śaivism. A tenth Rasa, Bhakti Rasa (devotional love), was articulated as a unique religious category by the Vaishnava theologian Rūpa Goswami in the sixteenth century.

In terms of communion with the divine and the experience of Rasa, over roughly a thousand years there was an immense outpouring of devotional poetry in vernacular dialects that addressed nearly every deity in the Hindu pantheon. Apart from classical singing, which is also religious (see Beck 2019), the most popular forms of devotional singing are known as Kīrtan and Bhajan. These may involve lyrics of praise or simply the repetition of divine names. For more information, see "Kīrtan and Bhajan in Bhakti Traditions" (Beck 2010).

The great Hindu poets were also singer-musicians, and the great musicians in India were devout Hindus. These include the Haridasa saints like Narahari Tirtha, Śrīpadarāya, and Purandara Dāsa who wrote songs or Kīrtanas in Kannada language expressing devotion to Lord Hari (Vishnu or Krishna), Annamāchārya in Telugu to Śrī Venkateśvara (Vishnu), Śyāma Śāstri in Telugu devoted to the Goddess, and Tyāgarāja in Telugu to Lord Rāma. In the North, Sūr Dās, Nanda Dās, Paramānand Dās, and Swami Haridās wrote songs in Braj Bhāshā about Lord Krishna; Śrī Hita Harivaṁśa in Braj Bhāshā about Rādhā and Krishna; Tulasi Dās in Avadhi to Lord Rāma; Tukarām and Nāmdev in Marathi expressing devotion to Krishna; Meera Bai in Hindi and Rājasthāni to Krishna; Govinda Dās in Brajbuli about Krishna, Chandi Dās in Bengali expressing devotion to Rādhaā and Krishna, and Rāmprasad Sen who wrote songs in Bengali in praise of the Goddess Kālī. While there are biographies of many of these singer-saints in the native languages, two of the most famous, Sūr Dās in the North and Tyāgarāja in the South, have been the topic of American scholarship in terms of music and religion: see John Stratton Hawley, *Sūr Dās: Poet, Singer, Saint* (1985), and William J. Jackson, *Tyāgarāja and the Renewal of Tradition; Translations and Reflections* (1994).

In traditional Hindu belief, music is understood to be present among the gods and the blessed in the Vedic and Hindu afterlife. In *The Hymns of the Rig Veda* (X.135.7: 636), Ralph T. H. Griffith (1973: 636) states in translation: "Here is the seat where Yama dwells, that which is called the Home of Gods: Here minstrels blow the flute for him: here he is glorified with songs." This reference is significant as music in most of the Hindu traditions is believed to continue after death in heaven or in the Home of the Gods. R. C. Zaehner, in *The Dawn and Twilight of Zoroastrianism* (2002: 132–133), describes this "musical heaven" of the Rig Veda, and noted similarities with the aforementioned Zoroastrian "House of Song":

> In the Rig Veda Yama is the first man only in the sense he is the first of the immortals to choose a mortal destiny . . . Yama chooses death of his own free will: he lays aside his immor-

tality so that, himself passing through the valley of death, he may once again join the immortals and feast and carouse with them forever "under the fair-leafed tree." This is the abode of Yama called the palace of the devas: [here] is his flute blown, and [here] is he surrounded with song (*gīrbhih*) . . . In these passages from the Rig Veda there are some curious parallels to the Avesta. Yama's path is also called *gavyuti* or "pasture-land," and the Avestan equivalent of this word, *gaoyaoiti*, is used of the "wide pastures" of Mithra . . . His palace is the abode (*māna*) of the devas (=Avestan daevas) and in it he is surrounded with song (*gīr-*). So too is Zoroaster's own heaven known as the House of Song (*garo (de)māna*) . . . As the House of Song is the highest heaven in the Zoroastrian literature, so is the abode of Yama in which the dead are assembled higher than the two heavens of the [Vedic] sun-god Savitr.

An interesting phenomenon regarding the divinity of the flute is in the Vaishnava division of Hindu theology and devotion. This involves the narrative of Krishna, his flute playing, and his eternal dance in the spiritual world, the famous Rāsa Dance. As a divine manifestation of God who appeared on earth roughly five thousand years ago, Krishna performed a sacred round dance accompanied by singing and playing of musical instruments. Krishna, one of the most beloved of Hindu deities, appears with flute in hand, inviting all devotees to join in this dance both in spirit on earth and as an eternal pastime in the afterlife.

Celebrated throughout India during the season of the full moon in mid-October, the earthly round dance known as the Rāsa Dance is a manifestation of the timeless celestial dance involving Krishna, Rādhā, and his Gopī companions. Saturated in eternal joy, the Rāsa Dance, as described by Vaishnava saints, was a superb musical event that entailed singing, playing instruments, and dancing. The aspiration of the advanced Krishna devotee is direct participation in or observation of the eternal pastime of the Rāsa Dance, wherein Krishna attracts all the ladies of his native Braj with his flute in a round-dance on a full-moon night of autumn. The original Sanskrit sources of Krishna's pastimes have been the object of study by generations of traditional Bhakti scholars. The literary narrative of the Rāsa Dance reached its final form within the Sanskrit Purana genre, in the *Bhāgavata-Purāna*, by the ninth century CE. The complete narrative in five chapters (10. 29–34), translated by Graham Schweig, is in *Dance of Divine Love: India's Classic*

Sacred Love Story: The Rāsa Līlā of Krishna (2005). As described by Schweig (2005: 182), "Among all scriptural texts of India, originating with the Vedas, the Rāsa Līlā episode becomes the most important revelation of supreme love. As a story, the Rāsa Līlā has a beginning and an end. As a sacred love story, however, it is the timeless dance in which God and the soul lose themselves forever in the *rhythms, melodies,* and movements of divine love. The drama of the Rāsa is a celebration of souls joining together to glorify God's unlimited power to love, and further, of God's capacity to love each soul intimately." Accenting the theme of divine love, Schweig (2005: 183) contends that the revelation of this event is paramount for the deepest understanding of the nature of God, which is grounded in musical and dance performance: "This love of the divine couple [Rādhā and Krishna] becomes a *song*, as well as a *dance*, and the reader is invited to join the celebration, along with the chorus of *celestial singers*."

A rare text of the sixteenth century, *Ānanda-Vrindāvana-Campū* by Kavi Karnapūr (Bhanu Swami 1999), reveals lesser-known information about the music of the Rāsa Dance. While Krishna is the musician and flute player *par excellence*, in this text Rādhā and the Gopīs as well as other participants are said to be very skilled in music: "At the end of the dance, all the lotus-eyed Gopīs tightly embraced Krishna. Trembling in ecstasy, they sang another Rāga in loud voices, conveying their intense longing" (1999: 328). Yet their skills dwarfed in comparison to those of Rādhā and Krishna: "In a mixture of joy, enthusiasm, and a desire to outdo each other, Rādhā and Krishna, overcome with attraction, sang the *ālāpa* (introductory part) with the initial note (*graha*) and the sixth note. They sang all the notes of the ascending and descending scales with *gamaka* (trills or wavering). This invoked various tastes, induced more singing and dancing, and spread auspiciousness all around. It did not however appear to be a manifestation of any material skill" (1999: 329). Moreover, the singing and dancing were accompanied by instruments: "The instrumentalists, situated outside the circle, assisted the pastime of the Lord by playing according to the dancing of the Gopīs" (1999: 328).

The *Saṅgīta Dāmodara* by Śubhaṅkara (1960), another sixteenth-century Vaishnava text, describes how all earthly music emerged out of the Rāsa Dance, and why there are thirty-six Rāgas. Saṅgīta began with the enchanting sound emanating from Krishna's flute (*muralī-nāda-mohitam*), which stimulated the creation of sixteen thousand Rāgas by the equally thousands of Gopīs: "The Rāgas are so-called because they attract the heart of all in the three worlds. Each of the sixteen thousand Gopīs started singing separately before Krishna and thus were born sixteen thousand Rāgas. Of them only thirty-six are well-known in the world and even of this number a gradual decline is noticed as time rolls by" (1960: 16). While Śubhankara lists the thirty-six Rāgas and Rāginīs, he acknowledges that the remaining Rāgas (out of 16,000) may still exist in other parts of the world: "Some affirm that all the Rāgas certainly exist and they are current in the countries north of the Meru [Himalaya] as well as in the countries situated in the east, west and south and those surrounded by the ocean." This notion helps one understand the perpetual aim to enlarge the repertoire of Rāgas in Indian classical music over the centuries by drawing upon regional tunes (i.e., folk songs) and "raising them up" or refining them as Rāgas, in a sense rescuing them from oblivion, such that there are now roughly six hundred Rāgas in the common stock among musicians. As an interesting comparative note, the tradition of Jewish mysticism known as Kabbalah teaches that the universe was torn into fragments at creation and must be repaired through a process known as Tikkun Olam. For the musician, this means that divine music in the form of "sparks" (melodies) remains scattered throughout the various countries, and the duty of the musician is to collect the fallen melodies that lie unredeemed throughout the world, perform them, and thus assist in re-assembling the cosmos.

Many types of sacred musical performance have developed in the Hindu tradition. One important genre of temple music still practiced in the Vaishnava realm is Samāj Gāyan, a form of group singing that closely follows the sacred text. The poems describing the Rāsa Dance are regularly sung as part of temple liturgy in the holy pilgrimage town of Vrindaban in northern India. Richard David Williams, in "Sounding Out the Divine: Musical Practice as Theology in Samāj Gāyan" (2020: 357), explains how singing this style of music is on par with theology: "Music, sound arts, and practices are not merely decorative: they also function as modes of 'doing' theology, in terms of how people make sense of another reality and engage with it meaningfully. Music can be a gift to a god, a bridge to another world, a tool for realigning the self, and many other things besides. By thinking in terms of a musical assemblage, rather than an autonomous musical object, it is possible to consider the social and intellectual relationships that give meaning to a sonic practice, and how a musical event can disrupt quotidian experience." For more information on this music, including audio recordings, see Beck (2011).

The subject of sacred sound and music in Hinduism is highly relevant to Musicology of Religion, especially since most elements of Indian music remain extant. While listeners in the West were first exposed to the mystical sounds of Rāga melodies played on the Indian Sitar and Sarod beginning in the 1960s, few at the time were cognizant of the links to the sacred syllable OM or the Mantras chanted alongside ancient fire sacrifices. In response to the growing desire of America's youth to reach out beyond traditional Western forms of religion and the arts, visiting Gurus and Yoga teachers from India began teaching about OM recitation, the chanting of Sanskrit Mantras, and the singing of Kīrtan and Bhajan songs as part of Yoga instruction. Some well-known figures of this period include Maharishi Mahesh Yogi (founder of Transcendental Meditation), Swami Vishnudevānanda (disciple of Swami Śivānanda and founder of Śivānanda Ashram), A. C. Bhaktivedānta Swami (founder of the Hare Krishna Movement or ISKCON, and promoter of the famous Hare Krishna Mahāmantra), and Swami Satchidānanda (disciple of Swami Śivānanda and founder of Integral Yoga Institute and Yogaville), each of whom established Ashrams or living communities to teach and propagate their methods of Yoga and self-realization. At the same time, celebrated Indian musicians such as Pandit Ravi Shankar and Ustad Ali Akbar Khan performed and taught their students classical music on instruments such as the Sitar and Sarod. And as the physical practice of Yoga became an international phenomenon, along with the singing of devotional chants and songs, it is possible now to reaffirm the original spiritual intention and formation of both Yoga and Indian music, and to further elucidate their close connection.

One of the first Yoga teachers to settle in America, in 1920, was Paramahansa Yogānanda (1893–1952), who developed what became known as the Self-Realization Fellowship. In his best-selling work, *Autobiography of a Yogi: The Classic Story of One of India's Greatest Spiritual Thinkers* (2016 [1946]: 131), Yogānanda suggests an ancient alliance between the syllable OM (AUM) and music or sound that can be heard through special faculties taught in Yoga: "The ancient Rishis discovered these laws of sound alliance between nature and man. Because nature is an objectification of AUM, the Primal Sound or Vibratory Word, man can obtain control over all natural manifestations using certain mantras or chants. The deeper aim of the early Rishi-musicians was to blend the singer with the Cosmic Song which can be heard through awakening of man's occult spinal centers."

The name of Swami Śivānanda (1887–1963) is key to the transmission of Yoga to the West and the principal link between the pre-1960 period and the present explosion of Yoga in the world. Though he did not visit the United States, Swami Śivānanda's teachings were a far-reaching influence through his disciples who brought his message to America and the Western world. His most renowned disciples in the West include Swami Vishnudevānanda, Swami Satchidānanda, Swami Chidānanda, and Swami Nādabrahmānanda. In his seminal book, *Music as Yoga* (1956: 6–7), Swami Śivānanda explained the relation between Yoga and music by means of OM: "What distinguished Indian music . . . It was always held to be but an extension and outward symbolization of the Omnipresent Praṇava Sound—OM—and utilized only for purposes of God attainment—a feature it has retained to the present-day, as will be evident from the fact that, up to the end of the last century, the subject of musical compositions has rarely been anything but God and his glories." He also introduced the notion of Nāda to Western readers: (17). "Music attracts every living being. Wherefrom has music derived this mighty power? From the Supreme Music of Brahman, the Sacred Praṇava [OM]. Listen to the vibration of the Tambura or the Veena: do you hear the majestic Praṇava-Nāda? All the musical notes are blended beautifully into this Praṇava. All the musical notes spring from this Praṇava. Music is intended to reverberate this Praṇava-Nāda in your heart." In terms of Yoga terminology, he identifies the physical Yoga with music (18): "Music is a synthesis of the various Yogas or paths to God-realization. Music itself is Haṭha Yoga Sādhana: for it involves a good amount of control and regulation of breath. There is deep and full breathing; and this greatly strengthens the lungs and purifies the blood, too." Delving with more depth into the esoteric aspects, he explained how musical notes corresponded to nerve centers or channels in the body (18–19): "The various musical notes have their own corresponding Nadis (subtle channels in the vital sheath of the body) in the vital centers within—the Kundalini Chakras—and music vibrates these Nadis, purifies them and awakens the psychic and spiritual power dormant in them."

In line with the teachings of the Yoga teachers, renowned sitarist Pandit Ravi Shankar (1920–2012) introduced sacred sound concepts like Nāda-Brahman in his autobiography, *My Music, My Life* (1968: 17): "Our tradition teaches us that sound is God—Nāda Brahma. That is, musical sound and the musical experience are steps to the realization of the self. We view music as a kind of spiritual discipline that raises one's inner being to divine peacefulness and bliss. We are taught that one of the fundamental goals a Hindu works toward in his lifetime is acknowledge of the true meaning of the universe—its unchanging, eternal essence—and this is realized first by a complete knowledge of one's self and one's own nature. The highest aim of our music is to reveal the essence of the universe it reflects, and the ragas are among the means by which this essence can be apprehended. Thus, through music, one can reach God."

As important practices of religious traditions that reflect and express theological principles and structures, the next chapter will discuss ritual and liturgy in relation to the Musicology of Religion.

Chapter Six

Liturgical Studies and Music

> Music is integral to the expression of liturgical content and bodily engagement. Text and music together—musical liturgy and sung prayer—are appreciated for their power to illuminate the mind and move the heart.
>
> —Mary M. Schaefer, "What is Liturgical Worship?"

> Sound—voice or music—constitutes a sacred link with the transcendent being. The religious significance of the sacrifice of sound is global, at once evocation and adoration, invocation, and praise, from the syllable "OM" which contains within it all the acoustic powers, to the vocal expression of a Kyrie or an Alleluia.
>
> —Joseph Gelineau, "The Path of Music"

> Ritual spaces of sound have a particular kind of acoustics, a special soundscape that transports any listener to another world . . . Music, in this context, . . . becomes a ritual.
>
> —Axel Michaels, *Homo Ritualis*

In the quest to understand the intrinsic bond between religion and music, one of the most promising areas of inquiry is the subfield of theology known as Liturgical Studies. This chapter will indicate fruitful directions of Liturgical Studies and how they enhance the Musicology of Religion. But while Liturgical Studies is often assumed to have connection to Ritual Studies, we begin with a brief outline of this area that has more broadly answered the call to explain and interpret the near universal tendency of human beings to engage in ritual behavior. Attaching itself primarily to anthropology, Ritual Studies scholarship has indeed revealed the central importance of ritual in nearly all human culture and civilization. Accordingly, we will first offer remarks about the study of ritual.

Ritual Studies

> Music-making and ritualization must be interpreted as an integrated whole. Music unfolds not only in ritual but as ritual, as a mode of ritual performance. An assembly's musical performance inevitably influences the whole ritual process.
>
> —Mary E. McGann, *Exploring Music as Worship and Theology*

Regarding the ubiquity of ritual, anthropologist Mary Douglas (1970: 78) observed that, "As a social animal, man is a ritual animal. If ritual is suppressed in one form it crops up in others, more strongly and more intense the social interaction." Taking this notion further by linking ritual directly to religion, new research in Ritual Studies scholarship lends more credence to the fact that ritual becomes increasingly identified with all religious behavior, even that which is normatively "anti-ritual." For example, dispelling older conceptions of the anti-ritual nature of Zen Buddhism, Steven Heine and Dale S. Wright, in *Zen Ritual: Studies in Zen Buddhist Theory in Practice* (2007), have clearly articulated the role of ritual in Zen. Although the Beat Poets had written about the demythologized, anti-ritualized spirit of Zen, this collection of essays reveals how Zen is inextricably associated with varieties of ritual behavior. Yet while the field of Ritual Studies includes broad and integrative approaches, attempts to incorporate music in ritual theory have remained sporadic and undeveloped within the discipline.

If there is a modicum of ritual in Zen Buddhism, then by comparison there is an immense surplus of ritual in Hinduism, as revealed in *Homo Ritualis: Hindu Ritual and its Significance for Ritual Theory* (2015), where author Axel Michaels develops the notion of *homo ritualis*, the ritual human. In a multitude of instances, Michaels (2015: 146–147) reveals the close identification of ritual and the arts, in this case music: "Ritual spaces of sound have a particular kind of acoustics, a special soundscape that transports any listener to another world. Such rituals are separations in space and time from daily life, and music enables the separation without simply being a background. Music, in this context, is neither just ornamental nor is it program music; rather, music itself becomes a ritual (at least in religious rituals) in that it creates singular, elevated spaces of sound that can be bodily sensed."

One comprehensive compendium of theories and methods in Ritual Studies is the volume of essays edited by Jens Kreinath, Jan Snoek, and Michael Stausberg, entitled *Theorizing Rituals: Issues, Topics, Approaches, Concepts* (2008). By way of a useful summation, Jan Snoek (2008: 13), in his article "Defining Rituals," offers a series of characteristics of ritual: "Ritual behavior is a particular mode of behavior, distinguished from common behavior. Its performers are (at least part of) its own audience. In general, all human actions can be part of ritual behavior, including speech acts. However, in each particular case the large majority of these will be traditionally sanctioned as proper ritual actions. Most ritual behavior takes place at specific places and/or specific times. Most ritual behavior is more formally stylized, structured, and standardized than most common behavior. Most ritual behavior is based on a script [written or oral]. Most ritual behavior is to some extent purposeful and symbolically meaningful for its participants. At least those playing an active part consider themselves to be participating in non-common behavior." While a ceremonial is the total configuration of ceremonies for any ritual occasion, the "ritual" may be the actual script or playbook, oral or written, outlining each step of any ritual procedure. The mysterious omission here, however, is the almost universal presence of chant and music in ritual.

Ritual Studies has been associated most importantly with the social sciences and the methods of anthropology. Although pursued in religious studies, the general viewpoint places it within the domain of the Mirror Theory of religion, in which religion and music are each considered as one of several "cases of culture." However, in the field of Liturgical Studies, as part of theological studies, there is a greater attention to the enduring and widespread sonic and musical dimension of ritual activity. This is also where an interest in phenomenology of religion and the work of Rudolf Otto and Mircea Eliade has been consistently on the rise, including an adherence to the Window Theory of religion and the close rapprochement between religion and music. Theologians and historians working in the field of Liturgical Studies, emerging in renewed form out of conservative reactions to the delimiting of the Sacred Liturgy after Vatican II, have expanded this field beyond its Christian base, and is one of the most developed and useful disciplines for the study of ritual and music as part of religion.

The phenomenology of religion has increasingly become the focus of theologians in their study of liturgy and ritual worship. For example, theologian J. D. Crichton, in *The Study of Liturgy* (1978: 5), endorsed Rudolf Otto's paradigm of the holy in relation to worship: "Worship is seen to have a value and significance of its own that cannot be explained or explained away as superstition or magic or the expression of fear. Worship is a religious phenomenon, a reaching out through the fear that always accompanies the sacred to the *mysterium* conceived as *tremendum* but also *fascinans*, because behind it and in it there is an intuition of the Transcendent. But if in this sense worship is profoundly religious it is also profoundly human."

Earlier, theologian Louis Bouyer, in *Rite and Man: Natural Sacredness and Christian Liturgy* (1963: 31), drew upon the work of Mircea Eliade in his treatment of ritual as a universal and permanent characteristic of human behavior: "More effectively than anyone else, Eliade has helped us to understand that the religious attitude is not merely a primitive attitude of man in the face of reality. It is a permanent attitude. For it is the relation of man to his whole experience. Through that relation man discovers the world as a totality which is also a unity, and a unity perceived as being at once both immanent and transcendent . . . The history of comparative religions has had to recognize the fact that religion is a permanent, irreducible, and generally dominating element in all human experience."

The raison d'etre of ritual is that rituals were originally the creation of the gods, as explained by Bouyer (1963: 66): "Rites exist precisely as rites because it is believed that if they can be instituted at all, it is the gods who have instituted them and are the real agents of the rites, working through and beyond the action of the priests . . . This is why at all times and in all places, rites are considered to be the work of the gods. The men who celebrate these rites would not celebrate them as they do if they thought that they were themselves their authors."

Parallel to the apparent connection between religion and music, Bouyer (1963: 53) reflected on the wider natural connection between words and deeds in ritual context: "Sacred words and sacred actions are as a matter of fact always found joined together. But in just as many ways as they are found joined together, so it would seem they have that many values and meanings. Their constant connection, however, already indicates their original bearing and, also, what is essentially permanent about them beneath the wide variety of forms in which they are found. If words and rites are distinct and are to a certain extent reciprocally opposed, their constant connection must mean a natural relationship."

There indeed appears to be a kind of "spiritual balance" between word and rite that Bouyer (1963: 61–62) claims must be recovered to experience the primordial mystery underlying the performance of ritual: "In the ritual itself actions must be spiritualized by the words. If the meaning of the ritual is not enlightened by an authentic divine word, it degenerates into magic or simple superstition. But the action should not on that account be reduced to a mere clothing of abstract ideas. Otherwise, there is no longer any ritual at all but at most a kind of pious charade. Therefore, it is the meaning of the ritual symbol which must first be recovered if the words themselves are to become again the words of the divine mystery and not a simple formula which, substituted for reality, can no longer attain it." Like the separation between music and religious experience, the negative effect for the ritual experience is the radical separation of word and rite, generating for Bouyer (1963: 65–66) a kind of "false intellectualism" that lacks the original divine inspiration: "Rituals are never artificial compositions, the work of theologians who first think in the abstract . . . Quite the contrary, it is everywhere evident that the rites are first and the theological constructions so subordinate to them that they regularly flow from them . . . Rites are not actions that are themselves more or less indifferent and which have been by sheer compulsion impregnated with a meaning for which they were in no way prepared. A ritual action, far from being a late offspring of a highly intellectualized religion that has to have recourse to gestures to regain contact with the simple-minded, is the most spontaneous and original manifestation of religion." In this sense, religion is not the result of speculation or abstract thought but derives only from lived experience: "From this ritual action, the later notions about religion itself are gradually derived. A living rite is not something that has been coldly worked out so that religious ideas which have been put together in the quiet of one's study may have some external manifestation. It is the immediate, primordial creation of religiously minded men in which they have actively realized their effective connection with the divinity before they explain this connection to themselves." Accordingly, Bouyer warned against two extremes of imbalance as situations to be avoided, namely meaningless rituals and its opposite, abstract speculation without ritual practice. The work of Bouyer is thus doubly significant in affirming the importance of seeing beyond the mere empirical manifestation of ritual and intuiting the depth of the sacred within ritual, and thus within the liturgical action involving music.

In similar fashion, scholars of liturgy have continued to stress the close association between myth (narrative words) and ritual. Aidan Kavanagh (1973: 148–149) supported this point by explaining that myth was the "conceiving" aspect, and ritual the "enacting" aspect: "Both myth and ritual thus appear to me as strictly correlative and inseparable junctions: their reciprocal union is what I mean by cult. The outcome of cult, so understood, is what I understand as culture." Marking a turning point for the Roman Catholic faith, as *Vatican Council II: The Conciliar and Post Conciliar Documents* (1963–1965) on "Sacred Music" reveal, the close and necessary connection between the divine word and musical expression became a directive for all types of liturgical activity, including the sacraments (1975: 82, 84): "Liturgical worship is given a more noble form when it is celebrated in song. . . . The unity of hearts is more commonly achieved by the union of voices . . . One cannot find anything more religious and more joyful in sacred celebrations than a whole congregation expressing its faith and devotion in song." To build a more solid case for all authentic liturgical activity that included music, the Church needed to situate its own liturgical tradition within the broader inherent sacrality of the universe. And to work this cause to its real fruition, the phenomenology of religion became an effective tool, as culled from the writings of Otto, van der Leeuw, and Mircea Eliade.

As the interest in Ritual Studies is continuing to blossom in the academic world, with special conferences and journals devoted to its research, social scientists have duly recognized the importance of religion as a signature component of ritual. In recent years, the famed anthropologist Roy A. Rappaport (1999: 1) has stated the unavoidable reason for its importance: "The absolute ubiquity of religion, however defined, supports the attribution of such profound significance to it. No society known to anthropology or history is devoid of what reasonable observers would agree is religion." As a social scientist, Rappaport's investigations into religion have yielded many profound insights relating to ritual, including the revelation that notions of the sacred and the numinous owe their very origin to ritual itself. In his important study *Ritual and Religion in the Making of Humanity* (1999: 3), he spearheaded the approach to ritual whereby the very concepts of the numinous and the sacred, as central elements of religion, are concluded to be "creations of ritual": "Religion's major conceptual and experiential constituents, the sacred, the numinous, the occult and the divine, and their integration into the Holy, are creations of ritual. To put the matter into logical rather than causal terms, these constituents are *entailments* of the *form* which constitutes ritual." And though music is not discussed in his work, Rappaport builds a clear case for the ubiquity of religion and its connection to ritual by drawing on the work of phenomenologists of religion such as Rudolf Otto among others.

Liturgical Studies

> All our singing is a singing and praying with the great liturgy that spans the whole of creation.
>
> —Joseph Cardinal Ratzinger, *The Spirit of the Liturgy*

As an active field grounded in Catholic and Protestant Christian tradition as well as in Judaism, Liturgical Studies is rapidly expanding to include non-Western traditions. When seen in cross-cultural perspective, the role of music often parallels the role of worship in religion. And when music is understood as sacred or "religious," it functions within the ritual or liturgy in a real relationship to what is of absolute value to believers, such as the sacred or a transcendent reality. Thus, almost all liturgical action in religion involves music and chant. The obvious presence of "liturgy" in many other religious traditions expands the theoretical possibilities for the presence of 'liturgical music' worldwide, as current opinions in Liturgical Studies are moving toward endorsement of music as a central element in all religious action. One impetus for this can be found in the statements of the Second Vatican Council, in the 1963 Constitution on the Sacred Liturgy: "In certain parts of the world, especially mission lands, there are people who have their own musical traditions, and these play a great part in their religious and social life. For this reason, due importance is to be attached to their music and a suitable place is to be given to it" (cited in Mary Collins 1989: 4). Accordingly, Roman Catholicism has embraced many varieties of folk and world music as part of the liturgy. The broader Christian tradition has also embraced diversity in liturgy, as found in the number of non-Christian entries in Paul Bradshaw's *The New Westminster Dictionary of Liturgy and Worship* (2002), which includes Jewish, Islamic, Hindu, Buddhist, Sikh, and Shinto worship. In each case, the presence of music and chant is briefly woven into the descriptions of the ritual and liturgical dimensions.

The term "liturgy" (from *laos*, "people," and *ergos*, "work" or "action") is understood within Liturgical Studies to be a series of rites that combine word, music, action, symbol, and/or object that is performed on behalf of a group. This most often refers to the public ritual or worship of a religious community performed by priests or other functionaries. The term "paraliturgical" denotes private or individual rituals that are nonetheless tied symbolically to larger public liturgies, such as rites of passage and other domestic ceremonies.

As a welcome introductory statement for the study of liturgy, theologian Joseph Gelineau (1978: 441) has affirmed the embedded nature of singing and music in all liturgies: "The liturgy is the shared activity of a people gathered together. No other sign brings out this communal dimension so well as singing." In fact, his ecumenical perspective indicates profound restructuring of the categories of sound, music, and sacrifice, as he states his premise with examples from the Bible and eastern religion (Gelineau 1989: 137): "Sound—voice or music—constitutes a sacred link with the transcendent being. The religious significance of the sacrifice of sound is global, at once evocation and adoration, invocation, and praise, from the syllable 'OM' which contains within it all the acoustic powers, to the vocal expression of a Kyrie or an Alleluia. The sacrifice of sound is at the root of all cults containing song and music. In the biblical revelation, it constitutes a force which carries us from blood sacrifices to the pure sacrifice of the lips, already present in the prophet Hosea (Hos 14:2) and taken up again by the Epistle to the Hebrews (Heb 13:15). It will culminate in the sacrifice of thanksgiving (*sacrificium laudis*) from Psalm 50, vv. 14 and 23, to the Christian Eucharist where it becomes the sacrament of spiritual sacrifice."

As a signal of the trend toward assimilating various academic disciplines in conversation with the study of liturgy, liturgical scholar Mary M. Schaefer (1998: 3) set the stage by establishing the basic premises of the Western tradition of religion: "In both Judaism and Christianity God is the Holy One and Creator of all that exists (Gen 1; Deut 6: 4; John 1: 1–3). By their very existence things praise their Creator; God is glorified by all creatures God has made. Human beings, endowed with reason and will, have been created according to God's image and likeness (Gen 1: 27)." Schaefer (1998: 6) then invited contributions from the social sciences and a variety of disciplines to "throw light on worship as a human cultural phenomenon": "Study of the Church at prayer should draw on contributions which the human sciences—anthropology, sociology, and psychology—can make. As Christian worship is a response to the mystery-dimension of life, phenomenology (especially study of where the holy is experienced), the meaning communicated by the aural and visual arts, qualitative studies (esthetics, or appreciation of the beautiful), the science of signs (semiotics), and the interaction of human beings with their environment (proxemics) throw light on worship as a human cultural phenomenon engaged in by those who seek communion with the divine." She (1998: 8) then elevated music to center stage in liturgical action: "Instead of being treated as decoration and extraneous to the 'real business' of worship, music is integral to the expression of liturgical content and bodily engagement. Text and music together—musical liturgy and sung prayer—are appreciated for their power to illuminate the mind and move the heart."

As a fertile example of the musicological approach to biblical texts, we may turn to the Psalms. Literary scholars and biblical interpreters have habitually praised works like the Psalms for their beautifully crafted verses. But according to specialized research they were much more than poetical creations—they were meant to be sung in ritual and liturgy. In fact, the Psalms are the quintessential example of how word, music, and ritual are bound together. Biblical scholar Sigmund Mowinckel, in *The Psalms in Israel's Worship* (1962: 8, 12), affirmed both the musical and cultic context of the Psalms: "In all ancient cults song, music and dance play an important role. So they do so in the Psalms . . . There can be no doubt that the Psalms were meant to be sung. They contain a number of allusions to singing, and they are often described in the title as songs rendered to music, or as hymns . . . The testimonies to the connection of the psalms with the cult and its ceremonies, is sacrifices and lustrations, its song, music, and dance are thus both numerous and strong." In fact, Mowinckel (1962: 9) observed, "In many languages the word for 'song' [or chant] originally betokened the powerful ritual word." Accordingly, many of the conclusions about the Psalms hold true for the Sanskrit Vedas in Hindu ritual, the Zoroastrian Avestan texts, the Qur'an in Islam, and Gregorian chant in Christian liturgy.

Having established that authentic religious ritual sustains a balance between word and action, and that sound and music play fundamental roles, we will now display the work of a scholar of liturgy who has outlined useful parameters for developing further insights into liturgy or ritual and music. Liturgical professor and scholar Edward Foley, Capuchin, has addressed salient issues regarding the role of music in ritual behavior in *Ritual Music: Studies in Liturgical Musicology* (1995). At the beginning of chapter 5 entitled, "Toward a Sound Theology," Foley (1995: 107) raises the basic question of why sound/music is integral to religious worship, noting that "even if one accepts the premise that music is integral to worship, few have attempted to explore why this is so. As a result, most commentators on the subject-be they musicians or liturgists-find themselves addressing questions of how music is integral to worship rather than questions of whether or why music is integral to worship." In this work Foley presents some resolution with careful insights into the meaning of sound and music in religious ritual and experience.

In his analysis of ritual, Edward Foley (1995: 115) is reminiscent of Mircea Eliade's notion of *homo religiosus*: "Ritual is patterned, shared, public behavior, expressing a meaning and purpose that cannot be put into words alone, in the face of some reality larger than ourselves." He then (1995: 116) brings music into the discussion with reference to the realm of symbols that inhabit a space beyond rational discourse: "Rituals achieve the inexpressible by means of symbols; and although all art is symbolic, opening up levels of reality which can be broached in no other way, the most highly developed type of such purely connotational semantic is music."

Employing a phenomenological method that he calls "Liturgical Musicology," or simply the "ritual-music approach," Foley (1995: 109–110) states that "[s]ound, as such, does not really exist in the world around us. What does exist is vibration . . . In other words, there is no sound until we hear it . . . it is not only a physical phenomenon, but also the response to that phenomenon and to a lesser degree the intentionality behind the phenomenon that enables us to distinguish between noise and communication."

Revealing the close connection between performer and audience, Foley (1995: 112) argues that sound-events "are not only active events in and of themselves, but dynamic to the extent that they engage the other and captivate the listener . . . sound events like human song are fundamentally unitive: uniting singer with the song, listener with the song, singer with the listener, the listener with other listeners, and even in a new way the listener with her or himself." He also reflects on the uniqueness characteristic of religion in its encounter with a personal "other" rather than an abstract One or essence. Speaking of religious music as "sound-events," he presented sound as an "experience of the personal" and sound-events as not simply "experiences of something other, but of another." Recalling Martin Buber's "I and Thou" approach, Foley stated that "sound encounters are keyed to personal encounters. They occur in the realm of acoustic space which is translated by the human imagination as an arena of personal presence. Thus, the sound-event by its very nature supports the revelation of God who is perceived as a person. Music, in particular, is an infallible indicator of human presence since music, properly speaking, is a human creation that does not otherwise occur in nature. Consequently, music serves as a special sound metaphor for the unnamable God who chooses to reveal Self in personal terms" (1995: 119)

Within the context of auditory phenomena, Foley (1990: 869) explains that since music is the most refined of all sound-events, it reflects the characteristics of all sound phenomena to the highest degree. Music is thus the most suitable feature for ritual worship because "[m]usic's temporality, human genesis, dynamism, and apparent insubstantial nature enable it to serve as a unique symbol of God, suggesting presence without confinement, eliciting wonder without distance, and enabling union which is both personal and corporate. More critical than any other characteristic for liturgy is music's capacity to wed itself to word and share in its power, for music like word is both event and utterance. Music can, therefore, be understood as necessary or integral to liturgy because it has the capacity to reveal images of God and the community as well as to realize the implications of those images in a unique and irreplaceable way."

With reference to the language of Rudolf Otto, Foley (1990: 868–869) affirmed that music comes closest to expressing the meanings associated with the numinous: "Music has symbolized the mysterious and wholly other since the dawn of creation . . . This elusiveness in form and content is part of the reason why music is so often used for communicating with the spirit world. In the Judeo-Christian tradition music is an effective means for communicating with a God who is both present and hidden." Foley (1995: 116) also explained the sublime context for the placement of music in ritual: "Music creates that acoustic space which—as much as any other environment—enables ritual precisely to express meaning and purpose that cannot be put into words alone, in the face of some reality larger than ourselves . . . Traditional societies have known that beautiful sounds convey feelings and thoughts more powerfully. More completely, and more exactly than does any word, and consequently is universally tied to their rituals. Thus, music's most important and frequent use is in religious rituals." Foley (1995: 120) even posited a kind of "natural alliance between text and tune . . . [whereby] music has a special capacity to heighten and serve the word which occupies a central place in worship."

The irreplaceable nature of music's contribution to religious worship is a function of its special acoustical properties, which enable it to engage the assembly, reveal the divine, and enact the communion between assembly and God or the sacred in ways unique to this art form. In this respect, Foley (1990: 868–869) has conveniently listed four acoustic properties that allow music to accomplish these results: music is time bound; music is the indicator of personal presence; music is dynamic; and music is intangible:

1. Music is time bound. Music requires performance in historical time for it to exist: "Sound as one of the basic ingredients of music is considered more real or existential than any other sense object and situates us in the midst of actuality and simultaneity (cf. Walter J. Ong 1967: 111, 128). Because of this existential quality, music can image a God who . . . intervened in time and reveals Self in human history. Furthermore, this time-bound art has the ability to engage the community in the present reality of worship."

2. Music is an indicator of personal presence. Music is one of the universal symbols of human civilization and a symbol of human presence: "Since it is a human creation, music is itself a symbol of human presence . . . God . . . is not only believed to be an abstract power intervening in history but a personal God who intervenes on behalf of a beloved . . . this intervention . . . took an auditory form . . . In view of this auditory bias in God's self-revelation . . . music as the most sophisticated form of sound has the capacity to symbolize the personal nature of God's self-will especially as it unites to the Word."

3. Music is dynamic. Sound and music announce presence and engage another in dialogue: "Because of sound's ability to resonate inside two individuals at the same time it has the capacity to strike a common chord and elicit sympathetic vibrations from those who hear it. It, therefore, is dynamic in its ability to enter the world of the other and elicit a response."

4. Music is Intangible. In deference to Otto, Foley states that "the paradox of all sound phenomena including music is that sound/music is perceivable but elusive, recognizable but

uncontainable. The apparently insubstantial nature of music is one of the reasons why it has symbolized the mysterious and wholly other since the dawn of creation. Music as a non-discursive symbol is not only perceived as insubstantial but itself seems to have an ambivalence of content . . . Furthermore, music offers itself as a powerful symbol for the Divine Self who is recognizable while remaining the unnamable. Music thus enables us to encounter and know God without presuming to capture or contain the divine Self."

Instead of simply prioritizing songs according to the religious importance of texts, as previous scholarship had done, Foley's ritual-music approach (1995: 113–115) establishes a fivefold typology of ritual music that we have tentatively applied cross-culturally:

1. Music alone: music without text or ritual action; examples: drums before a Buddhist ritual, organ prelude before the Eucharist, shehnai music before Hindu wedding, taps during a funeral, drums and hand cymbals between Hindu worship activities.

2. Music and ritual action: music without text but tied to ritual activity; examples: organ mass during preparation of the Eucharist, dirge or slow march at a funeral, "Hail to the Chief" during arrival of president, "Pomp and Circumstance" at graduation, "Wedding March" at a wedding.

3. Music and text: music tied to text without ritual action; examples: Gregorian chant (i.e., Vespers), Qur'an recitation, Torah cantillation, Christian hymns, Theravada Buddhist chanting, Vedic Stotra prayers preceding the fire sacrifice, the national anthem at sports events.

4. Music and text and ritual action: music united with words and tied to ritual activity; examples: Haveli Sangit in Hindu temple worship, Latin chants performed during the Mass, Tibetan Buddhist chanting during rituals, jazz funeral hymn "Just a Closer Walk with Thee" in procession.

5. Text and ritual action: without music, this would still be a

sound-event including speaking or reciting something during a ritual activity. Examples: pledge of allegiance, swearing of oaths on the Bible.

When these typologies are expanded with more examples from other religions, they provide a useful framework for substantive research in the Musicology of Religion. Although Foley outlined the above four acoustical properties and the five types of ritual music to analyze sound and music as part of Christian ritual and liturgy, he also indicated the need for more cross-cultural work in this field: "There is so little comparable work on the theology of music or liturgical music" (1995: 108).

Mary E. McGann, an American liturgical scholar, has endorsed Foley's advocacy for more comparative studies in liturgical music by orienting her academic approach around the need for a wider understanding of the central role of music in a variety of world religious cultures. In her efforts to develop the field of Comparative Liturgy and Music, McGann, in *Exploring Music as Worship and Theology: Research in Liturgical Practice* (2002: 11), calls for an interdisciplinary approach: "The method is necessarily interdisciplinary. Each of the three fields of Liturgical Studies, Ethnomusicology, and Ritual Studies offers us a different yet complementary view of what takes place when a liturgical assembly makes music. Taken together, the perspectives, theories, and methods of these three disciplines provide a basis for studying and interpreting music as an integral part of liturgical performance." She then proffers a persuasive call for more interdisciplinary work in the music and liturgy of various religious cultures: "It is my hope that other scholars will take up the work of studying worship music, using all or parts of this method, or developing comparable methods of their own. The approach I take can be used in a variety of cultural and denominational settings and can be adapted to a range of musical idioms."

According to McGann (2002: 20), music and the arts "are a compendium of religious, social, and cultural realizations of relatedness. From the perspective of liturgical theory, they are not embellishments but constitutive of what takes place in liturgy, affecting how all other elements are experienced and participating in the creation of meaning that takes place." Music and song are thus not meant as mere decoration or background ambience but express key cultural factors within the worship communities themselves. She stressed that the holistic approach is most effective in understanding the role of music as it is inseparable from ritual: "Music-making and ritualization must be interpreted as an integrated whole. Music unfolds not only in ritual but as ritual, as a mode of ritual performance. An assembly's musical performance inevitably influences the whole ritual process" (2002: 35).

In making a similar case for the importance of the ritual context for sacred music, Stephen A. Marini, in *Sacred Song in America: Religion, Music and Public Culture* (2003), argues that merely the mythic content of a song, that is, the lyrics and their narrative dimension, is not sufficient to make it sacred or "religious"; it must contain the ritual element. Marini (2003: 7) has given this explanation: "For a song to be sacred, it must possess not only belief content but also ritual intention and form. Ritual is the defining performance condition for sacred song, as mythic content is its defining cognitive condition . . . In order for song to be religious expression it must be presented with sacred intentionality as part of effective ritual action . . . Sacred song is an extraordinary vehicle for conducting believers into the ritual dimension. It may indeed be the single most powerful medium of the ritual process."

For both McGann and Marini, music and song are the key modes of ritual expressiveness. Music structures time in various ways, song inhabits the acoustical space, and the singing of songs permits specific words to take on the cultural resonances and style of a community. But while both are optimistic about the trends in Liturgical Studies toward increasing attention to the entirety of performance traditions rather than the mere study of texts, McGann (2002: 11) remains apprehensive about the lack of sophisticated research methods for examining the musical aspects of liturgies in different contexts: "Little has been done to develop methods for studying music within a community's worship performance, and for assessing how a community's musical performance affects the entire continuum of liturgical action, shaping and expressing an embodied theology."

In his insightful essay "Psalm, Bhajan, and Kirtan: Songs of the Soul in Comparative Perspective" (2001), Terry Muck has demonstrated the kind of comparative and interdisciplinary research into religious worship and music that both Foley and McGann have anticipated. In this essay, Muck (2001: 15–16) discusses three varieties of sacred song—one Western and two Indian—and finds that each reflects the "ineffable" or "sublime" realm in a unique way: "The difficulty in identifying defining characteristics of religious song is that these characteristics are precisely those that go beyond definition. Religious song refers one to the sublime dimensions of life, the ineffable, the beyond, the indefinable. Perhaps the best definition is one that acknowledges it is really no definition at all because it admits that its subject is indefinable . . . Religious songs, then, are those that have the capacity to present the unpresentable, the sublime . . . Clearly Psalms, Bhajan, and Kirtan have as their subject matter, their evocative basis, and their performance this area called the sublime." Psalms, Bhajans, and Kirtans each has its own religious context within a specific community of worship, whether in Judaism, Christianity, Hinduism, or Sikhism, and exemplify the notion of what Rudolf Otto and others have described as a personal encounter with God or the ineffable: "Psalm, Bhajan, and Kirtan speak truth and open one to God. Their singing represents one aspect of the quintessence of the religious act. But these religious, devotional songs are more than theology, worship, and liturgy. They are all of these together—and more . . . Religious, devotional songs are directed from human beings toward the object of devotion . . . Humans direct their religious songs to the transcendent object with awe and reverence in the face of sacred power; they are sung with confidence and trust that the transcendent is real; and they are sung with a single-minded concentration that befits the sincerity required of such an endeavor." Utilizing particular expertise, Muck (2001: 19) establishes the basis for advanced comparative discourse about music in religious worship: "Clearly the consensus in all three traditions is that religious, devotional songs may be used individually or in groups for purposes of worship, and/or petition with a wide variety of musical styles, as long as they are faithful to the religious traditions' understanding of the transcendent and effective in generating ways of connecting singers to that transcendent."

Asian Liturgical Traditions

> Song, according to the ancient concept, did not accompany the sacrifice but in fact formed the core of the sacrificial process. What resounds at the beginning of all things is a praise song. This song represents the first sacrifice . . . If this sacrifice is a sound sacrifice, a praise song, then man taps into the primordial acoustic energy of creation, which in the final analysis is the holy syllable AUM that "fastens" everything together: the past, the present, and the future.
>
> —Marius Schneider, "The Nature of Praise Song"

As the sequel to *Sonic Theology: Hinduism and Sacred Sound* (Beck 1993), the present author's *Sonic Liturgy: Ritual and Music in Hindu Tradition* (Beck 2012) built on the theoretical premises of the former book and pursued the practical application and exploration of the important commonalities associated with sacred sound in Hindu ritual and liturgy. This work developed the category of "sonic liturgy," conceived as "sacred sound in practice," as opposed to "sacred sound in theory." Topics examined in this work include the ancient practice of Vedic sacrifice and the liturgical music associated with worship of the Hindu gods. The groundwork for this kind of comparative liturgical study began several decades ago with Marius Schneider in Germany.

Among the early formulators of what became known as "comparative musicology" in Berlin in the early twentieth century, Marius Schneider (1903–1982) focused his attention on music and song in ancient India as indissolubly linked with sacrifice and liturgical action. In an article originally published in 1964, "The Nature of Praise Song" (1989: 37–38), Schneider proclaimed: "Song, according to the ancient concept, did not accompany the sacrifice but in fact formed the core of the sacrificial process. What resounds at the beginning of all things is a praise song. This song represents the first sacrifice." He then expounded on the ancient Hindu syllable of OM (AUM) as emblematic of the earliest notion of the sacrificial nature of sound: "Sacrifice is the crimson thread that runs through the whole of human life. If this sacrifice is a sound sacrifice, a praise song, then man taps into the primordial acoustic energy of creation, which in the final analysis is the holy syllable AUM that 'fastens' everything together: the past, the present, and the future. This is of great significance, insofar as all that is present actually issues from the sum total of the past. The way in which man carries out his life sacrifice, that is, his word, constitutes the holistic rhythm of his existence. For what he is today, he can thank his yesterdays" (Schneider 1989: 41). He also cited the authoritative Sanskrit text *Shatapatha Brahmana* (VIII 4. 3. 2) for the theology behind ritual action: "All that the gods do, they do through song . . . The praise song is the body of the invisible and the primordial matter of all that has come into being" (Schneider 1989: 41). The spiritual practitioner emulates the gods through liturgical action: "The priest must enunciate every one of his actions while he does it. He must sing or speak, for the heart of ritual lies not in concrete acts but in singing and speaking" (Schneider 1989: 49). We confirm Schneider's claims with a closer look at types of liturgical "sound-events" in India, including examples from Hinduism, Buddhism, Jainism, and Sikhism.

The sacred syllable "OM" (or "AUM") figures prominently in any understanding of ritual sound in South Asia, whether in Hinduism, Buddhism, Jainism, or Sikhism. OM first emerges in ancient Vedic religion, the predecessor of Hinduism, beginning with the Vedas and Upanishads. The Vedas are collections of Mantras and hymns for the purpose of sacrifice. OM in the Vedas is associated with ritual, specifically the fire sacrifice known as Yajna. OM was a practical sonic tool for invocation and application as a preface to the Mantras that accompanied oblations into the sacrificial fire. Before any ritual act, the intonation of sacred sound in the form of Mantra was necessary. Without Mantra, there was no sacrifice, and without OM there was no Mantra. OM prefaces the most sacred Mantra of Vedic and Hindu religion, the Gāyatrī Mantra, beginning "*OM bhūr bhuvah svah*," which petitions the power of the sun to illuminate the mind. Mantras are composed of words and syllables in Sanskrit (*saṁskrita*, "well formed"), considered the reproduction in sound of the nature and structure of reality. The ancient law codes of Hinduism known as the *Dharma-Sūtras* proclaim that since OM is the gateway to heaven, and the best means to remove defilements, it should be intoned at the beginning and end of all Mantras and rituals. OM, having immense significance from the beginning as an invocation of sacred power, heralded the continuing importance of the voice in all Indian religious practice.

Arising out of his deep study of Indian religion and Hindu experience, Rudolf Otto (1958 [1923]: 192–193) became one of the first Western theologians to recognize the numinous quality of the ancient syllable OM: "Another original sound in which numinous feeling is articulated is certainly the holy syllable 'OM' . . . sounding up from within as the quasi-reflex expression of profound emotion in circumstances of a numinous-magical nature, . . . almost physical in its constraining force. And this constraint and compulsion to expression are still recoverable to our feeling when we recapture this mood of submergence and absorption in the 'wholly other.'"

Recent research has confirmed the inherent tonal nature of OM and its value for understanding the sacred foundations of Indian music. Sanskrit scholar Finnian McKean Moore Gerety has thoroughly researched the origins and history of OM in Hindu thought and practice. An important conclusion for Gerety is the close association of the syllable OM with singing and music in ancient India. He states: "It was the singer-theologians . . . who did the most to foster OM's emergence. In my view, this is the single most important finding of the present study: that the history of the sacred syllable resounds with music and song" (Gerety 2015: 401). This finding helps to explain why the chanting of OM is always tonal, unless muttered in near silence. That is, OM has been recited in a kind of monotone on the tonic note of a scale for centuries. This method is still the foundation of most forms of South Asian worship and music performance.

The singing of hymns was also an important practice in Vedic India. Singing the hymns of the Sāma Veda, known as Sāma-Gāna, was not a mere supplement to the sacrifice. Sāma-Gāna was so essential to the sacrifice that without it no sacrificial offering can reach the gods. The singing played a central role, was highly respected, and even used with caution. The chanted hymns were believed to possess supernatural qualities capable of petitioning and summoning the deities in charge of the forces of nature. Vedic scholar G. U. Thite (1997: 68) has carefully described the powerful nature of Sāma-Gāna vis-à-vis the Vedic gods: "the poet-singers call, invoke, and invite the gods with the help of musical elements. In so doing they seem to be aware of the magnetic power of music and therefore they seem to be using that power in calling the gods." Even the Vedic gods appeared to have had a sense of music appreciation: "Gods are fond of music. They like music and enjoy it. The poet-singers sing and praise the gods with the intention that the gods may be pleased thereby and having become pleased they may grant gifts" (1997: 71). In addition, music functioned as an autonomous power substance that controlled natural phenomena and even the gods: "In the Veda, music is considered to be a power substance. By means of it one can control natural phenomena and perform miraculous deeds; the power of music is sometimes considered to be superior and sometimes inferior to gods; it can work sometimes independently and even upon gods; but sometimes it requires the help of gods for its effectiveness. Thus, the power of music is magico-religious" (1997: 61–62).

In Tibetan Buddhism, the most famous Mantra is the Maṇi Mantra, the six-syllable Mantra of Avalokiteśvara, the Bodhisattva of Compassion. Believed to date before the sixth century, it begins with the syllable OM: *OM Maṇi-Padme Hūm* ("OM, The Jewel is in the Lotus"). As in Hinduism, OM represents the totality of sound, existence, and consciousness for the Buddhists. Yet in Buddhist Tantra it functions as a focal point for meditation on Śūnyatā (Emptiness), and as a request of Buddhas and Bodhisattvas for assistance on the path toward Nirvāṇa. It is said that all the Buddha's teachings are contained in this Mantra. In Japanese Shingon, Mantras can be as short as OM, or very long as in the elegant Dharanis to various Buddhas. Eastern religions scholar John Blofeld, in *The Tantric Mysticism of Tibet: A Practical Guide* (1970: 194), outlined the significance of OM for the Tibetan Buddhists: "In common with all Mantras, the Maṇi has OM as its first syllable. OM stands for the totality of sound and, indeed, for the totality of existence. Originally written AUM, it starts at the back of the throat and ends with the lips. It is chief among the sounds to which a mystical creative quality is attached. A stands for consciousness of the external world; the U, for consciousness of what goes on inside our minds, and the M, for consciousness of the non-dual, unqualified emptiness of the void." In contrast to the Upanishads, in which OM represents the fullness of existence, the Maṇi Mantra including OM resonates with the principle of emptiness found in Mahāyāna philosophy, as stated by Blofeld (1970: 195): "This above all other mantric syllables symbolizes the central truth of the Vajrayāna—the truth of voidness [Śūnyatā, Emptiness] enclosed within the petals of the non-void." Here, each syllable relates to an area of the cosmos, whereby OM represents the realm of the gods, Ma the demons (asuras), Ni humans, Pad animals; Me hungry ghosts (pretas) and Hum the region of hell. For Buddhist chant and music, see Sean Williams (2006).

As part of the daily prayer in Jainism, practitioners recite the Namaskāra Mantra, *OM Namaskāram*, the most important Mantra in Jain practice. Without reference to a god or supernatural being, the Jain devotee offers this prayer to the moral qualities of teachers and saints. Jains do not ask favors or material benefits but instead display respect toward spiritually advanced beings as part of their quest to achieve liberation. Jainism scholar Padmanabh S. Jaini, in *The Jaina Path of Purification* (1979: 163–164), explains this Mantra further under the name Pañca-Namaskāra-Mantra and its relation to OM as part of Jain initiation services: "Jains sometimes venerate the holy syllable om as well, though their analysis of this utterance differs from that of the Brahmanical traditions. Whereas Vedic scripture suggests that the A, U, and M of which OM is composed represent earth, the atmosphere, and heaven, respectively, Jaina texts (probably post-canonical) derive the same sound by connecting the initial syllables of the epithets for each being addressed in the Namaskāra-Mantra: hence A (Arhat), A (Asarira [the Siddha], A (Ācārya), U (Upādhyāya), M (Muni [Sādhu]). Repetition of OM thus becomes a legitimate practice for the Jaina, serving to remind him of the five holy beings of his creed."

The Sikh religion was founded in north India in the sixteenth century by Guru Nanak (1469–1539 CE). As a form of monotheism devoted to the One True God, Sikhs recite the daily Morning Prayer known as the Japji. The Japji begins with the Mūla Mantra, the fundamental Mantra of Sikh religion that also appears as the opening words of the Śrī Gurū Granth Sahib, the Sikh scripture. The Mūla Mantra begins with OM in the form of *Ik Onkar Satnām* in the language of Gurmukhi. Ik Onkar functions as a statement of oneness, "There is but One God," and is a compound of the numeral one, Ik (Sanskrit eka, one) and Onkar (OM). Satnām refers to God, who is the "True Name" beyond all name and form. Guru Nanak wrote a poem called *Oankar* in which he attributes the origin of speech to OM. As a popular symbolic form, W. H. McLeod (2005: 97–98) explained how the Ik-Oankar represents the full adoption of the syllable OM throughout Sikh life: "A popular emblem used by Sikhs, a combination of the Gurmukhi figure 1 and the letter O, taken from the Ādi Granth where it is employed as the first part of various invocations. It represents the unity of God ("One Oankar" or One Being). The emblem is a common feature of Sikh logos and frequently appears on buildings, clothing, books, letterheads, and so on. "Oankar" is actually a cognate of 'Om' and can carry the same mystical meaning."

Aside from OM, Sikhs embrace the metaphysical notion of Nāda-Brahman as found in the Hindu music treatises. Inderjit Nilu Kaur (2011: 304) reveals how the theory of the "unstruck sound' underlies the Sikh spiritual quest: "The progression from ahat nad [Āhata Nāda] (struck sound, audible by the senses) to anhad [Anāhata Nāda] (un-struck mystical vibrations) is a significant theme in the Guru Granth. The ultimate purpose of Sikh shabad kirtan is to awaken in the participant vibrations sympathetic with anhad, and thereby to move beyond the sensory to the mystical—a state marked by peace and tranquility." Sikh scholar and practitioner Pashaura Singh (2006: 141) stressed the presence of Nāda-Brahman and its connection with the Rāgas in Sikh performance: "In line with the metaphysical theory of ancient Indian music and Hindu tradition of sacred sound, Sikh doctrine maintains that the inspired 'utterance of the Guru' (*gurbani*) embodies the divine word (*śabda* or *nāda*). In his Ramakali hymn, for instance, Guru Nanak proclaims: '*Gurbani* embodies all the scriptural knowledge (Veda) and the eternally sounding melodious vibration (*nāda*) that permeates all space.' This 'unstruck melody' (*anāhata nāda*) cannot be directly perceived or 'heard,' although it is the basis of the entire perceptible universe. The physical vibrations of musical sound are inextricably connected with the spiritual world of 'unstruck melody.' Likewise, all the Rāgas exist eternally and some of them are merely discovered from time to time by inspired musicians."

Indian music in the form of Rāgas is a central part of the daily ritual services of Sikhs. The fundamental hymnal text is the Śrī Gurū Granth Sahib, or the Ādi Granth, which is organized according to the Rāgas of

Indian music. As explained by Pashaura Singh (2006: 156), "The Ādi Granth is divided into three major sections. It begins with an introductory section containing liturgical texts and concludes with an epilogue consisting of a group of miscellaneous works. The bulk of the material, however, is arranged in the middle section and is based on Rāgas, which number thirty-one in the standard version of the Ādi Granth. Many of these Rāgas are the same as those sung by Hindu musicians in their temple worship." The mutual borrowing of sound-events and music in India, in what may be called "shared religious soundscapes," is much larger in scope because evidence shows that Muslim, Christian, and even Jewish communities have adopted Indian sonic and musical idioms. What we have presented here speaks to a much broader substratum among these groups beside simply doctrine, ethics, or ritual practice.

Ethnomusicologist Philip V. Bohlman, in "Music: Music and Religion in India" (2005, vol. 9: 6279), summarized a basic tenet of music and religion in India, an axiom that holds much wider application in the Musicology of Religion: "Just as music is inseparable from most rituals in Indian religions, so too is ritual meaning densely present in much musical activity. Music has the potential to recalibrate the temporal and social components of ritual, transposing them from the everyday to the sacred world."

As part of the broader substratum that we have established, we also note that the near universal association of religion and music is not fully credible as the result of independent arising in different regions of the world but owes as much to the dissemination of core ideas and practices from key locations in the ancient world. We have already documented the widespread adoption of Pythagorean conceptions of harmony throughout the ancient and medieval worlds of the West and Middle East. And as noted above, multiple examples exist within the South Asian context. Historically speaking, going beyond South Asia, scholars have surmised that at one time the Vedic and ancient Persian religions were considered a unity, referred to as the Indo-Iranian or Aryan tradition. Many Indo-Iranian prototypes in religion, ritual, and music, including musical instruments, have been dispersed over wide geographic areas spanning thousands of years. The Buddhist chanting of the Pali Canon, derived from Vedic models, has spread over Southeast Asia and, through its Mahāyāna counterpart, influenced countless types of religious chant and rituals in Central Asia, China, Korea, and Japan. Indo-Iranian influences are present, for example, in the subtle style of chanting the Qur'an in Islam, which is pre-Islamic and can be traced most directly to Persian or Zoroastrian roots. This Zoroastrian base, which is of family resemblance with Vedic chant and cantillation traditions, is also seminal in the oldest levels of Semitic and Hebrew recitation and prayer, reaching Christian chant and psalmody, both Byzantine and Latin, through the overlapping of liturgical traditions.

Understanding the role of ritual and liturgy in the performance of sacred chant and music worldwide is thus of paramount importance in the development of theories and methods in the Musicology of Religion. In the next chapter, the scientists will have their voices heard, offering credible evidence from neuroscience and cognitive studies that religion and music are not mere human inventions or contrivances but are each inextricably fused with the evolutionary and genetic make-up of the human species.

Chapter Seven

Cognitive Studies and Music

Humans are predisposed to detect, produce, remember, and enjoy music. This is a human universal. There is no human society without some musical tradition.

—Pascal Boyer, *Religion Explained: The Evolutionary Origins of Religious Thought*

No known human culture lacks music . . . All human beings are capable of creating and responding to music . . . Neurological studies demonstrate the brain's specificity for music, suggesting that musical capacity represents a specific biological competence rather than a generalized cultural function.

—Nils L. Wallin, *The Origins of Music*

Music is much more universal and ancient than literacy, and unlike literacy, basic musical abilities develop without any special instruction.

—Aniruddh D. Patel, *Music and the Brain*

Despite the strong trends in favor of cultural relativism, including musical relativism, in the social sciences and ethnomusicology, recent work in cognitive studies and neuroscience on the role of music in the biological development of the human species has significantly reinforced the value of the comparative study of music and religion. The prevalence of universals across cultures in both religion and music, when combined with cognitive studies that include biological and neurological factors, offers a positive harbinger for the Musicology of Religion. To automatically consign music or religion solely to nonuniversal domains of specific cultures is arbitrary at best and may obfuscate important cross-cultural and comparative potentialities that may reveal links to broader biological and psychological traits.

Cognitive sciences are developing new methodologies for establishing that religious and musical experiences involve unique sets of mental processes. Music and religion can now be viewed as permanent factors not only in human experience but in the mental capacities of human beings as developed through evolution. Cognitive research into religion is based on the conclusion that all human beings aspire toward transcendence in some form, thus offering a new platform for the re-unification of music and religion after their separation in recent decades, or since the neglect of music from the time of Otto and van der Leeuw in the phenomenology of religion. The new platform is centered on the human mind and its cognitive faculties under scientific observation and measurement. Let us first look at religion.

Religiosity

Over the past few decades, cognitive research has made great strides in establishing the human tendency toward religion or religiosity as a natural phenomenon arising out of human evolution. Yet an ideological current of anti-scientism in religious studies has hindered the appreciation and acceptance of neuroscience and cognitive studies. To approach and understand this tendency, Luther Martin, in "Religion and Cognition" (2010), has provided a useful summary of the historical emergence of cognitive studies in religion, pointing out why and how the above-described situation in religious studies has occurred. Before the rise of cognitive science in the late twentieth century, most views of human mental activity, including those of logical positivism and behavioral psychology, considered the brain to be a *tabula rasa* (blank slate) upon which environmental and cultural input was inscribed. Knowledge of the brain was thus limited to first-person accounts and limited stimulus-response observations. Although William James had earlier suggested a neurological approach to religious experience, not until seventy years later was more accurate data of mental activity provided by third-person reports and noninvasive technologies for imaging brain activity such as positron emission tomography, magnetic resonance imagery and functional magnetic resonance imagery. These observations and experiments revealed previously unknown patterns of brain activity that could be measured and tested with scientific precision. Yet despite these advances, according to Martin (2010: 528), "scholars of religion steadfastly resisted as reductionistic any scientific approach to their work, preferring instead to retain their largely theological (confessional) agendas." As religious studies expanded within or alongside philosophy, social science, and humanities departments, an air of anti-scientism permeated the academic study of religion. But by mid-century, when phenomenologists of religion had catalogued enormous amounts of data from religions around the world, the suggestion of universals was seriously reconsidered, especially regarding the notion of "the sacred" or holy that was viewed as *sui generis* or unique.

However, as Martin (2010: 529) explains, "evolutionary biologists, cognitivists and anthropologists began to argue that such patterned universals were shaped, rather, by the ordinary capacities of and constraints upon human brain functions, which, like the panhuman functioning(s) of any of our organs or systems, are the naturally selected consequences of our evolutionary history." Since the new scientific data seemed to corroborate the ethnographic data regarding patterns or categories of function and meaning, the probability of a naturalistic explanation for religion was tendered. For example, Pascal Boyer, an eminent pioneer in cognitive studies of religion, has argued (cited in Martin 2010: 531) that "representations of superhuman agency, documented from virtually every human society, are readily and easily produced by our ordinary cognitive equipment and are, consequently, as natural as are the actions they predicate." He likened religious phenomena to the widely documented phenomena of imaginary friends in children or the sci-fi and fantasy fictional worlds of adults. But while cognitive research does not interpret or explain meanings associated with specific constructions of religion in the world, it can help to clarify the ubiquity of religion among all human societies past and present. According to Martin (2010: 534), "It can offer naturalistic explanations of recurring patterns that have long been noted among the diversities of religious expressions. It can offer explanations for the modes of conservation and transmission employed by those particular constructions and for individual commitments to them. And it can express these explanations with some precision in ways that may be assessed from the wealth of ethnographic and historical data controlled by scholars of religion." In opposition to earlier hesitations regarding religion (and music), such that they resisted accurate measurement by scientific instruments, Martin attested that "[t]he evolved capacities and constraints of human cognition can provide a metric of universal human possibilities in terms of which the vast diversity of human cultures—and their religious expressions—might be measured and in terms of which they have been historically and socially constructed" (2010: 537).

New research associated with the name of neuroscientist Andrew Newberg has confronted the issue of the human brain and the unitary nature of religion. Based on scientific study, Andrew Newberg, Eugene d'Aquili, and Vince Rause, in *Why God Won't Go Away: Brain Science and the Biology of Belief* (2001), set the parameters for future investigations with a profound understanding of the religious impulse and its various manifestations in history. According to Newberg (2001: 129), "Evidence suggests that the deepest origins of religion are based in mystical experience, and that religions persist because the wiring of the human brain continues to provide believers with a range of unitary experiences that are often interpreted as assurances that God exists." With full confidence in his findings, Newberg (2001: 175) concluded that "all the world's great religions—and, we believe, all religious impulses—arise from the brain's ability to transcend the limited self and perceive a larger, more fundamental reality. Any attempt to create a biological theory of religion must address this point." Newberg (2001: 175–176) proceeds to address this challenge by envisioning a new discipline that he terms "neurotheology," designed "to understand the link between brain function and all important aspects of religion . . . A neurotheological approach, by its very nature, is universal. All human beings have a brain, and all these brains work in a similar fashion. So if we are ever going to get a sense of the universal aspects of religion, then the brain might be the best place to start . . . The neurotheological approach can help explore many critical ingredients of religion, including myth, ritual, and mystical experience." Precisely how this is to be accomplished conforms to a methodological framework proposed by Newberg (2001: 175) comprising categories such as "metatheology" and "megatheology": "A metatheology is a way to describe how the specific theological principles of any given religion may have arisen. A megatheology is a way of approaching religion that focuses on the universal elements that all religions seem to share." Many of these ideas and proposals have been assembled in the treatise *Principles of Neurotheology* (2010), in which Newberg (2010: 1) formally announced and defined the new discipline: "Neurotheology is the unique field of scholarship and investigation that seeks to understand the relationship specifically between the brain and theology, and more broadly between the mind and religion."

Since music has been established as a significant element in religion, neurotheology holds great promise in association with the Musicology of Religion.

For further exploration of the rapidly expanding field of cognitive studies in religion, see Pascal Boyer, *The Naturalness of Religious Ideas: A Cognitive Theory of Religion* (1994) and *Religion Explained: The Evolutionary Origins of Religious Thought* (2001); Scot Atran, *In Gods We Trust: The Evolutionary Landscape of Religion* (2002); Ilkka Pyysiainen and Veikko Antonnen, editors, *Current Approaches in the Cognitive Science of Religion* (2002); Ilkka Pyysiainen, *How Religion Works: Towards a New Cognitive Science of Religion* (2003); Dean Hamer, *The God Gene: How Faith is Hardwired into our Genes* (2004); Patrick McNamara, *The Neuroscience of Religious Experience* (2009); and Todd Tremlin, *Minds and Gods: The Cognitive Foundations of Religion* (2010).

Musicality

Cognitive research into the human tendency toward music or musicality has also reached new levels of advancement, forming commonalities with the cognitive study of religion. The contributions of cognitive research to the study of music are based on the realization that human beings are capable of learning music implicitly. Cognitive anthropologist Pascal Boyer, in *Religion Explained: The Evolutionary Origins of Religious Thought* (2001: 132), identified music as occupying a unique position in human evolution: "Humans are predisposed to detect, produce, remember, and enjoy music. This is a human universal. There is no human society without some musical tradition. Although the traditions are very different, some principles can be found everywhere. For instance, musical sounds are always closer to pure sound than to noise. The equivalence between the octaves and the principal role of particular intervals like fifths and fourths are consequences of the organization of the cortex."

While a few nonhuman species can make semi-musical sounds, distinctly human mental processes are associated with hearing and making music. Biomusicologist Nils L. Wallin (2000: 11) acknowledged that, "no known human culture lacks music and that all human beings are capable of creating and responding to music," and affirmed that "neurological studies demonstrate the brain's specificity for music, again suggesting that musical capacity represents a specific biological competence rather than a generalized cultural function." Wallin also lauded the growing momentum for this research: "Just as music brings us in touch with the very deepest levels of our emotions, so too the study of music evolution has the potential to bring us in touch with the very deepest aspects of our humanity, our origins, our reasons for being" (2000: 21).

A significant direction in cognitive research on music was inspired by linguist Noam Chomsky, who developed a generative grammar in linguistics. Just as the grammar of a language was shown to be a statement of what a person needs to know to recognize a speech utterance as grammatical, a generative grammar of music could identify key universal features of human cognition necessary for simple musical structures of melody and rhythm to occur. In the fall of 1973, composer and conductor Leonard Bernstein delivered a series of lectures at Harvard University that were published as *The Unanswered Question: Six Talks at Harvard* (1976). Motivated by the work of Noam Chomsky and his transformational-generative grammar in linguistics, Bernstein proposed the idea of a "musical grammar" that would explicate human musical capacity along similar lines. The Bernstein lectures eventually led to the work of Fred Lerdahl and Ray S. Jackendoff, in *A Generative Theory of Tonal Music* (1983), which attempted to create a generative theory of tonal music (GTTM), much like Chomsky's generative grammar theory of language. This theory has been successful to the degree that it has influenced scores of musicologists and theorists. Chomsky had argued that many of the properties of a generative grammar arose from a universal grammar innate to the human brain, rather than being learned from the environment. As summarized (1983: 5), generative linguistic theory "is an attempt to characterize what a human being knows when he knows how to speak a language, enabling him to understand and create an indefinitely large number of sentences, most of which he has never heard before. This knowledge is not on the whole available to conscious introspection and hence cannot have been acquired by direct instruction. Linguistic theory models this unconscious knowledge by a formal system of principles or rules called a grammar, which describes (or 'generates') the possible sentences of a language."

On the very first page, Lerdahl and Jackendoff (1983: 1) outlined the new approach of GTTM: "We take the goal of a theory of music to be a formal description of the musical intuitions of a listener who is experienced in a musical idiom." Defining a piece of music as "a mentally constructed entity, of which scores and performances are partial representations by which the piece is transmitted," this groundbreaking approach positioned itself squarely within the discipline of psychology (1983: 2): "In our view, the central task of music theory should be to explicate this mentally produced organization. Seen in this way, music theory takes a place among traditional areas of cognitive psychology such as theories of vision and language." Their approach was purely psychological since the concept of the unconscious mind is clearly introduced (1983: 3): "We are referring to the largely unconscious knowledge (the 'musical intuition') that the listener brings to his hearing—a knowledge that enables him to organize and make coherent the surface patterns of pitch, attack, duration, intensity, timbre, and so forth." Instead of simply measuring surface patterns of sound and tone perception, or comparatively looking for parts of speech in musical phrases, the generative approach posits the inclusion of what are called "innate ideas" or 'universal principles' associated with music within the mind of all human beings, suggesting a kind of *a priori* apparatus reminiscent of Kant (1983: 4): "A formal theory of musical idioms will make possible substantial hypotheses about those aspects of musical understanding that are innate; the innate aspects will reveal themselves as 'universal' principles of musical grammar." More specifically Lerdahl (1983: 6) explained musical factors: "The fundamental concepts of musical structure must instead involve such factors as rhythmic and pitch organization, dynamic and timbral differentiation, and motivic-thematic processes. These factors and their interactions form intricate structures quite different from, but no less complex than, those of linguistic structure." As such, since generative grammar in linguistics is not an algorithm to manufacture grammatical sentences, a musical generative grammar is not an algorithm to compose pieces of music. Generative here means to describe an infinite set of possibilities with a finite set of rules.

Two personal examples will help to illustrate how this works. As I sit down to play blues on the piano, I unconsciously know the rules of how to play blues and to create bluesy effects with notes and chord changes. Yet each time I play, the music comes out differently, with an infinity of new possibilities according to my use of the material to create blues songs. The same goes with non-Western idioms like Hindustani classical music and the employment of Rāgas. A Rāga is a defined melodic pattern of notes ascending and descending that through practice becomes part of a set of different melodic patterns in the unconscious mind. Each time I sit down to sing, I spontaneously create a fresh, "never-sung-before" presentation from the ingredients according to the rules of each Rāga. Neither result can be accurately predicted. In fact, almost all world musical systems can shore up a basic structural pattern of basic rules or grammar that generate performance variations. And what is truly encouraging about the theory of a generative musical grammar is that while the authors were conscious of the idioms of Western tonal music, Lerdahl and Jackendoff (1983: xi) foresaw the valuable corroborative possibilities from other world music systems: "As we develop our rules of grammar, we often attempt to distinguish those aspects of the rules that are peculiar to classical Western tonal music from those aspects that are applicable to a wide range of musical idioms. Thus, many parts of the theory can be tested in terms of musical idioms other than the one we are primarily concerned with here, providing a rich variety of questions for historical and ethnomusicological research." Following this line of inquiry, in terms of what appears to be a universal in music, that is, improvisation based on some initial rules or structure, the innovative collection of essays edited by Bruno Nettl and Melinda Russell, *In the Course of Performance: Studies in the World of Musical Improvisation* (1998), illuminates the culture of improvisation in world music traditions, like Javanese Gamelan, Arabic music, Modal Jazz, Louis Armstrong, Cantonese Opera, and Hindustani instrumental music.

Next, a provocative work on music and brain science is by neuroscientist Aniruddh D. Patel, *Music, Language, and the Brain* (2008). Rather than treating music and language as separate neural or syntactic systems, as in GTTM, Patel concluded they are closely related, and he develops his research to bring new findings that corroborate this position: "Comparing music and language provides a powerful way to study the mechanisms that the mind uses to make sense of sound" (2008: 417). His assertions are based on the premise that music perception engages regions of the brain far outside the auditory cortex, such as those that govern motor control, language, social cognition, and emotional responses. He describes how all human music engages complex mental processing involving universal musical capacities unique to humans. These include, for example, the ability to distinguish consonant notes from dissonant ones, the ability to recognize transposed melodies, the ability to move the body rhythmically, and the difference between male and female voice production.

Dane Harwood, in "Universals in Music: Perspectives from Cognitive Psychology" (1976), was one of the first ethnomusicologists to confront the issue of universals from the perspective of cognitive studies. Harwood (1976: 521) began by explaining that comparing facts are at the root of the social sciences and especially anthropology: "Human beings do notice similarities and differences between themselves and fellow humans. How to make sense, to describe and understand, this fact of man's world is one of the oldest and most profound of human activities. Such description and explanation, in fact, are the core of modern anthropology, and so it is hardly surprising to find that ethnographers and ethnomusicologists have raised this issue of 'human universals' with respect to our—the world's musics." Beside facts alone, Harwood (1976: 523) recognized that the cognitive apparatus with which humans engage with music may be closer to universal than originally thought and calls for a more sophisticated theory: "The process of understanding and engaging in musical behavior may be more universal than the content of musical knowledge or action. If so, we would like a psychological theory to help us investigate such processes." And if culture is a cognitive and interpersonal fact as well as physical artifact, then so is music, according to Harwood (1976: 523–524):

> The influence of culture on human behavior is strong and pervasive, the more so as we view activities like making music from levels of analysis broader and more comprehensive than sensation of sound. Culture is both the knowledge of the range of acceptable behaviors, shared by members of a community, and the behaviors and artifacts such knowledge produces in "public" . . . We may examine music as a complex auditory stimulus which is somehow perceived, structured, and made meaningful by the human perceptual and cognitive system. From this point of view, we can search for perceptual and cognitive processes which all human beings apply to musical sound, and thus identify some processing universals. Moreover, we may also search for those processes which are not universal but rather are context-dependent. We may also examine music as a complex cultural event in which various social contexts have important effects on perception and cognition. Given this second level of analysis, we may see if there are cultural processes operating on musical information.

After countering some of the skepticism regarding universals, Harwood (1976: 525–527) affirmed the reality of universals in five categories of analysis with salient examples: "At the level of sensing sound and distinguishing signals from noise, human auditory processing seems universal. Moreover, even at higher levels of perception, when sequences sounds are construed as being patterned, we notice some strong processing similarities across cultures." The five categories are pitch perception, octave generalization, discrete scale pitches, melodic fission, and melodic contour. Upon completing his analysis of these universals, Harwood concluded: "The above examples of 'universal' phenomena in the perceptual processing of music exist in cultural contexts. Pitch perception, scale construction, and melody perception are all affected by the particular musical tradition in which the music perceiver and performer operate. However, we have seen that, while both function and structure may vary across cultures, the process-the perceptual importance of pitch and contour categories for understanding what we have heard-is very similar. As the examples indicated, the process is one of grouping perceived information into meaningful categories to be (a) stored in memory, (b) used to understand new musical experience through active construction of the musical event, and (c) transmitted between members of a musical community." He then noted that the process universals in music are similar to those used in language.

The issue of universals for the psychology of music has remained active, since a decade later John A. Sloboda, in *The Musical Mind: The Cognitive Psychology of Music* (1985), outlined several specific universals in musical cognition. Sloboda (1985: 253) begins his exposition: "A very large number of cultures contain, both in theory and practice, the notion that music takes place with respect to fixed reference pitches. These pitches need not be fixed for all time but are usually fixed for the duration of a single piece of music. In many cultures, the principal reference pitch (or pitches) are maintained throughout the music in the form of a (usually instrumental) 'drone.' Even where drones are absent, we can usually see that certain pitches are 'privileged' in that the music often returns to them, circles around them." Different cultures maintain different tonal centers or tonic notes, yet the octave appears to remain more or less intact with coordinated subdivisions: "Although tonality, as we know it, is by no means universal, the notions of scale and tonic have formal analogies in most cultures . . . It seems that the subdivisions of the octave into scale steps follow common principles in most cultures. First, the number of subdivisions is always moderately small . . . Particularly common are five- and seven-note scales. In fact, the term octave derives from the fact that, in a seven-note scale, the eighth note marks the start of the repetition of the scale pattern at a pitch with a frequency of approximately double that of the first note" (1985: 254). The unequal fourth and fifth intervals are much more frequent or important, such that Sloboda (1985: 252) raised the question: "The ubiquity of this unequal interval principle leads one to ask whether it serves some fundamental psychological purpose." Another universal feature is that no culture has made scales entirely of whole tones: "A second similarity is that practically no scale divides the octave up into equal ratio steps. In other words, scales are almost never found where the pitch intervals between adjacent notes are the same for each and every pair" (1985: 254). This correlates with the observation that the whole-tone scale, as in the music of Debussy and other modern composers, as well as the chromatic scale or twelve-tone scale of Schoenberg, have never enjoyed wide or sustained popularity as a basis for music.

In his outlook for the future of cognitive studies and music, Harwood (1976: 531–532) advocated for more research in this direction:

> I have suggested a contemporary psychological paradigm-information processing-which seems to facilitate studying the processes of perceiving, understanding, and performing music . . . There is much research to do, of course, but we should be encouraged for two reasons germane to our concerns. First, the information approach has suggested perceptual and cognitive processes which operate on musical knowledge yet are so fundamental as to be identifiable across traditions. Too, the basic aspect of such processing allows us to tie musical behavior to other human behavior. The power of our discoveries is exactly that they derive from a general human information-processing system. Second, our concern for the process, not the content, of music-making allows us to see, even at the cultural level, common elements in most musical communities . . . Critical to musical learning at all levels of analysis are two basic cognitive behaviors, which I have tried to emphasize. (1) Humans "chunk" information into meaningful patterns, attach labels to those chunks, and use them to construct a meaningful world. (2) Humans "go beyond the information given" in understanding their world; we are active participators in how our world will look, drawing as much on hypotheses and conjecture as on data which impinge on our sensory systems.

Harwood concluded that these two logical processes must begin any search for universals in music.

Within the field of cognitive studies in recent decades the universality of musical experience—that is, musicality—has garnered attention by experts. Bennett Reimar and Jeffrey E. Wright, in *On the Nature of Musical*

Experience (1992), made a major contribution to this topic by examining the perspectives on musical experience of twenty prominent aestheticians, composers, theorists, and educators. Among the thinkers covered in this volume are Monroe Beardsley, Leonard Bernstein, John Blacking, John Cage, Thomas Clifton, Aaron Copland, Nelson Goodman, Paul Hindemith, Susanne K. Langer, Fred Lerdahl and Ray Jackendoff, Abraham Maslow, Leonard B. Mayer, James Mursell, Arnold Schoenberg, Roger Sessions, and Igor Stravinsky. While one of the purposes of the book is to further music education, salient points are shared regarding features of musical experience held in common or shared by humanity. Part II, "Features of Musical Experience Held in Common and Implications for Research," contains these fourteen features: intrinsicality, affect, expectation, meaning, intelligence, listening, sensuosity, time, reference, inspiration and creativity, greatness, universals, functionality, and musicality. One statement made by the editors (1992: 272–273) corroborates the scientific findings of cognitive studies regarding musicality—the ability to have musical experiences: "Many if not most writers on musical experience believe that the ability to experience music is so widespread that it must be considered an inborn capacity for all humans . . . Musical experience is not limited to the talented or elite. That is why all cultures have music and all people have musical experience by nature." Under the section labeled "Universals," Leonard Bernstein as well as Fred Lerdahl and Ray Jackendoff are most affirmative regarding the universality of musical experience. As representing the thought of Bernstein, the editors affirm that "[j]ust as different cultures of the world have constructed a large number of grammars or languages from the basic monogenetic materials, Bernstein believes that all types of music from the world's cultures are derived from a common origin that he calls the universal phenomenon of the harmonic series" (1992: 263–264). And for Lerdahl and Jackendoff, they explain that "[u]niversal principles of musical grammar (or musical universals) are hypotheses about those aspects of musical understanding that are innate to all humans. The musical universals are principles available to all experienced listeners for organizing the musical surfaces they hear, regardless of the idiom in which they are experienced" (1992: 262). An example of a universal principle of music noted by Lerdahl and Jackendoff is that of stress points: "The comprehension of regular or irregular stress points in music is an innate aspect of hearing and comprehending music. This rule can apply in every idiom and is therefore considered a universal rule" (1992: 265). Related to musicality, the origin of music is the subject of the next section.

Origin of Music

In the zealous probing into the origins of religion and language, many scholars have previously overlooked the enormous significance of music in the early stages of human development, much to the detriment of history, anthropology, and especially musicology. But now that such interest in the issue of the "origin of music" has re-emerged among scientists, there is a new confidence based on cognitive research that supports the biological and evolutionary significance of music. Before examining some of the new perspectives in cognitive studies on the origin of music, however, we pause to recall the view of ethnomusicology conveyed by Bruno Nettl (2000: 463): "The point is that ethnomusicologists today have no special claim to be concerned with or to know something about the origins of music. They are really more concerned with beliefs or myths of the world's societies about the origins of music, and with what these myths may tell us about the way each of the world's peoples conceives of music and its role in culture." Appropriately, both points of view are accommodated in the Musicology of Religion.

In *The Descent of Man* (1871), which reshaped all human biological history with its theory of human evolution and sexual selection, Charles Darwin (1809–1882) devoted ten pages to music (see Darwin 2004: 417, 429, 632–639). Asserting a continuity with pre-human species, Darwin (2004: 636) placed music in the oldest layers of human history: "Whether or not the half-human progenitors of man possessed, like the singing gibbons, the capacity of producing, and therefore no doubt of appreciating, musical notes, we know that man possessed these faculties at a very remote period . . . The arts of singing and of dancing are also very ancient." Darwin (2004: 639) also believed that musicality was linked with sexual selection in its early stages, a tendency that lingers on inadvertently in the succeeding historical process: "The impassioned orator, bard, or musician, when with his varied tones and cadences he excites the strongest emotions in his hearers, little suspects that he uses the same means by which is half-human ancestors long ago aroused each other's ardent passions, during their courtship and rivalry."

Neuroscientist Aniruddh D. Patel, in *Music and the Brain* (2015: 31, 349), interprets Darwin's relevance in the current context: "Darwin believed that music was ancient, universal, and powerful, and that its origins must lie in some biological function that musical behavior had for our ancestors . . . Charles Darwin felt that there was a deep connection between our singing and the songs of other animals. He theorized that our ancestors sang wordless songs before they spoke to help them attract mates the way many birds use song today." In fact, scientific experiments conducted within the past twenty years have shown that birdsongs display melodic contour, fireflies communicate with pulsing patterns of sound, whales deliver songlike communication, and some primates engage in vocalizations that resemble wordless singing. Yet despite these discoveries, and others, clear differences remain between human and nonhuman music-making, such that much more research must be done to resolve many of the debates concerning the origin of music. In effect, Darwin's influence has even prompted several scholars to argue for a kind of "proto-musicality" in the human species that predates the arrival of language communication. Patel (2015: 28) grounds music in the ancient adaptive mechanisms of survival that, according to Darwin, predate language and literacy by thousands of years: "Music is much more universal and ancient than literacy, and unlike literacy, basic musical abilities develop without any special instruction." In favor of the primacy of music over literacy, it may be noted that literacy has been around for only about 5,000 years, and evidence of musical instruments exists as far back as 40,000 years. Supporting this position, Patel advanced theories that point to a biological specialization or predisposition for music that predate similar types of specializations for language learning that develop later in the human chronology.

Prior to the rise of neuroscience and the renewal of Darwinian thought in recent decades, an earlier twentieth-century work by music historian Siegfried Nadel attempted to set some initial guidelines for the development of the new field of evolutionary musicology without reference to Darwin. In his article "The Origins of Music" published in *Musical Quarterly* (1930), Nadel summarized the basic theories of the day followed by his own conclusion. After dismissing theories of music deriving from speech and language, from sexual selection (Darwin), and social cohesion, Nadel (1930: 542–543) firmly located the origin of all music within the emotional religious experiences of ancient peoples:

> Another highly significant factor plays a part here-the strong, thrilling emotional effect of music on the human spirit, which in all ages has provoked comparison with the state of ecstasy (the Greeks knew and feared the "*ethos ekstatikon*" of music), and the state of intoxication. The musical usages of the primitives, as well as those of many highly developed Oriental civilizations,

and even our own "romantic" conception of music, recognize only this state of ecstasy and strongest psychic emotion in the enjoyment of music. Bear in mind how intimately this state of entrancement has been connected, in every period, with the mystic and religious experiences of mankind. In this state we again see the principle of the supernatural, the out-of-the-ordinary, illustrated. This emotional effect of music should, therefore, have still more firmly knit the bond between religious cult and music, and have made the "music as intoxicant" a collaborator in the creation of the "music as art."

Ethnomusicologist Bruno Nettl, in *The Study of Ethnomusicology: Thirty-one Issues and Concepts*, recognized the profound implications of Nadel's assessment. Nettl (2005 [1983]: 262–263) explained how his own work carried forth similar conclusions: "We are drawn to a suggestion by Nadel. Noting the close association in all cultures between music and religion, as well as the tendency to render the most serious and formal aspects of rituals musically, he hypothesized the beginnings of music as a result of a need for establishing a particular way of communicating with the supernatural, a way of sharing certain major characteristics of speech—the ordinary human communication—that is nonetheless readily distinct from it." Yet without the new scientific research brought out by neuroscience on the universality of human musicality, the directions indicated by Nadel and Nettl would not carry the consensus in ethnomusicology, which was moving more and more in the direction, like William James and unlike Darwin, toward musical relativism, the view of music as a purely cultural construct, reinforcing the diverse particularity of music rather than its universal characteristics within the species.

Despite tendencies toward particularism (non-universalism) in ethnomusicology, however, recent work in cognitive science on the role of music in the biological development of the human species has significantly reinforced the universalist claim. The implications here for music in psychology of religion are apparent, especially those arising from the subfields of evolutionary musicology and "bio-musicology." In the monumental volume derived from a European conference and edited by Nils L. Wallin, Bjorn Merker, and Steven Brown, *The Origins of Music* (2000), groundwork was laid for the future of the scientific approach to music as a fundamental dimension of human consciousness. The description of the book speaks for itself:

What biological and cognitive forces have shaped humankind's musical behavior and the rich global repertoire of musical structures? What is music for, and why does every human culture have it? What are the universal features of music and musical behavior across cultures? In this groundbreaking book, musicologists, biologists, anthropologists, archaeologists, psychologists, neuroscientists, ethologists, and linguists come together for the first time to examine these and related issues. The book can be viewed as representing the birth of evolutionary bio-musicology—the study of which will contribute greatly to our understanding of the evolutionary precursors of human music, the evolution of the hominid vocal tract, localization of brain function, the structure of acoustic-communication signals, symbolic gesture, emotional manipulation through sound, self-expression, creativity, the human affinity for the spiritual, and the human attachment to music itself.

From the outset, *The Origins of Music* (Wallin 2000: 3) builds an ironclad case for the inclusion of music in any form of evolutionary study of the human species: "The language-centered view of humanity has to be expanded to include music, first, because the evolution of language is highly intertwined with the evolution of music, and second, because music provides a specific and direct means of exploring the evolution of human social structure, group function, and cultural behavior. Music making is the quintessential human cultural activity, and music is an ubiquitous element in all cultures large and small." Whereas in previous studies language was isolated as a unique phenomenon, in the new approach, as also discussed in Patel (2008, 2015), music and language are genetically related (2000: 8): "Many parallels exist between music and language at the structural level . . . In fact, the distinction between speaking and singing is best thought of as a difference in degree rather than a difference in kind." And while music is still neglected by some scientists in favor of language or creativity as the only truly unique human trait, a single precursor to both music and language has been identified by Steven Brown as "musilanguage," as discussed in "The Musilanguage Model of Human Evolution" (2000). The entire issue of the interrelationship of language and music—including the three theories that music evolved from speech, that speech evolved from music, or that both evolved from a common ancestor—is also of paramount concern to the future of key disciplines impacting the study of music in the psychology of religion: "We predict that this will become one of the central issues in the areas of music psychology, intonational phonology, and bio-musicology in years to come" (Brown 2000: 8). In fact, this approach to music illumines several features of vocal and gestural behavior that are changing the narrative of linguistics and human history: "The study of music evolution promises to shed light on such important issues as evolution of the hominid vocal tract; the structure of acoustic communication signals; human group structure; division of labor at the group level; the capacity for designing and using tools; symbolic gesturing; localization and lateralization of brain function; melody and rhythm in speech; the phrase-structure of language; parent-infant communication; emotional and behavioral manipulation through sound; interpersonal bonding and synchronization mechanisms; self-expression and catharsis; creativity and aesthetic expression; the human affinity for the spiritual and the mystical; and finally, of course, the universal human attachment to music itself" (2000: 3).

The new perspectives on music evolution raise questions regarding the claims of many ethnomusicologists, influenced by anthropology, namely, that every musical culture is qualitatively different and unique, and that there are no universals in music theory or history. This is clearly indicated in Wallin (2000: 13): "In the case of ethnomusicology, universals have been a subject of great skepticism, as they are seen as smacking too much of biological determinism, and therefore of denying the importance of historical forces and cultural traditions in explaining the properties of musical systems and musical behavior." The editors boldly defend their case in this way (2000: 14): "It is simply wrong to say that a demonstration of musical universals denies anything of the uniqueness or richness of any culture's particular forms of musical expression. If anything, it protects this uniqueness against ethnocentric claims that some cultures' musics are 'more evolved' than those of other cultures, claims frequently heard even in contemporary times." Moreover, ethnomusicologists are alleged to have overlooked the rapidly growing mass of information gathered by other disciplines (2000: 20): "The cultural evolutionary issues, including musical universals, classification, replicators, and the musical map of the world, are critical concerns that contemporary ethnomusicology has either ignored or simply rejected." The positive elements of musical universals are required for any balanced scientific approach to music in psychology, as stated (2000: 13): "The idea of musical universals does nothing if not place all of humankind on equal ground, acting as a biological safeguard against ethnocentric notions of musical superiority. In this balancing act between biological constraints and historical forces, the notion of musical universals merely provides a focus on the unity that underlies the diversity present in the world's musical systems and attributes this unity to neural constraints underlying musical processing."

There are thus clear directives for musicologists and ethnomusicologists to heed the call of evolutionary and cognitive science, as expressed by Wallin (2000: 18): "Comparative musicology must seriously return to the issues of musical universals and classification to understand not only the deep evolutionary roots of music but how contemporary musical systems undergo change and stasis from historical and geographic perspectives." Examples of the features of music that support the universalist approach are in fact legion, and most do not delimit the intrinsic value of specific musical cultures. A few examples have been provided (2000: 14): "As a preview to a universal theory, let us just mention that octaves are perceived as equivalent in almost all cultures, that virtually all scales of the world consist of seven or fewer pitches (per octave), that most of the world's rhythmic patterns are based on divisive patterns of twos and threes, and that emotional excitement in music is universally expressed through loud, fast, accelerating, and high-registered sound patterns." Based on this current research, the ground is fertile for more discussion and serious consideration of universals in music as germane to the Musicology of Religion.

Yet detractors such as Steven Pinker, in *How the Mind Works* (1997), have proclaimed music to be a kind of "auditory cheesecake" derivative of other faculties and but a mere human invention for purposes of entertainment. Debunking this theory and building on the cogency of the points presented in the Wallin anthology discussed above, Steven Mithen, in *The Singing Neanderthals: The Origins of Music, Language, Mind, and Body* (2006), begins his analysis in chapter 1, "The Mystery of Music: The Need for an Evolutionary History of Music" (2006: 1): "The appreciation of music is a universal feature of humankind; music-making is found in all societies, and it is normal for everyone to participate in some manner; the modern-day West is quite unusual in having significant numbers of people who do not actively participate and may even claim to be unmusical. Rather than looking at sociological or historical factors, we can only explain the human propensity to make and listen to music by recognizing that it has been encoded into the human genome during the evolutionary history of our species."

Furthermore, in the essay "Music and the Miraculous: The Neurophysiology of Music's Emotive Meaning" (2008), C. S. Alcorta shared research into the supernatural features of music from the viewpoint of a neuroscientist. Paraphrasing the conclusions, Alcorta explains how the human ability to make and be moved by music is a universal human trait shared across cultures throughout the world as a central element of religious ritual. Like miracles, music is intimately interconnected with a sense of the sacred, the numinous, and the divine. Music not only represents the sacred but also calls it forth and embodies it. Among the Mbuti pygmies of Africa, the haunting music of the sacred bull roarer is not just the symbol of the divine; this music is the divine as it embodies the "voice" of the forest. For the Mbuti, music has the miraculous power to transform a rusty pipe into a sacred presence that evokes joy, fear, and awe. The ability of music to invest the profane with sacred significance by eliciting feelings of joy, fear, and awe lies at the heart of music's central role in all religions. When combined with communal ritual, the intense emotions stirred by music become powerful motivational forces.

As demonstrated in the few examples given in this section, the fields of neuroscience and cognitive studies have only begun to unravel the ultimate questions about religion and music. We look forward to their continuing revelations through the lens of science.

This chapter completes Part II. In Part III, in the form of chapter 8, many of the themes and concerns from the previous chapters are assembled into a coherent argument and strategy for implementing the field of Musicology of Religion. This includes examining the academic concepts of Homo Religiosus, Homo Musicus, and their connecting link, Homo Ritualis. When combined as a kind of "triune human being," these three foci offer useful categories that serve to unify the ordinarily disparate sectors of religious studies, musicology, and aesthetics. This is followed by discussion of ways of resolving the apparent division between universal and relativistic interpretations of religion and music, the broadening of phenomenology of religion as well as music, and the need for the inclusion of theology and liturgical studies to furnish important data for the Musicology of Religion.

III

Homo Religiosus and Homo Musicus

Chapter Eight

Musicology of Religion

Homo Religiosus always believes that there is an absolute reality, the sacred, which transcends this world but manifests itself in this world, thereby sanctifying it and making it real. He [she] further believes that life has a sacred origin, and that human existence realizes all of its potentialities in proportion as it is religious—that is, participates in reality.

—Mircea Eliade, *The Sacred and the Profane: The Nature of Religion*

Homo Musicus, of man the musician, the being that requires music to realize itself fully. This dimension of our humanity has largely been in shadow over the course of Western thought. It is time to bring it into the light.

—Victor Zuckerkandl, *Man the Musician*

For the *Homo Ritualis*, the religious feeling of space and time is absolute, not relative; it creates identities (or distinctions)—rather than similarities—between spaces.

—Axel Michaels, *Homo Ritualis*

The descriptions in the foregoing chapters of the role of music, whether great or small, in religious studies, the social sciences, philosophy, theology, liturgical studies, and cognitive studies, as well as the rapid rise of interest by the public sector, should awaken us to the need for a creative resolution involving religion and music as a singular unit of study and research. As indicated at the outset, just as one encounters the sociology of religion, anthropology of religion, sociology of religion, and psychology of religion, we now hear the beckoning of a new field, Musicology of Religion. The principal object of Musicology of Religion is the connection between religion and music covering a broad spectrum, and its approach and methods are necessarily comparative and geared toward finding cross-cultural patterns and insights that are otherwise concealed or less obvious. The successful pursuit of Musicology of Religion thus requires a refined strategy that draws on a variety of disciplines and accomplishes results despite minor challenges posed by critics of musical universalism and comparative religion. We will now attempt to establish guidelines based on the terrain covered in the previous chapters and determine how to shape and structure a Musicology of Religion.

Our true aim is to develop a "meta-conversation" involving religion and music that rises above specific methods and traditions. One may study and discuss Jewish religious music, Navaho religious music, Hindu religious music—the examples are endless—but what is needed is more conversation about the universal and abiding connections between music and religion throughout the human condition, while at the same time taking note of differences. And while one may subscribe to the methods of anthropology of music, sociology of music, philosophy of music, and even a theology of music, our vision is to gain conclusions from the successes of all disciplines to foster and develop a Musicology of Religion that does not limit its methods or theories to one or another approach.

Arriving before Musicology of Religion, other "new disciplines" or "field neologisms" related to sound, music, and religion have emerged over the course of the past few decades. They include akumenal phenomenology or phenomenology of music (F. Joseph Smith 1979), theological aesthetics (Hans von Balthasar 1982, Patrick Sherry 1992, Richard Viladesau 1999), religious aesthetics (Frank Burch Brown 1989), sonic theology (Guy L. Beck 1993), theomusicology (Jon Michael Spencer 1994), ritual musicology (Edward Foley 1995), acoustemology (Steven Feld 1996), musical theology (Jeremy S. Begbie 2005), rhythmic theology (Eben Graves 2009), neurotheology (Andrew B. Newberg 2010), sonic liturgy (Guy L. Beck 2012), and musical religiosity (Martin Hoondert 2015). The Musicology of Religion as outlined in this book is not just another new subfield designed to supplant other proposed fields. The hope is that the research and content of these new fields, at best, will be channeled into the broader template of the Musicology of Religion, which will be strengthened and sustained in conversation with the other new fields. Thus, Musicology of Religion, drawing on a panoply of disciplines, old and new, is an effective and decisive moniker to encompass research into what we have posited as a central core of the human experience of the sacred, that is, music in combination with religion.

One underlying "structure" that seems to endure throughout the entire domain of religion and music is worthy of recollection here. Without attaching the qualifier "sacred" to every noun in our analysis, it seems plausible to accept that most religions involve "word" in combination with "rite," "rite" in combination with "music," and "music" in combination with "word," forming a kind of triune circularity (triangularity!) that may be viewed from many angles, like a prism. The foresight of Frank Burch Brown (2014: 109) is recalled: "The music that is most easily identified as religious is usually combined with words or with ritual action." While there are exceptions, it appears habitual and even predictable that ritual is tied to word and music, word is tied to ritual and music, and music is tied to word and ritual. The inverse bears some attention, as virtually no religious tradition exists in which rite exists in silence without word, or in which word exists in isolation from rite and music, or one that completely divorces music from rite and word. Specialized training in several disciplines is required to grasp the implications of these phenomena in their entirety. Academically, the theological or religious studies approach will focus on revelation, "scripture," and religious experience, the anthropological or liturgical studies approach will examine the practical dimension of ritual or liturgy, and a musicological approach will examine the sonic and musical dimensions including voice and instruments. But since all three are connected, to construct a competent "morphology" and analysis of sacred sound and music one needs a multipronged approach, with training in multiple fields.

For purposes of articulating this triune theme as a foundation for Musicology of Religion, we will now recall established notions of human nature as essentially religious, musical, and ritualistic. As the word "homo" means both man and woman and is related to the word humanity, these concepts appear in the form of homo religiosus, homo musicus, and homo ritualis.

Homo Religiosus

Throughout the study of religion, one of the recurring themes is that religiosity—the capacity for religious experiences—is part of human existence as a permanent nature or essence. This concept is known as Homo Religiosus and has been reaffirmed by research in cognitive studies. Yet even before the advancements in neuroscience that places both the religious and musical impulses directly in the mainstream of human evolution, we have the harbingers in the form of statements in both phenomenology of religion and history of religions. Following the line of Rudolf Otto, Mircea Eliade described the idea of *homo religiosus*, religious man, as a feature of the sacred history of humanity that is opposed by the profane world of modernity. The term *homo religiosus* refers to the idea that human existence is inherently religious, and that religiosity is somehow embedded in human nature. While this idea predates Otto and Eliade, of course, they have done the most to make it a signature of the phenomenology of religion. With roots in Plato and Greek philosophy, many modern philosophers have proposed similar ideas, including Hegel, Schleiermacher, Kierkegaard, William James, Gerardus van der Leeuw, Max Scheler, Karl Jaspers, and Paul Tillich. In most of these cases, the concept of *homo religiosus* is not about creedal beliefs or institutional affiliations but is predicated on the human existential drive toward transcendence, freedom, and higher meaning regardless of the differences of cultural or religious backgrounds or perspectives.

When Swedish botanist Carl Linnaeus (1707–1778), in *Systema Naturae*, coined the term *homo sapiens* ("the wise human") to designate the human species, he based this on eighteenth-century notions of humans as essentially rational beings. But the Romantic movement, influenced by emotional factors and concepts drawn from Antiquity, responded with characterizations that differed from the rational. Gregory D. Alles (1987: 443) explained this phenomenon: "Perhaps the nineteenth century's growing awareness of the universality of religion, especially in the realm of the 'primitives' (as they were then known), made it inevitable that a phrase would emerge to express that aspect of humanity that the Enlightenment's ideal had so opposed: *homo religiosus*, the 'religious human.'"

Historian of religion Gregory D. Alles, in "Homo Religiosus" (1987: 442–445), described three different meanings of "homo religiosus." The first one recognizes *homo religiosus* as a religious leader, an exceptional human being in communication with the supernatural. This was based on Greek and Latin writers of Antiquity, like Cicero (*De natura deorum*), who recognized *homines religiosi* as specialists in the sacred. Among the Romantics, this idea of the "religious human" was later revived under Schleiermacher with an emphasis on the individual and self-consciousness. In the twentieth century, Max Scheler, in *On the Eternal in Man* (1960: 134), fully encapsulated this view of *homo religiosus* as a particular type of human personality: "The fount of all religious truth is not scientific utterance but *faith* in the words of the *homo religiosus*, the 'holy man'—that is, a type of man that may be known by the following signs: 1. As a *whole and undivided person* he possesses a *charismatic quality* peculiar to no other outstanding type of humanity, such as the genius or hero. By virtue of this quality, he encounters belief simply because it is *he*—the bearer of this quality—who is talking, acting, expressing himself. 2. He lives in his own peculiar, real and vital relationship to the divine, as the eternal source of salvation, and bases his utterances and precepts, deeds and authority on this relation." Influenced by Scheler and Max Weber, Joachim Wach represented this view in modified form. The second type of Homo Religiosus was more generic and was a moniker for all humanity. Gerardus van der Leeuw developed this view in opposition to Scheler, whereby all human beings are potentially religious according to their nature.

The third type, though sometimes confused with the second, is when *homo religiosus* is viewed as a premodern condition opposed to modern secular consciousness. Noting that this was the position of Eliade, Alles (1987: 444) summarized Eliade's position regarding *homo religiosus*, especially as it is contrasted with the human condition in modernity:

> Eliade is struck by the difference between the nature and use of symbols in the ancient classical religions and especially among archaic cultures as opposed to the modern Western intelligentsia. He contrasts two distinct modes of existing in and experiencing the world. His *homo religiosus* is driven by a desire for being; modern humanity lives under the dominion of becoming. *Homo religiosus* thirsts for being in the guise of the sacred. *Homo religiosus* attempts to live at the center of the world, close to the gods and in the eternal present of the paradigmatic mythic event that makes profane duration possible. The experience of time and space for *homo religiosus* is characterized by a discontinuity between the sacred and profane. Modern humanity, however, experiences no such discontinuity. For *homo religiosus*, neither time nor space is capable of distinctive valorization. *Homo religiosus* is determined indiscriminately by all the events of history and by the concomitant threat of nothingness, which produces a profound anxiety.

Mircea Eliade explained in *The Quest: History and Meaning in Religion* (1969: 8) that, since *homo religiosus* refers to the "total man," the study of religion must orient itself around this permanent human capacity: "*Homo Religiosus* represents the 'total man'; hence, the science of religions must become a total discipline in the sense that it must use, integrate, and articulate the results obtained by the various methods of approaching a religious phenomenon." In *The Sacred and the Profane: The Nature of Religion* (1959: 15), Eliade earlier pointed to religious behavior as the substratum for this primordial capacity: "The man of traditional societies is admittedly a *homo religiosus*, but his behavior forms part of the general behavior of mankind and hence is of concern to philosophical anthropology, to phenomenology, to psychology." This behavior crosses all levels of humanity and behooves the attention of all comparative study: "We realize the validity of comparisons between religious facts pertaining to different cultures; all these facts arise from a single type of behavior, that of *homo religiosus*" (1959: 17–18). What is the nature of the beliefs of *homo religiosus*? Eliade explains: "Whatever the historical content in which he is placed, *homo religiosus* always believes that there is an absolute reality, the sacred, which transcends this world but manifests itself in this world, thereby sanctifying it and making it real. He further believes that life has a sacred origin, and that human existence realizes all of its potentialities in proportion as it is religious—that is, participates in reality. The gods created man and the world, the culture heroes completed the Creation, and the history of all these divine and semidivine works is preserved in myths. By re-actualizing sacred history, by imitating the divine behavior, man puts and keeps himself close to the gods—that is, in the real and the significant" (1959: 202).

The concept of *homo religiosus* has indeed been expanded in the thought of Mircea Eliade beyond several of his predecessors. In several ways, the individual as *homo religiosus* becomes humanity as *homines religiosi*. According to David Cave (1993: 92), "Eliade uses the term *homo religiosus* to refer to all humans. It is not meant for only the charismatic individual, such as the mystic, as it does for Schleiermacher, Max Scheler, and Joachim Wach. For Eliade, *homo religiosus* designates a quality of the human condition. The phenomenologist of religion Gerardus van der Leeuw uses it this way, but, in contrast to him, Eliade says the quality of *homo religiosus* remains in the secularized person, though obscured or camouflaged. The structural condition of *homo religiosus* manifests itself through the secularized person's nostalgias, dreams, ambitions, fictions, initiations, political movements, New Year festivals, etc." When referring to the total human person as *Homo Religiosus*, Eliade is thus, in part, reifying in expanded form the religious vision of Schleiermacher, of perceiving the infinite within the finite. Cave (1993: 94) seems to intuit this idea: "By positing the human as homo *religiosus*, Eliade infuses the dimension of meaning as a necessary and serviceable construct into all other characteristics that make up the totality of the human person."

For Eliade, *homo religiosus* becomes much more than a mere academic category but also the signature and touchstone for what he calls a "new humanism." David Cave has outlined this vision in *Mircea Eliade's Vision for a New Humanism* (1993: 92): "The presupposition that a human being is by nature *homo religiosus* underlies Eliade's theories of the behavior of humans toward the world in which they live. Humans have an essential desire to *be*, to live in Being, to live in a world that has meaning and is taken as sacred. It is this ontological view which makes the new humanism into a decidedly 'spiritual' enterprise. The new humanism involves the spirit, the eternal, and the nonchanging in human life."

One of the most sustained criticisms of *homo religiosus* came from a University of Chicago colleague Jonathan Z. Smith, in *Map is Not Territory: Studies in the History of Religions* (1978). For Eliade, the activities of archaic humans as *homo religiosus* reflect their understanding of the cosmogony or divine creation and were directed toward reenactment or repetition. In place of *homo religiosus*, Smith preferred the concept of *homo faber*, "human as toolmaker." Cave (1983: 144) explains this difference: "The fundamental distinction between Smith and Eliade is Smith's assertion that human's essential nature is firstly *homo faber*. That is, humans, in the order of things, first fashion their tools, domesticate the landscape, and construct their world and only later do they designate certain actions and certain places as special, different, sacred, as having religious meaning." Hence religion is not primary but only a secondary phenomenon based on historical situations and not divine revelation (1983: 144–145): "Humans do not inherently require the need to establish and understand their place within the cosmos. Meaning is a later imposition, being principally done for establishing power relations . . . For Smith, humans construct sacred place. It is not founded upon any cosmogony." Thus, the concept of *homo religiosus* is misguided and does not portray human consciousness at the beginning of time. And since Eliade stood in stark contrast to the scenario of *homo faber*, Smith viewed his work as flawed (1978: 91): "Eliade implies a fundamental reversal . . . man's fundamental mode is not freedom and creativity but rather repetition."

Yet there is a post-Kantian element in Smith's understanding of freedom that raises questions, as pointed out by Cave (1983: 119): "In being dependent upon an *a priori* ontology, the human as *homo religiosus* differs from the autonomously free *homo faber* in the post-Kantian view of human nature." In this post-Kantian view, archaic humans, as "free and autonomous" beings, first chose to make tools and develop technology by necessity as they wandered and settled according to their freedom of choice. Only later were religion and myth introduced as expressions of human power and social hierarchy, corresponding, as it were, to the Mirror Theory. Smith's assessment is thus problematic since it relies solely on post-Kantian notions of freedom in which humans are totally autonomous in the modern sense. His misinterpretation of Eliade is in fact based on his acceptance that since Kant, philosophers and scientists have proposed authentic theories based on the proposition that "man makes himself" (Cave 1983: 120): "Smith's misgiving concerning *homo religiosus* rests on the Kantian notion that humans stand over against nature as subjects to object . . . Nature becomes what humans make it to be." In Eliade's defense, then, Cave (1983: 122) explained how freedom for *homo religiosus* rests on a much wider perspective of freedom: "Smith is misleading in ascribing freedom to *homo faber* and insinuating its absence in *homo religiosus* . . . To speak of freedom for Eliade, who operated from a Goethian paradigm rather than a Kantian, we find that freedom includes not just our Western perceptions of the term but archaic and Eastern ones as well."

In a 1985 article. "*Homo Faber* and *Homo Religiosus*," Mircea Eliade indirectly responds to the argument of Smith. After recounting the history of toolmaking and metallurgy and how these skills have always been associated with the revelation of the sacred and hence *homo religiosus*, Eliade (1985: 11) explained how even in the modern world the two concepts of *homo faber* and *homo religiosus* are closely intertwined: "In the last analysis, we discover that the latest activities and conclusions of scientists and technologists—the direct descendants of *homo faber*—reactualize, on different levels and perspectives, the same fears, hopes, and convictions that have dominated *homo religiosus* from the very beginning: the fear of death, and even the catastrophic destruction of life; the hope of conquering death through a ritually constructed post-existence; and, finally, the certitude that the indestructibility of life and the immortality of the soul are to be accepted as they are, as a series of states of consciousness."

Bryan S. Rennie, one of the foremost interpreters of Eliade's thought, has also discussed *homo religiosus* in relation to all humanity. In *Reconstructing Eliade: Making Sense of Religion*, Rennie (1996: 43) states: "If it is to be accepted that the religious person is the person in specific relation to the sacred, and that the sacred is equated with the real, then *homo religiosus* must be seen as humanity insofar as we apprehend the real and apprehend ourselves as standing in some specific relationship to reality." More recently, Andreas Nehring (2016: 99) has further clarified Eliade's position on *homo religiosus*, arguing that if the study of religion employs this concept in the sense of the total human person, almost by definition the discipline must include a myriad of approaches: "Because *homo religiosus* represents the 'total man,' as Eliade argues, the science of religions can never be reductionistic, but must become a total discipline in the sense that it must use, integrate and articulate the results gained from various methods of approaching a religious phenomenon." There is here a natural and inevitable congruence with Musicology of Religion.

Over the years, a renewal of interest has continued in the idea of *homo religiosus*, which serves to validate it in religious studies with the support of cognitive studies. Timothy Samuel Shah and Jack Friedman, in *Homo Religiosus? Exploring the Roots of Religion and Religious Freedom in Human Experience* (2018: 1), state at the outset that the case is affirmative in favor of *homo religiosus*: "This volume invites a renewed inquiry into an enduring question: are humans naturally religious? Do they possess a set of common characteristics transcending time, place, and culture that incline them toward religion? The answer, according to a growing body of research in the cognitive and evolutionary sciences of religion, appears to be yes."

Homo Musicus

Throughout the study of music, a recurring theme is that musicality—the capacity for musical experiences—is fundamental to human existence and part of the essence of human nature. The concept of Homo Musicus, "the musical human," though not as widely circulated as Homo Religiosus, generates its own respect and signification nowadays due to advances in the cognitive study of music. The term was established by the famed Austrian musicologist Victor Zuckerkandl, in *Man the Musician*, based partly on an interpretation of a message originally conveyed in a dialogue of Plato. The context involves a confidential statement made by Socrates as he awaited execution. During the closing hours of his life, Socrates shared a dream that came to him while asleep in his prison cell, and which his student Plato had recorded in the *Phaedo*. The statement of Socrates is given here in the 1914 translation of *Phaedo* (60e) by Harold North Fowler (Plato 1966: 211–213): "The same dream came to me often in my past life, sometimes in one form and sometimes in another, but always saying the same thing: 'Socrates,' it said; 'make music and work at it.' And I formerly thought it was urging and encouraging me to do what I was doing already and that just as people encourage runners by cheering, so the dream was encouraging me to do what I was doing, that is, to make music, because philosophy was the greatest kind of music and I was working at that. But now, after the trial and while the festival of the god delayed my execution, I thought, in case the repeated dream really meant to tell me to make this which was ordinarily called music, I ought to do so and not to disobey . . . So first I composed a hymn to the god whose festival it was."

The Fowler translation above complies with the earlier nineteenth-century version of Benjamin Jowett (Plato 2007: 38): "In the course of my life I have often had intimations in dreams 'that I should make music.' The same dream came to me sometimes in one form, and sometimes in another, but always saying the same or nearly the same words: 'Make and cultivate music,' said the dream. And hitherto I had imagined that this was only intended to exhort and encourage me in the study of philosophy, which has been the pursuit of my life, and is the noblest and best of music." This message was taken to be of high importance since it purports to say that music should be considered the greatest philosophy and the noblest pursuit of human beings—pointing to the appropriate identification of the human species as "Homo Musicus." But while two later translations have lessened music's position by replacing the word "music" with either "the arts" (Plato 1971: 103) or simply "art" (Plato 1993: 5), a closer look at the original Greek, "make music and work at it," confirms the original meaning: *mousikēn poiei kai ergazou: mousikēn poiei* = "make music/serve the art of music," and *kai ergazou* = "and work."[1]

Based on this pronouncement of Socrates, as well as other discussions in Plato's dialogues regarding the harmony of the spheres and the corresponding harmony of the soul, Zuckerkandl (1973: 2–3) regarded music as fundamental to human nature: "Music still is, just as it has always been, the other power which, along with language, fully defines man as a spiritual being. No one who has not recognized and honored music as such can be said to have paid his full debt in the world, to himself, to mankind. The notion to which the *Phaedo* gives expression is that of *homo musicus*, of man as musician, the being that requires music to realize itself fully. This dimension of our humanity has largely been in shadow over the course of

---

1. Thanks to classical scholar Dr. Eleni Boliaki (personal communication, April 2022).

Western thought. It is time to bring it into light." Here Zuckerkandl implies that the human life is not complete without music, as music reaches into the interiority of the self and consciousness and provides something invaluable that no other art can give. We have seen the immense importance given to music through the ages by scholars of multiple disciplines, and with the reinforcement of cognitive studies, musicality, along with religiosity, virtually defines the human condition.

Zuckerkandl (1973: 7–8) further amplified the idea of Homo Musicus in terms of an assessment of all humanity regarding musicality, or as the universal tendency to make music: "Musicality is not the property of individuals but an essential attribute of the human species. The implication is not that some men are musical while others are not, but that man is a musical animal, that is, a being predisposed to music and in need of music, a being that for its full realization must express itself in tones and owes it to itself and to the world to produce music. In this sense, musicality is not something one may or may not have, but something that—along with other factors—is constitutive of man." Accordingly, music is a universal endowment like reason or will: "So defined, the concept cannot have a negative counterpart; to call a man unmusical would be meaningless, self-contradictory. Nobody is being singled out and set apart. Music is the concern of all, not of a privileged elite, and if musicality represents an asset, it is not the prerogative of a chosen few, but an endowment of man as man."

Writers and scholars from outside of religious studies have corroborated the connection of music with human nature, such as intellectual historian George Steiner (1991: 6), who concluded: "I believe the matter of music to be central to that of the meanings of man, of man's access to or abstention from metaphysical experience . . . To ask 'what is music?' may well be one way of asking 'what is man?'" And coupled with observations in cognitive studies, such as that of Pascal Boyer (2001: 132), the status of Homo Musicus is reinforced: "Humans are predisposed to detect, produce, remember, and enjoy music. This is a human universal. There is no human society without some musical tradition."

Most recently, Russian music psychologist Dina Kirnarskaya has researched the preeminent value of music as part of education and concluded that Homo Musicus (Musical Man) must have predated Homo Sapiens (Reasoning Man). In *The Natural Musician: On Abilities, Giftedness, and Talent*, Kirnarskaya (2009: 351) provides support with reference to cognitive history: "*Homo musicus*—Musical Man, who creates, performs, and listens to music—is older than *Homo sapiens* [Reasoning Man]." She revealed how

"Man made music of a sort even when he did not know how to measure things or count them properly, and the very concept of numbers was still but a glimmer in his brain. He made music when he could not find the reason for natural phenomena, the rain, hail, and drought around him. He made music before he had learned to work the land and before he could build a boat to cross the sea. Music was already, in the most distant antiquity, the concentration on feeling and thought in our primitive ancestor." Rational thought of various dimensions was even prefigured in the structure of music itself (2009: 351): "Before the formulation of mathematics as a science, there was present in the rhythm of music the essence of proportions, symmetry, and the relationship of things in time; geometry did not exist, yet in the songs man sang there was already a concept of higher and lower, of different 'points in space' which indicated different ranges of sound." Abstract thought as exemplified in Homo Sapiens was hence the result of long evolutionary cycles that were predated by musical activity (2009: 351): "Earliest man thought with the help of music even before he came upon abstract thought and learned to use concepts. Man's mental abilities were assembled over thousands of years in the framework provided by the art of Music, a framework left distinct as evolution moved on." Kirnarskaya (2009: 352) suggests that, since the germs of thought existed in the musical mind of prehistory, the proper understanding of the mind must include a return to its source, musical thought: "Thinking as such and the procedures of thought—comparison, apposition, analysis, and synthesis, the division of things and their assembly into a whole—exist organically in music. Indeed, it is entirely possible that these functions proceeded from music to the realm of abstract thought, creating a psychological bridge between the world of art and that of science . . . a man wishing to order his thoughts naturally, wishing to return to the psychological sources of thought, and to give thought over completely to nature—such a man must inevitably turn to music. He must become *Homo musicus* in order to return in future to *Homo sapiens*—such was the process of the evolution of the human brain, and there is nothing more sensible in the development of one's mental powers than to turn to their musical source."

Music is also included with the other arts in the historical scenario described by Kirnarskaya (2009: 351), which indicates how the arts preceded rational thought processes in humankind: "Art and music are older than science, and indeed older than thought itself; in art man expresses his relationship to nature and life, with the ideational process dissolving into sensation and blending into it entirely. Art as the creative self-expression of man and the method of interaction with the world arose earlier than abstract thought and science. This means that the human brain was originally formed in the venues of art—songs, dances, and rituals. It was formed when man covered the walls of his cave with magical drawings, it was made when he made rhymes and sang songs—and only then, after the passing of many millennia, did this brain chart the course of the planets, open the secrets of matter, and discover the laws of natural evolution." Many of her observations and conclusions are benchmarks in the development of the Musicology of Religion.

Homo Ritualis

In the search for the elusive "missing link" between religion and music, we have identified ritual and liturgy as probable candidates in our discussion of Ritual Studies and Liturgical Studies. But while anthropologists and scholars in religion have accented the critical importance of ritual as part of human nature, until very recently there has not been a proper moniker for this "link" that could be juxtaposed with Homo Religiosus and Homo Musicus. In addition to religiosity and musicality, the capacity for ritual is also considered by scholars to be fundamental to human existence. Thus, we have the concept of Homo Ritualis, the "ritual human," which has come to our attention through the work of Axel Michaels (2015). But in fact, despite the multiple behaviors performed by human beings, Louis Bouyer (1963: 57) had earlier explained that ritual is the most fundamental characteristic of human existence, especially in relation to the divine: "A rite is not simply one type of action among many others. It is the typical human action, in as much as it is connected with the word as the expression and realization of man in the world, and to the degree that this expression and realization are immediately and fundamentally religious . . . A rite is a human action in which man apprehends himself as a religious being . . . what a man does in the rite is a divine action, an action which God performs through and in man, as much as man himself performs it in and through God."

Ritual studies pioneer Catherine Bell (1998: 205) has reaffirmed this position and amplified the critical need for more attention to ritual by academic scholars in both religious studies and the social sciences: "Most theories of religion since the Enlightenment have tended to emphasize the more cognitive aspects of religion no matter how rooted these were thought to be emotional, doctrinal, or communal experience . . . In the last several decades, however, religious studies has become (as have other fields such as anthropology, history, and psychology) increasingly concerned to give more attention to the actual 'doing' of religion."

Taking firm hold of this direction, anthropologist Roy A. Rappaport, in his monumental study *Ritual and Religion in the Making of Humanity* (1999: 31), emphasized that ritual is fundamental to the human species: "The ubiquity of ritual . . . approaches universality: no society is devoid of what a reasonable observer would recognize as ritual . . . I therefore take ritual to be the social fact basic to humanity." Rappaport analyzes the ramifications of his theory of ritual by positing that while the particulars are different throughout the world, the "form" of ritual is universal and is sustained through what he calls "metamessages": "If, in contrast to the infinite variety of ritual contexts, the ritual form is universal, then it is plausible to assume that the metamessages intrinsic to that form are also universal." The sacred "metamessages" that are considered universal and intrinsic to ritual are termed "Ultimate Sacred Postulates" by Rappaport (1999: 371): "The locus of the sacred, in bodies of religious discourse, lies in certain expressions, labelled Ultimate Sacred Postulates, enunciated in ritual and sometimes elsewhere as well. These expressions are peculiar in that they are typically absolutely unfalsifiable and objectively unverifiable, but are nonetheless taken to be unquestionable." Examples of such postulates in the West are cited as the Jewish *Shema*, the Lord's Prayer in Christianity, and the Call to Prayer in Islam ("There is no God but God"). But one might also include Asian examples, such as Hindu Mantras and the Buddhist Four Noble Truths. What Rappaport is saying is that all religions contain some form of linguistic assertion or statement as a sacred postulate (1999: 278): "Equivalent expressions are implicit if not explicit in the rituals of all religions, even those claiming to postulate no spiritual beings, or to espouse no creed. It is, in fact, by the presence of such sacred postulates, implicit or explicit, that we finally take liturgical orders to be religious."

Bridging religion and ritual in theory is one thing; realizing and establishing its truth through practical observation in a specific religious tradition is quite another. Recent work in Asian studies has accomplished this feat of cementing the divide between ritual and religion: this is done by establishing the term and concept of Homo Ritualis, the "ritual human." Focusing on the Hindu tradition as a prime exemplar of ritualistic religion, Axel Michaels, in *Homo Ritualis: Hindu Ritual and its Significance for Rit-*

ual Theory (2015: 70), develops the theme of Homo Ritualis as a kind of archetype for the generic human being who is preordained to conduct and perform rituals no matter how large or small: "For the *homo ritualis*, the religious feeling of space and time is absolute, not relative; it creates identities (or distinctions)—rather than similarities—between spaces." Ritual is indissolubly bound to sound and music when it enters the realm of religion (2015: 150): "Ritual music is sacred or mythical music, and so what is true for mythical spaces and times is also true for it. Ritual music and ritual are thus not complementary, but rather form a unit. Music, then, exists not only in space and time but also outside both. It is not in the ritual, or during the ritual, but forms itself the whole strength of the ritual. Ritual music is therefore a sacred potency which different things may possess at the same time; the sacred arena and sacred space, the priest, the statue, or, precisely, a piece of music." As a central part of religion, the close bond between music and ritual is made crystal clear by Michaels (2015: 150), who explains the experience of the religious *homo ritualis*: "Ritual music, in this sense, is unique, for the religious *homo ritualis* does not know of similarities in the context of spaces, only of identities or differences therein. Every perceivable equivalence is identity, the expression of the same sacred potency. Equally, it is no coincidence for the religious *homo ritualis*, or only an external feature, where and when something exists; rather, for this person, a binding relationship exists between the object and its expression—in this case, between ritual and music." When ritual and music (and dance) are wedded, the gods come into play (2015: 159): "For the person bound to ritual, the *homo ritualis*, in ritual dances it is the gods who dance, not man." Current interest in this link or "bridge" between ritual and music is exemplified by a volume of essays compiled by editors Raquel Jimenez, Rupert Till, and Michael Howell, *Music and Ritual: Bridging Material and Living Cultures* (2013).

In many respects, then, the formerly separate portrayals of human nature as religious, musical, or ritualistic find their unified expression in the Musicology of Religion as the triune combination of Homo Religiosus, Homo Musicus, and Homo Ritualis.

More Issues of Method

Setting up guidelines for the Musicology of Religion requires that we take a closer look at some methodological issues that warrant attention. As a case in point, Isabel Laack, in "Sound, Music and Religion: A Preliminary Cartography of a Transdisciplinary Research field" (2015), reviews several recent works in music and religion. Laack (2015: 222) then outlines the prospects for a new research field involving what she calls "transdisciplinarity": "The study of sound, music and religion is best undertaken as a transdisciplinary endeavor, considering diverse disciplines from the humanities, social sciences, and natural sciences. The academic study of religion has been pursued from many distinctive perspectives since its beginnings: from within science-oriented traditions as much as within humanistic and hermeneutical academic schools such as the phenomenology of religion or the history of religions as understood by Mircea Eliade. Accordingly, we tend to group these approaches into so-called 'subdisciplines' such as sociology of religion or psychology of religion." So far so good, but she then stops short of endorsing a "musicology of religion" due to stated concerns for a broader dialogue and less specialization: "Following this line of thought, we could simply call for a musicology (or acoustemology) of religion. However, this avenue might lead us to over-specialization and thus to a further seclusion of the field rather than opening the way to interdisciplinary dialogue and knowledge transfer. Therefore, I suggest joining the current movement towards transdisciplinary thinking. Concisely, transdisciplinarity represents a way of working on a particular topic or research field in which traditional boundaries of academic disciplines are transcended and in which their distinctive perspectives are combined to gain more holistic knowledge on a complex aspect of human life." However, although advocating for a broad interdisciplinary field of study, Laack (2015: 241) concedes in favor of pursuing a "critical secular approach" that dismisses theological, religious, and phenomenological methods and directions: "I opted for a transdisciplinary perspective that is open to contributions from many disciplines within the humanities, social sciences, and natural sciences. Epistemologically, I believe that a critical secular approach rather than a phenomenological, theological, or religious approach contains more potential for dialogue among the disciplines." This is the point of difference from what we are proposing here, which is a field of study that would give equal weight to all forms of academic inquiry and research, including theology and phenomenology. In addition, though the terms "interdisciplinarity" or "transdisciplinarity" may appeal to advanced scholars, I would wager that neither would attract or persuade newcomers to the subject matter.

For true transdisciplinarity, all perspectives are necessary, including especially phenomenology and theology, as discussed in previous chapters.

No one perspective or vantage point is sufficient to encompass the broad range of music and religion. The earlier example of the five blind men may be recalled here, with an additional example that clearly reveals the result of deficiency in approach. We have discussed both the Window Theory and the Mirror Theory. The latter, as exemplified in the social sciences and its critical secular approach, engages in the "etic" or outsider vantage point to bring discovery of objective information about religion or music that reflects the human socio-psychological condition. The Window Theory, as an "emic" approach exemplified in phenomenology of religion and theology, views the natural world as a place of religious experience, as a "window" into the sacred or divine realm that may or may not be defined as real. What people do not understand is that the Window Theory approaches are not meant to be dogmatic or necessarily confessional—only to temporarily suspend judgment of truth value as a means toward empathetic understanding. With a salient example, Eric J. Sharpe (1983: 60–61) compares both theories to hearing a Beethoven sonata on the piano:

> On the individual level, it may be argued that unless one has some "religious experience" of one's own, one is unable to understand the depths and heights of religion as a deaf man is to understand a Beethoven piano sonata. If one's ear is physically unable to capture the sounds, appreciation cannot even begin; there is an insuperable barrier to understanding. A deaf man could however "explain" a piano sonata in a fashion, in terms of the wood, wire and ivory out of which the piano is made, the movements of the pianist's fingers and feet, and the mechanical processes which take place inside the instrument—all of which are accessible to anyone who takes the trouble to look. And the explanation would be a "true" one, as far as it went; every statement would be verifiably accurate, measurable, and repeatable—ideal material for scientific investigation. All that would be missing would be the music, passing along the line of communication from composer, through performer, to listener.

All that is missing is the music; all that is missing is the religious experience. Sharpe then explains how students and scholars of religion often proceed in this way, describing and analyzing rituals, texts, and other paraphernalia without paying attention to the inner meaning of the experience that animates everything. A similar situation arises within ethnomusicology, wherein students and scholars pursue fieldwork to gather data about scales, rhythms, tuning, instruments, social class, performance practices, genres of song and composition, and so on without considering the spiritual or religious depth of what it is that the musicians are doing or experiencing. This point is driven home by citing an aphorism from Wilfrid Cantwell Smith: "The Hindus do not worship the cow that we see, they worship the cow that they see."

Accordingly, both phenomenology of religion and theology are necessary components of a Musicology of Religion. Although these fields are supported, we recognize that the phenomenology of religion has undergone harsh criticism in recent years, as pointed out by Laack (2015: 221): "After the phenomenology of religion had fallen into disgrace, scholars of religion hesitated to focus on religious experience and thus on the role of music in religions or simply felt insufficiently competent in both religious studies and musicology." One of the most trenchant critiques had been about the tendency of phenomenologists of religion to separate and reify the sacred or religion as sui generis, an autonomous category outside of history. Despite these setbacks, however, Jason N. Blum and others have already sought to reform or revitalize it as a viable method in the study of religion. After discussing some of the key points in a revived phenomenology of religion, we argue that it is the most ideal method for the study of religion and music, situated at a point beyond the dualities of etic and emic, relativism and universalism, and the hermeneutics of either recollection and suspicion.

Blum, in "Retrieving Phenomenology of Religion as a Method for Religious Studies" (2012: 1026), argues that the discipline of religious studies would be seriously compromised without phenomenology and recommends three avenues of reform: "The reorganization of religious studies suggested by these critics would significantly narrow methodology in the discipline and, I suggest, truncate the study of religion. In an attempt to offer some balance to this discussion, and building on the insights of others who have defended or sought to clarify phenomenology of religion, I suggest three related ways in which this approach may be reconceptualized as a viable and defensible method for religious studies. The version of phenomenology of religion I propose avoids problematic claims often associated with it, such as the positing of a sui generis, irreducible religious essence (such as 'the sacred'), the assumption that religion is radically autonomous from history, and the appearance of endorsing the religious subject's perspective." He states explicitly that, "In this revised form, I argue that phenomenology of religion offers a necessary and unique dimension to the study of religion:

interpretation of the meaning of religion from the perspective of religious experience and consciousness."

Conceptualized in this fashion, phenomenology of religion, instead of positing the existence of the transcendent, religion, or the sacred, or assuming the truth of religion, employs *epoché* and suspends judgment by focusing on interpreting the consciousness and experience of the immanent religious subject. Regarding *epoché*, Blum (2012: 1032) explains that it provides a midway point between the extremes of theological dogmatism and the pure empiricism associated with naturalism: "This interpretive posture is achieved through *epoché*, which maps out a middle road between the Charybdis of crypto-theology and the Scylla of naturalism. Rather than assuming either the existence or non-existence of religious realities, the phenomenologist of religion suspends or brackets this question in order to disclose meanings as constructed and experienced from the perspective of religious consciousness." Blum concludes here by stating, "This interpretive endeavor underscores the fact that phenomenology of religion need not—and, indeed, ought not—construe religion as a radically ahistorical and autonomous domain. In fact, it utilizes history, texts, and contextual research as the essential guide to interpretation" (2012: 1043).

Contrary to some unfounded assumptions, such as the perception of its uncritical advocacy of religion or the sacred, phenomenology does not dismiss the data collected by empirical studies as expressed by the Mirror Theory. Blum (2012: 1044–1045) has indeed clarified this position: "A primary virtue of this formulation is that it does not demand the blanket rejection of social scientific, psychological, and/or reductionist approaches to the study of religion. Whereas phenomenology of religion, in this perspective, focuses on the interpretation of religious consciousness and experience, other methods focus on the explanation of religion, often in naturalistic terms. Phenomenology of religion need not—indeed, cannot justifiably—reject such explanations out of hand. Rather, I suggest that phenomenology of religion pursues a different end than reductive or explanatory methods. While these interrogative goals are distinct from each other, neither need necessarily reject the other as inherently illegitimate . . . Explanations in terms of the categories of the social sciences are a necessary aspect of a full analysis of religion."

On the other hand, in contrast to the method of naturalism espoused by social science and ethnomusicology scholars employing the Mirror Theory, Blum explains how both the natural and supernatural worlds are required as fields of study in phenomenology: "It is this interpretive attempt to disclose the meaning of religion from the perspective of religious consciousness that prompts the phenomenologist's resistance to naturalism. In seeking to disclose such meanings, the phenomenologist of religion is required to refer to non or supernatural categories, entities, etc. The terms 'natural' and 'supernatural' are dichotomous and parasitic on each other; the supernatural is conceived as that which is not natural, and vice-versa. In seeking to interpret the meaning of religion from the perspective of religious consciousness, the phenomenologist has little choice but to forego naturalistic categories and explanations if he is to accurately represent the perspective he seeks to understand. The interpretive endeavor to disclose the meaning of religion as experienced by religious consciousness therefore requires reference to supernatural or theological entities and concepts" (2012: 103).

The other contested domain, theology, is often separated out due to reservations about the researcher's faith commitment or orientation. Though discussed in this book as part of the Window Theory, theology is usually associated with ecclesiastical institutions and denominational doctrines. Modern theologians Karl Barth (a critic of Schleiermacher), Emil Brunner, and Rudolf Bultmann (a critic of Otto) have given little importance to the general study of religion or comparative religion. For Rudolf Otto, however, theology was always intimately connected with the study of religion in a broad comparative framework. His continuing relevance for both theology and comparative religion (and music) is evident in the study of Otto by Philip C. Almond, *Rudolf Otto: An Introduction to His Philosophical Theology* (1984). In this work, Almond (1984: 111) revives the conversation around phenomenology of religion by recognizing the value of Otto's sense of the Holy as religious *a priori*: "Otto's most original contribution to the study of religion lies in his attempt to apply the principles contained in the religious a priori to the history and comparison of religions." Almond then reveals how for Otto the religious *a priori* functions as a kind of common denominator ("mutual interplay") to bring various forms of religious experience toward a shared or universal human perspective: "The relationship between religion in general and the specific phenomena of the various religious traditions is one of mutual interplay. On the one hand, the universality of the religious phenomenon, that is, that religion occurs at all times and at all places, is explained for Otto by the fact that the specific phenomena of religion are so many manifestations of the universal human capacity for religion." The unifying factor is always the religious *a priori*: "The recognition of the similarities between religions in their respective historical evolutions points toward the necessity of understanding them in a conceptually unified way, that is, of seeing them as so many manifestations of the operation of the religious a priori." The ease with which the word "music" may be substituted for "religion" in these phrases speaks to the mutual standing of religion and music in comparative theological discourse. Moreover, as phenomenology of religion talks of religious *a priori*, neuroscience affirms both religious *a priori* and musical *a priori*.

The religious *a priori* for Otto is the logical conjunction between theology and the history of religions, according to Almond (1984: 112): "For Otto the history and comparison of religions is itself a theological exercise . . . Theology and the history and comparison of religions meet in the analysis of the religious consciousness which has come into effect through the operation of the category of the Holy. The religious a priori is, so to speak, the 'point of connection' between the Holy apprehended through its operation and the religions as the various expressions of this apprehension . . . The only means by which any religion can be understood as a religion, and in relation to other religions, is by its connection to that religious a priori by whose operation it came into effect. The religious a priori is, so to speak, the logical possibility for the study of religions." Thus, Otto viewed the phenomenology of religion as both theological and philosophical, as affirmed by Almond (1984: 130): "The religious *a priori* provides a philosophically grounded objective criterion for the comparative assessment of religions, and this comparative assessment is at the same time a theological one."

As a salient example of how Otto's influence has been realized in comparative religion and theology, we refer to Harvard professor John B. Carman, who in *Majesty and Meekness: A Comparative Study of Contrast and Harmony in the Concept of God* (1994: 35), evokes valuable insights in his discussion of the concept of God in Christianity and Hinduism: "My debt to Rudolf Otto is very great . . . I believe that Otto remains one of the 'role models' for a Christian who wishes to approach the religion of Hindus both as a historian of religion and as a theologian. Otto intends to distinguish between these roles but to exercise them both." To those critics of Otto for his "Christian perspective," Carman (1994: 35–36) responds: "It is important to recognize that Otto himself thinks that his philosophical analysis of religion does not depend on his Christian theology. He believes that the experience of ultimate reality as holy—that is, as a mysterious combination of the terrifying and the fascinating, the awesome and the attractive—is a possibility for all human beings and is at the heart of all genuine religion. Each particular religion, according to Otto, combines this common nonrational core of awesome awareness of the ultimate mystery with a rational apprehension of that same reality's moral character."

Religion and Aesthetics

We have identified ritual as the "missing link" between religion and music, yet another less tangible relationship remains to be discussed in the form of aesthetics and the experience of beauty. Indeed, while ritual serves as an external link between religion and music, it may be conceded that the experience of beauty operates as a kind of internal "missing link" within human consciousness. According to the Window Theory, religion is a unique aspect of human experience that is a potential "window" into the divine or transcendent reality. But does the same hold for music, and if so, how? In partial reference to the Mirror Theory, one may hold the view that while religion of faith may access the divine, music may be seen as a mere art or skill, a human construct. One asks, does beauty in the form of music provide access to the divine? To address this issue, we turn to the field of aesthetics where the relation between religion and the arts, including music, has been a significant yet often controversial focal point.

The arts and religion were closely connected in ancient times. One of the principal aspects of divinity among the ancient Greeks was beauty, which was equated with the ultimate Good. In fact, the Greek term *kalos* can mean both "good" and "beautiful." The idea of aesthetics, as understood by the ancient Greeks, was the appreciation of beauty through the arts. Yet the use of the term "aesthetics" to designate a distinct province of philosophical inquiry was first introduced in the eighteenth century by Alexander Baumgarten in *Aesthetica* (1750–1758). Bernard Bosanquet, in *A History of Aesthetic* (1904: 1), has clarified this issue: "The thing existed before the name; for reflection upon beauty and upon fine art begins among Hellenic thinkers at least as early as the time of Socrates, if not, in a certain sense, with still earlier philosophers." Aesthetics hence came, "to accept as its immediate subject-matter the succession of systematic theories by which philosophers have attempted to explain or connect together the facts that relate to beauty."

For Plato, the ultimate truth was known as the Good, which also reflected ultimate Beauty, leading to the understanding that just as all things are good insofar as they reflect the highest Good, so all things are beautiful insofar as they resemble the highest Beauty. The driving force behind Socratic inquiry was not mere curiosity but love (*eros*), the desire to behold ultimate Beauty. In the *Symposium*, there is the analogy known as the "ladder of beauty," better known as the Platonic "ladder of love," whereby earthly beauty is the bottom rung of a ladder from which one ascends through several steps to perfect Beauty through the power of love. Plato's *Symposium* (209e–212c) contains the exposition on this ascent as taught by the priestess Diotima to Socrates. To fully grasp the analogy, we cite a key passage from the translation of Walter Hamilton (Plato 1951: 94): "This is the right way of approaching or being initiated into the mysteries of love, to begin with examples of beauty in this world, and using them as steps to ascend continually with that absolute beauty as one's aim, from one instance of physical beauty to two and from two to all, then from physical beauty to moral beauty [beauty of the Soul], and from moral beauty to the beauty of knowledge, until from knowledge of various kinds one arrives at the supreme knowledge whose sole object is that absolute beauty, and knows at last what absolute beauty is. This above all others, . . . is the region where a man's life should be spent, in the contemplation of absolute beauty."

The argument for absolute beauty is clarified by utilizing geometric forms. For example, in nature there is no perfect form of a triangle; it only exists as something "intelligible," that is, as an abstract entity seen with the "mind's eye." The reasoning is that since in the physical world there are also no earthly perfections of truth, goodness, or beauty, only gradations, there must also exist in the intelligible realm perfect forms of Truth, Goodness, and Beauty.

The direct link between beauty and absolute goodness is made in the *Symposium*, resulting in immortality (Plato 1951: 95): "Do you not see that in that region alone where he sees beauty with the faculty capable of seeing it, will he be able to bring forth not mere reflected images of goodness but true goodness, because he will be in contact not with a reflection but with the truth? And having brought forth and nurtured true goodness he will have the privilege of being beloved of God, and becoming, if ever a man can, immortal himself." Patrick Sherry (1992: 4) notes the significance of this trinity of Truth, Goodness, and Beauty: "Philosophers from Plato onwards have recognized the power of beauty . . . This power and the wonder it evokes explain why they have often listed beauty together with truth and goodness as subjects of utmost importance." For more discussion of this text with commentaries, see Plato (1993b).

The implicit connection between beauty and divinity was further enunciated by the philosopher Plotinus (204–270 CE), the founder of

Neo-Platonism who dedicated a section of his work, *The Enneads* (I.6), to Beauty. For Plotinus, Beauty emanates from the Good to the Soul and all of creation, as indicated in the translation of Stephen MacKenna (Plotinus 1991: 52): "Beauty which is also The Good, must be posed as The First: directly driving from the First is the Intellectual-Principle which is pre-eminently the manifestation of Beauty; through the Intellectual-Principle Soul is beautiful. The beauty in things of a lower order—actions and pursuits for instance—comes by operation of the shaping Soul which is also the author of the beauty found in the world of sense. For the Soul, a divine thing, a fragment as it were of the Primal Beauty, makes beautiful to the fullness of their capacity all things whatsoever that it grasps and moulds." As both Plato and Plotinus identified true beauty with goodness, they posited a "ladder of beauty," that is, the stepwise "ascent" of the mind to the divine from the beauty encountered in the physical world. And while this idea is an ancient one, it recurs frequently in the Western religious traditions. Richard Viladesau (1999: 107) describes how this concept became a cornerstone of Christian faith through the teachings of Augustine: "Combining the Platonic tradition with a Christian awareness of creation, Augustine holds . . . that the beauty of creation reveals its Maker . . . Augustine argues for the necessity of God from the incompleteness of the intelligibility that the mind finds in itself; and he explicitly connects this reasoning with the steps of the Platonic 'ascent': from external beauty to the beauty of the soul, and finally to the supreme source of all beauty, which is also the ultimate truth."

However, the modern intellectual climate changed the dynamic, leading to the eventual separation of religion from the arts. When the late eighteenth-century German philosopher Kant postulated a separate realm of aesthetics from religious experience, he forged a distinction that endured into the early twentieth century. For Kant, beauty was a matter of individual "taste" within the realm of phenomena, but religion was cordoned off into the realm of the *noumena,* inaccessible to human inquiry. This meant that religion and aesthetics were largely distinct areas of human existence; in terms of music, the temple and the concert hall are to be considered separate venues for different experiences, one for religious and the other for aesthetic. Frank Burch Brown, in *Religious Aesthetics: A Theological Study of Making and Meaning* (1989: 47), has articulated this phenomenon: "Since the time of Kant that part of the point in calling something of aesthetic at all is to say or imply that, in this respect at least, it is not to be evaluated in terms of religion or morality . . . Insofar as something is appreciated for aesthetic reasons, it is to be appreciated for its own sake, not for the good it can do or the understanding or devotion it can enhance. Or so the usual thinking goes." After Kant, many Kantian and neo-Kantian thinkers continued with the dichotomy of religious and aesthetic experiences, including Kierkegaard, Benedetto Croce, R. G. Collingwood, Suzanne Langer, John Dewey, and many others. Accordingly, aesthetics should be viewed as a separate aspect of the human enterprise divorced from moral, ethical, or religious factors. Paul Weiss, in *Religion and Art* (1963: 10), held this view: "Both religion and art will suffer if they allow themselves to be merged or used as supplements to one another, unless they continue at the same time to be pursued as basic, independent enterprises."

Despite this persistent dichotomy, an intellectual movement in theology and religion has generated a re-convergence of religion and the arts in recent times. Influenced by Schleiermacher, Schelling (see Schelling 1989), and Hegel (see Desmond 1986) among the German Romantics who had directly tied art with the Infinite, God, or the Absolute, Rudolf Otto challenged the Kantian distinction in the early twentieth century by bringing the aesthetic dimension of music back into closer proximity to the religious experience, in this case, with the "numinous," much current thought in religious studies and theology has rejected this strict separation, since religion and the arts are believed to permeate all cultures and societies. And with reference to Western and Asian traditions, art historian and philosopher Ananda K. Coomaraswamy (2014: 62) proclaimed in 1934: "Art is religion, religion art, not related, but the same."

In twentieth-century Protestant theology, Paul Tillich, in *Theology of Culture* (1959), and David Harned, in *Theology and the Arts* (1966), argued that religion is the substance of culture, and that culture is the form of religion, whereby ultimately no irreligious art is possible. In Russian Orthodox thought, Nicolas Berdyaev viewed art as essentially a religious phenomenon. Combining religion and art, academic philosophers followed these steps. F. David Martin, in *Art and the Religious Experience: The "Language" of the Sacred* (1972: 67), spoke in existentialist terms under the influence of Heidegger: "Art is a gift of *Being*. That is why art, despite its autonomy, has always served as the principal sacred bridge . . . to the religious experience, and continues to do so even in these apparently post-religious times." Thomas R. Martland, in *Religion as Art* (1981: 1, 5, 9), incorporating the thought of J. L. Austin and the concept of 'performative utterance,' concluded that religion and art were largely indistinguishable in terms of function: "What art does, religion does . . . religion does what art does . . . I consider art and religion not as cultural components actively functioning in society but as carriers of other meanings or purposes beyond themselves, to the 'given' which they 'represent;' to the feelings, goals, or techniques they wish to conserve." Furthermore, Doug Adams and Diane Apostolos-Cappadona, in *Art as Religious Studies* (1987), have effectively brought art into religious studies. Henceforth, the arts and music are no longer marginal to religious experience or gratuitous to a theological enterprise but must be seen as integrated at very primary levels of religious meaning.

Drawing on the ancient Greek traditions of an ascent to divinity through beauty, theologians and religion scholars in recent times have revived this sense of aesthetics, advancing the field of 'theological aesthetics.' These include Hans Urs von Balthasar, *The Glory of the Lord: Theological Aesthetics* (1982), Frank Burch Brown, *Religious Aesthetics: A Theological Study of Making and Meaning* (1989), James Alfred Martin, *Beauty and Holiness: The Dialogue between Aesthetics and Religion* (1990), Patrick Sherry, *Spirit and Beauty: An Introduction to Theological Aesthetics* (1992), and Richard Viladesau, *Theological Aesthetics: God in Imagination, Beauty, and Art* (1999). Martin (1990) and Sherry (1992) provide the historical context for the relation between aesthetics and religion. Martin discusses beauty and holiness in The Bible, Plato, Aristotle, Augustine, Aquinas, Jonathan Edwards, Hume, Kant, Schiller, Schlegel, Schelling, Schleiermacher, Otto, Eliade, van der Leeuw, Tillich, Geertz, Santayana, Dewey, Whitehead, Heidegger, Wittgenstein, as well as in Eastern thought: India, China, Japan, while Sherry examines aesthetics in the early Church Fathers, Plotinus, St. Gregory of Nazianzus, Calvin, Balthasar, and Barth.

The prominent Swiss theologian Hans Urs von Balthasar was one of the first modern Catholic theologians to sound the alarm regarding the absence of beauty and aesthetics in theology. In *The Glory of the Lord: A Theological Aesthetics* (1982: 17), Balthasar declared that the divine must approached in multiple ways: "God's truth is, indeed, great enough to allow an infinity of approaches and entryways." Yet he bemoaned the fact that the sense of beauty had all but disappeared from theological discourse (1982: 17–18): Beauty is "a word from which religion, and theology in particular, have taken their leave and distanced themselves in modern times by a vigorous drawing of the boundaries . . . No longer loved or fostered by religion, beauty is lifted from its face as a mask, and its absence exposes features on that face which threaten to become incomprehensible to man." To his credit, Balthasar's vision for a renewed theology of beauty included the eastern religions, according to John O'Donnell SJ, in *Hans Urs von Balthasar* (1992: 7): "At root, Balthasar's approach is meant to open a dialogue with the great Western philosophical tradition as well as with the great mystical tradition of the East." A much needed and rigorous analysis of Balthasar's 'theological aesthetics' is provided by W. T. Dickens in *Hans Urs von Balthasar's Theological Aesthetics: A Model for Post-Critical Biblical Interpretation* (2003).

Aware of the uneven relation between religion and the arts in modernity, Frank Burch Brown sought to redress the situation. In *Religious Aesthetics: A Theological Study of Making and Meaning* (1989: 193), Brown attests to a natural relation between religious language and the arts: "The fact that the primary language of religion is markedly poetic, mythic, and otherwise aesthetic means that it is with such language that theology repeatedly begins and that it is to such language that theology must often return." And the relation between theology and aesthetics may take the form of a dialectic (1989: 42): "A more adequate understanding of the relation of the aesthetic realm and its truth(s) to that of theological concepts is that they exist in mutually transformative dialogical relationship." In terms of the dialogue between aesthetics and theology, Clyde J. Steckel (1994: 16–17) describes Brown's positive approach of "neo-aesthetics: "Frank Burch Brown argues in *Religious Aesthetics* [1989] that aesthetic experience and religious experience have so much in common that the traditional separation of these domains in Western thought has resulted in a significant impoverishment for each. He challenges the notion of a formally independent aesthetic realm, an idea advanced by Kant and continuing to hold sway in the twentieth century as represented by formalists such as Suzanne Langer. Burch Brown also challenges postmodern and deconstructionist aesthetics in their claim that a work of art is only another cultural text to be decoded. In place of both these approaches, he offers his 'neo-aesthetics,' which seeks to place theologians, religious studies scholars, and philosophers in a shared dialogue about religious and aesthetic experience that have much in common." Brown (2014: 5) continues to advocate for more interaction between theology and the arts: "In view of how widespread and prominent the arts are in the terrain of religion, it can be surprising how little attention has been paid in the past to putting the arts on the map of religion, or to exploring them once they are located there."

Inspired by Balthasar and Brown, Anthony Monti, in *A Natural Theology of the Arts: Imprint of the Spirit* (2003), showcased the important role of the arts in natural theology. The author describes the subject in the description: "A natural theology of the arts contends that the arts are theological by their very nature and not simply when they are explicitly religious—thereby constituting a distinctive kind of 'natural theology.' Borrowing from science the stance of 'critical realism' to justify truth claims in art and theology, it argues that works of art are complex metaphors that convey the 'real presence' of God, even when not labeled as such."

The combined study of music and theology has been greatly enriched by the work of Jon Michael Spencer, who has formed a new category of study called "theomusicology." Spencer's major work, *Theological Music: An Introduction to Theomusicology* (1991), described theomusicology as a unique discipline in the description: "Theomusicology is musicology as a theologically informed discipline. Borrowing thought and method from anthropology, sociology, psychology, and philosophy, it has as its subject the myriad cultural worlds of ethical, religious, and mythological belief. Theomusicological research into cultural/intercultural reflections on the ethical, the religious, and the mythological involves the study of music in the domain or communities of the sacred, the secular, and the profane. By examining the depths of sacrality, secularity, and profanity in the music of civilization's many cultures, the theomusicologist can increasingly discern how particular peoples perceive the universal mysteries that circumscribe their mortal existence, and how the ethics, theologies, and mythologies to which they subscribe shape their worlds." Focusing on a variety of music, including African American Christianity, gospel, jazz, and blues, Spencer has developed a methodology to study the general human musical experience and analyze it theologically. An aspect of theomusicology that is quite relevant to the phenomenological approach involves the acceptance of traditional or mythic descriptions regarding the divine origin of music and the arts and necessitates bracketing (*epoché*) rational attitudes and evolutionary models.

Theology is also key to understanding music in a wide variety of contexts. Clyde J. Steckel, in "How Can Music Have Theological Significance?" (1994: 13), explains how theology is intertwined with culture and simply cannot be ignored or neglected in the study of music: "The task of discerning and articulating theological meanings in music involves an analysis of both religious music and music that is not overtly religious by text or usage, in order to determine how music expresses and mediates the dominant values of a culture and how music is an experience of encounter with whatever is taken to be divine or of ultimate importance." The encounter with the supernatural or the divine is key to theology. A study of religion and music must account for the role of these aspects in not only religious music but *all* music. Steckel (1994: 15) also affirmed the natural connection between music and theology by stressing that they tend to nourish each other: "For the musician who is wary about any extramusical claims upon the arts, finding theological significance in music may seem a peril to be resisted. But for those who cherish music as a deeply expressive and communicative art, and who cherish music in religious life for all that music can do in ways that are different from other modes of experience, discovering theological significance in music can integrate theology and music in ways that will bring illumination and enjoyment to both disciplines."

Richard Viladesau, in *Theology and the Arts: Encountering God through Music, Art, and Rhetoric* (2000: 41), set parameters for a cross-cultural approach to music as part of religion and theology by utilizing the category of the "Holy" or numinous, as earlier introduced by Rudolf Otto in *The Idea of the Holy* (1923): "There is an underlying implicit or transcendental dimension of religious experience. Its object—the *mysterium tremendum et fascinans,* the numinous—would then be ontologically identical with the ultimate object of aesthetic or moral or intellectual experience; it would never be experienced simply in itself as a categorical object but would always be 'co-experienced' as the dimension of mystery implicit in all human knowing and loving . . . In this perspective, the ultimate reason for music's ability to mediate the spiritual is not merely that it echoes emotions that are felt in religious experience, but also and more profoundly that its object is the beautiful, which itself is godly and thus leads toward God." In this sense, recalling Plato and Plotinus, music becomes a potential window into the divine since it partakes of the numinous.

For centuries in cultures and traditions, music has held theological significance to the degree that for musicologists to focus solely on the musical and sociological aspects would, applying Blum's phrase, "truncate the study of music." In fact, the study of music is incomplete without theology. Music requires theology because music is associated cross-culturally with transcendental states of consciousness beyond ordinary experience and beyond language. The theological traditions are well-designed to articulate these states as well as other experiences of the divine within an empathetic context. Likewise, theology requires music to express what lies deep within the soul, beyond the spoken and written word. Theologian Don E. Saliers, in *Music and Theology* (2007: 4), elaborates on this notion by describing music as the language of the soul made audible: "Music confers upon human language addressed to God the appropriate silence and mystery required by prayer. Music is the language of the soul made audible especially as music is the performative mode of the prayer and ritual engagement of a community." The individual human voice in union with other voices becomes the quintessential theological motif and is something inherently relevant to comparative study (2007: 5): "If music is the language of the soul made audible, then human voices conjoined in community are primary instruments of the collective soul—a medium for what transcends the immediately common-sense world. In such cases the hearing and the sound itself encode more than what is heard. This is a profoundly cross-cultural fact." With a simple phrase, Saliers (2007: vii) says it all: "In the final analysis, music and theology may require one another."

Comparative Studies and Musicology of Religion

Throughout the foregoing chapters, the issue of universalism versus non-universalism has been mooted from the viewpoints of several disciplines. Without minimizing non-universalism, our intention is to upgrade the importance of some form of universalism to validate the method and process of comparative study of religion and music. The Musicology of Religion requires such a balanced vantage point. For this, scholarship in religious studies is pertinent. Paul Roscoe, in "The Comparative Method" (2009: 25), has provided the context: "Applied with varying degrees of analytical rigor, the comparative method has been a staple of Western thought since the days of Herodotus . . . Comparison came later to the social sciences, but it is now widely employed in sociology, economics, political science, psychology, and anthropology." But while some in religious studies have rejected comparativism, according to Roscoe (2009: 25), comparative studies is foundational to the discipline despite recent reservations: "In religious studies, comparison has a distinguished ancestry in the work of William Robertson Smith and, more recently, of Mircea Eliade. Notwithstanding this pedigree, scholars of religion now tend to spurn the comparative method, not least because of their unease over the excesses they see in the work of two early practitioners, Robertson Smith himself and, even more, J. G. Frazer. As Robert Segal has argued, these concerns may be misplaced." Even anthropology, which one normally associates with cultural relativism, has widely utilized the comparative method (2009: 26): "Anthropology, the social science that has as its enduring goal a holistic understanding of all human societies and . . . consequently has made by far the greatest use of the comparative method." In a special sense, comparativism is unavoidable, according to Roscoe (2009: 27): "Even opponents of comparison are closet comparativists. No matter how emphatically they oppose comparison, no matter how forcefully they insist that their aim is to study another culture 'in its own terms,' they have no option but to render their descriptions in Eurocentric terms if their descriptions are to remain intelligible to the anthropological community."

Arvind Sharma offers an innovative perspective on the comparative study of religion in *Religious Studies and Comparative Methodology: The Case for Reciprocal Illumination* (2005), in which he, in addition to comparing the methods of W. C. Smith and Mircea Eliade, develops a method of mutual interaction or "reciprocal illumination" among religions that has wide implications for religion and music. Regarding comparison in general, Sharma (2005: ix) first states its importance in religious studies: "It was central to the emergence of the study of religion as an academic discipline and has remained a key ingredient of the discipline since its inception." Sharma (2005: 254) describes the process of "reciprocal illumination" as a productive enterprise in the interests of comparison: "Reciprocal illumination seeks to see how one datum may shed light on another, or two data on each other, rather than on a common or transcendent category, and further seeks to show that apparently different phenomena may also unexpectedly shed similar light . . . Comparison is not meant to serve some other end, but is used to clarify the items under comparison themselves. Because these data are not used in this method to illuminate anything other than the data themselves, it has been described as reciprocal illumination." In this book, Sharma very fruitfully compares a multitude of aspects of Hinduism, Judaism, Christianity, Islam, Confucianism, and Buddhism.

One of the basic axioms promoted by advocates of cultural relativism is that musics, like religions, are best studied and defined according to their own terms. Following this direction, however, one faces at best only a vast "sea of particulars," at worst an enormous set of "mutually unintelligible approaches." This is neither adequate nor appropriate for comparative study. Instead, Ter Ellingson, in "Music and Religion" (1987: 165), offers a compromise between cultural relativism and universalism by recognizing the over-arching factors: "Along with aspects of musical sounds and their structural relationships, religious definitions frequently take into consideration such factors as cosmological and mathematical laws, divine origin or inspiration, psychological and emotional effects, social and ethical implications, relations or contrasts between religious and secular musics, and a wide range of other elements." With these factors in place, Ellingson (1987: 165) recommended a broad comparative approach that considers a network of shared elements: "For want of a better solution, we must discuss music and religion in the terms most widely shared by the full range of musical and religious traditions; and these, in the first place, require attention to the technical elements of music and of the paramusical phenomena found in religious contexts." He outlines three areas of attention: "Technical Features," encompassing issues of melody, rhythm, vocal versus instrumental music, classification of instruments, and organization of music in terms of solo or group performance; "Origin, Myth, and Symbolism," and "Time, Space, and Ritual."

A common consensus is that, metaphorically speaking, music is "like" religion. Moving beyond mere metaphor, religion and music scholar Albert L. Blackwell has advocated a new comparative method of religious and musical experiences through the use of analogy. Drawing upon German scholarship on Schleiermacher (see Scholtz 1981), Blackwell (1991: 124) explains how this is to occur: "For Schleiermacher, the relations between musical and religious experience . . . are relations of analogy, indeed a rich variety of analogies. The difference is that that while a metaphor tends to be merely descriptive of certain similar effects, an analogy serves to clarify the essential nature of both experiences. That is, to analyze the one kind of experience brings corresponding new understanding and appreciation of the analogous experience." Examples are that both music and religion are universal, and that both involve experiences of immediacy. Developing this further, Blackwell (1991: 123) presents a typology of comparative analogies culled from Schleiermacher: "Schleiermacher suggests at least four distinct kinds of musical experience, though all, he says, 'spring from one impulse.' They are musical composition, musical performance, musical participation, and musical listening. We can correlate these four kinds of musical experience more or less directly with four distinct kinds of religious experience: musical composition with religious inspiration, musical performance with religious liturgy, musical participation with congregational worship, and musical listening with what Schleiermacher calls religious self-consciousness."

In his interpretation of Schleiermacher, Blackwell (1991: 137) offered a profound insight by way of analogy into the nexus between music and religion: "In a most intriguing simplification, Schleiermacher suggests that in music the octave is given by universal nature, while various scales are relative to particular cultures. Analogously in religion: the fundamental religious feeling of absolute dependence is given in our universal relation to God, while the varieties of religious expression are as diverse as the varieties of human culture."

Considering the voluminous ethnographic data available on music and chant in religious rituals, a special comparative area of study for music and religion is thus timely. Advancements in ethnomusicology also provide prospective methods of analysis regarding vocal and instrumental expression within religious communities. The range of flexible systems of classification of scale systems, rhythmic patterns, musical instruments, and singing styles provides structural methods that may be applied in the cross-cultural study of diverse musical traditions. One example that has stood the test of time is the Sachs–Hornbostel system of instrument classification developed in 1914, which offers systematic terminology (chordophones, aerophones, etc.) for a large variety of musical instruments used in religious ceremonies and rituals. The "test of time" can be stretched back to ancient India where this type of classification first arose.

Although begun in the mid–twentieth century, the program of "canto-metrics," designed by Alan Lomax for the comparative study of vocal music, needs to be further integrated with and applied to the study of music and religion. Lomax, in "Folk Song Style" (1959: 929), outlined the numerous aspects of his comparative study:

> The study of musical style should embrace the total human situation which produces the music. (1) The number of people habitually involved in a musical act, and the way in which they cooperate. (2) The relation between the music makers and the audience. (3) The physical behavior of the music makers-their bodily stance, gestures, facial expressions, muscular tensions, especially those of the throat. (4) The vocal timbres and pitch favored by the culture, and their relationship to the factors under three. (5) The social function of the music and the occasion of its production. (6) Its psychological and emotional content as expressed in the song texts and the culture's interpretation of this traditional poetry. (7) How songs are learned and transmitted. (8) Finally, we come to the formal elements in the situation: the scales, the interval systems, the rhythmic patterns, the melodic contours, the techniques of harmony used; the metric patterns of the verse, the structure of the poetry, and the complex interplay between poetic and musical patterns, the instruments and instrumental techniques.

Lomax described his unified approach to music and culture: "Only when the behavioral patterns covered by points 1–7 are taken into account can the formal elements under eight be properly understood, for they are symbols which stand for the whole. A musical style is learned as a whole and responded to as a whole by a member of any culture. If some familiar element is absent in a performance, the music gives far less satisfaction. Conversely, the very magic of music lies in the fact that its formal elements can conjure up the total musical experience."

As a comprehensive grid for comparison of vocal music cross-culturally, Alan Lomax, in "Song Structure and Social Structure" (1962), presented charts of thirty-seven categories of musical styles and social organization of music as part of "canto-metrics," which he then further described with examples. The basis for Lomax's comparison of song structure of large regions is made according to social structure (despotism, hierarchy, loose governance, etc.). For example, bardic solo singing is more prevalent under despotism and authoritarian regimes (Middle east, China, India, Islamic kingdoms); complex interactive singing aligns with collective social groupings in tribal or smaller societies (Pygmies). In Musicology of Religion, these indices would be enlarged and applied to new categories such as religious belief (monotheism, polytheism), types of ritual (fire ceremonies, icon worship, initiations), and modes of experience (trance, ecstasy, meditation), as well as aspects of sacred space and sacred time.

Suggested new approaches to the study of sacred vocal music might involve the comparative calculation of the number of notes per syllable, or syllables per note, in a chanted or sung composition, and the identification of metrical versus non-metrical styles of singing. When there are many syllables (words) per note, the term used is "cantillation," as in Hebrew Psalms, Vedic chant, Sanskrit Mantras, Sikh Japjī prayers, and Shinto Norito prayers. When there is an almost one-to-one relationship between syllable and note, the term "syllabic" is used, as in Protestant hymnody, Hindu Dhrupad, Greek hymns, and Japanese Buddhist Shōmyo. And when there are many notes per syllable, the term "melismatic" is applied, as in Gregorian chant, Qur'an recitation, Hindu temple songs, and Sufi Qawwali singing. This is related to the further identification of metrical and non-metrical styles of music and chant. Non-metrical examples of singing or chanting include the Hebrew Psalms, the Qur'an, Gregorian chant, the Buddhist Pali Canon, and some Sikh prayers. Metrical patterns involving fixed time durations of syllables or words are found in the Rig Veda and other Sanskrit prayers in Hinduism, the Avesta in Zoroastrianism, and some Buddhist chant. Sacred songs labeled as hymns ("praise songs") are often metrical texts, as in Greek hymns, Protestant hymnody, Dhrupad and Kīrtan in Hinduism, Japanese Shōmyo, and Sikh Shabads.

As an ethnomusicologist, Edith Gerson-Kiwi, in "Religious Chant: A Pan-Asiatic Conception of Music" (1961), demonstrated the ideal type of research aligned with the objectives of Musicology of Religion. Comparing a large body of material, Gerson-Kiwi (1961: 64) explained the cross-cultural nature of Asian religious chant as consisting of a one-note structure: "As in the accentual forms of Gregorian chant, especially in the lesson and psalms, the natural flow of the speaker's voice, with its constant change of pitch is channeled into a magico-hypnotic one-note recitation. Strangely enough, music is born at this moment." At this point, Gerson-Kiwi identifies some of the distinct features of religious music: "Clearly it is not melody (in the sense of mere pitch variation) alone which makes music, but the spiritual message that the voice carries. In chant the singer becomes the messenger of Divinity. As such he is no longer himself; he represents a being of superhuman stature." Thus the singer becomes a medium through whom Divinity announces its presence by the miraculous transformation of the singer into that "other man" of prophetic dimensions of which we are told in I Samuel x. 5,6. Samuel prophesies to Saul that he will "meet a company of prophets coming down from the high place with a psaltery and tabret, and a pipe and a harp before them, and they shall prophesy: And the spirit of the Lord will come upon thee and thou shalt prophesy with them, and shalt be turned into another man." As such, Gerson-Kiwi (1961: 64–65) proclaimed the similarities of style throughout much of the world's religious traditions: "The one-note chant should be regarded as one of the most refined musical manifestations of ancient civilizations, in particular of those of the Asian continent. Religious chant is an "artefact"—an artistic construction for delivering texts of the highest religious and moral quality . . . Most of Asia's types of cantillation [chant] form a class by themselves, bridging national boundaries and, to some extent, even those of race and religion. Thus Shintoist, Buddhist, Brahman [Hindu], Moslem and Hebrew sacred chant reveal a striking similarity to one another, while they differ greatly from the secular musics of their respective countries." This research reveals that religious music and chant are often in separate categories of their own, apart from folk or secular songs, and require a broad yet distinct set of methods and terminologies for analysis and comparison. As a step in this direction, we have suggested an inclusive glossary of terms for Musicology of Religion in Appendix B.

Returning to Ellingson (1987: 168), we pause to reflect on his most compelling statement regarding the common ground in musical and religious experience: "Music enhances, intensifies, and . . . transforms almost any experience into something felt not only as different but also a somehow better. In this transformative power, music resembles religion itself; and when the energies of music and religion are focused on the same object in an isofunctional adaptation of both toward a common meaning or goal, intensification reaches a peak greater perhaps than either might achieve by itself. Thus, the 'otherness' of music and the 'other' levels of reality and beings encountered in religion merge into a heightened synthesis of religious-musical experience." At this point, we bring this presentation to an end with my own closing remarks.

Conclusion

It should not be surprising that scholars in religion are "religious" or "theological," yet in current times theological perspectives are frequently disparaged in religious studies and, especially, in the social sciences. Combined with the neglect of music as a significant element in religious practice and experience, this has led to an impoverishment of both religious studies and the phenomenology of religion. Despite this, we have shown that when the study of religion includes music, the results are enhanced and nourished by the perspectives of theology and liturgical studies, not only as theory or method but as data for a revived or "reformed" phenomenology of religion. In fact, we have established in this book that the study of religion is incomplete without music, and that the phenomenology of religion is not comprehensive without music, especially in terms of the idea of the numinous or the sacred. With the numinous comes music, and since the numinous experience can be shown through many examples validated by the experience of music, discussing the numinous without engaging the musical experience is imprecise at best. The theoretical foundation for music as part of religious experience has been established by Schleiermacher, Dilthey, Otto, van der Leeuw, and other pioneers in religious studies. But while music has receded in later scholarship in religion and phenomenology, and even in theology, the recent upsurge in interest in religion and music is cause for a reassessment, supported by recent research in cognitive studies, ethnomusicology, and the phenomenology of religion.

Inversely, the study of music is incomplete without theology. As discussed above, music requires theology because music is associated cross-culturally with transcendental states of consciousness beyond ordinary experience and beyond language. The theological traditions have been able to articulate these states as well as other experiences of the divine within an empathetic context. Beside many theological works of yore dealing with sacred music, the close relation between music and theology is also amply supported by the fact that the preponderance of great musicians in the world, though perhaps not theologians themselves, has been men and women of deep religious faith and commitment. This applies not only to the music of Europe but to the Middle East, India, and Asian countries. With music and theology come worship and liturgy. We recall the poignant statement by Ninian Smart (1972: 74): "The substantive concept of God is indissolubly linked to the practice of worship."

We thus have come to our conclusion: religion, music, and liturgical worship are indissolubly bound together in various ways, and, as we have demonstrated, needs to be studied and researched as a unitary phenomenon from diverse perspectives, including the social sciences and ethnomusicology but also theology, phenomenology of religion, aesthetics, and cognitive studies. The data and insights provided by all the disciplines discussed herein thus furnish a solid ground for the Musicology of Religion.

In a special sense, Musicology of Religion is inevitable. With all the emerging information, rising self-awareness, and research interests in both religion and music as a combined topic, the previously invisible "elephant in the room" becomes the Holy Grail or the Golden Fleece in the study of humanity. Despite advocates of the Mirror Theory and their frequent claims of non-universalism, we can envision the benefits of avoiding extremes and balancing these claims with those on the side of the Window Theory who embrace the free comparativist and sophisticated universalist methodologies presented in the past few chapters. The many-faceted approaches of all concerned cry out for a new "third realm" or discipline in academia: from Pythagorean harmony to phenomenology of music, from the evidence of primal monotheism among thousands of prehistoric cultures to insightful theories of the "sense of God" inherent in all peoples, from the Window Theory to the Mirror Theory, from the "signals of transcendence" of sociologist Berger to the universal presence of music-making as part of the human cognitive apparatus, from the ascent to divinity through beauty to the case for "theological aesthetics," from the powerful influences on the production of religious music by a theology of music as Divine Gift to the manifestation of music as emanating from Brahman in Indian metaphysics. And from the multifarious forms of music in ancient cultures to the biological nexus of music and human evolution.

Looking forward, let me offer some personal remarks on the future of the study of religion and music. Previously, we talked about religions of the world as being composite, with each religion comprising a rich blend of historical and cultural elements drawn from diverse sources. One of these elements is certainly music, however defined. In fact, ample documentation supports the transference of musical styles, instruments, and even scale types and rhythms across cultural and religious boundaries over the course of time. It is noteworthy that, as have been shown, many or most of the academic accounts of world religions and the history of religion, whether in the form of textbooks, dictionaries, scholarly anthologies, and monographs, have generally omitted music from the narratives that they present and analyze. This situation has created a degree of vulnerability to the field, such that defenders of the reality of "religion" as a universal phenomenon are frequently forced to rely solely on the particularities of language, belief, ritual, scripture, and social organization to make their case for the efficacy of comparison. As the rising tide of cultural relativism seems to sweep away all attempts at universal thinking, the alleged reality of the "sacred," the "numinous," or "religious experience" as plausible categories of comparative thinking have become susceptible to criticism, and worse, are frequently subsumed and erased in the long march toward absolute differentiation in the arena of culture. That is, however, until the element of music is introduced. Music is the "wildcard" that makes pure cultural relativism impossible. Knowledge of music is the "master key" that unlocks the mystery of a variety of religious experiences and allows entry to previously unknown dimensions of the comparative study of religious community engagement. As a provable universal feature of civilization, music is immune to the challenges of Neo-Marxism, Postmodernism, Deconstruction, or Postcolonialism, simply because music is part of all humanity, because it appeals to all humanity. Hence, in the study of religion, music should not be something extraneous that is sometimes discussed, sometimes not, occasionally heard, often not, or seldom compared, whether in teaching or research. In fact, religious studies *is* the principal discipline that needs to *own* music in the sense of claiming special jurisdiction over something widely recognized as having divine origins and utilized in religious rituals and ceremonies throughout the world. Thus, as a central and pervasive ingredient of religious thought and practice, music, when aesthetically appreciated and intellectually understood within the phenomenology of religion and the history of religions, solidifies the status of comparative religion, and necessitates the Musicology of Religion. And with the assistance of multiple disciplines as well as focused research on ethnographic data, Musicology of Religion, being phenomenological and comparative, will foster advancement in the study of religion and music.

We end by recalling the timely words of Finnish scholar Martin Hoondert cited in our Introduction. Hoondert (2015: 128) poses a compelling challenge that can effectively be met by the Musicology of Religion: "I want to defend the thesis that music is by its nature religious, or rather, that it has qualities that correspond well with what religion aspires to be. If we listen intensely, we participate in the movement and in the 'now' of the music . . . Music can be heard in many different ways in relation to religion, but music is always there, whether it is the recitation of Psalms or verses of the Qur'an, the communal singing of a strophic hymn, the listening to a melodious motet by Bruckner or the singing of a Mantra. There is a close connection between music, rituality and religiosity, a connection which I believe is also logical and explicable." Hence, we celebrate the advent of a long-awaited Musicology of Religion.

Finally! The reunion of Homo Religiosus and Homo Musicus has begun.

Appendix A

Resources and Current Outlook

Appendix A cites recent work and resources relevant to the subject of Musicology of Religion, including individual contributions, reference works, and scholarly collaborations. While the corpus of material is expanding, areas for further research remain abundant.

We begin with the larger reference works and proceed to specialized topics. Despite its centenary age, the twelve-volume *Encyclopedia of Religion and Ethics* (1908–1921), edited by James Hastings, contains a surprisingly comprehensive entry on Music (v. 9: 5–61) with separate articles on ancient and living religions: Primitive and Savage (J. A. MacCulloch), American (H. R. Alexander), Babylonian and Assyrian (T. G. Pinches), Buddhist (C.A.F. Rhys-Davids), Celtic (J. A. MacCulloch), Chinese (J. Dyer Ball), Christian (H. Westerby), Egyptian (J. Baikie), Greek and Roman (E. Graf), Hebrew (G. Wauchope Stewart), Indian (E. Clements), Japanese (H. Muraoka), Jewish (F. L. Cohen), Muhammadan (J. D. Prince), Slavic (L. A. Magnus), and Teutonic (M. E. Seaton).

After Hastings, the next large reference work to include music is *The Encyclopedia of Religion* (1987), edited by Mircea Eliade. This work in sixteen volumes contains in-depth articles (vol. 10, 163–215) on the role of music in diverse religious traditions. Including the lead article by Ter Ellingson, "Music and Religion" (1987: vol. 10: 163–172), eleven articles by expert scholars cover separate geographic areas: Sub-Saharan Africa (J. H. Kwabena Nketia); Australia and Oceania (Richard Moyle); the Americas (David P. McAllester); the Middle East (Amnon Shiloah); India—including Vedic, Buddhism, and Hindu and Islamic devotional music (David Roche); Southeast Asia (Martin Hatch); China, Korea, and Tibet (Isabel

Wong); Japan (Kishibe Shigao); Greece, Rome, and Byzantium (Eric Werner); and Religious Music in the West (Alexander L. Ringer). The second edition (2005) in fifteen volumes, edited by Lindsay Jones, contains updated revisions by the same authors as well as new or rewritten articles by new authors (vol. 9: 6248–6314). The new or rewritten articles are "Indigenous Australia" (Elizabeth Mackinlay and John Bradley), "Mesoamerica" (Arnd Adje Both), "South America" (Acacio Tadeu de Camargo Piedade and Deise Lucy Oliviera Montardo), "India" (Philip V. Bohlman), "Southeast Asia" (David Harnish), "Japan" (Kishibe Shigeo and Ogi Mitsuo), and "Religious Music in the West" (Frank Burch Brown).

As the most comprehensive resource on world music traditions, the ten-volume *Garland Encyclopedia of World Music* (2000), edited by Bruno Nettl and Ruth M. Stone, contains multiple articles that describe and explain music in various religious contexts. The reader is also well rewarded by consulting the twenty-volume *New Grove Dictionary of Music and Musicians* (1980), edited by Stanley Sadie. There is also a single-reference work on sacred music in world religions: Joseph P. Swain, *The A to Z of Sacred Music* (2010). In a welcome reference tool compiled by Gardner E. Rust, *The Music and Dance of the World's Religions: A Comprehensive, Annotated Bibliography of Materials in the English Language* (1996), one finds an extensive collection of sources for the study of music and religion.

Three anthologies in the past thirty years have attempted to grapple comprehensively with the topic of music and world religions. The first, *Sacred Sound: Music in Religious Thought and Practice* (1983), edited by Joyce Irwin, was a breakthrough collection of articles by experts who explored theoretical aspects of the intersection of music and religion in specific cases: Music and Theology (Oskar Sohngen), Islam (Lois Ibsen al Faruqi), Jewish Liturgical Music (Judith K. Eisenstein), Lutheran Theology (Joyce Irwin), American Christianity (Stephen Marini), Sufi Islam (Bruce B. Lawrence), Ghana (Barbara L. Hampton), Theravada Buddhism (John Ross Carter), and Music in India (Donna Marie Wulff). Next, *Enchanting Powers: Music in the World's Religions* (1997), edited by Lawrence E. Sullivan, provides excellent articles on music in selected religious traditions: Javanese Gamelan (Judith Becker), World Music (Philip V. Bohlman), Ghana (John Chernoff), African American Christianity (Michael W. Harris), Shamanism in Venezuela (Jonathan D. Hill), Jewish Mysticism (Moshe Idel), Choctaw (Victoria Lindsay Levine), Islam (Seyyed Hossein Nasr), Confucianism (Rulan Chao Pian), Islam (Regula Burckhardt Qureshi), and Jewish Music (Kay Kaufman Shelemay). A more recent anthology, *Sacred Sound: Experiencing Music in World Religions* (2006), edited by Guy L. Beck, contains individual chapters on six major world religions: Judaism (Joseph Levine), Christianity (Gerald Hobbs), Islam (Regula Qureshi), Hinduism (Guy L. Beck), Sikhism (Pashaura Singh), and Buddhism (Sean Williams). The chapters are by scholar/performers with performances by the authors themselves on a CD. An appendix contains an extensive discography of recommended recordings. This work is an ideal teaching companion to Harold Coward's edited volume, *Experiencing Scripture in World Religions* (2000), wherein the oral nature of scripture is discussed and evaluated in each of these six religions.

Collections of individual essays elicit our attention regarding music and religious experience, as well as targeted studies. One of the first to set the stage for fruitful investigation is *Music and the Experience of God* (1989), edited by Mary Collins, David Power, and Mellonee Burnim. Siglind Bruhn has edited a volume, *Voicing the Ineffable: Musical Representations of Religious Experience* (2002), containing essays on St. Jerome, St. Augustine, the Romantics, Adorno, and Derrida. The contributors to *Resounding Transcendence: Transitions in Music, Religion and Ritual* (2016), edited by Jeffers Engelhardt and Philip V. Bohlman, provide innovative analyses of music in ritual contexts, including Taiwan Buddhist festivals, Byzantine chant at Mt. Athos, Christian worship in Indonesia and South India, Evangelical hymn singing, Tunisian devotion, post-secular Europe, Jewish experience, and the music of composer Arvo Part. More recently, *Music and Transcendence* (2020), edited by Ferdia J. Stone-Davis, presents penetrating essays ranging from Schleiermacher to Gadamer, and from Bach to Beethoven.

The tradition of Pythagoras and its relation to literature, while often elusive, has been given careful and exacting treatment in terms of the Renaissance by S. K. Heninger Jr. in *Touches of Sweet Harmony: Pythagorean Cosmology and Renaissance Poetics* (1974). Beside the works of Joscelyn Godwin cited in chapter 4, two recent books, one as an introduction to harmony of the spheres by Jamie James (1993), and another on Pythagorean numbers and music by Eli Maor (2018), are worth notice. For music and esoteric traditions, see the edited volume by Lawrence Wuidar, *Music and Esotericism* (2010), and for the "ineffable" in music, see Vladimir Jankelevitch's *Music and the Ineffable* (2003), a valued contribution.

Richard Viladesau (1999, 2000) and Anthony Monti (2003) have explored issues involving the arts, including music, and theology. Frank Burch Brown, as editor of *The Oxford Handbook of Religion and the Arts* (2014), brought together scholars in the visual and performing arts to create an excellent introduction to this rapidly expanding field. For women and music, see Ellen Koskoff, ed., *Women and Music in Cross-cultural Perspective* (1987), and Sarah Weiss (2019). In addition, the complex interface between religion and popular music is well introduced by Robin Sylvan (2002), with more specialized studies in Michael J. Gilmour (2005) and Christopher Partridge (2014). For a recent survey of diverse new directions in religion and music, see Dustin D. Wiebe (2021), "Music and Religion: Trends in Recent English-Language Literature (2015–2021)."

Chant often brings us to the core of religion. As Gregorian chant forms an integral part of Western music history, Richard L. Crocker, in *An Introduction to Gregorian Chant* (2000), provides a lucid introductory study. Peter Jeffery, in *Re-Envisioning Past Musical Cultures: Ethnomusicology in the Study of Gregorian Chant* (1992), has demonstrated the fruits of collaboration between the study of Gregorian chant and ethnomusicology. Tala Jarjour, in *Sense and Sadness: Syriac Chant in Aleppo* (2018), recaptures the essence of an ancient chant tradition. Liturgical traditions in context can also reveal treasures of sacred chant, as in Margot Fassler's *The Virgin of Chartres: Making History through Liturgy and the Arts* (2010). In *Singing the Right Way: Orthodox Christians and Secular Enchantment in Estonia* (2014), Jeffers Engelhardt details the resilience of traditional Orthodox Christian chant and its complex interface with modernity in Estonia.

Sacred musical traditions in Judaism and Christianity share a reliance on the Biblical literature. Siobhan Dowling Long and John F. A. Sawyer, in *The Bible in Music: A Dictionary of Songs, Works, and More* (2015), offer a useful introductory reference work on the relation between the Bible and music over the centuries. Wilfrid Mellers, in *Celestial Music? Some Masterpieces of European Religious Music* (2001), provides expert analyses of the European classical tradition of religious music. For focused treatment on Judeo-Christian traditions of liturgical music, excellent chapter/articles appear in *Sacred Sound and Social Change: Liturgical Music in Jewish and Christian Experience* (1992), edited by Lawrence A. Hoffman and Janet R. Walton. For a thorough presentation of music in ancient Israel, see Alfred Sendrey (1969), and for a valuable study of ancient Jewish and Christian liturgical traditions, see Eric Werner, *The Sacred Bridge: Liturgical Parallels in Synagogue and Early Church* (1960). More details of Jewish music and its cultural history appear in Emanuel Rubin and John H. Baron (2006). For early Christianity, see James McKinnon (1987). The volume by Amnon Shiloah covering Jewish music (1992) is an excellent introductory text. And for the significant contributions of Jews to modern music, see Arthur Holde (1974).

For a description and analysis of types of sacred music in America, refer to Stephen A. Marini, *Sacred Song in America: Religion, Music, and Public Culture* (2003), and David W. Stowe, *How Sweet the Sound: Music in the Spiritual Lives of Americans* (2004). For a useful reference on current Christian music, see M. A. Powell (2001). The recent work of Monique Ingalls (2018) in congregational music accompanies the previous edited volume of Monique Ingalls, Carolyn Landau, and Tom Wagner, *Christian Congregational Music: Performance, Identity, and Experience* (2013). Tim Dowley, in *Christian Music: A Global History* (2011), introduces the diversity of Christian music in the world. Studies of the music of specific Christian communities appear in Marc Gidal, *Spirit Song: Afro-Brazilian Religious Music and Boundaries* (2016), Vicki L. Brennan, *Singing Yoruba Christianity: Music, Media, and Modernity* (2018), and Melvin Butler, *Island Gospel: Pentecostal Music and Identity in Jamaica and the United States* (2019).

After the excellent work on Islamic music by Henry George Farmer (1957) and Amnon Shiloah (1995), historical studies on sound and music in Islam appear in Michael Frishkopf and Federico Spinetti's compilation *Music, Sound, and Architecture in Islam* (2018). Islamic Sufi music is a prominent part of Islamic devotion; for Qawwali, see Regula Qureshi (1986, 2006), and for Mevlevi Whirling Dervish music, see Shems Friedlander (1992). The rich tradition of Islamic music in South Asia is in Richard K. Wolf, *The Voice in the Drum: Music, language, and Emotion in Islamicate South Asia* (2014).

For the Hindu tradition, *Sonic Theology* (Beck 1993) and *Sonic Liturgy* (Beck 2012) discuss the primary and secondary sources on sacred sound and music. For more information on the history, theories, and methods related to Mantras, see the edited volume by Harvey P. Alper, *Understanding Mantras* (1989). Regarding religious music, two articles in *Garland Encyclopedia of World Music*, vol. 5, introduce and describe the major types of religious music in India, north and south: "Religious and Devotional Music: Northern Area" (Beck 2000), and "Religious and Devotional Music: Southern Area" (William Jackson 2000). For the genres of Kīrtan and Bhajan, see Beck (2010), and for musical instruments, Beck (2013). A collection of Vaishnava temple music songs and hymns is available in *Vaishnava Temple Music in Vrindaban: The Rādhāvallabha Songbook* (Beck 2011), with eighteen CDs. For the role of music in twentieth-century Hindu nationalism, see Anna Schultz, *Singing a Hindu Nation: Marathi Devotional Performance and Nationalism* (2012).

A paucity of sources on music in Zoroastrianism was reversed by the welcome work of Raiomond Mirza (2004). For music in Buddhism, see Sean Williams (2006), and for Sikhism, Pashaura Singh (2006). Erica Fox Brindley examines Chinese ceremonial music in the breakthrough study,

Cosmology, and the Politics of Harmony in Early China (2012). A text of readings in Karen Ralls-McLeod and Graham Harvey (2000) contains useful examinations of rare and lesser-known forms of Indigenous religious music. Gilbert Rouget (1986) is important in relation to the psychological states of musical trance and possession.

Additional studies in Asian religion and music contribute to the detailed research objectives of Musicology of Religion: Sukanya Sarbadhikary, in *The Place of Devotion: Siting and Experiencing Divinity in Bengal Vaishnavism* (2015), describes the rich symbolism of musical activity in Bengal. Eben Graves, in *Rhythmic Theology: Khol Drumming in Caitanya Vaisnava Kirtan* (2009), provides a complement with a close analysis of religious drumming in Bengal. For the Baul singing tradition of Bengal, see Carola Lorea, *Folklore, Religion and the Songs of a Bengali Madman: A Journey Between Performance and the Politics of Cultural Representation* (2016). The esoteric ritual music of Tibetan Buddhism is well documented by Jeffrey W. Cupchik in *The Sound of Vultures' Wings: The Tibetan Chöd Ritual Practice of the Female Buddha Machik Labdrön* (2018). Two studies of Southeast Asian music are also significant contributions revealing the sacred context of music: Sean Williams, in *Sounds of the Ancestral Ship: Highland Music of West Java* (2001), and Brita Renée Heimarck, in *Balinese Discourses on Music and Modernization: Village Voices and Urban Views* (2003).

The issue of universals in aesthetics as the basis for comparative study is another contributing factor to the Musicology of Religion. Denis Dutton's "Aesthetic Universals" (2001) is a good starting point. For a perspective from the social sciences, focusing on African traditions, see Wilfried van Damme, *Beauty in Context: Toward an Anthropological Approach to Aesthetics* (1996). The evolutionary and cognitive aspects of aesthetics, outlining human nature as *homo aestheticus*, have been explored by Ellen Dissanayake in *Homo Aestheticus: Where Art Comes From and Why* (1995). Pioneering work in 'comparative aesthetics,' with an India-West basis, is found in Dr. Kanti Chandra Pandey's two-volume work, *Comparative Aesthetics: Indian Aesthetics*, v. 1, (1959); *Comparative Aesthetics: Western Aesthetics*, v. 2 (1972), followed by a comparative aesthetics of the music of India and Japan in Lewis Rowell's *Thinking about Music: An Introduction to the Philosophy of Music* (1983: 190–210).

Inaugurated in 2015, a periodical devoted to music and religion, *Yale Journal of Music and Religion*, publishes articles covering specialized topics relevant to the Musicology of Religion. As an important venue for studies in religion and music, this journal is published twice yearly by the Yale Institute of Sacred Music, a research and teaching facility based at Yale University in New Haven, Connecticut. For more information, visit the website: https://elischolar.library.yale.edu/yjmr.

Academic conferences devoted to religion and music as well as other coordinated efforts are also on the rise. A group of scholars in the American Academy of Religion contributed to a *Religious Studies News* issue devoted to teaching religion and music, edited by Tazim Kassam: *AAR Religious Studies News* supplement: "Spotlight on Teaching/Religion and Music," vol. 16, no. 2 (Spring 2001): 1–12. The consensus of the authors was that since chant and music are intrinsically related to religion, the topic of music belongs within classroom and scholarly presentations of religion. As an outgrowth, a new section of the American Academy of Religion, "Music and Religion," is now hosting panels and papers on this important topic.

In 2006, Lidia Guzy organized a "Religion and Music" conference at the Freie Universitat in Berlin. The proceedings were published in 2008 as *Religion and Music: Proceedings of the Interdisciplinary Workshop at the Institute for Scientific Studies of Religions*. Lidia Guzy (2008: 8–9) outlined the format in the form of two questions with broader implications: "In its transdisciplinary and culturally comparative perspective the volume focuses on the following questions: How are religious ideas in diverse religions and societies transmitted through music? How can we translate the cultural meaning of music in the rituals of diverse religions into an analysis of religions and rituals in general?"

In 2010, a special symposium, "Sound In/As Religion," was held at the XXth World Congress of the International Association for the History of Religions (IAHR) at the University of Toronto. Organized by Rosalind Hackett, the symposium stimulated a renewed focus on the acoustic, auditory, and sonic dimensions of religion. New research represented a concerted effort to overhaul the discipline of religious studies in the direction of both ritual and sonic expression.

The Andrew W. Mellon project of "Religion across the Disciplines" (2010–2012) involved a working group on Music and Religion headed by Peter Jeffery of the University of Notre Dame. This group included Stephen Marini, Philip V. Bohlman, Margot Fassler, Kay K. Shelemay, Melvin Butler, Carolyn Landau, and Guy L. Beck, who discussed the integration of the study of religion with music on several levels, including theology, history of religions, musicology, and ethnomusicology. Results included panel sessions presented in 2012 at the newly formed Music and Religion Group of the American Academy of Religion (AAR) in Chicago, and at the Society for Ethnomusicology (SEM) in New Orleans. Strategies were envisioned to close the gap between religious studies and music that included a collection of articles and a website.

In recent years, this author participated in three international conferences relating to sacred music. In August 2011, an Eranos Conference on "Love and the Musical Arts" was held in Ascona, Switzerland, and assembled delegates from several religious traditions. The event was hosted by the Eranos Foundation and the Fetzer Institute under the direction of Lawrence E. Sullivan, Harvard University Professor Emeritus.

Second, in June 2016 the author represented Hinduism at the conference on "Sacred Voices," sponsored by the International Christian University in Tokyo, Japan, and organized by Matt Gillan. The announcement for the conference included chant from four religions: "Combining performances and lectures, this event will provide a chance to experience the vocal chant traditions of Hinduism, Buddhism, Christianity, and Islam in performance with lecture-demonstrations." The third conference, held at Tubingen University, Germany, January 2020, was organized by Heike Oberlin and Peter Gietz of the Tubingen Institute of Asian and Oriental Studies and the Department of Indology and Comparative Religion. Titled, "From Sacred Hymns to Devotional Songs: A Diachronic and Transcultural Study of Religious Singing in India," the conference included papers covering a wide range of Indian religious vocal music.

A recent project involves this author as Guest Editor of a Special Issue of the online journal *Religions*, entitled "Tuning In the Sacred: Studies in Music and World Religions." Religions | Special Issue: Tuning In the Sacred: Studies in Music and World Religions (mdpi.com).

This issue complements the earlier Special Issue of *Religions*, "Music in World Religions," with Guest Editor, Dr. Heather MacLachlan. Religions | Special Issue : Music in World Religions (mdpi.com).

Appendix B

Glossary of Terms for Musicology of Religion

To advance the study of religion and music, I have created a glossary of terms drawn from various disciplines and from religious traditions. These terms aim to establish a greater degree of precision in identifying sound or music events as they occur in the context of religious ritual or experience. While many of these terms derive from Greek and Latin, and have been used in Christian theology, there is ample reason to include terms from other languages such as Sanskrit, Hebrew, Arabic, and Chinese that may provide further nuance in articulating how music functions in worship and in religious experience worldwide. As to the author's own field, Sanskrit or Indian terms represent additional categories of religious music.

The researcher's role in applying these terms is not only to identify which term goes with which ritual or tradition but also to foster further engagement in comparative analysis about how, when, and where the terms may apply, for example, in the context of monotheism, polytheism, or animism. It is about locating which genres of music, patterns of melody, or rhythmic structures correspond with certain kinds of religious belief systems and hierarchies; it is about how and why diverse kinds of instruments and musical ensembles are organized around belief in the supernatural; it is about which types of music are portrayed in religious texts dealing with life after death. In reference to traditional phenomenology of religion, it may be about documenting how experiences of the "numinous" or the "sacred" appear and reappear in dialectical manner within the multilayered texture of the world of religion and music. In any case, while several terms or concepts may overlap, with some traditions comprising multiple categories, we posit that a neutral interpretive lexicon helps to locate the role of music in a large variety of ritual contexts, enables the transfer of understanding from one tradition to another, and determines specific patterns that will facilitate successful and creative studies in the Musicology of Religion.

Anamnesis—Music performed for the purpose of remembrance of a past historical or religious event, whether as instrumental or vocal, and containing lyrics that provide a narration. Examples are the musical commemorations of Jewish Passover, Christ's Passion, or Lord Rāma's Victory over demon Rāvana in the Hindu epic *Rāmāyaṇa*.

Ānanda-kāraṇa (Sanskrit)—Music performed with the express desire of achieving personal bliss or transcendental happiness (ānanda). Experiencing musical bliss is the goal, such that it is synonymous with religious experience. Examples are Hindu Bhakti traditions, Sufi dance, forms of African drumming, and spiritualist music.

Ancestor based—Music performed along with ancestral rites to communicate with deceased ancestors, to please or placate them or to establish a bond. Widely practiced, examples are ancient Shang China and Confucian ceremonies, Japanese Shinto, Indonesian and Balinese Gamelan, and in Africa.

Apotheosis—Music as capable of elevating the human being to divine status, as in mystery cults, theurgy, or magical rites. This includes music that transforms participants into observers of sacred pastimes of the gods, as in forms of Hindu devotional temple music.

Apotropaia—Music for the removal of unwanted spirits or demons, accomplished through the chanting of specific texts or the playing of percussive instruments. Examples of this effect are Hindu Mantra chant, Theravada Buddhist Paritta chant, Shinto chant, and in the native religions of Africa and Southeast Asia.

Bhakti-kāraṇa (Sanskrit)—Music for the cultivation of intense devotion (Bhakti) to a deity or God. In cases where the objective is (Prema), this music becomes a self-perpetuating ideal, as found in Hindu theistic traditions of Vaishnavism or Saivism, and Sufi traditions. Examples are mystical piety in all three Western monotheistic religions.

Catharsis—Purification from sin or defilement, usually with the aid of scripture or a saint or deity. Examples are the chant of Gnostic sects, scripture chanting in Hinduism, and in Buddhist recitation of the Pali Canon.

Cosmogony—Music that reenacts the creation myth. Examples include the music of New Year ceremonies as well as in ritual combat. Selected Vedic sacrifices reenact the cosmogony and involve complex styles of chant and the singing of hymns.

Demonology—Music directed toward the invocation or manipulation of demonic or evil forces. Besides the use of instruments, this includes various forms of chant and intonation practices to conjure demons or evil spirits and direct them for sinister purposes. Examples of these aspects are in Shamanism, Satanism, witchcraft, black magic, sorcery, and native religions associated with animism.

Didactic—Music or chant of sacred texts involved in teaching doctrine, as found in Jewish lessons, Hindu Puranic recitation, Jain Stavan, and the chanting of the Buddhist Pali Canon.

Diegesis—Music that accompanies a narration from a sacred text, often involving a degree of creative improvisation; opposed to Mimesis, which is music that imitates music in the heavens, as in, for example, ancient Indian Gandharva music.

Doxology—Music associated with the praise or glorification of God or a deity. In response to receiving the gift of life from their Creator, humans offer praise. This function is termed Doxological (*doxa*, "glory") because music is used to glorify or praise the divine, as in most forms of Psalmody, the Zoroastrian Gathas, and Vedic hymns. Music as "Doxology" is also present in Bhajan in Hinduism, Qawwali in Islam, and Shabad in Sikhism.

Epektasis—"Traveling toward the infinite," in the sense that music acts as a vehicle to move or proceed toward God or the divine. Examples are in mystery cults or traditions influenced by Neo-Platonism, Neo-Pythagoreanism, Gnosticism, and Shamanism.

Epiclesis—Music associated with the invitation of a god or divine being to a sacrifice or worship occasion. Borrowed from classical pagan vocabulary, this term is used in Catholicism to depict the priestly action of inviting the Holy Spirit into the sacramental bread and wine. In a broader sense, it may refer to the action of Mantras in a Vedic sacrifice, Hindu devotional music, and other forms of invitational singing in religions of the world.

Eschatology—Expressing the end times, music that is "eschatological" represents or expresses a future state of being, such as found in the Biblical books of Isaiah (6:3) and Revelation (5:8–10). Examples of this type are in certain Jewish messianic songs, Christian hymns, Hindu Bhajans, Buddhist prayers, or Sikh Shabads.

Eucharistic—Music that gives thanks for a variety of reasons, as found in Christianity, Judaism, Sikhism, and Hinduism.

Expiation—Music that serves to request forgiveness of sins or transgressions from a deity or divine being. All religions have rituals for purification and removal of sins or offenses.

Exstasis—Music employed to achieve states of ecstasy, termed *Exstasis* in the texts of mystery religions. Examples are in Sufism, Hasidism, Hindu Bhakti, and some Buddhist sects.

Gender based—Music that is gender-specific to either men or women in terms of structure and performance. For women, this includes female initiation music found in mystery religions and sacred orders of sisterhood, as well as music that is composed for female voices, especially those in the upper registers (soprano, alto), such as, for example, in Bulgarian singing and the music of Hildegard of Bingen. This also includes Psalmody performed by women in Catholic monasteries, forms of Wicca chant, Jain Stavans, and special songs of Hindu women as part of devotional worship. For men, this includes male initiation chants or hymns found in mystery religions and sacred fraternal orders, as well as music composed for or oriented toward male voices, especially those in the lower register (bass, tenor), such as for Tibetan monks and those in the Russian Orthodox Church.

Harmonia—While not necessarily performed as "music" in the typical sense, Harmonia refers to the philosophical "tuning the soul" with the greater cosmos through meditation on the pure notes, intervals, and their corresponding numbers. While recommended in Plato's works and in ancient Greece, this process is also present in mystery cults, Neo-Pythagoreanism, esoteric traditions, and in some forms of Neo-Platonism.

Katanyxis—Music that expresses or accompanies contrition or remorse for grave sins. Beside Christianity, this is found in some forms of Hindu Bhakti poetry and Sikh Shabads.

Koinonia—Music that enacts or expresses communion between the human and divine world. Notions of musical unity among human beings, martyrs, and saints appear in Christianity but also in archaic and Asian religions where music celebrates a communal meal of humans and the gods, as practiced in ancient Vedic India or in temple Hinduism.

Litaneia—Music as petitionary prayer, as in the Catholic Mass (Kyrie eleison, "Lord Have Mercy"), in Judaism, temple Hinduism, and in Sikh Shabads.

Loka-rañjana (Sanskrit)—Music as entertainment, for oneself, for group pleasure, or for the pleasure of others as a prelude to religious experience.

Mimesis—Music that seeks to imitate nature, in this case heavenly music or divine archetypes. Examples are in the ancient Indian Gandharva music as well as the Sufi Whirling Dervish tradition of replicating the motions of the stars or heavenly bodies.

Mukti-kāraṇa (Sanskrit)—Performing music with the intention of securing liberation or release from this transitory world or the cycle of transmigration. This is present in Hindu traditions of devotional music, Jewish Kabbalah, and Buddhism, and in certain Pythagorean traditions in Greco-Roman Antiquity.

Pavitra-kāraṇa (Sanskrit)—Music performed in conjunction with ritual so that one becomes purified of sins or transgressions, with or without the aid of a deity or God. Examples are in most religious traditions.

Propitiation—Seeking the favor or blessing from a deity or divine being. This is a widely accepted notion in all world religions.

Śānti-kāraṇa (Sanskrit)—Music performed for the attainment of spiritual peace, either for oneself, for gatherings of musicians and listeners, or for the general uplift of humanity.

Soteriology—Music oriented toward achieving existence in heaven or a realm beyond death, performed solo and in musical ensembles. This includes forms of Christian choral music, Hindu temple music, Sufi songs, and Celtic singing.

Upahāra (Sanskrit)—Music offered solely as a gift to please a deity or God without requesting a favor or something in exchange. This occurs in the Bhakti tradition of Hinduism, the hymn singing in Lutheran Pietism, and in the songs of the Sufi Whirling Dervishes.

Works Cited

Adams, Doug, and Diane Apostolos-Cappadona, eds. 1987. *Art as Religious Studies*. New York: Crossroad.
Adorno, Theodor W. 1976. *Introduction to the Sociology of Music*. New York: The Seabury Press.
Alcorta, C. S. 2008. "Music and the Miraculous: The Neurophysiology of Music's Emotive Meaning." In *Miracles: God, Science, and Psychology in the Paranormal: Parapsychological Perspectives*. Edited by J. H. Ellen. Westport, CT: Praeger, 230–252.
Allen, Douglas. 2010. "Phenomenology of Religion." In *The Routledge Companion to the Study of Religion*. 2nd edition. Edited by John Hinnells. London & New York: Routledge, 203–224.
Allen, Warren Dwight. 1962 [1939]. *Philosophies of Music History: A Study of General Histories of Music 1600–1960*. New York: Dover Publications.
Alles, Gregory D. 1987. "Homo Religiosus." In *The Encyclopedia of Religion*. Edited by Mircea Eliade. New York: Macmillan Publishing, Vol. 6, 442–445.
Alles, Gregory D., trans. and ed. 1996. *Rudolf Otto: Autobiographical and Social Essays*. Berlin and New York: Mouton de Gruyter.
Almond, Philip C. 1984. *Rudolf Otto: An Introduction to His Philosophical Theology*. Chapel Hill and London: University of North Carolina Press.
Alper, Harvey P., ed. 1989. *Understanding Mantras*. Albany, NY: SUNY Press.
Alston, William P. 1991. *Perceiving God: The Epistemology of Religious Experience*. Ithaca, NY: Cornell University Press.
Alves, William. 2012. *Music of the Peoples of the World*. 3rd edition. Boston: Cengage Learning.
Ānanda-Vrindāvana-Campū by Kavi Karnapūr. 1999. Translated from Sanskrit by Bhanu Swami and Subhag Swami. English edited by Mahanidhi Swami. Vrindavana, UP: Mahanidhi Swami.
Anderson, Warren D. 1966. *Ethos and Education in Greek Music: The Evidence of Poetry and Philosophy*. Cambridge, MA: Harvard University Press.
Anderson, Warren D. 1994. *Music and Musicians in Ancient Greece*. Ithaca & London: Cornell University Press.

Antilla, Miikka E. 2017. *Luther's Theology of Music: Spiritual Beauty and Pleasure*. Berlin, Germany: Walter de Gruyter.
Antweiler, Christoph. 2016. *Our Common Denominator: Human Universals Revisited*. Translated by Diane Kerns. New York & Oxford: Berghahn Books.
Atran, Scot. 2002. *In Gods We Trust: The Evolutionary Landscape of Religion*. New York: Oxford University Press.
Baillie, John. 1928. *The Interpretation of Religion: An Introductory Study of Theological Principles*. New York & Nashville: Abingdon Press.
Bakan, Michael B. 2007. *World Music: Traditions and Transformations*. New York: McGraw-Hill.
Balthasar, Hans Urs von. 1982. *The Glory of the Lord: A Theological Aesthetics. Volume 1: Seeing the Form*. Translated by Erasmo Leiva-Merikakis. Edited by Joseph Fessio, SJ, and John Riches. San Francisco: Ignatius Press.
Bannan, Nicholas, ed. 2012. *Music, Language, and Human Evolution*. New York & Oxford: Oxford University Press.
Barth, Karl. 1986 [1956]. *Wolfgang Amadeus Mozart*. Eugene, OR: Wipf & Stock.
Beard, David, and Kenneth Gloag. 2016. *Musicology: The Key Concepts*. Second Edition. London and New York: Routledge.
Beck, Guy L. 2019. "All Roads Lead to OM: From Ancient Roots to Hindu, Buddhist, Jain, and Sikh Dharma." *Journal of Vaishnava Studies*, Vol. 28, No. 1: 51–67.
Beck, Guy L. 2013. "Divine Musical Instruments." In *Brill's Encyclopedia of Hinduism*. Edited by Knut A. Jacobsen. Leiden: Brill Academic Publishers, Vol. 5, 36–44.
Beck, Guy L. 2014. "Hinduism and Music." In *The Oxford Handbook of Religion and the Arts*. Edited by Frank Burch Brown. New York: Oxford University Press, 358–366.
Beck, Guy L. 2010. "Kirtan and Bhajan in Bhakti Traditions." In *Brill's Encyclopedia of Hinduism*. Edited by Knut A. Jacobsen. Leiden: Brill Academic Publishers, Vol. 2, 585–598.
Beck, Guy L. 2021. "Music." In *The Wiley Blackwell Companion to the Study of Religion*. 2nd edition. Edited by Robert A. Segal and Nickolas P. Roubekas. West Sussex, UK: John Wiley & Sons, Ltd., 335–347.
Beck, Guy. 2000. "Religious and Devotional Music: Northern Area." In *Garland Encyclopedia of World Music*, Vol. 5, Indian Subcontinent. Edited by Alison Arnold. New York and London: Garland Publishing, 246–258.
Beck, Guy L. 2019. "Sacred Music and Hindu Religious Experience: From Ancient Roots to the Modern Classical Tradition." In *Religious Experience in the Hindu Tradition*. Edited by June McDaniel. Basel Switzerland: MDPI *Religions*, Vol. 10, No. 2: 111–124. https://doi.org/10.3390/rel10020085. www.mdpi.com/2077-1444/10/2/85
Beck, Guy L. 2012. *Sonic Liturgy: Ritual and Music in Hindu Tradition*. Columbia: University of South Carolina Press.
Beck, Guy L. 1993. *Sonic Theology: Hinduism and Sacred Sound*. Columbia: University of South Carolina Press.

Beck, Guy L., ed. 2006. *Sacred Sound: Experiencing Music in World Religions.* Waterloo, Ontario: Wilfrid Laurier University Press (with CD).
Beck, Guy L., ed. 2011. *Vaishnava Temple Music in Vrindaban: The Rādhāvallabha Songbook.* Kirksville, MO: Blazing Sapphire Press. With 18 CDs.
Beck, Kajal Dass. 2016. *Nava Alpana: New Decorative Designs of India.* Kirksville, MO: Blazing Sapphire Press.
Becker, Judith. 2001. "Anthropological Perspectives on Music and Emotion." In *Music and Emotion: Theory and Research.* Edited by John A. Sloboda and P. N. Juslin. Oxford, England: Oxford University Press, 135–160.
Becker, Judith. 2004. *Deep Listeners: Music, Emotion, and Trancing.* Bloomington: Indiana University Press.
Begbie, Jeremy. 2013. *Music, Modernity, and God: Essays in Listening.* Oxford, UK: Oxford University Press.
Begbie, Jeremy S. 2013. "Natural Theology and Music." In *The Oxford Handbook of Natural Theology.* Edited by Russell Re Manning. New York: Oxford University Press, 566–580.
Begbie, Jeremy S. 2000. *Theology, Music, and Time.* Cambridge, UK: Cambridge University Press.
Begbie, Jeremy S. 2005. "Theology and Music." *In The Modern Theologians: An Introduction to Christian Theology since 1918.* Third edition. Edited by David F. Ford and Rachel Muers. Oxford, UK: Blackwell Publishing, 719–735.
Bell, Catherine. 1998. "Performance." In *Critical Terms for Religious Studies.* Edited by Mark C. Taylor. Chicago: University of Chicago Press, 205–224.
Belzen, Jacob. A. von. 2013. "Music and Religion: Psychological Perspectives and their Limits." *Archive for the Psychology of Religions,* Vol. 35: 1–29.
Berendt, Joachim-Ernst. 1987. *Nada Brahma: The World is Sound; Music and the Landscape of Consciousness.* Rochester, VT: Destiny Books.
Berger, Peter L.1970. *A Rumor of Angels: Modern Society and the Rediscovery of the Supernatural.* Garden City, NY: Doubleday Anchor Books.
Berger, Peter L. 1967. *Sacred Canopy: Elements of a Sociological Theory of Religion.* Garden City, NY: Doubleday.
Bernard, Patrick. 2004. *Music as Yoga: Discover the Healing Power of Sound.* San Rafael, CA: Mandala Publishing.
Bernstein, Leonard. 1981 [1976]. *The Unanswered Question: Six Talks at Harvard.* Cambridge, MA: Harvard University Press.
Blacking, John. 1973. *How Musical Is Man?* Seattle: University of Washington Press.
Blacking, John. 1977. "Can Musical Universals be heard?" *The World of Music,* Vol. 19, No. 1–2, UNIVERSALS: 14–22
Blacking, John. 1995. *Music, Culture, and Experience: Selected Papers of John Blacking.* Chicago: University of Chicago Press.
Blackwell, Albert L. 1999. *The Sacred in Music.* Louisville, KY: Westminster John Knox Press.

Blackwell, Albert L. 1991. "Schleiermacher on Musical Experience and Religious Experience: 'What Hath Vienna to do with Jerusalem?' " In *Friedrich Schleiermacher and the Founding of the University of Berlin: The Study of Religion as a Scientific Discipline.* Edited by Herbert Richardson. Lewiston, NY: The Edwin Mellen Press, 121–139

Bleeker, C. J. 1963. *The Sacred Bridge: Researches into the Nature and Structure of Religion.* Leiden: E. J. Brill.

Bloch, Ernst. 1985. *Essays on the Philosophy of Music.* Translated by Peter Palmer with an Introduction by David Drew. Cambridge, UK: Cambridge University Press.

Blofeld, John. 1970. *The Tantric Mysticism of Tibet: A Practical Guide.* New York: E.P. Dutton.

Blum, Jason N. 2012. "Retrieving Phenomenology of Religion as a Method for Religious Studies." *Journal of the American Academy of Religion,* Vol. 80, No. 4 (December): 1025–1048.

Bohlman, Philip V. 1994. "Is All Music Religious?" In *Theomusicology.* Edited by Jon Michael Spencer. Durham, NC: Duke University Press, 3–12.

Bohlman, Philip V. 2005. "Music: Music and Religion in India." In *The Encyclopedia of Religion,* 2nd edition. Editor in Chief, Lindsay Jones. New York: Macmillan, Vol. 9, 6278–6287.

Bohlman, Philip V. 2020 [2002]. *World Music: A Very Short Introduction.* Oxford: Oxford University Press.

Bosanquet, Bernard. 1904 [1892]. *A History of Aesthetic.* Second edition. London: Macmillan.

Bowie, Andrew. 2003 [1990]. *Aesthetics and Subjectivity: from Kant to Nietzsche.* Manchester & New York: Manchester University Press.

Bowie, Andrew. 2020 [2015]. "Music, Transcendence, and Philosophy." In *Music and Transcendence.* Edited by Ferdia J. Stone-Davis. New York: Routledge, 213–223.

Bowker, John. 1997. *The Oxford Dictionary of World Religions.* Oxford: Oxford University Press.

Bowker, John. 1995 [1971]. *The Sense of God: Sociological, Anthropological and Psychological Approaches to the Origin of the Sense of God.* Oxford: Oneworld Publications.

Bouyer, Louis. 1963. *Rite and Man: Natural Sacredness and Christian Liturgy.* South Bend, IN: Notre Dame University Press.

Boyer, Pascal. 1994. *The Naturalness of Religious Ideas: A Cognitive Theory of Religion.* Berkeley: University of California Press.

Boyer, Pascal. 2001. *Religion Explained: The Evolutionary Origins of Religious Thought.* New York: Basic Books.

Bradshaw, Paul, ed. 2002. *The New Westminster Dictionary of Liturgy & Worship.* Louisville, KY: Westminster John Knox Press.

Brandon, S.G.F., ed. 1970. *A Dictionary of Comparative Religion.* New York: Charles Scribners & Sons.

Brattico, E., P. Brattico, and T. Jacobsen. 2009. "The Origins of the Aesthetic Enjoyment of Music—A Review of the Literature." *Musicæ Scientæ,* 13: 15–39.

Braun, Willi, and Russell T. McCutcheon. 2000. *Guide to the Study of Religion.* London & NY: Cassell.
Brennan, Vicki L. 2018. *Singing Yoruba Christianity: Music, Media, and Modernity.* Bloomington: Indiana University Press.
Brindley, Erica Fox. 2012. *Cosmology, and the Politics of Harmony in Early China.* Albany, NY: SUNY Press.
Brown, Donald E. 1991. *Human Universals.* Philadelphia: Temple University Press.
Brown, Frank Burch. 2013. "Aesthetics and the Arts in Relation to Natural Theology." In *The Oxford Handbook of Natural Theology.* Edited by Russell Re Manning. New York: Oxford University Press, 523–538.
Brown, Frank Burch. 2014. "Introduction: Mapping the Terrain of Religion and the Arts." In *The Oxford Handbook of Religion and the Arts.* Edited by Frank Burch Brown. Oxford University Press, 1–21.
Brown, Frank Burch. 2008. "Music." In *The Oxford Handbook of Religion and Emotion.* Edited by John Corrigan. New York: Oxford University Press, 200–222.
Brown, Frank Burch. 2014. "Musical Ways of Being Religious." In *The Oxford Handbook of Religion and the Arts.* Edited by Frank Burch Brown. New York: Oxford University Press, 109–129.
Brown, Frank Burch. 1989. *Religious Aesthetics: A Theological Study of Making and Meaning.* Princeton, NJ: Princeton University Press.
Brown, Frank Burch, ed. 2014. *The Oxford Handbook of Religion and the Arts.* New York: Oxford University Press.
Brown, Steven. 2000. "The Musilanguage Model of Music Evolution." In *The Origins of Music.* Edited by Nils. L Wallin, Bjorn Merker, and Steven Brown. Cambridge, MA: MIT Press, 271–300,
Bruhn, Siglind, ed. 2002. *Voicing the Ineffable: Musical Representations of Religious Experience.* Hillsdale, NY: Pendragon Press.
Brunner, Emil, and Karl Barth. 2002 [1946]. *Natural Theology: Comprising 'Nature and Grace' by Professor Dr. Emil Brunner and the Reply 'No!' by Dr. Karl Barth.* Eugene, OR: Wipf and Stock Publishers.
Burrows, David. 1990. *Sound, Speech, and Music.* Amherst: University of Massachusetts Press.
Bussanich, John. 2016. "Plato and Yoga." In *Universe and Inner Self in Early Indian and Early Greek Thought.* Edited by Richard Seaford. Edinburgh: Edinburgh University Press, 87–103.
Butler, Melvin. 2019. *Island Gospel: Pentecostal Music and Identity in Jamaica and the United States.* Urbana, Chicago, & Springfield: University of Illinois Press.
Calvin, John. 2008 [1536 CE]. *Institutes of the Christian Religion.* Translated by Henry Beveridge. Peabody, MA: Hendrickson Publishers.
Campbell, Don. 1997. *The Mozart Effect: Tapping the Power of Music to Heal the Body, Strengthen the Mind, and Unlock the Creative Spirit.* New York: Avon Books.
Campbell, Don, ed. 1991. *Music Physician for Times to Come.* Wheaton, IL: Quest Books.

Cantz, Paul. 2013. "A Psychodynamic Inquiry into the Spiritually Evocative Potential of Music." *International Forum of Psychoanalysis*, Vol. 22, No. 2: 69–81.

Capetz, Paul E. 2003. *God: A Brief History*. Minneapolis: Fortress Press.

Capleton, Brian. 2015. *The Harmony of the Spheres*. Studies in Musical Science & Philosophy, Volume 4. Amarilli Books

Caputo, John D. 1997. *The Prayers and Tears of Jacques Derrida: Religion without Religion*. Bloomington: Indiana University Press.

Carman, John B. 1994. *Majesty and Meekness: A Comparative Study of Contrast and Harmony in the Concept of God*. Grand Rapids, MI: Eerdmans Publishing.

Cave, David. 1993. *Mircea Eliade's Vision for a New Humanism*. New York: Oxford University Press.

Christian, C. W. 1979. *Friedrich Schleiermacher*. Makers of the Modern Theological Mind. Waco, TX: Word Books.

Clark, L. S., ed. 2006. "Introduction to a Forum on Religion, Popular Music, and Globalization." *Journal for the Scientific Study of Religion*, Vol. 45: 475–479.

Clifton, Thomas. 1983. *Music as Heard: A Study in Applied Phenomenology*. New Haven, CT: Yale University Press.

Clooney, Francis X, SJ. 2010a. *Comparative Theology: Deep Learning Across Religious Borders*. London: Wiley-Blackwell.

Clooney, Francis X., SJ, ed. 2010b. *The New Comparative Theology: Interreligious Insights from the Next Generation*. London: T & T Clark International.

Clynes M., ed. 1982. *Music, Mind and Brain: The Neuropsychology of Music*. New York: Plenum.

Collins, Mary, David Power, and Mellonee Burnim, eds. 1989. *Music and the Experience of God*. Edinburgh: T & T Clark.

Comtois, Pranada. 2022. *Prema Kirtan: Journey into Sacred Sound*. St. Augustine, FL: Chandra Media.

Cook, Nicholas, and Mark Everist, eds. 2001. *Rethinking Music*: Oxford: Oxford University Press.

Coomaraswamy, Ananda K. 2014 [1934]. *The Transformation of Nature in Art*. New Delhi: Munshiram Manoharlal.

Corduan, Winfried. 2013. *In the Beginning God: A Fresh Look at the Case for Original Monotheism*. Nashville, TN: B & H Publishing Group.

Cornille, Catherine. 2020. *Meaning and Method in Comparative Theology*. West Sussex, UK: Wiley Blackwell.

Corsini, Raymond J., ed. 1999. *The Dictionary of Psychology*. Philadelphia, PA: Brunner/Mazel.

Coward, Harold. 1988. *Sacred Word and Sacred Text: Scripture in World Religions*. Maryknoll, NY: Orbis Books.

Coward, Harold. 2019. *Word, Chant and Song: Spiritual Transformation in Hinduism, Buddhism, Islam, and Sikhism*. Albany, NY: SUNY Press.

Coward, Harold, ed. 2000. *Experiencing Scripture in World Religions*. Maryknoll, NY: Orbis Books.

Crichton, J. D. 1978. "A Theology of Worship." In *The Study of Liturgy*. Edited by Cheslyn Jones, Geoffrey Wainwright, and Edward Yarnold, SJ. New York: Oxford University Press, 1–29.

Crocker, Richard L. 2000. *An Introduction to Gregorian Chant*. New Haven, CT: Yale University Press.

Cross, Ian. 2009. "The Nature of Music and its Evolution." In *The Oxford Handbook of Music Psychology*. Edited by Susan Hallam, Ian Cross, and Michael Thaut. New York: Oxford University Press, 3–13.

Cumont, Franz. 1922. *After Life in Roman Paganism*. New Haven, CT: Yale University Press.

Cupchik, Jeffrey W. 2018. *The Sound of Vultures' Wings: The Tibetan Chöd Ritual Practice of the Female Buddha Machik Labdrön*. Albany, NY: SUNY Press.

Dahlhaus, Carl. 1989. *The Idea of Absolute Music*. Chicago: University of Chicago Press.

Darwin, Charles. 2004 [1871]. *The Descent of Man, and Selection in Relation to Sex*. With an Introduction by James Moore and Adrian Desmond. London: Penguin Books.

Davie, Martin, Tim Grass, Stephen A. Holmes, John McDowell, and T.A. Noble, eds. 2016. *New Dictionary of Theology: Historical and Systematic*. Downers Grove, IL: InterVarsity Press.

Davis, Stephen F., and William Buskist, eds. 2008. *21st Century Psychology: A Reference Handbook*. 2 vols. Los Angeles & London: Sage Publications.

Demarest, Bruce A. 1982. *General Revelation: Historical Views and Contemporary Issues*. Grand rapids, MI: Zondervan Publishing House.

De Rosen, Lawrence. 2014. "Music and Religion." In *Encyclopedia of Psychology and Religion*. Edited by David A. Leeming. Boston: Springer, 1156–1160.

Desmond, William. 1986. *Art and the Absolute: A Study of Hegel's Aesthetics*. Albany: NY: SUNY Press.

Deutsch, Diana, ed. 2013 [1982]. *The Psychology of Music*. 3rd edition. London: Academic Press.

DeVale, Sue Carole. 1988. "Musical Instruments and Ritual: A Systematic Approach." *Journal of the American Musical Instrument Society*, Vol. 14: 126–160.

DeVale, Sue Carole. 1989. "Power and Meaning in Musical Instruments." In *Music and the Experience of God*. Edited by Mary Collins, David Power, and Mellonee Burnim. Edinburgh: T & T Clark, 94–110.

Dickens, W. T. 2003. *Hans Urs von Balthasar's Theological Aesthetics: A Model for Post-Critical Biblical Interpretation*. Notre Dame, IN: Notre Dame University Press.

Dissanayake, Ellen. 1995 [1992]. *Homo Aestheticus: Where Art Comes From and Why*. Seattle and London: University of Washington Press.

Doniger, Wendy. 2000. "Post-Modern and Colonial Structural Comparisons." In *A Magic Still Dwells: Comparative Religion in the Postmodern Age*. Edited by Kimberly C. Patton and Benjamin C. Ray. Berkeley & London: University of California Press, 63–74.

Doniger, Wendy, ed. 1999. *Merriam-Webster's Encyclopedia of World Religions*. Springfield, MA: Merriam-Webster Incorporated.

Dorrien, Gary. 2000. *The Barthian Revolt in Modern Theology: Theology Without Weapons*. Louisville, KY: Westminster John Knox Press.

Douglas, Mary. 1970 [1966]. *Purity and Danger: An Analysis of Concepts of Pollution and Taboo*. Baltimore, MD: Penguin Books.

Dowley, Tim. 2011. *Christian Music: A Global History*. Minneapolis, MN: Fortress Press.

Dowling Long, Siobhan, and John F. A. Sawyer. 2015. *The Bible in Music: A Dictionary of Songs, Works, and More*. New York & London: Rowman and Littlefield.

Dubuisson, Daniel. 2003. *The Western Construction of Religion: Myths, Knowledge, and Ideology*. Baltimore, MD: Johns Hopkins University Press.

Durkheim, Emile. 2008 [1912]. *The Elementary Forms of Religious Life*. A New Translation by Carol Cosman. Abridged with an Introduction by Mark S. Cladis. New York: Oxford University Press.

Dutton, Denis. 2001. "Aesthetic Universals." In *The Routledge Companion to Aesthetics*. Edited by Berys Gaut and Dominic Mclver Lopes. London and New York: Routledge, 203–214.

Edgar, William. 1986. *Taking Note of Music*. Minneapolis MN: Fortress Press.

Eliade, Mircea. 1985. "*Homo Faber* and *Homo Religiosus*." In *The History of Religions: Retrospect and Prospect*. Edited by Joseph M. Kitagawa. New York: Macmillan, 1–12.

Eliade, Mircea. 1958. *Patterns in Comparative Religion*. New York: Sheed & Ward.

Eliade, Mircea. 1959. *The Sacred and the Profane: The Nature of Religion*. New York: Harcourt Brace & World.

Eliade, Mircea. 1964. *Shamanism: Archaic Techniques of Ecstasy*. Princeton NJ: Princeton University Press.

Eliade, Mircea. 1969. *The Quest: History and Meaning in Religion*. Chicago: University of Chicago Press.

Eliade, Mircea, ed. 1987. *The Encyclopedia of Religion*. 16 vols. New York: Macmillan.

Ellingson, Ter. 1987. "Music and Religion." In *The Encyclopedia of Religion*. Editor-in-Chief, Mircea Eliade. New York: Macmillan, Vol. 10, 163–172.

Ellis, Alexander. 1885. "On the Musical Scales of Various Nations." *Journal of the Society of Arts*, Vol. 33, No. 1688 (March 27): 485–527.

Ellis, John M. 1989. *Against Deconstruction*. Princeton, NJ: Princeton University Press.

Ellwood, Robert S., and Barbara A. McGraw. 2005. *Many Peoples, Many Faiths: Women and Men in the World Religions*. 8th edition. Upper Saddle River, NJ: Prentice-Hall.

Engelhardt, Jeffers. 2014. *Singing the Right Way: Orthodox Christians and Secular Enchantment in Estonia*. New York: Oxford University Press.

Engelhardt, Jeffers, and Philip V. Bohlman, eds. 2016. *Resounding Transcendence: Transitions in Music, Religion and Ritual*. New York: Oxford University Press.

Epstein, Heidi. 2004. *Melting the Venusberg: A Feminist Theology of Music*. London: Bloomsbury Academic.

Farmer, Henry George. 1957. "The Music of Islam." In *The New Oxford History of Music. Vol. I. Ancient and Oriental Music*. Edited by Egon Wellesz. Oxford, UK: Oxford University Press, 421–477.

Fassler, Margot. 2010. *The Virgin of Chartres: Making History through Liturgy and the Arts*. New Haven, CT: Yale University Press.

Feder, Stuart, Richard L. Karmel, and George H. Pollock, eds. 1990. *Psychoanalytic Explorations in Music*. Madison, CT: International Universities Press.

Feder, Stuart, Richard L. Karmel, and George H. Pollock, eds. 1993. *Psychoanalytic Explorations in Music*. Second Series. Madison, CT: International Universities Press.

Feld, Steven, and Keith H. Basso, eds. 1996. *Senses of Place*. New York: School of American Research.

Fenton, John Y. et al. 2001. *Religions of Asia*. 3rd edition. New York: St. Martin's Press.

Feuerbach, Ludwig. 1957 [1841]. *The Essence of Christianity*. Translated from the German by George Eliot. Introductory essay by Karl Barth. Foreword by H. Richard Niebuhr. New York: Harper & Row.

Fideler, David R., ed. 1987. *The Pythagorean Sourcebook and Library: An Anthology of Ancient Writings which relate to Pythagoras and Pythagorean Philosophy*. Compiled and translated by Kenneth Sylvan Guthrie. Grand Rapids, MI: Phane Press.

Fink, S.J, Peter E., ed. 1990. *The New Dictionary of Sacramental Worship*. Collegeville, MN: The Liturgical Press.

Fiorenza, Francis Schussler, and Gordon D. Kaufman. 1998. "God." In *Critical Terms for Religious Studies*. Edited by Mark C. Taylor. Chicago: University of Chicago Press, 136–159.

Fisher, Mary Pat. 2002. *Living Religions*. 5th edition. Upper Saddle River, NJ: Prentice-Hall. In the 9th edition (2014: 15), the present author (Beck 2006) is cited regarding sacred music.

Fitzgerald Timothy. 2000. *The Ideology of Religious Studies*. New York: Oxford University Press.

Fletcher, Peter. 2001. *World Musics in Context: A Comprehensive Survey of the World's Major Musical Cultures*. New York: Oxford University Press.

Flood, Gavin. 1999. *Beyond Phenomenology: Rethinking the Study of Religion*. London & New York: Cassell.

Flood, Gavin. 2016. "Religious Practice and the Nature of the Human." In *Interreligious Comparisons in Religious Studies and Theology: Comparison Revisited*. Edited by Perry Schmidt-Leukel and Andreas Nehring. London: Bloomsbury Academic, 130–141.

Foley, Edward.1998. "Liturgical Music: A Bibliographic Essay." In *Liturgy and Music: Lifetime Learning*. Edited by Robin A. Leaver and Joyce Ann Zimmerman. Collegeville, MN: The Liturgical Press, 411–452.

Foley, Edward. 1990. "Music, Liturgical." In *The New Dictionary of Sacramental Worship*. Edited by Peter E. Fink, SJ. Collegeville, MN: The Liturgical Press. 854–870.

Foley, Edward. 1995. *Ritual Music: Studies in Liturgical Musicology.* Beltsville, MD: The Pastoral Press.

Foley, Edward. 1993. "Toward a Sound Theology." *Studia Liturgica*, Vol. 23, No. 2: 121–139.

Foley, Edward, ed. 2015. *Music and Spirituality. Religions Special Issue.* Basel, Switzerland: MDPI, Introduction, ix–xii.

Foley, Edward, ed. 2000. *Worship Music: A Concise Dictionary.* Collegeville, MN: The Liturgical Press.

Ford, David F. 2013 (1999). *Theology: A Very Short Introduction.* Second edition. New York: Oxford University Press.

Frazier, Jessica. 2013. "Natural Theology in Eastern Religions." In *The Oxford Handbook of Natural Theology.* Edited by Russell Re Manning. New York: Oxford University Press, 166–181.

Freud, Sigmund. 1966. *The Complete Introductory Lectures on Psychoanalysis.* Translated and Edited by James Strachey. New York: W.W. Norton.

Freud, Sigmund. 2010 [1955]. *The Interpretation of Dreams.* The Complete and Definitive Text. Translated from the German and edited by James Strachey. New York: Basic Books.

Friedlander, Shems. 1992. *Whirling Dervishes: Being an Account of the Sufi Order known as the Mevlevis and its Founder the Poet and Mystic Jalalu'ddin Rumi.* Albany, NY: SUNY Press.

Frishkopf, Michael, and Federico Spinetti, eds. 2018. *Music, Sound, and Architecture in Islam.* Austin: University of Texas Press.

Gallope, Michael. 2017. *Deep Refrains: Music, Philosophy, and the Ineffable.* Chicago, IL: University of Chicago Press.

Garside, Charles. 1979. "The Origins of Calvin's Theology of Music: 1536–1543." *Transactions of the American Philosophical Society*, Vol. 69: 4–35.

Gass, Robert, and Kathleen Brehony. 1999. *Chanting: Discovering Spirit in Sound.* New York: Broadway Books.

Geertz, Clifford. 1984. "Anti Anti-Relativism," *American Anthropologist*, Vol. 86: 263–78.

Gelineau, Joseph. 1978. "Music and Singing in the Liturgy." In *The Study of Liturgy.* Edited by Cheslyn Jones, Geoffrey Wainwright, and Edward Yarnold, SJ. New York: Oxford University Press, 440–454.

Gelineau, Joseph. 1989. "The Path of Music." In *Music and the Experience of God.* Edited by Mary Collins, David Power, and Mellonee Burnim. Edinburgh: T & T Clark, 135–147.

Gerety, Finnian McKean Moore. 2015. *This Whole World is OM: Song, Soteriology, and the Emergence of the Sacred Syllable.* PhD dissertation, Harvard University, Cambridge, Massachusetts.

Gerson-Kiwi, Edith. 1961. "Religious Chant: A Pan-Asiatic Conception of Music." *Journal of the International Folk Music Council*, Vol. 13: 64–67.

Gidal, Marc. 2016. *Spirit Song: Afro-Brazilian Religious Music and Boundaries*. New York: Oxford University Press.

Gilmour, Michael J., ed. 2005. *Call Me Seeker: Listening to Religion in Popular Music*. New York: Continuum.

Godwin, Joscelyn. 1984. "The Golden Chain of Orpheus: A Survey of Musical Esotericism in the West." *Temenos* 4: 7–25; *Temenos* 5: 211–239.

Godwin, Joscelyn. 1987. *Harmonies of Heaven and Earth: The Spiritual Dimension of Music from Antiquity to the Avant-Garde*. Rochester, VT: Inner Traditions.

Godwin, Joscelyn, ed. 1989. *Cosmic Music: Musical Keys to the Interpretation of Reality. Essays by Marius Schneider, Rudolf Haase, Hans Erhard Lauer*. Rochester, VT: Inner Traditions.

Godwin, Joscelyn, ed. 1992. *The Harmony of the Spheres: A Sourcebook of the Pythagorean Tradition in Music*. Rochester VT: Inner Traditions.

Godwin, Joscelyn, ed. 1986. *Music, Mysticism, and Magic: A Sourcebook*. New York & London: Routledge.

Gracyk, Theodore, and Andrew Kania, eds. 2011. *The Routledge Companion to Philosophy and Music*. London and New York: Routledge.

Gradenwitz, Peter. 1996 [1949]. *The Music of Israel: From the Biblical Era to Modern Times*. 2nd edition. Portland, OR: Amadeus Press.

Graves, Eben. 2009. *Rhythmic Theology: Khol Drumming in Caitanya Vaisnava Kirtan*. Boston: Tufts University.

Green, Garrett. 2010. "Hermeneutics." In *The Routledge Companion to The Study of Religion*. 2nd edition. Edited by John R. Hinnells. London: Routledge, 411–425.

Griffith, Ralph T. H., trans. 1973 [1889]. *The Hymns of the Rig Veda*. New Delhi: Motilal Banarsidass.

Gurney, Edmund. 1880. *The Power of Sound*. London: Smith, Elder.

Guzy, Lidia. 2008. *Religion and Music: Proceedings of the Interdisciplinary Workshop at the Institute for Scientific Studies of Religions, Freie Universität Berlin, May 2006*. Berlin, Germany: Weißensee Verlag.

Haar, James. 1960. "Musica Mundana: Variations on a Pythagorean Theme." PhD dissertation, Harvard University, Cambridge, Massachusetts.

Hackett, Rosalind J. 2012. "Review: Sound, Music, and the Study of Religion." *Temenos* 48: 11–27.

Hallam, Susan, Ian Cross, and Michael Thaut, eds. 2009. *The Oxford Handbook of Music Psychology*. Oxford, UK: Oxford University Press.

Halpern, Steven, and Louis Savary. 1985. *Sound Health: The Music and Sounds that Make us Whole*. New York: HarperCollins.

Hamel, Peter Michael. 1987. *Through Music to the Self*. Element Books.

Hamer, Dean. 2004. *The God Gene: How Faith is Hardwired into our Genes*. New York: Anchor Books.

Harned, David. 1966. *Theology and the Arts*. London: Westminster Press.

Harrison, Everett F., ed. 1960. *Baker's Dictionary of Theology*. Grand Rapids, MI: Baker Book House.

Harrison, Frank. 1977. "Universals in Music: Towards a Methodology of Comparative Research." *The World of Music*, Vol. 19, No. 1–2, UNIVERSALS: 30–36.

Harvey, Van A. 1995. *Feuerbach and the Interpretation of Religion*. Cambridge, UK: Cambridge University Press.

Harwood, Dane L. 1976. "Universals in Music: Perspectives from Cognitive Psychology." *Ethnomusicology* 20.3 (September), 521–533.

Hastings, James, ed. 1908–1921. *Encyclopedia of Religion and Ethics*. 12 vols. Edinburgh.

Hawley, John Stratton. 2011. "Foreword." In *Vaishnava Temple Music in Vrindāban: The Rādhāvallabha Songbook*. Edited by Guy L. Beck. Kirksville, MO: Blazing Sapphire Press, xxi–xxiii.

Hawley, John Stratton. 1985. *Sūr Dās: Poet, Singer, Saint*. Seattle: University of Washington Press.

Heimarck, Brita Renée. 2003. *Balinese Discourses on Music and Modernization: Village Voices and Urban Views*. London: Routledge.

Heine, Steven, and Dale S. Wright, eds. 2007. *Zen Ritual: Studies in Zen Buddhist Theory in Practice*. New York: Oxford University Press.

Heninger, Jr., S. K. 2013 [1974]. *Touches of Sweet Harmony: Pythagorean Cosmology and Renaissance Poetics*. Tacoma, WA: Angelico Press.

Hicks, Stephen R. C. 2011. *Explaining Postmodernism: Skepticism and Socialism from Rousseau to Foucault*. Ockham's Razor Publishing.

Hinnells, John, ed. 2010. *The Routledge Companion to the Study of Religion*. 2nd edition. London & New York: Routledge.

Hirschkind, Charles. 2006. *The Ethical Soundscape: Cassette Sermons and Islamic Counterpublics*. New York: Columbia University Press.

Hodges, D. A., and D. C. Sebald. 2011. *Music in the Human Experience: An Introduction to Music Psychology*. New York: Routledge.

Hoffman, Lawrence A., and Janet R. Walton, eds. 1992. *Sacred Sound and Social Change: Liturgical Music in Jewish and Christian Experience*. South Bend & London: University of Notre Dame Press.

Holde, Arthur. 1974. *Jews in Music: From the Age of the Enlightenment to the Mid-Twentieth Century*. New York: Bloch Publishing.

Hood, Mantle. 1977. "Universal Attributes of Music." *The World of Music*, Vol. 19, No. 1–2, UNIVERSALS: 63–69.

Hoondert, Martin. 2015. "Musical Religiosity." *Temenos* 51.1: 123–136.

Hopfe, Lewis M., and Mark R. Woodward. 2001. *Religions of the World*. 8th edition. Upper Saddle River, NJ: Prentice-Hall.

Hughes, Aaron W., and Russell T. McCutcheon. 2022. *Religion in 50 Words: A Critical Vocabulary*. London: Routledge.

Hughes, Aaron W., and Russell T. McCutcheon. 2022. *Religion in 50 More Words: A Critical Vocabulary*. London: Routledge.

Husserl, Edmund. 1964. *The Phenomenology of Internal Time-Consciousness*. Bloomington: Indiana University Press.
Ingalls, Monique. 2018. *Singing the Congregation: How Contemporary Worship Music Forms Evangelical Community*. New York: Oxford University Press.
Ingalls, Monique, Carolyn Landau, and Tom Wagner, eds. 2013. *Christian Congregational Music: Performance, Identity, and Experience*. London: Routledge.
Irwin, Joyce L. 1993. *Neither Voice nor Heart Alone: German Lutheran Theology of Music in the Age of the Baroque*. Eugene, OR: Wipf & Stock.
Irwin, Joyce, ed. 1983. *Sacred Sound: Music in Religious Thought and Practice*. Chico, CA: Scholars Press.
Jackson, William. 2000. "Religious and Devotional Music: Southern Area." In *Garland Encyclopedia of World Music*, Vol. 5, Indian Subcontinent. Edited by Alison Arnold. New York & London: Garland Publishing, 259–271.
Jackson, William J. 1994. *Tyagaraja and the Renewal of Tradition; Translations and Reflections*. New Delhi: Motilal Banarsidass
Jaeger, Werner. 1967. *The Theology of the Early Greek Philosophers*. The Gifford Lectures 1936. Oxford: Oxford University Press.
Jaini, Padmanabh S. 1979. *The Jaina Path of Purification*. New Delhi: Motilal Banarsidass.
James, E. O. 1961 [1938]. *Comparative Religion: An Introductory and Historical Study*. New York: Barnes & Noble.
James, E. O. 1950. *The Concept of Deity: A Comparative and Historical Study*. London: Hutchinson's University Library.
James, Jamie. 1993. *The Music of the Spheres: Music, Science, and the Natural Order of the Universe*. New York: Copernicus Books.
James, William. 1982 [1902]. *The Varieties of Religious Experience: A Study in Human Nature*. New York: Penguin.
Jankelevitch, Vladimir. 2003. *Music and the Ineffable*. Translated by Carolyn Abbate. Princeton, NJ: Princeton University Press.
Janz, Denis R. 2010. *The Westminster Handbook to Martin Luther*. Westminster John Knox Press.
Jarjour, Tala. 2018. *Sense and Sadness: Syriac Chant in Aleppo*. New York: Oxford University Press.
Jastrow, Jr., Morris. 1981 [1901]. *The Study of Religion*. Chico, CA: Scholars Press.
Jeffery, Peter. 1989. "Chant East and West: Toward a Renewal of the Tradition." In *Music and the Experience of God*. Edited by Mary Collins, David Power, and Mellonee Burnim. Edinburgh: T & T Clark, 20–29.
Jeffery, Peter. 1992. *Re-Envisioning Past Musical Cultures: Ethnomusicology in the Study of Gregorian Chant*. Chicago: University of Chicago Press.
Jimenez, Raquel, Rupert Till, and Michael Howell, eds. 2013. *Music and Ritual: Bridging Material and Living Cultures*. Berlin: Ekho Verlag.
Johnsen, Linda, and Maggie Jacobus. 2007. *Kirtan! Chanting as a Spiritual Path*. St. Paul, MN: Yes International Publishers.

Jones, Cheslyn, Geoffrey Wainwright, and Edward Yarnold, SJ, eds. 1978. *The Study of Liturgy*. New York: Oxford University Press.

Jourdain, Robert. 1997. *Music, the Brain, and Ecstasy: How Music Captures Our Imagination*. New York: William Morrow.

Juslin, Patrick N., and John A. Sloboda, eds. 2010. *Oxford Handbook of Music and Emotion*. New York: Oxford University Press.

Karp, Theodore C. 1983. "Music." In *The Seven Liberal Arts in the Middle Ages*. Edited by David L. Wagner. Bloomington: Indiana University Press, 169–195.

Kaur, Inderjit Nilu. 2011. "Musical Aesthetic in the Guru Granth and Implications for the Performance Practice of Sikh Shabad Kirtan." *Sikh Formations*, Vol. 7, No. 3: 297–312.

Kavanagh, Aidan. 1990. *Elements of Rite: A Handbook of Liturgical Style*. Collegeville, MN: Liturgical Press.

Kavanagh, Aidan. 1973. "The Role of Ritual in Personal Development." In *The Roots of Ritual*. Edited by James Shaughnessy. Grand Rapids, MI: Wm. B. Eerdmans Publishing, 145–160.

Kavanaugh, Patrick. 1996 [1992]. *Spiritual Lives of the Great Composers*. Grand Rapids, MI: Zondervan Publishing House.

Kayser, Hans. 1970 [1964]. *Akroasis: The Theory of World Harmonics*. Boston: Plowshare Press.

Kazdin, Alan E., ed. 2000. *Encyclopedia of Psychology*, 8 volumes. American Psychological Association. New York: Oxford University Press.

Khan, Hazrat Inayat. 1962. *The Sufi Message of Hazrat Inayat Khan*. 2 Vols. Geneva: International Headquarters of the Sufi Movement.

Kichlu, Vijay. 1987. "Gharanas in Hindustani Vocal Music." In *Aspects of Indian Music: A Collection of Essays*. Edited by Sumati Mutatkar. Delhi: Sangeet Natak Academy, 106–112.

Kirnarskaya, Dina. 2009. *The Natural Musician: On Abilities, Giftedness, and Talent*. Oxford, UK: Oxford University Press.

Knitter, Paul F. 2002. *Introducing Theologies of Religions*. Maryknoll, NY: Orbis Books.

Kolb, Robert, Irene Dingel, and Lubomir Batka, eds. 2014. *The Oxford Handbook of Martin Luther's Theology*. Oxford and New York: Oxford University Press.

Koskoff, Ellen. 1984. "Thoughts on Universals in Music." *The World of Music*, Vol. 26, No. 2: 66–87.

Koskoff, Ellen, ed. 1987. *Women and Music in Cross-Cultural Perspective*. Westport, CN: Greenwood Press.

Kreinath, Jens, Jan Snoek, and Michael Stausberg, eds. 2008. *Theorizing Rituals: Issues, Topics, Approaches, Concepts*. Leiden & Boston: Brill.

Kung, Hans. 1993 [1991]. *Mozart: Traces of Transcendence*. Grand Rapids, MI: Wm. B. Eerdmans.

Kunst, Jaap. 1974 [1950]. *Ethnomusicology: A Study of Its Nature, Its Problems, Methods, and Representative Personalities to which is Added a Bibliography*. The Hague: Martinus Nijhoff. Main Bibliography, 79–215; Supplement Bibliography 5–24.

Laack, Isabel. 2015. "Sound, Music and Religion: A Preliminary Cartography of a Transdisciplinary Research Field." *Method and Theory in the Study of Religion* 27: 220–246.

Lamm, Julia A. 1996. *The Living God: Schleiermacher's Theological Appropriation of Spinoza*. University Park, PA: Penn State University Press.

Lang, Andrew. 2007 [1898]. *The Making of Religion*. Fairfield, IA: 1st World Library.

Leaver, Robin A. 1992. "Christian Liturgical Music in the Wake of the Protestant Reformation." In *Sacred Sound and Social Change: Liturgical Music in Jewish and Christian Experience*. Edited by Lawrence A. Hoffman and Janet R. Walton. South Bend & London: University of Notre Dame Press, 124–144.

Leaver, Robin A. 2017. *Luther's Liturgical Music: Principles and Implications*. Minneapolis, MN: Fortress Press.

Leaver, Robin A., and Joyce Ann Zimmerman, eds. 1998. *Liturgy and Music: Lifetime Learning*. Collegeville, MN: The Liturgical Press.

Lehrich, Christopher I. 2014. "The Unanswered Question: Music in Theory of Religion." *Method and Theory in the Study of Religion*, 26, No. 1: 22–43.

Le Mée, Katharine. 1994. *Chant: The Origins, Form, Practice, and Healing Power of Gregorian Chant*. New York: Bell Tower.

Lerdahl, Fred, and Ray S. Jackendoff. 1983. *A Generative Theory of Tonal Music*. Cambridge, MA: MIT Press.

Levine, Joseph A. 2006. "Judaism and Music." In *Sacred Sound: Experiencing Music in World Religions*. Edited by Guy L. Beck. Waterloo, Ontario: Wilfrid Laurier University Press, 29–59.

Lewis, James R., and Evelyn Dorothy Oliver. 2002. *Angels A to Z*. Canton, MI: Visible Ink Press.

Lindbeck, George A. 2009 [1984]. *The Nature of Doctrine: Religion and Theology in a Postliberal Age*. Louisville, KY: Westminster John Knox Press.

List, George. 1971. "On the Non-Universality of Musical Perspectives." *Ethnomusicology* 15,3: 399–402.

List, George. 1984. "Concerning the Concept of the Universal in Music." *The World of Music*, Vol. 26, No. 2: 40–49.

Livingston, James C. 2005. *Anatomy of the Sacred*. 5th edition. Upper Saddle River, NJ: Prentice-Hall.

Lomax, Alan. 1959. "Folk Song Style." *American Anthropologist*, New Series, Vol. 61, No. 6 (December): 927–954.

Lomax, Alan. 1962. "Song Structure and Social Structure." *Ethnology* 1: 425–451.

Lomax, Alan. 1977. "Universals in Song." *The World of Music*, Vol. 19, No. 1–2, UNIVERSALS: 117–130.

Lorea, Carola. 2016. *Folklore, Religion and the Songs of a Bengali Madman: A Journey Between Performance and the Politics of Cultural Representation*. Leiden: Brill Academic Publishers.

Lundblad, Jonas. 2020. "Theomusical Subjectivity: Schleiermacher and the Transcendence of Immediacy." In *Music and Transcendence*. Edited by Ferdia J.

Stone-Davis. London & Oxford: Ashgate, 2015 and New York: Routledge, 85–104.

McAllester, David. 1971. "Some Thoughts on 'Universals' in World Music," *Ethnomusicology* 15: 379–380.

McClain, Ernest G. 1978. *The Pythagorean Plato: Prelude to the Song Itself*. York Beach, ME: Nicholas-Hays Inc.

McCollum, Jonathan, and David G. Hebert, eds. 2014. *Theory and Method in Historical Ethnomusicology*. Lanham, MD: Lexington Books.

McCutcheon, Russell T. 1997. *Manufacturing Religion: The Discourse on Sui Generis Religion and the Politics of Nostalgia*. New York: Oxford University Press.

McEvilley, Thomas. 2002. *The Shape of Ancient Thought: Comparative Studies in Greek and Indian Philosophies*. New York: Allworth Press.

McGann, Mary E. 2002. *Exploring Music as Worship and Theology: Research in Liturgical Practice*. Collegeville, MN: The Liturgical Press.

MacGregor, Geddes. 1988. *Angels: Ministers of Grace*. New York: Paragon House Publishers.

Mackie, J. L. 1982. *The Miracle of Theism: Arguments for and against the Existence of God*. Oxford, UK: Clarendon Press.

McKinnon, James. 1987. *Music in Early Christian Literature*. Cambridge, UK: Cambridge University Press.

McLeod, W. H. 2005. *Historical Dictionary of Sikhism*. 2nd edition. Lanham, MD: The Scarecrow Press.

McNamara, Patrick. 2009. *The Neuroscience of Religious Experience*. Cambridge, UK: Cambridge University Press.

Makkreel, Rudolf A. 1975. *Dilthey: Philosopher of the Human Sciences*. Princeton, NJ: Princeton University Press.

Margulis, Elizabeth Hellmuth. 2019. *The Psychology of Music: A Very Short Introduction*. New York: Oxford University Press.

Maor, Eli. 2018. *Music by the Numbers: From Pythagoras to Schoenberg*. Princeton, NJ: Princeton University Press.

Marini, Stephen A. 2003. *Sacred Song in America: Religion, Music, and Public Culture*. Urbana & Chicago: University of Illinois Press.

Markham, Ian S. 2009. "Theology." In *The Blackwell Companion to the Study of Religion*. Second edition. Edited by Robert A. Segal and Nickolas P. Roubekas. West Sussex, UK: Wiley Blackwell, 152–167.

Martin, F. David. 1972. *Art and the Religious Experience: The "Language" of the Sacred*. Lewisburg, PA: Bucknell University Press.

Martin, James Alfred. 1990. *Beauty and Holiness: The Dialogue between Aesthetics and Religion*. Princeton, NJ: Princeton University Press.

Martin, Luther. 2010. "Religion and Cognition." In *The Routledge Companion to the Study of Religion*. 2nd edition. Edited by John Hinnells. London & New York: Routledge, 526–542.

Martland, Thomas R. 1981. *Religion as Art*. Albany, NY: SUNY Press.
Masuzawa, Tomoko. 2005. *The Invention of World Religions: Or, How European Universalism Was Preserved in the Language of Pluralism*. Chicago: University of Chicago Press.
May, Elizabeth, ed. 1983. *Musics of Many Cultures: An Introduction*. Berkeley: University of California Press.
Mellers, Wilfrid. 2001. *Celestial Music? Some Masterpieces of European Religious Music*. Rochester, NY: Boydell Press.
Mendieta, Eduardo, ed. 2005. *The Frankfurt School on Religion: Key Writings by the Major Thinkers*. New York & London: Routledge.
Mendl, R. W. S. 1957. *The Divine Quest in Music*. Salisbury Square, London: Rockliff Publishing.
Merkur, Dan. 2010. "Psychology of Religion." In *The Routledge Companion to the Study of Religion*. 2nd edition. Edited by John Hinnells. London & New York: Routledge, 186–201.
Merriam, Alan P. 1964. *The Anthropology of Music*. Evanston, IL: Northwestern University Press.
Merriam, Alan P. 1982. "On Objections to Comparison in Ethnomusicology." In *Cross-cultural Perspectives on Music*." Edited by Robert Falck and Timothy Rice. Toronto: University of Toronto Press, 174–189.
Meyer, Leonard B. 1956. *Emotion and Meaning in Music*. Chicago: University of Chicago Press.
Meyer, Leonard B. 1960. "Universalism and Relativism in the Study of Ethnic Music." *Ethnomusicology*, Vol. 4: 49–54.
Meyer-Baer, Kathi. 1970. *Music of the Spheres and the Dance of Death: Studies in Musical Iconology*. Princeton, NJ: Princeton University Press.
Michaels, Axel. 2015. *Homo Ritualis: Hindu Ritual and its Significance for Ritual Theory*. New York and Oxford: Oxford University Press.
Miller, Terry E. 2016. *World Music: A Global Journey*. 4th edition. London: Routledge.
Mirza, Raiomond. 2004. *The House of Song: Musical Structures in Zoroastrian Prayer Performance*. PhD Thesis, Ethnomusicology. School of Oriental and African Studies (SOAS), University of London.
Mithen, Steven. 2006. *The Singing Neanderthals: The Origins of Music, Language, Mind, and Body*. Cambridge, MA: Harvard University Press.
Monti, Anthony. 2003. *A Natural Theology of the Arts: Imprint of the Spirit*. Burlington, VT: Ashgate Publishing.
Mowinckel, Sigmund. 1962. *The Psalms in Israel's Worship*. Oxford UK: Basil Blackwell.
Muck, Terry. 2001. "Psalm, Bhajan, and Kirtan: Songs of the Soul in Comparative Perspective." In *Psalms and Practice: Worship, Virtue, and Authority*. Edited by Stephen Breck Reid. Collegeville, MN: The Liturgical Press, 7–27.

Mugglestone, Erica. 1981. "Guido Adler's 'The Scope, Method, and Aim of Musicology' (1885): An English Translation with an Historico-Analytical Commentary," *Yearbook for Traditional Music*, Vol. 13: 1–21.
Murdock, George Peter. 1932. "The Science of Culture." *American Anthropologist* New Series, Vol. 34, No. 2 (April–June): 200–215.
Murdock, George Peter. 1971. "Anthropology's Mythology." *Proceedings of the Royal Anthropological Institute of Great Britain and Ireland.*
Nadel, Siegfried. 1930. "The Origins of Music." *Musical Quarterly*, Vol. 16, No. 4: 531–546.
Nagel, Julie Jaffee. 2013. *Melodies of the Mind: Connections between Psychoanalysis and Music.* London: Routledge.
Nasr, Seyyed Hossein. 1978 [1964]. *An Introduction to Islamic Cosmological Doctrines: Conceptions of Nature and Methods Used for its Study by the Ikhwan al-Safa, al-Biruni, and Ibn Sina.* Boulder, CO: Shambhala.
Nasr, Seyyed Hossein. 1997. "Islam and Music: The Legal and Spiritual Dimensions." In *Enchanting Powers: Music in the World's Religions.* Edited by Lawrence E. Sullivan. Cambridge, MA: Harvard University Press, 219–235.
Needham, Rodney. 1967. "Percussion and Transition." *Man*, Vol. 2: 606–614.
Nehring, Andreas. 2016. "Camouflage of the Sacred: Can We Still Branch Off from Eliade's Comparative Approach?" In *Interreligious Comparisons in Religious Studies and Theology: Comparison Revisited.* Edited by Perry Schmidt-Leukel and Andreas Nehring. London: Bloomsbury Academic, 95–109.
Nettl, Bruno. 2000. "An Ethnomusicologist Contemplates Universals in Musical Sound and in Musical Culture." In *The Origins of Music.* Edited by Nils L. Wallin, Bjorn Merker, and Steven Brown. Cambridge, MA: MIT Press, 463–472.
Nettl, Bruno. 2001. *Excursions in World Music.* 3rd edition. Upper Saddle River, NJ: Prentice-Hall.
Nettl, Bruno. 2001. "The Institutionalization of Musicology: Perspectives of a North American Ethnomusicologist." In *Rethinking Music.* Edited by Nicholas Cook and Mark Everist. Oxford: Oxford University Press, 287–310.
Nettl, Bruno. 1977. "On the Question of Universals." *The World of Music*, Vol. 19, No. 1–2: 2–7.
Nettl, Bruno. 2005 [1983]. *The Study of Ethnomusicology: Thirty-one Issues and Concepts.* Champaign: University of Illinois Press.
Nettl, Bruno, and Melinda Russell, eds. 1998. *In the Course of Performance: Studies in the World of Musical Improvisation.* Chicago: University of Chicago Press.
Nettl, Bruno, and Philip V. Bohlman, eds. 1991. *Comparative Musicology and Anthropology of Music: Essays on the History of Ethnomusicology.* Chicago: University of Chicago Press.
Nettl, Bruno, and Ruth M. Stone, eds. 2000. *Garland Encyclopedia of World Music.* 10 vols. New York & London: Garland Publishing
Nettl, Paul. 1948. *Luther and Music.* Russell & Russell.

Neville, Robert Cummings, ed. 2000. *The Comparative Religious Ideas Project*. Vol. I: *The Human Condition*. Vol. II: *Ultimate Realities*. Vol. III: *Religious Truth*. Albany, NY: SUNY Press.

Newberg, Andrew B. 2010. *Principles of Neurotheology*. Routledge Science and Religion Series. London & New York: Routledge.

Newberg, Andrew, Eugene d'Aquili, and Vince Rause. 2001. *Why God Won't Go Away: Brain Science and the Biology of Belief*. New York: Ballantine Books.

Niebuhr, H. Richard. 1957. "Foreword." In *The Essence of Christianity*, by Ludwig Feuerbach. Translated by George Eliot. New York & London: Harper & Row, vii–ix.

Nielson Jr., Niels C. et al. 1993. *Religions of the World*. 3rd edition. New York: St. Martin's Press.

Nongbri, Brent. 2013. *Before Religion: A History of a Modern Concept*. New Haven, CT: Yale University Press.

North, A. C., and D. J. Hargreaves. 2008. *The Social and Applied Psychology of Music*. Oxford, England: Oxford University Press.

Noss, David S. 2003. *A History of the World's Religions*. 11th edition. Upper Saddle River, NJ: Prentice-Hall.

O'Donnell SJ, John. 1992. *Hans Urs von Balthasar*. Collegeville: MN: The Liturgical Press.

Olson, Carl., ed. 2003. *Theory and Method in Religious Studies: A Selection of Critical Readings*. Belmont, CA: Thomson Wadsworth.

Ong, Walter J. 1967. *The Presence of the Word: Some Prolegomena for Cultural and Religious History*. New Haven, CN: Yale University Press.

Ostrem, Eyolf. 2002. "Music and the Ineffable." In *Voicing the Ineffable: Musical Representations of Religious Experience*. Edited by Siglund Bruhn. Hillsdale, NY: Pendragon Press, 287–312.

Otto, Rudolf. 1958 [1923]. *The Idea of the Holy*. New York: Oxford University Press.

Paden, William E. 2010. "Comparative Religion" In *The Routledge Companion to the Study of Religion*. 2nd edition. Edited by John Hinnells. London & New York: Routledge, 225–242.

Paden, William E. 2016. *New Patterns for Comparative Religion: Passages to an Evolutionary Perspective*. London: Bloomsbury Academic.

Paley, William. 2006 [1802]. *Natural Theology: or Evidences of the Existence and Attributes of the Deity Collected from the Appearances of Nature*. Edited with an Introduction and Notes by Matthew D. Eddy and David Knight. New York: Oxford University Press.

Pals, Daniel L. 1987. "Is Religion a Sui Generis Phenomenon?" *Journal of the American Academy of* Religion, Vol. 55, No. 2: 259–282.

Paloutzian, Raymond F., and Crystal L. Park, ed. 2013. *Handbook of The Psychology of Religion and Spirituality*. Second. New York & London: The Guilford Press.

Pandey, Dr. Kanti Chandra. 2008 [1959]. *Comparative Aesthetics: Indian Aesthetics.* Vol. I. Varanasi, India: Chaukhamba Sanskrit Series Office.

Pandey, Dr. Kanti Chandra. 2015 [1972]. *Comparative Aesthetics: Western Aesthetics.* Vol II. Varanasi, India: Chaukhamba Sanskrit Series Office.

Pargament, K. I. 1999. "The Psychology of Religion *and* Spirituality? Yes and No." *The International Journal for the Psychology of Religion* 9, 3–16.

Parrinder, Geoffrey, ed. 1971. *World Religions: From Ancient History to the Present.* New York: Facts-on-File.

Partridge, Christopher. 2014. *The Lyre of Orpheus: Popular Music, the Sacred, and the Profane.* New York: Oxford University Press.

Patel, Aniruddh D. 2015. *Music and the Brain.* Chantilly, VA: The Teaching Company.

Patel, Aniruddh D. 2008. *Music, Language, and the Brain.* New York: Oxford University Press.

Patton, Kimberley C., and Benjamin C. Ray, eds. 2000. *A Magic Still Dwells. Comparative Religion in the Postmodern Age.* Berkeley: University of California Press.

Paul, Russill. 2004. *The Yoga of Sound: Healing & Enlightenment through the Sacred Practice of Mantra.* Novato, CA: New World Library.

Pavry, Jal Dastur Cursetji. 1929 [1926]. *The Zoroastrian Doctrine of a Future Life: From Death to the Individual Judgment.* 2nd edition. New York: Columbia University Press.

Pelikan, Jaroslav. 1986. *Bach Among the Theologians.* Eugene, OR: Wipf & Stock Publishers.

Pelikan, Jaroslav. 1988. *The Melody of Theology: A Philosophical Dictionary.* Cambridge, MA: Harvard University Press.

Pike, Alfred. 1970. *A Phenomenological Analysis of Musical Experience and Other Related Essays.* New York: St. John's University Press.

Pike, Alfred John. 1953. *A Theology of Music.* Toledo, OH: The Gregorian Institute of America.

Pinker, Steven. 1997. *How the Mind Works.* New York: W.W. Norton.

Plantinga, Alvin. 1990 [1967]. *God and Other Minds: A Study of the Rational Justification of Belief in God.* Ithaca & London: Cornell University Press.

Plato. 2007. *Six Great Dialogues: Apology, Crito, Phaedo, Phaedrus, Symposium, and the Republic.* Translated by Benjamin Jowett. Mineola, NY: Dover Publications, Inc.

Plato. 1993a. *Phaedo.* Translated by David Gallop. New York: Oxford University Press.

Plato. 1993b. *The Symposium and the Phaedrus: Plato's Erotic Dialogues.* SUNY Series in Ancient Greek Philosophy. Translated with Introduction and Commentaries by William S. Cobb. Albany, NY: SUNY Press.

Plato. 1971 [1954]. *The Last Days of Socrates: Euthyphro, The Apology, Crito, Phaedo.* Translated and with an Introduction by Hugh Tredennick. Middlesex, UK: Penguin Books.

Plato. 1966. *Plato in Twelve Volumes*, Vol. 1. Translated by Harold North Fowler. Introduction by W. R. M. Lamb. Cambridge, MA: Harvard University Press & London: William Heinemann Ltd.

Plato. 1963. *Timaeus and Critias*. Translated by Desmond Lee. Middlesex, UK: Penguin Books.
Plato. 1951. *The Symposium*. Translated by Walter Hamilton. Middlesex, UK: Penguin Books.
Plotinus. 1991 [1956]. *The Enneads*. Translated by Stephen MacKenna. Abridged with an Introduction and Notes by John Dillon. London: Penguin Books.
Portnoy, Julius. 1954. *The Philosopher and Music: A Historical Outline*. New York: The Humanities Press.
Powell, M. A. 2001. *The Encyclopedia of Contemporary Christian Music*. Peabody, MA: Hendrickson Publishers.
Preus, J. Samuel. 1987. *Explaining Religion: Criticism and Theory from Bodin to Freud*. New Haven, CT & London: Yale University Press.
Proudfoot, Wayne. 1985. *Religious Experience*. Berkeley: University of California Press.
Przywara, Erich. 2014 [1932]. *Analogia Entis: Metaphysics—Original Structure and Universal Rhythm*. Grand Rapids, MI: William. B. Eerdmans.
Pulvermacher, Gunter. 1991. "Carl Gustav Jung and Musical Art." In *Jung in Modern Perspective: The Master and His Legacy*. Edited by Renos K. Papadapoulos and Graham S. Saayman. Dorset, UK: Prism Press, 256–267.
Pyysiainen, Ilkka. 2003. *How Religion Works: Towards a New Cognitive Science of Religion*. Leiden: Brill.
Pyysiainen, Ilkka, and Veikko Antonnen, eds. 2002. *Current Approaches in the Cognitive Science of Religion*. London: Bloomsbury Academic.
Quasten, Johannes. 1983. *Music & Worship in Pagan & Christian Antiquity*. Washington DC: National Association of Pastoral Musicians.
Qureshi, Regula Burckhardt. 1986. *Sufi Music of India and Pakistan: Context and Meaning in Qawwali*. Cambridge UK: Cambridge University Press.
Qureshi, Regula Burckhardt, ed. 2002. *Music and Marx: Ideas, Practices, Politics*. New York: Oxford University Press.
Radano, Ronald, and Philip V. Bohlman, eds. 2000. *Music and the Racial Imagination*. Chicago: University of Chicago Press.
Ralls-MacLeod, Karen. 2000. *Music and the Celtic Otherworld: From Ireland to Iona*. Edinburgh: Polygon.
Ralls-Macleod, Karen, and Graham Harvey, eds. 2000. *Indigenous Religious Music* (with CD). London: University of London.
Randal, Don Michael, ed. 1986. *The New Harvard Dictionary of Music*. Cambridge, MA: Harvard University Press.
Rangacharya, Adya, trans. 2003. *The Nāṭya-Śāstra: English Translation With Critical Notes*. New Delhi: Munshiram Manoharlal.
Rappaport, Roy A. 1999. *Ritual and Religion in the Making of Humanity*. Cambridge, UK: Cambridge University Press.
Ratzinger, Joseph Cardinal. 2000. *The Spirit of the Liturgy*. San Francisco: Ignatius Press.

Raynor, Henry. 1978. *A Social History of Music: From the Middle Ages to Beethoven*, Vol. 1; *Music and Society: Since 1815*, Vol. 2. New York: Taplinger Publishing.
Re Manning, Russell. 2013. "Introduction." In *The Oxford Handbook of Natural Theology*. Edited by Russell Re Manning. New York: Oxford University Press, 1–5.
Redeker, Martin. 1973. *Schleiermacher: Life and Thought*. Philadelphia, PA: Fortress Press.
Reik, Theodor. 1953. *The Haunting Melody: Psychoanalytic Experiences in Life and Music*. New York: Grove Press.
Reimar, Bennett, and Jeffrey E. Wright, eds. 1992. *On the Nature of Musical Experience*. Niwot: University Press of Colorado.
Rennie, Bryan S. 1996. *Reconstructing Eliade: Making Sense of Religion*. Albany, NY: SUNY Press.
Rice, Timothy. 2014. *Ethnomusicology: A Very Short Introduction*. Oxford: Oxford University Press.
Ricoeur, Paul. 1970. *Freud and Philosophy: An Essay on Interpretation*. New Haven, CT: Yale University Press.
Riesebrodt, Martin. 2010. *The Promise of Salvation: A Theory of Religion*. Chicago: University of Chicago Press.
Ringer, Alexander L. 1987. "Religious Music in the West." *The Encyclopedia of Religion*. Editor-in-Chief, Mircea Eliade. New York: Macmillan, Vol. 10, 209–216.
Robertson, Alec. 1950. *Sacred Music*. New York: Chanticleer Press.
Rodrigues, Hillary, and John S. Harding. 2009. *Introduction to the Study of Religion*. London & New York: Routledge.
Roscoe, Paul. 2009. "The Comparative Method." In *The Blackwell Companion to the Study of Religion*. Edited by Robert A. Segal. Oxford: Wiley-Blackwell, 25–46.
Rose, Gilbert J. 2004. *Between Couch and Piano: Psychoanalysis, Music, Art, and Neuroscience*. New York: Brunner-Routledge.
Rose, Kenneth. 2016. "The Singular and the Shared: Making Amends to Eliade after the Dismissal of the Sacred." In *Interreligious Comparisons in Religious Studies and Theology: Comparison Revisited*. Edited by Perry Schmidt-Leukel and Andreas Nehring. London: Bloomsbury Academic, 110–129.
Rosen, Steven. 2008. *The Yoga of Kirtan: Conversations on the Sacred Art of Chanting*. New York: Folk Books.
Rouget, Gilbert. 1986. *Music and Trance: A Theory of the Relation between Music and Possession*. Chicago, IL: University of Chicago Press.
Rowell, Lewis. 1983. *Thinking about Music: An Introduction to the Philosophy of Music*. Amherst, MA: The University of Massachusetts Press.
Rubin, Emanuel, and John H. Baron. 2006. *Music in Jewish History and Culture*. Sterling Heights, MI: Harmonie Park Press.

Ruitenbeck, Hendrik M., ed. 1973. *Freud As We Knew Him*. Detroit, MI: Wayne State University Press.
Rust, E. Gardner. 1996. *The Music and Dance of the World's Religions: A Comprehensive, Annotated Bibliography of Materials in the English Language*. Westport, CN: Greenwood Press.
Ryba, Thomas. 2009. "Phenomenology of Religion." In *The Blackwell Companion to the Study of Religion*. Edited by Robert A. Segal. Oxford: Wiley-Blackwell, 91–121.
Rytting, Bryce. 2010. "Music." In *The Routledge Encyclopedia of Religion, Communication, and Media*. Edited by Daniel A. Stout. London & New York: Routledge, 275–279.
Sachs, Curt. 1949. *A Short History of World Music*. London: Dennis Dobson LTD,
Sacks, Oliver. 2007. *Musicophilia: Tales of Music and the Brain*. New York: Alfred A. Knopf.
Sadie, Stanley, ed. 1980. *New Grove Dictionary of Music and Musicians*. 20 vols. New York: Macmillan.
St. Vincent, Justin, ed. 2009–2012. *The Spiritual Significance of Music*. 3 vols. New Zealand: Xtreme Music.
Saliers, Don E. 2007. *Music and Theology*. Nashville, TN: Abingdon Press.
Samuels, David W., Louise Meintjes, Ana Maria Ochoa, and Thomas Porcello. 2010. "Soundscapes: Toward a Sounded Anthropology." *Annual Review of Anthropology* 39: 329–345.
Saṅgīta Dāmodaraḥ of Śubhaṅkara.1960. Edited by Gaurinath Shastri and Govinda Gopal Mukhopadhyaya. Calcutta: Sanskrit College.
Saṅgīta Ratnākara of Śārṅgadeva. 1978. Edited and translated by R. K. Shringy and Prem Lata Sharma. New Delhi: Munshiram Manoharlal, Vol. 1.
Śaraṇa, Gopāla. 1975. *The Methodology of Anthropological Comparisons: An Analysis of Comparative Methods in Social and Cultural Anthropology*. Tucson: University of Arizona Press.
Sarbadhikary, Sukanya. 2015. *The Place of Devotion: Siting and Experiencing Divinity in Bengal Vaishnavism*. Berkeley: University of California Press.
Schaefer, Mary M. 1998. "What is Liturgical Worship?" In *Liturgy and Music: Lifetime Learning*. Edited by Robin A. Leaver and Joyce Ann Zimmerman. Collegeville, MN: The Liturgical Press, 3–18.
Schafer, R. Murray. 1994 [1977]. *The Soundscape: Our Sonic Environment and the Tuning of the World*. Rochester, VT: Destiny Books.
Schalk, Carl F. 1988. *Luther on Music: Paradigms of Praise*. St. Louis, MO: Concordia Publishing House.
Scheler, Max. 1960. *On the Eternal in Man*. London: Routledge.
Schelling, F. W. J. 1989. *The Philosophy of Art*. Edited, translated, and introduced by Douglas W. Stott. Minneapolis, MN: University of Minnesota Press.

Schilbrack, Kevin. 2010. "Religions: Are There Any?" *Journal of the American Academy of Religion*, Vol. 78: 1112–1138.
Schleiermacher, Friedrich. 1996 [1811]. *Dialectic: or, the Art of Doing Philosophy*. A Study Edition of the 1811 Notes. Translated, with Introduction and Notes by Terrence N. Tice. Atlanta, GA: Scholars Press.
Schleiermacher, Friedrich. 1958 [1899]. *On Religion: Speeches to its Cultured Despisers*. Edited and translated by John Oman, with Centenary Introduction by Rudolf Otto. New York: Harper & Row.
Schleiermacher, Friedrich. 1969. *On Religion: Addresses to its Cultured Critics*. Translated with introduction and notes by Terrence N. Tice. Richmond, VA: John Knox Press.
Schleiermacher, Friedrich. 2010 [1988]. *On Religion: Speeches to its Cultured Despisers*. Edited and translated by Richard Crouter. Cambridge, UK: Cambridge University Press.
Schmidt, Wilhelm. 2014 [1931]. *The Origin and Growth of Religion: Facts and Theories*. Proctorville OH: Wythe-North Publishing.
Schmidt-Leukel, Perry and Andreas Nehring, eds. 2016. *Interreligious Comparisons in Religious Studies and Theology: Comparison Revisited*. London: Bloomsbury Academic.
Schneider, Albrecht. 1991. "Psychological Theory and Comparative Musicology." In *Comparative Musicology and Anthropology of Music: Essays on the History of Ethnomusicology*. Edited by Bruno Nettl and Philip V. Bohlman. Chicago: University of Chicago Press, 293–317.
Schneider, Albrecht, ed. 2008. *Systematic and Comparative Musicology: Concepts, Methods, Findings*. Frankfurt am Main: Peter Lang.
Schneider, Marius. 1989. "The Nature of Praise Song." In *Cosmic Music: Musical Keys to the Interpretation of Reality*. Edited by Joscelyn Godwin. Rochester, VT: Inner Traditions, 35–52.
Scholtz, Gunter. 2010. "Schleiermacher." In *Music in German Philosophy: An Introduction*. Edited by Stefan Lorenz Sorgner and Oliver Furbeth. Chicago: University of Chicago Press, 47–67.
Scholtz, Gunter. 1981. *Schleiermachers Musikphilosophie*. Gottingen: Vandenhoeck & Ruprecht.
Schopenhauer, Arthur. 1995 [1819]. *The World as Will and Idea*. Abridged in One Volume. Edited by David Berman and translated by Jill Berman. London: J. M. Dent.
Schultz, Anna. 2012. *Singing a Hindu Nation: Marathi Devotional Performance and Nationalism*. New York: Oxford University Press.
Schweig, Graham. 2005. *Dance of Divine Love: India's Classic Sacred Love Story: The Rāsa Līlā of Krishna*. Princeton, NJ: Princeton University Press.
Scott, Cyril. 2013 [1933]. *Music and Its Secret Influence Throughout the Ages*. Rochester, VT: Inner Traditions.

Scott, Walter, ed. 1985 [1924]. *Hermetica: The Ancient Greek and Latin Writings which contain Religious or Philosophic Teachings ascribed to Hermes Trismegistus.* Vols. 1–4. Boston: Shambhala.

Scruton, Roger. 1999. *The Aesthetics of Music.* Oxford: Clarendon Press.

Scruton, Roger. 2020 [2015]. "Music and the Transcendental." In *Music and Transcendence.* Edited by Ferdia Stone-Davis. London & Oxford: Ashgate, Routledge, 75–84.

Seaford, Richard. 2020. *The Origin of Philosophy in Ancient Greece and Ancient India: A Historical Comparison.* Cambridge, UK: Cambridge University Press.

Seaford, Richard, ed. 2016. *Universe and Inner Self in Early Indian and Early Greek Thought.* Edinburgh: Edinburgh University Press.

Seeger, Charles. 1941. "Music and Culture." *Proceedings of the Music Teachers National Association for 1940*, Vol. 64: 112–122.

Seel, Thomas Allen. 1995. *A Theology of Music for Worship Derived from the Book of Revelation.* Studies in Liturgical Musicology No. 3. Metuchen, NJ: The Scarecrow Press.

Segal, Robert A. 2010. "Theories of Religion." In *The Routledge Companion to the Study of Religion.* 2nd edition. Edited by John Hinnells. London & New York: Routledge, 75–92.

Segal, Robert A. ed. 2009. *The Blackwell Companion to the Study of Religion.* Oxford: Wiley-Blackwell.

Sendrey, Alfred. 1969. *Music of Ancient Israel.* New York: Philosophical Library.

Shah, Timothy Samuel and Jack Friedman, eds. 2018. *Homo Religiosus? Exploring the Roots of Religion and Religious Freedom in Human Experience.* Cambridge UK: Cambridge University Press.

Shankar, Ravi. 1968. *My Music, My Life.* New York: Simon and Schuster.

Sharma, Arvind. 2005. *Religious Studies and Comparative Methodology: The Case for Reciprocal Illumination.* Albany, NY: SUNY Press.

Sharpe, Eric. J. 1986 [1975]. *Comparative Religion: A History.* 2nd edition. La Salle, IL: Open Court.

Sharpe, Eric J. 1971. *Fifty Key Words: Comparative Religion.* Richmond, VA: John Knox Press.

Sharpe, Eric. J. 1983. *Understanding Religion.* London: Duckworth.

Shelemay, Kay Kaufman. 2001. *Soundscapes: Exploring Music in a Changing World.* New York: W.W. Norton.

Sherry, Patrick. 1992. *Spirit and Beauty: An Introduction to Theological Aesthetics.* Oxford: Clarendon Press.

Sheveland, John N. 2010. "Solidarity through Polyphony." In *The New Comparative Theology: Interreligious Insights from the Next Generation.* Edited by Francis X. Clooney, S. J. London: T & T Clark International, 171–190.

Sheveland, John N. 2014. "What has Renaissance Polyphony to Offer Theological Method?" In *Understanding Religious Pluralism: Perspectives from Religious*

Studies and Theology. Edited by Peter C. Phan and Jonathan S. Ray. Eugene, OR: Wipf & Stock, 264–276.

Shiloah, Amnon. 1992. *Jewish Musical Traditions.* Detroit, MI: Wayne State University Press.

Shiloah, Amnon. 1995. *Music in the World of Islam: A Socio-Cultural Study.* Detroit, MI: Wayne State University Press.

Singh, Pashaura. 2006. "Sikhism and Music." In *Sacred Sound: Experiencing Music in World Religions.* Edited by Guy L. Beck. Waterloo, Ontario: Wilfrid Laurier University Press, 141–167.

Śivānanda, Swami. 1956. *Music as Yoga.* Śivānandanagar, U.P.: Divine Life Society.

Slaughter, J. W. 1905. "Music and Religion: A Psychological Rivalry." *International Journal of Ethics*, Vol. 15: 353–361.

Sloboda, John. 2000. "Music and Worship: A Psychologist's Perspective." In *Creative Chords: Studies in Music, Theology and Christian Tradition.* Edited by Jeff Astley, Timothy Hone and Mark Savage. Herefordhshire, UK: Gracewing, 110–125.

Sloboda, John A. 1985. *The Musical Mind: The Cognitive Psychology of Music.* Oxford UK: Oxford University Press.

Sloboda, John A. and P. N. Juslin, eds. 2001. *Music and Emotion: Theory and Research.* Oxford UK: Oxford University Press.

Smart, Ninian. 1972. *The Concept of Worship.* London: Macmillan.

Smart, Ninian. 1973. *The Phenomenon of Religion.* New York: Herder and Herder.

Smith, F. Harold. 1937. *The Elements of Comparative Theology.* New York: Charles Scribner's.

Smith, F. Joseph. 1979. *The Experiencing of Musical Sound: Prelude to a Phenomenology of Music.* New York & London: Gordon and Breach.

Smith, Huston. *The Religions of Man.* 1964 [1958]. New York: Harper Torchbooks. Revised in 1991 as *The World's Religions: Our Great Wisdom Traditions.* New York & San Francisco: Harper SanFrancisco.

Smith, Jonathan Z. 1982. *Imaging Religion: From Babylon to Jonestown.* Chicago: University of Chicago Press.

Smith, Jonathan Z. 1978. *Map is Not Territory: Studies in the History of Religions.* Leiden: E. J. Brill.

Smith Jonathan Z., and William Scott Green, eds., with the American Academy of Religion. 1995. *The Harper Collins Dictionary of Religion.* New York & San Francisco: Harper San Francisco.

Smith, Wilfrid Cantwell. 1963. *The Meaning and End of Religion: A New Approach to the Religious Traditions of Mankind.* New York: The New American Library.

Smith, Wilfrid Cantwell. 1981. *Towards a World Theology: Faith and the Comparative History of Religion.* Philadelphia, PA: The Westminster Press.

Snodgrass, Cynthia. 2002. *The Sonic Thread: Sound as a Pathway to Spirituality*. New York: Paraview Press.

Snoek, Jan. 2008. "Defining Rituals." In *Theorizing Rituals: Issues, Topics, Approaches, Concepts*. Edited by Jens Kreinath, Jan Snoek, and Michael Stausberg. Leiden: Brill, 3–14.

Sohngen, Oskar. 1983. "Music and Theology: A Systematic Approach." In *Sacred Sound: Music in Religious Thought and Practice*. Edited by Joyce Irwin. Chico, CA: Scholars Press, 1–19.

Sorgner, Stefan Lorenz and Oliver Furbeth. 2010. "Introduction." In *Music in German Philosophy: An Introduction*. Edited by Stefan Lorenz Sorgner and Oliver Furbeth. Chicago: University of Chicago Press, 1–25.

Sorgner, Stefan Lorenz, and Oliver Furbeth, eds. 2010. *Music in German Philosophy: An Introduction*. Chicago: University of Chicago Press.

Spencer, Jon Michael. 1994. "Musicology as a Theologically Informed Discipline." In *Theomusicology*. Edited by Jon Michael Spencer. Durham, NC: Duke University Press, 36–63.

Spencer, Jon Michael. 1991. *Theological Music: An Introduction to Theomusicology*. Westport, CN: Greenwood Press.

Spitzer, Leo. 1944, 1945. "Classical and Christian Ideas of World Harmony: Prolegomena to an Interpretation of the Word 'Stimmung.'" Part I. *Traditio* 2: 409–464, and Part II. *Traditio* 3: 307–364.

Stark, Rodney. 2007. *Discovering God: The Origins of the Great Religions and the Evolution of Belief*. New York: Harper Collins.

Stark, Rodney. 2021. "Economics of Religion." In *The Wiley-Blackwell Companion to the Study of Religion*. 2nd edition. Edited by Robert A. Segal and Nockolas P. Roubekas. West Sussex, UK: John Wiley & Sons, 2021, 25–43.

Stausberg, Michael, and Steven Engler, eds. 2013. *The Routledge Handbook of Research Methods in the Study of Religion*. London: Routledge.

Steckel, Clyde J. 1994. "How Can Music Have Theological Significance?" In *Theomusicology*. Edited by Jon Michael Spencer. Durham, NC: Duke University Press, 13–35.

Steiner, George. 1991. *Real Presences*. Chicago: University of Chicago Press.

Stewart, R. J. 1990. *The Spiritual Dimension of Music: Altering Consciousness for Inner Development*. Rochester, VT: Destiny Books.

Stoltzfus, Philip E. 2006. *Theology as Performance: Music, Aesthetics and God in Modern Theology*. New York & Edinburgh: T & T Clark.

Stone, John R., ed. 2002. *The Essential Max Muller: On Language, Mythology, and Religion*. New York: Palgrave Macmillan.

Stone-Davis, Ferdia J., ed. 2020 [2015]. *Music and Transcendence*. London & Oxford: Ashgate, New York: Routledge.

Storr, Anthony. 1992. *Music and the Mind*. New York: Free Press.

Stowe, David W. 2004. *How Sweet the Sound: Music in the Spiritual Lives of Americans*. Cambridge, MA: Harvard University Press.

Strenski, Ivan. 2015. *Understanding Theories of Religion: An Introduction*. 2nd edition. West Sussex, UK: Wiley Blackwell.

Sullivan, Lawrence E. 1984. "Sacred Music and Sacred Time." *The World of Music*, Vol. 26, No. 3: 33–52.

Sullivan, Lawrence E., ed. 1997. *Enchanting Powers: Music in the World's Religions*. Cambridge, MA: Harvard University Press.

Swain, Joseph P. 2010. *The A to Z of Sacred Music*. Lanham, MD: Scarecrow Press.

Swidler, Leonard, ed. 1987. *Toward a Universal Theology of Religion*. Maryknoll, NY: Orbis Books.

Swinburne, Richard. 1993 [1977]. *The Coherence of Theism*. Oxford, UK: Oxford University Press.

Swinburne, Richard. 2004 [1979]. *The Existence of God*. Oxford, UK: Oxford University Press.

Swinburne, Richard. 2005 [1981]. *Faith and Reason*. Oxford, UK: Oxford University Press.

Sydnor, Jon Paul. 2011. *Ramanuja and Schleiermacher: Toward a Constructive Comparative Theology*. Princeton Theological Monograph Series. Eugene, OR: Pickwick Publications.

Sylvan, Robin. 2002. *Traces of the Spirit: The Religious Dimensions of Popular Music*. New York: New York University Press.

Sziborsky, Lucia. 2010. "Adorno." In *Music in German Philosophy: An Introduction*. Edited by Stefan Lorenz Sorgner and Oliver Furbeth. Chicago: University of Chicago Press, 233–251.

Tame, David. 1984. *The Secret Power of Music: The Transformation of Self and Society through Musical Energy*. Rochester, VT: Destiny Books.

Taves, Ann. 2009. *Religious Experience Reconsidered: A Building Block Approach to the Study of Religion and Other Special Things*. Princeton, NJ: Princeton University Press.

Taylor, Mark C., ed. 1998. *Critical Terms for Religious Studies*. Chicago: University of Chicago Press.

Thandeka. 1995. *The Embodied Self: Friedrich Schleiermacher's Solution to Kant's Problem of the Empirical Self*. Albany, NY: SUNY Press.

Thite, G.U. 1997. *Music in the Vedas: Its Magico-Religious Significance*. Delhi: Sharada Publishing House.

Thomas, Downing A. 1995. *Music and the Origins of Language: Theories from the French Enlightenment*. Cambridge UK: Cambridge University Press.

Thompson, William Forde. 2009. *Music, Thought, and Feeling: Understanding the Psychology of Music*. New York: Oxford University Press.

Tillich, Paul. 1959. *Theology and Culture*. New York: Oxford University Press.

Titon, Jeff Todd and Timothy J. Cooley. 2016. *Worlds of Music: Introduction to the Music of the World's Peoples*. Boston: Cengage Learning.

Tremlin, Todd. 2010. *Minds and Gods: The Cognitive Foundations of Religion*. New York: Oxford University Press.

Troeltsch, Ernst. 1913. "The Dogmatics of the Religionsgeshichtliche Schule." *The American Journal of Theology*, Vol. 17, No. 1 (Jan 1913): 1–21.

Twiss, Sumner B., and Walter H. Conser, Jr., eds. 1992. *Experience of the Sacred: Readings in the Phenomenology of Religion*. Hanover & London: University Press of New England.

Van Damme, Wilfried. 1996. *Beauty in Context: Toward an Anthropological Approach to Aesthetics*. Leiden: Brill.

Van der Leeuw, Gerardus. 1963. *Sacred and Profane Beauty: The Holy in Art*. New York: Holt, Rinehart, and Winston.

Van der Leeuw, Gerardus. 1967 [1938]. *Religion in Essence and Manifestation*. Vols. 1 & 2. Gloucester: Peter Smith.

Vanden Bos, Gary R., editor-in-chief. 2007. *APA Dictionary of Psychology*. Washington, DC: American Psychological Association.

Van Khe, Tran. 1977. "Is the Pentatonic Scale Universal? A Few Reflections on Pentatonicism." *The World of Music*, Vol. 19, No. 1–2, UNIVERSALS: 76–84.

Vatican Council II: The Conciliar and Post Conciliar Documents.1975. Edited by Austin Flannery, O.P. Northport, NY: Costello Publishing Company.

Viladesau, Richard. 1999. *Theological Aesthetics: God in Imagination, Beauty, and Art*. New York: Oxford University Press.

Viladesau, Richard. 2000. *Theology and the Arts: Encountering God through Music, Art, and Rhetoric*. Mahwah, NJ: Paulist Press.

Waardenburg, Jacques, ed. 1999 [1971]. *Classical Approaches to the Study of Religion: Aims, Methods, and Theories of Research*. New York & Berlin: Walter de Gruyter.

Wach, Joachim. 1944. *Sociology of Religion*. Chicago: University of Chicago Press.

Wach, Joachim. 1951. *Types of Religious Experience: Christian and Non-Christian*. Chicago: University of Chicago Press.

Wainwright, Geoffrey. 1980. *Doxology: The Praise of God in Worship, Doctrine and Life. A Systematic Theology*. New York: Oxford University Press.

Wallin, Nils L., Bjorn Merker, and Steven Brown, eds. 2000. *The Origins of Music*. Cambridge: MIT Press.

Ward, Keith. 1998. *Religion and Human Nature*. Oxford, UK: Oxford University Press.

Ward, Keith. 1994. *Religion and Revelation: A Theology of Revelation in the World's Religions*. Oxford, UK: Oxford University Press.

Weber, Max. 2002 [1904–1905]. *The Protestant Ethic and the "Spirit" of Capitalism and Other Writings*. Edited and Translated with an Introduction by Peter Baehr and Gordon C. Wells. London: Penguin Books.

Weber, Max. 1958 [1921]. *The Rational and Social Foundations of Music*. Carbondale: Southern Illinois University Press.

Weiss, Paul. 1963. *Religion and Art*. The Aquinas Lecture. Milwaukee, WI: Marquette University Press.

Weiss, Sarah. 2019. *Ritual Soundings: Women Performers and World Religions*. Urbana, Chicago, & Springfield: University of Illinois Press.

Welton, Donn, ed. 1999. *The Essential Husserl: Basic Writings in Transcendental Phenomenology*. Bloomington & Indianapolis: Indiana University Press.

Werner, Eric. 1960. *The Sacred Bridge: Liturgical Parallels in Synagogue and Early Church*. Vol. 1. *The Sacred Bridge: The Interdependence of Liturgy and Music in Synagogue and Church During the First Millennium*. New York: Columbia University Press.

Whitehouse, Mary, and Rick Hollings. 2008. "Psychology of Religion." In *21st Century Psychology: A Reference Handbook*. Edited by Stephen F. Davis and William Buskist. Los Angeles, London: Sage Publications, Vol. 2., 475–482.

Whitehurst, Richard. 2011. *Mahamantra Yoga: Chanting to Anchor the Mind and Access the Divine*. Rochester, VT: Destiny Books.

Wiebe, Donald. 1999. *The Politics of Religious Studies: The Continuing Conflict with Theology in the Academy*. New York: Palgrave.

Wiebe, Dustin D. 2021. "Music and Religion: Trends in Recent English-Language Literature (2015–2021)." *Religions*, Vol. 12: 833. https://doi.org/10.3390/rel12100833

Wildman, Wesley J. 2013. "Comparative Natural Theology." In *The Oxford Handbook of Natural Theology*. Edited by Russell Re Manning. New York: Oxford University Press, 370–394.

Williams, Richard David. 2020. "Sounding Out the Divine: Musical Practice as Theology in Samāj Gāyan." In *The Oxford History of Hinduism: Hindu Practice*. Edited by Gavin Flood. New York and Oxford: Oxford University Press, 342–361.

Williams, Robert R. 1978. *Schleiermacher the Theologian: The Construction of the Doctrine of God*. Philadelphia, PA: Fortress Press.

Williams, Sean. 2006. "Buddhism and Music." In *Sacred Sound: Experiencing Music in World Religions*. Edited by Guy L. Beck. Waterloo, Ontario: Wilfrid Laurier University Press, 169–189.

Williams, Sean. 2001. *Sounds of the Ancestral Ship: Highland Music of West Java*. New York: Oxford University Press.

Wolf, Richard K. 2014. *The Voice in the Drum: Music, language, and Emotion in Islamicate South Asia*. Urbana, Chicago, & Springfield: University of Illinois Press.

Wright, J. Edward. 2000. *The Early History of Heaven*. Oxford and New York: Oxford University Press.

Wuidar, Lawrence, ed. 2010. *Music and Esotericism*. Leiden: Brill.

Wulff, David M.1991. *Psychology of Religion: Classic and Contemporary Views.* New York: John Wiley & Sons.
Yogananda, Paramahansa. 2016 [1946]. *Autobiography of a Yogi: The Classic Story of One of India's Greatest Spiritual Thinkers.* London: Arcturus Publishing Ltd.
Young, William A. 2005. *The World's Religions.* 2nd ed. Upper Saddle River, NJ: Prentice-Hall.
Zaehner, R. C. 2002 [1961]. *The Dawn and Twilight of Zoroastrianism.* London: Pheonix Press.
Zuckerkandl, Victor. 1973. *Man the Musician.* Princeton, NJ: Princeton University Press.
Zuckerkandl, Victor. 1956. *Sound and Symbol: Music and the External World.* Princeton, NJ: Princeton University Press.

Index

Adiaphora (music as neutral), 198
Adler, Guido: musicology, 123; comparative musicology, 124
Adorno, Theodor W. (Frankfurt School, Marxism and music), 2, 29–30, 117, 118–120, 305
Aesthetics, 18, 20, 25, 33, 38, 40, 49, 85, 104, 146, 150–151, 159, 160, 162, 175, 178–179, 181, 203–204, 259, 264, 284–289, 299; *homo aestheticus*, 308; Indian, 209–210; comparative, 308
Affect theology (Thandeka), 61–62
Alcorta, C. S. (neuroscience and music), 258–259
Allen, Douglas (phenomenology of religion), 79–80
Almond, Philip C. (Otto), 282–283
Analogy of Being (*analogia entis*), 173, 192–193
Analytical philosophy, 162–163
Ānanda-Vrindāvana-Campū by Kavi Karṇapūr (Sanskrit religious text), 212
Anderson, Warren D., (music in ancient Greece), 145
Anthropology, 89–98; and music, 103–105, 125–126
Antilla, Miikka E. (Luther and music), 181

Antweiler, Christoph (anthropology, universals), 89, 104
Aristotle, 151–152, 169, 171, 172–173, 198, 288
Augustine, St., 4, 152, 172, 187, 194, 198, 286, 288, 305

Bach, J. S. (composer), 5, 9, 71, 193, 202–203
Baillie, John (theology), 167–168
Balthasar, Hans Urs von (theological aesthetics), 264, 288–289
Bannan, Nicholas (cognitive studies, musical universals), 128
Barth, Karl (theology), 4, 22, 61, 65, 177–178, 203, 282, 288
Baumgarten, Alexander G. (aesthetics), 284
Becker, Judith (anthropology and music), 104, 304
Begbie, Jeremy S. (theology and music), 5, 178, 181, 198, 264
Bell, Catherine (ritual studies), 275–276
Belzen, Jacob (psychology and music), 105–106
Benjamin, Walter (Frankfurt School), 29
Berendt, Joachim-Ernst (Nada Brahma), 11

Berger, Peter L. (sociology), 101–102, 299
Bernstein, Leonard (music performance, Harvard lectures), 246, 252
Bhagavad Gītā (Hindu sacred text), 176–177
Blacking, John (ethnomusicology), 126, 131, 133, 136, 252
Blackwell, Albert L. (sacred music), 2, 181, 294
Bleeker, C. J. (history of religions), 59, 77
Bloch, Ernst (Marxism and music), 29, 30, 117
Blofeld, John (Buddhism), 235–236
Blum, Jason N. (phenomenology of religion), 53, 280–282, 290
Bohlman, Philip V. (ethnomusicology), 125, 182–183, 238
Bosanquet, Bernard (aesthetics), 284
Bowie, Andrew (philosophy, aesthetics), 162
Bowker, John (comparative religion), 1, 63, 64, 74–75, 78, 91–93, 101
Bouyer, Louis (theology, ritual studies), 220–222, 275
Boyer, Pascal (cognitive studies, musical universals), 241, 243, 273
Brahms, Johannes (composer), 13, 203
Brandon, S. G. F. (comparative religion), 18, 79
Brown, Donald E. (anthropology, universals), 103–104
Brown, Frank Burch (religious aesthetics), 35, 178, 264–266, 288, 289, 304, 305
Brown, Steven (cognitive studies, "musilanguage"), 256–257
Buddhism, 36, 134, 160, 181, 189, 218, 235–236, 238
Burrows, David (music history), 37

Bussanich, John (comparative philosophy), 157
Calvin, John, 4, 37, 173–174, 177, 198, 288
Campbell, Don ("Mozart effect"), 8, 9
Capetz, Paul E., 59
Capleton, Brian (Pythagoras), 155
Caputo, John D. (Derrida), 29, 31
Carman, John B. (Hindu theology), 253–254
Cave, David (religious studies, Eliade), 268–270
Chomsky, Noam (generative grammar), 246
Christianity, 4, 5, 22, 29, 51, 60–61, 152–154, 161–163, 167, 172–175, 177, 179, 180, 186–189, 194–195, 223, 225, 283, 306–307; Lutheran theology and music, 197–205
Clifton, Thomas (musicology), 87
Clooney SJ, Francis X. (comparative theology), 5
Cognitive Studies, 241–259
Comparative musicology, 122–124, 258
Comparative philosophy, 156–158
Comparative religion, 18, 24, 26, 27, 40, 48, 59–65, 67, 73, 89, 99, 220, 264, 282, 283, 300
Comparative theology, 5, 6, 62, 174–175
Coomaraswamy, Ananda K. (religion and art), 287
Corduan, Winfried (primal monotheism), 100
Cornille, Catherine (comparative theology), 5–6, 177
Coward, Harold (religious studies), 16, 37–38, 305
Crichton, J. D. (liturgy), 220
Cross, Ian (psychology and music, cultural relativism), 95

Crouter, Richard (Schleiermacher), 54, 58
Cultural relativism, 28, 93–96
Cultural universalism, 97–103
Cumont, Franz (Roman paganism), 194

Dahlhaus, Carl (absolute music), 69–71
Darwin, Charles (human evolution), 23, 92, 174, 253–254, 255
Davis, Stephen F. (psychology), 108–109, 110
Deism, 46, 174
Demarest, Bruce A. (natural theology, general revelation), 172–174
Derrida, Jacques (postmodernism), 30, 31–32
DeVale, Sue Carole (musical instruments), 138
Dilthey, Wilhelm, 18, 20, 28, 48, 56, 71, 73, 159, 298
Dionysius the Areopagite (angels), 188
Doniger, Wendy (history of religions), 2, 32, 94
Douglas, Mary (anthropology, ritual studies), 218
Durkheim, Emile (sociology), 19, 22, 49, 50, 52, 90, 92–93, 97, 103, 117

Edgar, William (music history), 181–182
Eliade, Mircea (history of religions, homo religiosus), 2, 18, 20, 23–26, 27, 28, 33, 48, 58, 59, 63–67, 71, 73, 82, 99, 139, 219–221, 226, 263, 266, 267–271, 278, 288, 292, 293, 303
Ellingson, Ter (musicology), 7, 33, 36, 293, 297, 303
Ellis, Alexander J. (musicology, musical relativism), 128–130

Epoché ('suspension of judgment'), 75–78, 84, 281, 290
Ethnomusicology, 6, 16, 27, 103, 111, 124–127

Feld, Steven (acoustemology), 140, 264
Feuerbach, Ludwig (Mirror Theory), 19, 21, 22, 49, 50–52, 90, 91, 101–102, 113, 159, 178
Fideler, David R. (Pythagoras), 143, 147–150, 152
Fiorenza, Francis Schussler, 175
Fitzgerald, Timothy, 24
Fletcher, Peter (musicology), 27
Flood, Gavin (religious studies), 31, 82
Foley, Edward (liturgy, ritual musicology), 43, 140, 225–230, 231, 264
Ford, David F. (theology), 167
Frankfurt School (Critical Theory), 28–30, 118
Frazier, Jessica (Hindu studies, natural theology), 176
Freud, Sigmund (psychoanalysis), 19, 22, 28, 29, 49, 50–53, 90–93, 97, 102, 105, 107–108, 112–115, 160
Friedlander, Shams (Islam, Sufism), 10, 307

Gallup Poll (Religion in America), 108
Gass, Robert (chant), 10
Geertz, Clifford (anthropology, cultural relativism), 26, 94, 288
Gelineau, Joseph, 179, 217, 224
General revelation: *see* Natural theology
Generative Theory of Tonal Music (GTTM), 246–248, 252
Gerety, Finnian M. M. (Hindu studies, OM), 234
Gerson-Kiwi, Edith (ethnomusicology), 297

352 | Index

Gillan, Matt (Japan), 309–310
Godwin, Joscelyn (Pythagorean tradition), 143, 144, 153–154, 188, 195, 305
Gradenwitz, Peter (Judaism), 183
Graves, Eben (rhythmic theology), 264, 308
Green, Garrett (hermeneutics), 51
Gregorian Chant, 9–10, 225, 229, 296, 297, 306
Griffith, Ralph T. H. (Rig Veda), 210
Guido of Arezzo (Solfeggio), 184
Guzy, Lidia, 309

Hackett, Rosalind J. (religion, sound, and music), 34, 309
Harrison, Frank (musical universals), 113, 133, 136–137
Harvey, Van A. (Feuerbach), 50–52, 90–91, 178
Harwood, Dane L. (cognitive studies and music), 248–257
Hastings, James (*Encyclopedia of Religion and Ethics*), 2, 33, 303
Hawley, John S. (Hindu studies, Bhakti poets), 17, 210
Hegel, 51, 90–91, 98, 101, 159, 161, 162, 202, 266
Hermeneutics (methods of interpretation), 50–51
Hermetic tradition (Poimandres, *Corpus Hermeticum*), 195–196
Hinduism: 16, 36, 166, 189, 213–216, 218, 232–235, 283, 293, 296, 309; Hindu theology and music, 205–217
History of Religions, 18, 20, 22, 23, 38, 39, 58–68, 79, 89, 99, 105, 177, 181, 204, 266, 269, 278, 283, 300
Homo Musicus, 6, 40, 116, 263, 271–275, 301

Homo Religiosus, 6, 40, 67, 226, 263, 265–271, 301
Homo Ritualis, 6, 218–219, 263, 275–277
Hood, Mantle (ethnomusicology, musical relativism), 133–134
Hoondert, Martin (religion and music), 34, 264, 301
Hornbostel, Erich von (comparative musicology), 84, 123–124, 295
House of Song (Zoroastrianism), 197, 210–211
Husserl, Edmund (phenomenology), 20, 28, 73–77, 83–84, 86, 118, 123, 159, 192

Indian Music (saṅgīta), 207–209; kirtan and bhajan, 210, 231–232; rāga, 207–208, 212–214, 216, 237–238, 247; samāj gāyan, 213
Irwin, Joyce L (Lutheran theology and music), 16, 34, 181, 185, 198, 304
Islam, 10, 140, 154, 190–192, 276, 307; Qawwali, 10, 181, 296, 307

Jackson, William, J. (South Asian musicology), 210
Jaeger, Werner (theology in ancient Greece), 169–172
Jaini, Padmanabh S. (Jainism), 236
Jainism, 236–238
James, E. O. (comparative religion), 99–100
James, Jamie (harmony of the spheres), 9
James, William (religious experience), 3–4, 103, 105, 107, 163, 242, 255, 266
Jastrow, Morris Jr. (religious studies), 56–57
Jeffery, Peter (musicology), 306, 309

Jung, Carl G. (analytical psychology), 105, 107, 112, 115
Judaism: 22, 33, 37, 152, 165–166, 185, 190, 223, 224, 232, 293, 305, 306, 313, 314; Talmud, 190; Kabbalah, 213

Kant, 18, 28, 48–49, 54–56, 62, 64, 69, 84, 90, 159–163, 203, 247, 270, 286–287, 288, 289
Karp, Theodore C. (medieval quadrivium and music), 145,
Kassam, Tazim (religion and music, Islam), 308
Kaur, Inderjit Nilu (Sikhism and music), 239
Kavanagh, Aidan (liturgical studies), 222
Kayser, Hans (Pythagoras, akroasis, world harmonics), 154–155
Kichlu, Vijay (Indian music, Agra Gharana), 14
Kirnarskaya, Dina (homo musicus), 273–274
Koskoff, Ellen (ethnomusicology), 16, 121, 134, 306
Krishna (Hinduism, Rāsa Dance), 211–213
Kung, Hans (theology), 4–5
Kunst, Jaap (ethnomusicology), 125
Kunst religion (religion of art), 70
Kyrie, 217, 224, 314

Laack, Isabel (religion and music), 21, 34–35, 43, 278, 280
Ladder of Beauty (Plato, Plotinus), 284–286
Lang, Andrew (anthropology, primal monotheism), 97–98
Leaver, Robin A. (Lutheran theology and music), 181, 198, 200–202
Lehrdahl, Fred (GTTM), 246–247, 252
Lehrich, Christopher I. (music and religion), 7, 72
Le Mée, Katherine (Gregorian chant), 10
Levine, Joseph A. (Judaism), 70
Lewis, James R. (religious studies, angels), 192
List, George (ethnomusicology, musical relativism), 134
Liturgical musicology, 226
Liturgical studies, 217, 223–232
Liturgy, 220, 224
Lomax, Alan (ethnomusicology, cantometrics), 137, 295–296
Lundblad, Jonas, 204
Luther, Martin, 4, 65, 71, 173–174, 197–205
Lutheran, 5, 40, 53, 60, 62, 65, 90, 159, 161, 163, 167, 181, 185, 304; Lutheran theology and music, 197–205

McAllester, David P. (ethnomusicology), 126, 130–131, 133, 303
McCutcheon, Russell T. (study of religion), 3, 23–25
McGann, Mary E. (liturgical studies), 218, 230–231
MacGregor, Geddes (angels), 189–190
McLoed, W. H. (Sikhism), 237
Makkreel, Rudolf A. (Dilthey), 56, 71
Maor, Eli (mathematics and music), 155–156
Margulis, Elizabeth H. (psychology of music), 111–112, 127
Marini, Stephen A. (American sacred music), 231, 306, 309
Markham, Ian (theology), 166
Martin, F. David (aesthetics), 287
Martin, James Alfred (aesthetics), 288
Martin, Luther, 242–244

354 | Index

Martland, Thomas R. (religion and art), 287–288
Marx, Karl, 19, 22, 29, 49, 51–52, 90, 102, 139, 159
Max Muller, Friedrich (comparative religion), 48–49, 62–63, 97, 204
Merkur, Dan (psychology and religion), 106–107
Merriam, Alan P. (ethnomusicology), 2, 103, 103, 125–127, 130, 135
Meyer, Leonard B. (musicology), 129–130
Meyer-Baer, Kathi (harmony of the spheres), 186–188, 190, 194–195
Michaels, Axel (Hindu studies, homo ritualis), 217, 218, 263, 275–277
Mirror Theory, 19, 47, 49, 50, 52, 89–90, 91, 97, 113, 126, 162, 281, 284, 299
Mithen, Steven (cognitive studies and music), 258
Monti, Anthony (natural theology and the arts), 178, 289, 305
Mowinckel, Sigmund (Psalms), 225
Mozart, W. A. (composer), 4–5, 8, 9, 113
Muck, Terry (religion and music), 231–232
Murdock, George (anthropology), 95–96
Music and the afterlife, 194–197, 210–211
Music as Divine Gift (*musica creatura, donum Dei*), 166, 181–185
Musica practica, 199
Musica speculativa, 143, 198
Musical angels, 185–193
Musical instruments, 138–139, 238, 295
Musical relativism, 127–131
Musical universalism, 131–139
Musicality: neuroscience, 245–252; Zuckerkandl, 273

Musicology, 122–124; *see* Comparative musicology, Ethnomusicology
Musicology of Religion, 263–298
Musilanguage, 256–257

Nāda-Brahman, 11, 107, 158, 206–209, 215, 237
Nadel, Siegfried (musicology), 254–255
Nārada Rishi (Hinduism; leader of the Gandharva musicians), 208
Nasr, Seyyed H. (Islamic studies), 190–191, 304
Natural theology (*theologia naturalis*), 61, 65, 149, 166–169, 171–179, 289–290
Nātya Śāstra (Sanskrit text on drama and music), 206, 207, 208–209
Nehring, Andreas (comparative theology), 67–68, 271
Neo-Marxism (Marxism), 28–29, 30, 32, 90, 101, 117–118, 119, 120, 178, 300
Nettl, Bruno (ethnomusicology), 1, 6, 121–122, 125–126, 128, 131–133, 135–136, 137–139, 248, 253, 255, 304
Nettl, Paul (Lutheran studies), 199
Neurotheology (Anthony B. Newberg), 244
New Age (esotericism), 9, 10, 108
Newberg, Anthony B. (neuroscience, neurotheology), 108, 244, 265
Niebuhr, H. Richard, 178
Numinous (Rudolf Otto), 48, 64, 72, 79–80, 86, 102, 103, 234, 227, 291

Oberlin, Heike (Hindu aesthetics, performance), 310
O'Donnell SJ, John, 288–289
OM (AUM), 36, 206, 207, 215, 217, 224, 233–237
Ong, Walter J., 37, 228

Origin of music, 252–259
Otto, Rudolf (phenomenology of religion, numinous), 3, 18, 20, 24, 26, 28, 46, 48, 50, 56, 58, 60, 63–67, 68, 75, 77, 79, 80, 86, 90, 99, 103, 107, 115, 123, 204–205, 219, 220, 222, 223, 227, 228, 232, 234, 242, 266, 282–283, 287, 288, 291, 299

Paden, William, E. (comparative religion), 32
Paley, William (natural theology), 174
Pals, Daniel L (religious studies), 57, 59
Pargament, K. I., (psychology of religion), 106
Patel, Aniruddh D. (neuroscience and music), 241, 248, 253–254, 256
Paul, Russill (Yoga), 11
Pavry, Jal Dastur Cursetji (Zoroastrianism), 197
Phenomenology of music, 83–87; see F. Joseph Smith
Phenomenology of religion, 73–83, 107, 283
Pike, Alfred J. (theology of music), 179–180, 182
Plato, 85, 116, 137, 143, 146, 150–153, 157, 160–161, 165, 171, 172, 175, 186–187, 192, 198, 266, 271–272, 284–286, 288, 291
Plotinus (Neo-Platonism), 152, 172, 285–286, 288, 291
Portnoy, Julius (philosophy and music), 144, 145–146, 150–152, 154, 184
Preus, J. Samuel (naturalism in religion), 52
Primal monotheism ("High Gods"), 97–100
Proudfoot, Wayne (religious studies), 3, 53, 57, 61

Przywara, Erich (analogy of being), 192–193
Psalms, 168, 185, 202, 225, 231
Psychoanalytical musicology, 114
Psychology and music, 105–116; religion, 106–109
Pulvermacher, Gunter (Jung), 115
Pythagoras (*harmonia*), 9, 69, 111, 145–156, 157, 186, 199, 200

Quasten, Johannes (music as Divine Gift), 181, 182
Qur'an, 35–36, 190–192

Ralls-MacLeod, Karen (Celtic religion), 196
Rao, Doreen B., 87
Rappaport, Roy A. (anthropology), 102–103, 222–223, 276
Rasa (Indian aesthetics), 209
Ratzinger, Joseph Cardinal (Roman Catholicism), 185, 193, 223
Reik, Theodor (psychoanalysis and music), 114
Reimar, Bennett (musical experience), 121, 251–252
Relativism: cultural, 93–96; musical, 127–131
Religiosity (in neuroscience), 242–245
Religious experience, 52–59
Religious Studies, 43–59
Re Manning, Russell (natural theology), 178
Rennie, Bryan S. (history of religions, Eliade), 270–271
Revealed theology (*theologia revelata*), 167, 175
Revelation (New Testament), 194–195
Rice, Timothy (ethnomusicology), 128
Ricoeur, Paul (hermeneutics), 50
Rig Veda (Sanskrit text of ancient India), 189, 206, 210–211, 296

Riesebrodt, Martin (religious studies), 31
Ritual studies, 218–223, 275–277
Robertson, Alec (sacred music), 183–184
Rodrigues, Hillary (religious studies), 107
Roscoe, Paul (comparative religion), 292–293
Rose, Kenneth (religious studies), 25–27
Ryba, Thomas (phenomenology of religion), 80, 82

Sachs, Curt (musicology), 84, 123–124, 295
Sacks, Oliver (musicology), 11–12
Saliers, Don E. (theology and music), 165, 291–292
Sāma Veda (Sanskrit text of ancient India), 206, 209, 235
Saṅgīta Dāmodara of Śubhaṅkara (Sanskrit musical text), 209
Saṅgīta Ratnākara of Śārṅgadeva (Sanskrit musical text), 158, 208
Śaraṇa, Gopāla (social sciences), 94–95
Schaefer, Mary M. (liturgical studies), 217, 224–225
Schafer, R. Murray (soundscape), 139–140
Schalk, Carl F. (Luther), 198–200
Scheler, Max (phenomenology of religion), 266–267, 268
Schilbrack, Kevin (religious studies), 25
Schleiermacher, Friedrich (religious experience, theology), 4, 18, 19–20, 22, 28, 45, 48–49, 51, 53–59, 61–64, 65, 66, 68–71, 72, 73–74, 80, 90, 107, 159–163, 163, 174, 203–205, 266–269, 282, 294, 298
Schmidt, Wilhelm (ethnology, primal monotheism), 98–99, 100

Schneider, Albrecht (ethnomusicology), 123
Schneider, Marius (musicology, sound sacrifice), 232–233
Schopenhauer, Arthur (philosophy of music), 69, 154, 158, 159–162
Schweig, Graham (Hindu studies), 211–212
Scruton, Roger (philosophy, aesthetics), 30, 205
Seeger, Charles (ethnomusicology), 129, 133
Segal, Robert A. (religious studies), 17, 81–82, 292
Shah, Timothy S. (homo religiosus), 271
Shankar, Ravi (Indian music, Sitar), 215–216
Shared religious soundscapes, 238
Sharma, Arvind (comparative religion), 293
Sharpe, Eric J. (comparative religion), 18, 44–48, 50, 61, 62–63, 90, 92, 279
Sherry, Patrick (theological aesthetics), 264, 285, 288
Sheveland, John N. (theology and music), 181
Sikhism, 14, 15, 16, 35, 36, 38, 40, 224, 232–234, 236–238, 296, 305, 307
Singh, Pashaura (Sikhism), 237–238
Śivānanda, Swami (Yoga and music), 205, 214–215
Slaughter, J. W. (psychology, music and religion), 116
Sloboda, John A. (psychology and music), 110, 116, 250
Smart, Ninian (religious studies), 21, 23, 24, 73, 299
Smith, F. Harold (comparative theology), 174

Smith, F. Joseph (phenomenology of music), 84–86, 264
Smith, Jonathan Z. (study of religion), 22–23, 26, 67, 269–270
Smith, Wilfrid C. (religious studies), 4, 22–24, 26, 45, 293
Snoek, Jan (ritual studies), 219
Sociology, 116–120
Sohngen, Oscar (Lutheran theology and music), 181, 202, 304
Solfeggio (scale systems), 184, 207
Spencer, Jon M. (theomusicology), 264, 290
Spitzer, Leo (medieval studies), 151, 153
Steckel, Clyde, J. (theology and music), 289, 290
Steiner, George (intellectual history), 273
Stoltzfus, Philip E. (theology, music, performance), 149–150, 153, 156–157, 175, 180
Storr, Anthony (psychology), 89, 113
Strenski, Ivan (religious studies), 24
Stumpf, Carl (comparative musicology), 83–84, 123
Sui generis (autonomy of religion), 23–25, 66, 81, 83, 243, 280
Sullivan, Lawrence E. (history of religions), 1, 16, 34, 304, 309
Sziborsky, Lucia (Adorno), 118

Thandeka (affect theology), 61–62
Theological aesthetics, 72, 179, 288–289
Theology, 4–5; 165–216, 282–292
Theology in ancient Greece, 169–172
Theology of music, 179–181
Theomusicology, 290
Thite, G. U. (Vedic studies), 235
Tice, Terrence N. (Schleiermacher), 54
Tillich, Paul (theology and culture), 180–181, 209, 266, 287, 288

Troeltsch, Ernst (theology, history of religions), 60–61, 203
Twiss, Sumner B. (phenomenology of religion), 73
Tylor, E. B. (anthropology), 92–97

Universals: cultural, 97–103; musical, 131–139
Upanishads (Hindu sacred texts), 176, 205–206, 209

Van der Leeuw, Gerardus (phenomenology of religion), 18, 20, 28, 48, 67, 72, 73, 77, 204, 222, 242, 266–267, 268, 298
Van Khe, Tran (ethnomusicology, musical universals), 137
Vatican Council II: The Conciliar and Post Conciliar Documents, 222–223
Vedanta (Indian philosophy), 156–157, 176–177
Viladesau, Richard (theology and aesthetics), 264, 286, 288, 291

Wach, Joachim (history of religions), 20, 26, 27, 53, 59, 62, 64–66, 204, 267, 268
Wainwright, Geoffrey (theology), 166
Wallin, Nils L. (origins of music), 241, 245–246, 255–258
Ward, Keith (theology, philosophy of religion), 47, 58, 64, 174
Weber, Max (sociology), 117, 267
Weiss, Paul (religion and art), 287
Wiebe, Donald (religious studies), 22–23
Wildman, Wesley J. (comparative natural theology), 175
Williams, Richard D. (Hindu studies), 165, 213
Williams, Robert R. (Schleiermacher), 29, 55–56, 73

Williams, Sean (Buddhism and music), 236
Window Theory, 18, 19, 47, 48, 89, 162, 284, 299
Wright, Edward J. (heaven), 190–191
Wulff, David (psychology and religion), 107

Yoga, 11, 14, 157, 214–215

Yogānanda, Paramahansa, 214

Zarlino, Gioseffo (musicology), 184–185
Zaehner, R. C. (comparative religion), 210–211
Zoroaster, 189, 197, 210–211
Zuckerkandl, Victor (psychology and music, homo musicus), 28, 115–116, 263, 271–273

www.ingramcontent.com/pod-product-compliance
Ingram Content Group UK Ltd.
Pitfield, Milton Keynes, MK11 3LW, UK
UKHW032212220125
454039UK00001B/31